The Faith of Jesus Christ

The Faith of Jesus Christ

Exegetical, Biblical, and Theological Studies

Edited by
MICHAEL F. BIRD
and
PRESTON M. SPRINKLE

Paternoster:
thinking faith

MILTON KEYNES ● COLORADO SPRINGS
● HYDERABAD

HENDRICKSON
PUBLISHERS

15 14 13 12 11 10 09   7 6 5 4 3 2 1

First published jointly, 2009, in the United Kingdom by Paternoster and in the
United States by Hendrickson Publishers Marketing, LLC
P.O. Box 3467, Peabody, Massachusetts 01961, USA

Paternoster is an imprint of Authentic Media
9 Holdom Avenue, Bletchley, Milton Keynes, Bucks, MK1 1QR, UK
1820 Jet Stream Drive, Colorado Springs, CO 80921, USA Medchal
Road, Jeedimetla Village, Secunderabad 500 055, A.P., India
www.loveauthentic.com

Authentic Media is a division of Biblica UK, previously IBS-STL UK. Biblica UK is
limited by guarantee, with its registered office at Kingstown Broadway, Carlisle,
Cumbria, CA3 0HA. Registered in England & Wales No. 1216232. Registered charity
in England & Wales No. 270162 and Scotland No. SCO40064

British Library Cataloguing in Publication Data
A catalogue record for this book is available from the
British Library
ISBN 978-1-84227-606-8

Library of Congress Cataloging-in-Publication Data
The Faith of Jesus Christ—exegetical, biblical, and theological studies/edited by
Michael F. Bird, Preston M. Sprinkle
p. cm
Includes bibliographical references (p.   ) and indexes.
ISBN 978-1-59856-429-7
1. Bible.; N.T. Epistles of Paul—Theology—Congresses. 2. Jesus Christ—Spiritual
life—Biblical teaching—Congresses. I. Bird, Michael F. II. Sprinkle, Preston M.,
1976—
BS2651.F25 2010
227'.06–dc22   2009027420

Design by James Kessell for Scratch the Sky Ltd (www.scratchthesky.com)

Printed in the United States of America

Contents

III. Pauline Exegesis, Hermeneutics, and Theology: Mediating Proposals and Fresh Approaches

IV. The Witness of the Wider New Testament

Abbreviations

AB	Anchor Bible
ABD	*Anchor Bible Dictionary*
ABRL	Anchor Bible Reference Library
ACCS	Ancient Christian Commentary on Scripture
AJBI	*Annual of the Japanese Biblical Institute*
AJP	*American Journal of Philology*
AnBib	Analecta Biblica
ANTC	Abingdon New Testament Commentaries
AUSS	*Andrews University Seminary Studies*
BDAG	Bauer, W., F.W. Danker, W.F. Arndt, and F.W. Gingrich. *Greek-English Lexicon of the New Testament and Other Early Christian Literature*. 3rd ed. Chicago, 2000
BECNT	Baker Exegetical Commentary on the New Testament
BETL	Bibliotheca Ephemeridum Theologicarum Lovaniensium
BHT	Beiträge zur Historischen Theologie
Bib	*Biblica*
BJRL	*Bulletin of the John Rylands University Library of Manchester*
BNTC	Black's New Testament Commentaries
BT	*The Bible Translator*
BWANT	Beiträge zur Wissenschaft vom Alten (und Neuen) Testament
BZNW	Beihefte zur Zeitschrift für die Neutestamentliche
CBQ	*Catholic Biblical Quarterly*
CBR	*Currents in Biblical Research*
CSEL	Corpus Scriptorum Ecclesiasticorum Latinorum
CurBS	*Currents in Research: Biblical Studies*
EKKNT	Evangelisch-katholoischer Kommentar zum Neuen Testament

EvQ	*Evangelical Quarterly*
EvRTh	*Evangelical Review of Theology*
ExpTim	*Expository Times*
FC	Fathers of the Church. Washington, DC, 1947–
FCI	Foundations of Contemporary Interpretation
Greg	*Gregorianum*
HDR	Harvard Dissertations in Religion
HeyJ	*Heythrop Journal*
HNT	Handbuch zum Neuen Testament
HTKNT	Herders theologischer Kommentar zum Neuen Testament
HTR	*Harvard Theological Review*
ICC	International Critical Commentary
Int	*Interpretation*
ISV	International Standard Version of the Bible
JBL	*Journal of Biblical Literature*
JES	*Journal of Ecumenical Studies*
JETS	*Journal of the Evangelical Theological Society*
JMALS	*Journal of the Midland Association for Linguistic Studies*
JSNT	*Journal for the Study of the New Testament*
JSNTSup	Journal for the Study of the New Testament: Supplement Series
JTS	*Journal of Theological Studies*
L&N	*Greek-English Lexicon of the New Testament: Based on Semantic Domains.* Edited by J.P. Louw and E.A. Nida. 2nd ed. New York, 1989
LNTS	Library of New Testament Studies
LS	*Louvain Studies*
LSJ	Liddell, H.G., R. Scott, H.S. Jones, *A Greek-English Lexicon.* 9th ed. with revised supplement. Oxford, 1996
Lum	*Lumen*
NCBC	New Cambridge Bible Commentary
NET	New English Translation of the Bible
NIB	*The New Interpreter's Bible*
NICNT	New International Commentary on the New Testament
NIGTC	New International Greek Testament Commentary
NIVAC	NIV Application Commentary
NKZ	*Neue kirchliche Zeitschrift*
NovT	*Novum Testamentum*
NovTSup	Supplements to Novum Testamentum

NPNF	*Nicene and Post-Nicene Fathers*, Series 1 and 2
NSBT	New Studies in Biblical Theology
NTF	Neutestamentliche Forschungen
NTS	*New Testament Studies*
PG	Patrologia graeca [= Patrologiae cursus completus: Series graeca]. Edited by J.-P. Migne. 162 vols. Paris, 1857–86
PNTC	Pelican New Testament Commentaries
RB	*Revue Biblique*
RHR	*Revue de l'Histoire des Religions*
RTAM	*Recherches de Théologie Ancienne et Médiévale*
RTR	*Reformed Theological Review*
SBJT	*Southern Baptist Journal of Theology*
SBLDS	Society of Biblical Literature Dissertation Series
SBLSP	*Society of Biblical Literature Seminar Papers*
SC	Sources chrétiennes. Paris: Cerf, 1943–
SCJ	*Stone-Campbell Journal*
SNTSMS	Society for New Testament Studies Monograph Series
SP	Sacra Pagina
SUNT	Studien zur Umwelt des Neuen Testaments
TDNT	*Theological Dictionary of the New Testament*. Edited by G. Kittel and G. Friedrich. Translated by G.W. Bromiley. 10 vols. Grand Rapids, 1964–76
Them	*Themelios*
Theol	*Theologica*
THKNT	Theologischer Handkommentar zum Neuen Testament
TJ	*Trinity Journal*
TLG	*Thesaurus Linguae Graecae: Canon of Greek Authors and Works*. Edited by Berkowitz and K.A. Squitier. 3rd ed. Oxford, 1990
TLZ	*Theologische Literaturzeitung*
TNIV	Today's New International Version of the Bible
TS	*Theological Studies*
TSK	*Theologische Studien und Kritiken*
TynBul	*Tyndale Bulletin*
WBC	Word Biblical Commentary
WTJ	*Westminster Theological Journal*
WUNT	Wissenschaftliche Untersuchungen zum Neuen Testament
ZTK	*Zeitschrift für Theologie und Kirche*

Preface

This volume is an attempt to wrestle with one of the enduring discussions in New Testament scholarship, namely the *pistis christou* debate. Should key phrases in the Pauline letters be translated as "faith in Christ" or the "faithfulness of Christ"? How does this debate relate to the wider New Testament and what does it matter theologically? Those questions are, in a nutshell, the reason why this book was written. We have been fortunate enough to assemble a group of top scholars (with a good mix of older and younger contributors) to engage this disputed topic from their respective vantage points, and we believe that the results speak for themselves. This book does not propound any single view of the *pistis christou* debate but provides a survey and analysis of the various issues, factors, and arguments that have shaped the discussion. We hope that this volume will lead others to understand more properly what the debate is about, what the main options are, what is at stake, and why there is a debate in the first place.

There are a number of people we need to thank for their help with this project. Dr Robin Parry of Paternoster first of all took the time to listen to our proposal and then encouraged us in the publication of this volume. Second, we have to thank the various contributors who wrote some fine papers, many of which were presented orally at the Society of Biblical Literature annual meeting in San Diego in November 2007. The discussions that followed were cordial, enjoyable, and highly stimulating (Dr Douglas Campbell in particular made sure that there was never a dull moment). Third, and as always, our families have very much shared the journey with us and often wondered what the "PX" thingy that we kept talking about even was. We remain thankful for their continued support.

Both editors are active in different faith communities where they have experienced the virtues of *pistis* ("faith" or "fidelity") in a variety of ways. Accordingly, Michael Bird would like to dedicate this book to his colleagues at the Highland Theological College who have provided a collegial setting and warm Christian atmosphere for the teaching of the New Testament. Likewise, Preston Sprinkle would like to dedicate this book to his colleagues at Eternity Bible College for their rich friendship and zeal for the faith. We would also like to thank Mr John and Mrs Amanda McGill for their work in compiling the indices for this volume. Together with our friends, co-workers, and family (regardless of whether they are proponents of an objective or subjective genitival reading of *pistis christou*), we entrust ourselves to the faithfulness of Jesus Christ.

Michael F. Bird and Preston M. Sprinkle
June 2008

Foreword

The πίστις Χριστοῦ debate has been almost entirely limited to English-speaking New Testament scholarship. Our German colleagues observe it with some bemusement since the objective sense ("faith in Christ") remains the consensus more-or-less taken-for-granted view. Ill-advisedly, they suspect that the subjective genitive alternative is part of an English-language attack on the Lutheran emphasis on justification by faith, largely ignoring the fact that Richard Hays' influential statement of the case for a subjective rendering ("the faith[fulness] of Christ") was entirely independent of "the new perspective on Paul".[1] But a large part of the value of the debate is precisely that it has broken through the old categories which had tramlined exegesis of the Pauline letters and prevented the rich diversity of Paul's theology from coming through. If truth be told, in academic circles prior to the early 1980s Pauline theology had become rather boring and turgid, a repetition and rehearsal of long-established truths – or, rather, of long-established interpretations. The πίστις Χριστοῦ debate helped shatter the moulds which unwittingly had so predetermined the exegesis and interpretative options which Paul's letters offer.

In a recent further contribution to the debate,[2] I have noted particularly two ways in which Richard Hays' contribution helped break the older mould.

---

[1] R.B. Hays, *The Faith of Jesus Christ: The Narrative Substructure of Galatians 3:1–4:11* (SBLDS 56; Chico, CA: Scholars Press, 1983). My "The New Perspective on Paul" appeared in the same year, *BJRL* 65 (1983): 95–122, and drew more attention only when reprinted in my *Jesus, Paul and the Law* (London: SPCK/Louisville, KY: Westminster John Knox, 1990), 183–214. I attempt to reassure German suspicion of "the new perspective" in *The New Perspective on Paul* (WUNT 185; Tübingen: Mohr Siebeck, 2005/Grand Rapids, MI: Eerdmans, 2008), ch. 1.

[2] Fittingly, if somewhat ironically, in Richard Hays' Festschrift, "*EK PISTEŌS*: A Key to the Meaning of *PISTIS CHRISTOU*", in *The Word Leaps the Gap: Essays on Scripture*

One was the main intention of his *The Faith of Christ* thesis, to highlight "the narrative elements that undergird Paul's thought".[3] This has been somewhat lost to sight by the spotlight focus on the phrase πίστις Χριστοῦ. But it needed and still needs to be stressed that Paul's theology presupposes a story about Jesus Christ – particularly about his death and resurrection, but including the memory of one "born under the Law" (Gal. 4:4) who "became a servant of circumcision" (Rom. 15:8). And behind that story also is the story of Israel, and the story of God's dealings with his creation. In my most recent work on Romans I have found it more than helpful to see the structure of the main section (1:18–11:36) as a threefold telling of the story of God's righteousness: the story of God's impartial judgment on all humankind, Jew first but also Gentile (1:18–5:11); the cosmic and apocalyptic story of the entrance, machinations and overcoming of the powers of Sin and Death, not by Torah but by Spirit (5:12–8:39); and the story of Israel, from call to completion (9:1–11:36).[4]

The question which has to be asked, however, is whether this important dimension of Paul's theology is dependent on πίστις Χριστοῦ being read as a subjective genitive – whether, indeed, the emphasis on "the faith of Christ" given by the subjective genitive reading is integral to the acknowledgement of the story/ies assumed by Paul. Would the theological/christological narrative be lost to sight without πίστις Χριστοῦ? Of course not! As already noted, the fact that Jesus was a Jew was an important part of the gospel story for Paul (Rom. 15:8; Gal. 4:4–5). His living out what he taught in the love command was taken for granted by Paul (Rom. 15:1–3; Gal. 6:2).[5] Paul speaks of Christ's "obedience" to the death of the cross more than once (Rom. 5:19; Phil. 2:8). What we don't find is that Paul made a point of stressing Jesus' "faithfulness" as such, apart from the disputed πίστις Χριστοῦ phrases,

---

and Theology in Honor of Richard B. Hays (ed. J.R. Wagner, et al.; Grand Rapids, MI: Eerdmans, 2008), 351–66.

[3] *The Faith of Christ* (2nd edn; Grand Rapids, MI: Eerdmans, 2002), xxiii.

[4] J.D.G. Dunn, "Paul's Letter to Rome: Reason and Rationale", in *Logos – Logik – Lyrik: Engagierte exegetische Studien zum biblischen Reden Gottes* (ed. V.A. Lehnert and U. Rüsen-Weinhold; Leipzig: Evangelische Verlagsanstalt, 2007), 185–200.

[5] Rom. 15:2 is the only passage in which Paul speaks of "the neighbour (*plēsion*)" apart from the two references to Lev. 19:18: "you shall love your neighbour as yourself" (Rom. 13:9–10 and Gal. 5:14); so it is most probable that he had in mind Jesus' teaching which uniquely (for his time) prioritized Lev. 19:18 (Mark 12:29–31); see my *Jesus Remembered* (Grand Rapids, MI: Eerdmans, 2003), 584–6.

whereas he was quite ready to stress God's Πίστις ("faithfulness") on various occasions.[6]

So what must not be lost to sight here is the danger of overloading the significance of the "faith of Christ" interpretation of πίστις Χριστοῦ. The Pauline emphasis on Christ's mission as a Jew and his obedience to his commission is not dependent on the "faith of Christ" rendering of πίστις Χριστοῦ. That emphasis is quite clear and should be given appropriate attention in modern restatements of Paul's theology, regardless of what decision is made about πίστις Χριστοῦ. Let us not make the mistake of suggesting that without the "faith of Christ" interpretation of πίστις Χριστοῦ we have lost sight of that important emphasis which Paul (and other NT writings) place on Christ as the pattern for the "obedience of faith".

A second feature brought out by the "faith of Christ" rendering of πίστις Χριστοῦ as promoted by Richard Hays is the added emphasis and dimension it gives to the Pauline theology of salvation as participation in Christ. To believe in Christ is to share in his faithfulness, "his gracious self-sacrificial death on a cross".[7] Here we see the benefit of breaking the old mould of a purely forensic interpretation of "justification by faith". For although Calvin was more successful than the Lutheran tradition in holding together both the forensic and the "in Christ" motifs in Paul, the Reformation tradition generally has found it difficult to integrate Paul's participation in Christ ("in Christ") emphasis with "justification by faith" as the article by which the church stands or falls. This is highly surprising, since Paul himself seems to have found no difficulty in doing so, as passages like 2 Corinthians 5:21 and Philippians 3:7–11 clearly show.[8] This seems to be another case where Paul was able to hold together (and evidently thought it important to do so) what later commentators have insisted must be held apart (continuity / apocalyptic,[9] justification / participation) with an insensitivity of exposition which has only muddied the scholarly debate and confused the faithful.

But again there is some danger that this entirely proper emphasis might be overshadowed and skewed by the πίστις Χριστοῦ debate. For once again, Paul's participation in Christ ("in Christ") emphasis is not dependent on a "faithfulness of Christ" rendering of πίστις Χριστοῦ.

---

[6] Rom. 3:3; 1 Cor. 1:9; 10:13; 2 Cor. 1:18; 1 Thess. 5:24.

[7] *The Faith of Christ*, xxx.

[8] See *The New Perspective on Paul*, ch. 22.

[9] I refer particularly to J. Louis Martyn, *Galatians: A New Translation with Introduction and Commentary* (AB 33A; New York: Doubleday, 1997).

There is, in fact, only one Pauline passage which really integrates the subjective genitive rendering of a Πίστις phrase into the participation in Christ (or Christ in us) theme – Galatians 2:20. And the Pauline emphasis on the gracious self-sacrifice of the cross is more clearly and more powerfully drawn in passages like Romans 5:6–11, 2 Corinthians 5:16–21 and Philippians 2:6–11, where again I find myself wondering why Paul did not include reference to Christ's faithfulness in such passages if it was indeed such an important motif for Paul. All of this raises for me the question whether so much can, or should be, rested on a phrase which is at best allusive and undeveloped (in the "faithfulness of Christ" interpretation) in its usage.

It will be evident that I myself remain unpersuaded by the "faith of Christ" rendering of πίστις Χριστοῦ. Of the following essayists, I find myself most "at home" with Francis Watson, and to some extent with Preston Sprinkle. As my contribution to the Hays Festschrift indicates, like Watson I see the *ek pisteōs* phrase as the key which unlocks the πίστις Χριστοῦ phrase, and Sprinkle's last two sentences resonate strongly, since I think the most obvious exegesis of Galatians 3:6–7 more or less settles the issue.

I also want to rescue (is that the appropriate term?) the emphasis on human faith which is so clear in Paul[10] yet which seems to be somehow denigrated by some defences of the "faith of Christ" interpretation. Of course, Paul's emphasis on human faith as the response to the gospel is no more dependent on the "faith in Christ" rendition of πίστις Χριστοῦ than is his emphasis on the obedience of Christ dependent on the "faith of Christ" rendition. But the fact that "faith" – that is, faith in Christ – is Paul's shorthand for the human response to the gospel for which he looked (Rom. 10:4–17) must not be lost to sight or shrouded by the πίστις Χριστοῦ debate. And the Reformation re-emphasis that God's grace comes to its most effective effect through faith alone, through trustful dependence on God alone (Rom. 4), quite apart from and without any added condition of "works of the Law" (Gal. 2:16; 3:2, 5), needs to be clearly reaffirmed in a day when different church traditions increasingly take the place of the "works of the Law" against which Paul warned so fiercely.

Overall, however, I am excited and stimulated by the range of essays which follow and which indicate so clearly how stimulating and properly creative (in terms of exegesis, that is, openness to the richness within

---

[10] Rom. 1:5, 8, 12, 17; 3:27, 28, 30, 31; 4:5, 9, 11–14, 16, 19, 20; 5:1, etc.

the texts being interpreted) these ancient letters can be. We don't simply want new tramlines to replace the old. Nor do we want to encourage retreat into different bastions from which we snipe at "the others". We want that openness and a truth-seeking dialogue which will help bring ourselves and others to new insights and a fresh grasp of the profundity and richness of the gospel. These essays will help achieve that.

James D.G. Dunn

1

Introduction: Problems and Prospects for a New Testament Debate

MICHAEL F. BIRD

Since Richard Hays published his doctoral dissertation *The Faith of Jesus Christ: The Narrative Substructure of Galatians 3:1–4:11*, there has been considerable debate in New Testament studies concerning whether or not the expression πίστις Χριστοῦ (*pistis christou*, lit., the "faith of Christ") should be interpreted as an objective genitive (i.e., faith in Christ), as a subjective genitive (i.e., the faithfulness of Christ), or as something in between (e.g., the faith that is of Christ). The phrase, and slight variations thereof, occurs at key junctures in the Pauline letters including Romans, Galatians, Philippians, and Ephesians. Far from being insignificant, this short expression is crucial for understanding the Apostle's conception of righteousness by faith and how Paul construed the story of salvation in relation to the Mosaic Law. It is little wonder, then, that such a short grammatical expression has prompted so much attention and discussion. Despite the fact that nearly thirty years have passed since Richard Hays effectively re-opened the debate, it remains in full swing and shows no sign of abating. Interest in the subject remains firm and this is evidenced not only by the appearance of this volume but also by the publication of three dissertations in 2007 that all focus quite specifically on this very subject.[1]

The πίστις Χριστοῦ debate continues, no doubt, because it is significant on a variety of levels. It is significant exegetically because it affects how Paul's syntax and arguments are construed in their literary

---

[1] Desta Heliso, *Pistis and the Righteous One: A Study of Romans 1:17 against the Background of Scripture and Second Temple Jewish Literature* (WUNT 2.235; Tübingen: Mohr Siebeck, 2007); Benjamin Schließer, *Abraham's Faith in Romans 4: Paul's Concept of Faith in Light of the History of Reception of Genesis 15:6* (WUNT 2.224; Tübingen: Mohr Siebeck, 2007); Karl Friedrich Ulrichs, *Christusglaube: Studien zum Syntagma pistis Christou und zum paulinischen Verständnis von Glaube und Rechtfertigung* (WUNT 2.227; Tübingen: Mohr Siebeck, 2007).

context, which in turns impacts exegetical observations and even Bible translations.[2] The debate is also significant theologically because at stake is nothing less than the very architecture of the Christ-event and the nature of the summons to faith and the life of discipleship that flows from it. As Sigve Tonstad writes: "The notion that 'the righteousness of God' has come to light in 'the faithfulness of Jesus Christ' cuts a wide swath in the theological landscape and rearranges the perspective around a new center." He adds, "Radical as it may seem our reading of πίστις Χριστοῦ [i.e., the subjective genitive], which on the surface may seem like a minor revision, lays the groundwork for an entirely different paradigm in the theology of the NT."[3] Mark Reasoner further outlines what is at stake in this debate:

---

[2] Contrast the following translations of the TNIV, NET, and ISV:

	TNIV	NET	ISV
Rom. 3:21–22	But now apart from the law the righteousness of God has been made known, to which the Law and the Prophets testify. This righteousness is given **through faith in Jesus Christ** to all who believe.	But now, apart from the law, God's righteousness of God (which is attested by the law and the prophets) has been disclosed – namely, the righteousness of God **through the faithfulness of Jesus Christ** for all who believe.	But now, apart from the law, God's righteousness is revealed and is attested by the Law and the Prophets – God's righteousness **through the faithfulness of Jesus Christ** for all who believe.
Gal. 2:15–16	We who are Jews by birth and not sinful Gentiles know that a person is not justified by observing the law, but by **faith in Jesus Christ**. So we, too, have put our faith in Christ Jesus that we may be justified by **faith in Christ** and not by observing the law, because by observing the law no one will be justified.	We are Jews by birth and not Gentile sinners, yet we know that no one is justified by the works of the law but by **the faithfulness of Jesus Christ**. And we have come to believe in Christ Jesus, so that we may be justified by **the faithfulness of Christ** and not by the works of the law, because by the works of the law no one will be justified.	We ourselves are Jews by birth and not Gentile sinners, yet we know that a person is not justified by works of the law but by the **faithfulness of Jesus Christ**. We, too, have believed in Christ Jesus so that we might be justified by **the faith of Christ** and not by the works of the law, for no human being will be justified by the works of the law.

[3] Sigve Tonstad, "πιστις χριστου: Reading Paul in a New Paradigm", *AUSS* 40 (2002): 56, 57.

Why does it matter whether we read *pistis Christou* as objective (faith in Jesus) or subjective (Jesus' faith)? First, the degree to which we emphasize faith in the human affects how we present the gospel. Proponents of the subjective genitive, who hold that Christ's faith is what saves, will not call for a distinct, conversion-constituting act of placing one's faith in Jesus. They will rather call people to join the church that lives out in a concentric pattern the faith that Jesus displayed. Second, we will begin to read Paul's gospel not as primarily based around the dichotomy of works and faith, which both have a human subject, but rather as a dichotomy between law and Christ. Third, this view of *pistis Christou* moves students of Paul's letters to see that justification by faith is part of a bigger theme in Paul, participation in Christ.[4]

As one can plainly see, the arguments are about far more than syntax and grammar. The interpretation of πίστις Χριστοῦ affects a whole constellation of issues about the nature of salvation, the person and work of Christ, the contents of faith, the character of the church, and even Bible translations.

Moreover, while this may appear to be a deliberation restricted to studies in the minutiae of Pauline exegesis, it is worth pointing out that there are several other places in the New Testament that seem to reflect a similar grammatical ambiguity regarding the relationship of Jesus Christ to faith. Consider the following examples: (1) In Acts 3:16 we find reference to "the faith that is through him [i.e., Jesus] (ἡ πίστις ἡ δι' αὐτοῦ) has given him this complete health"; (2) Revelation 14:12 states: "Here is a call for the endurance of the saints, those keeping the commandments of God and holding fast to the faith of Jesus (τὴν πίστιν Ἰησοῦ)"; (3) James 2:1 says: "My brothers, do you with your acts of favoritism really have the faith of our glorious Lord Jesus Christ? (τὴν πίστιν τοῦ κυρίου ἡμῶν Ἰησοῦ Χριστοῦ τῆς δόξης)". The translations, meanings, and significance of these passages are disputed – but they all contain a similar grammatical ambiguity about "faith" and "Jesus Christ" analogous to that found in Romans 3:22 and Galatians 2:15–16. It is quite evident, then, that the discussion about the relationship between "faith" and "Jesus" goes far beyond isolated phrases in Galatians and Romans and incorporates the wider New Testament as well.[5]

---

[4] Mark Reasoner, *Romans in Full Circle: A History of Interpretation* (Louisville, KY: Westminster John Knox, 2005), 39–40.

[5] Unfortunately restrictions of length prevented us from being able to include more substantive analyses of the Catholic Epistles, esp. Hebrews, the Petrine Epistles,

In addition, if the debate is not restricted to Paul's letters it cannot be limited to grammatical argumentation either. The notion that Jesus' faithfulness and obedience have intrinsic saving value is an evidently important theme in Pauline theology and even for New Testament theology as a whole.[6] If one chooses to identify the faithfulness of Jesus as an expression of the faithfulness of God then one will very naturally arouse the interest of systematic theologians for this discussion as well. If we take into account the *Wirkungsgeschichte* (effective-history) of the New Testament in the ancient church, including its translation and reception, then further vistas of study open up as to how the key phrases were interpreted by Christian exegetes and how patristic authors understood Jesus' faithfulness and obedience operating in relation to the economy of salvation. Thus, the debate about the faithfulness of Jesus Christ revolves around far more than grammatical, syntactical, and contextual matters restricted to Paul's epistles. It encompasses a whole range of exegetical, biblical, historical, and theological issues as well.

The upshot of all this is that the purpose of this volume is to attempt to give a global and panoramic perspective on the debate by demonstrating the dividing lines, showing the points of contention, and illustrating how the debate has developed in recent years in order to allow readers to make up their own minds about this ongoing conversation in New Testament studies. As such, no particular view of the πίστις Χριστοῦ debate is being singularly propounded. Rather, what follows are discussions that present the various arguments for each particular position and highlight the different factors that shape the discussion.

In *Part I* several background issues are brought forward. Debbie Hunn presents a brief survey of the debate in the twentieth century and notes how the discussion has largely orbited around the areas of lexical word studies, grammatical and syntactical arguments, and theological models. She observes that arguments based on grammar and language have singularly failed to provide an adequate answer for either side of the

---

Jude, and the Johannine Epistles. On Hebrews, see Todd D. Still, "*Christos* as *Pistos*: The Faith(fulness) of Jesus in the Epistle to the Hebrews", *CBQ* 69 (2007): 746–55.

[6] Cf. Richard Longenecker, "The Obedience of Christ in the Theology of the Early Church", in *Reconciliation and Hope New Testament Essays on Atonement and Eschatology Presented to L.L. Morris on his 60th Birthday* (ed. R. Banks; Exeter: Paternoster/Grand Rapids, MI: Eerdmans, 1974), 142–52; idem, "The Foundational Conviction of New Testament Christology: The Obedience/Faithfulness/Sonship of Christ", in *Jesus of Nazareth Lord and Christ: Essays on the Historical Jesus and New Testament Christology* (ed. Joel B. Green and Max Turner; Grand Rapids, MI: Eerdmans, 1994), 473–88.

debate. Subsequent exegetical studies on the key texts have multiplied questions as to how πίστις Χριστοῦ relates to a plethora of other concepts in Paul's letters. Hunn also raises a legitimate question as to whether or not the subjective, objective, and adjectival readings of πίστις Χριστοῦ really create the theological dichotomies related to justification and the New Perspective on Paul that some scholars allege.

Stanley E. Porter and Andrew W. Pitts engage the subject from the vantage point of lexical and syntactic considerations. They focus on the role of lexical semantics in sense disambiguation, offer a description of the Greek case system, reframe the debate in terms of lexis and case, and then present an analysis of the results. They advocate that lexical, grammatical, and syntactical factors are immediately relevant – though they are often minimized in the πίστις Χριστοῦ debate in favour of exegetical and theological observations. In their view, the imprecision of the debate is due to a failure to grasp the lexical relationship between genitives and their head term since the genitive case restricts the meaning of the head term but does not determine it. Much of the exegetical discussion assumes a grammatical choice between "subject" and "object", whereas the real issue lies in the various forms of modification and their relation to a head term like πίστις. Porter and Pitts maintain that, in light of case semantics, every time πίστις functions as an anarthrous head term with a preceding prepositional modifier it has an abstract function. Therefore Χριστοῦ delineates "Christ" as the realm of faith rather than specifying Christ's own faith. They do not think that the contours of the discussion can be settled exclusively by Greek linguistics. Nonetheless, they draw attention to the fact that a linguistic approach seems to favour the sense in pertinent texts that Christ was the object of faith.

Part II brings to the forefront some new and innovative analyses of the primary texts of contention from the Pauline corpus. Two scholars argue for the subjective genitive interpretation of πίστις Χριστοῦ and similar phrases. Two other scholars argue for an objective genitive reading of the same material. Douglas A. Campbell, who is now a veteran in this debate, sets a cracking pace. His essay on Romans 3:22 begins by noting that Paul's prepositional qualifiers to πίστις in Romans and Galatians indicate instrumentality, and the quotation of Habakkuk 2:4 in Romans 1:17 must be correlated with this. Moreover, Paul's emphasis on instrumentality in Romans 3:21–22, whereby the δικαιοσύνη Θεοῦ is disclosed or revealed by means of the πίστις of Jesus Christ, can only be adequately accounted for by a subjective genitive interpretation of the "faithfulness of Christ". Campbell, following Hays, argues that Paul refers to the story of Christ's passion metonymically so that one element may evoke a wider narrative discourse. Furthermore, he finds grounds for plausibly regarding Habakkuk 2:4 as a messianic proof-text for Paul which references ὁ δίκαιος with a christological meaning. It is crucial for Campbell that the act of faith is firm evidence of God's saving action, but human faith is entirely unable to disclose the revelation of the δικαιοσύνη Θεοῦ. That implies that Paul has to be talking about something other than human faith when he refers to the πίστεως Ἰησοῦ Χριστοῦ. For Campbell, the programmatic texts of Romans 1:17 and 3:22 state that the faithfulness of Christ – understood broadly as his obedience, death, and resurrection – has revealed the saving righteousness of God.

R. Barry Matlock attributes the persistence (and inconclusiveness) of the πίστις Χριστοῦ debate to its having become a "proxy war" between a corporate, participationist reading of Paul and an individual, forensic reading. Matlock resists the ideological bind that this imposes on πίστις Χριστοῦ ("detheologizing" the debate); and he persists in seeking out evidence that can be debated across or irrespective of such boundaries, particularly linguistic semantic evidence regarding the sense of πίστις ("faith", "faithfulness" or whatever) and the relation of Χριστός to πίστις ("subject", "object" or whatever). He focuses on the four πίστις Χριστοῦ texts that include additional πίστις / πιστεύω phrases: Galatians 2:16; 3:22; Romans 3:22; and Philippians 3:9. This rhetorical phenomenon of repetition has often been supposed to favour the subjective genitive reading. On Matlock's analysis, these additional phrases offer semantic information, directly or indirectly, about Paul's πίστις Χριστοῦ phrases, helping to select the sense, the subject, and the object of πίστις as according to the objective genitive reading. Matlock posits that these and related features of the Pauline contexts were sufficient to establish this reading among Paul's early readers, native Greek speakers for whom the subjective reading of πίστις Χριστοῦ was not explicitly rejected but rather literally unheard of.

Paul Foster presents an array of arguments for the subjective genitival reading of Philippians 3:9 and Ephesians 3:12. He finds the case for the subjective genitive in Philippians 3:9 to be finely balanced, but he is persuaded by the use of πίστις language with names or pronouns where it signifies the faith *of* an individual, rather than faith *in* an individual. What is more, he claims that the context of Philippians 3:3–9 suggests that righteousness is imputed on the basis of Christ's act of fidelity. Foster alleges that an even stronger case for the subjective genitive can be made in Ephesians 3:12 given the presence of the definite article and the similarities with Ephesians 2:18, which together indicate that the access to God that the Gentiles enjoy is a consequence of Christ's faithfulness in undergoing a sacrificial death.

In contrast to Foster, Richard Bell in turn argues for the objective genitive of faith in Christ in Philippians 3:9 and Ephesians 3:12. He advocates that, in Philippians 3:2–11, Paul writes of two different attitudes: one is concerned with a righteousness which comes by Law (which gives rise to confidence in the flesh), and the other is concerned with a righteousness which comes from God. Philippians 3:9, like Romans 10:3, contrasts one's own righteousness with the righteousness that comes from God and contrasts righteousness "by Law" with that "through faith in Christ". The objective genitive is suggested not only by the proposed structural analysis of Philippians 3:9, but also by the parallel objective genitive of "knowledge of Christ" in 3:8 and the parallel of Philippians 3:9–10 with Philippians 1:29. He also faults the subjective reading on several points, including the assumed relationship between human faith and Christ's faithfulness and the mistaken view that faith is the result of participation in Christ. "Faith in Christ", he argues, is the correlate of "the gospel concerning Christ" and it is this gospel, this word of reconciliation, which creates faith in the hearer. In regard to Ephesians 3:12, Bell contends for an objective translation based on parallels with Romans 5:1–2 and Ephesians 4:13. He then proceeds to contest the subjective genitive reconstructions of Paul Foster, Markus Barth, and Peter T. O'Brien. In his concluding remarks he suggests that some advocates of the subjective genitive have mistakenly read ideas of Jesus as the "faithful one" found in Hebrews and Revelation into Paul.

Part III includes some mediating perspectives and further proposals as they relate to Pauline exegesis, Pauline hermeneutics, and Pauline theology more broadly. Mark Seifrid takes up an interpretation of "the faith of Christ" that was prominent in earlier phases of the debate but has been largely overlooked in recent discussion. He argues that the expression describes Christ as the author and source of faith. In an attempt to lend grammatical precision to earlier proposals, he claims that the phrase πίστις Χριστοῦ is not best described as bearing either a "subjective" or "objective" genitive (which presuppose a purely verbal noun). Rather, he says, it is more helpful to describe it in terms of categories such as quality, source, and possession that are associated with a nominal sense of πίστις. He proceeds to give examples from Josephus, Philo, Ignatius, and Acts that illustrate this very point. Seifrid argues for the anticipation of the concept in Romans 1:17 where faith has its source in the faithfulness of God. He understands Romans 3:26 to indicate that God justifies the one who has the faith that comes from Jesus Christ. The same nominal genitives can be found in Galatians where, for example, Galatians 2:16 implies a genitive of authorship since just as works arise from the Law, so faith arises from Christ. Seifrid takes the "righteousness of God" in Philippians 3:9 to denote the righteousness that God effects through the faith which comes from Christ. He concludes by saying that, for the Apostle Paul, to believe in Jesus Christ is not merely to act, but to be acted upon by God in his work in Jesus Christ. If Seifrid is correct, this could potentially dissolve many of the dichotomies in the πίστις Χριστοῦ debate as to how faith(fulness) is effected by God through Christ – and it would give the entire discussion a theocentric shot in the arm at the same time.

Francis Watson brings his expertise on Pauline hermeneutics to the topic and focuses on Paul's use of the faith-formulations (e.g., ἐκ πίστεως and διὰ πίστεως) in order to refute the subjective genitive interpretation that has gained currency in English-speaking scholarship. He argues that in Galatians and Romans these faith-formulations all derive from the ἐκ πίστεως ("from/by faith") of Habakkuk 2:4. This is Paul's basic formulation, which is then extended into the double genitive ἐκ πίστεως Χριστοῦ ("from/by faith of Christ") in order to counterbalance ἐξ ἔργων νόμου ("from/by works of the Law"). Watson also rejects a messianic reading of Habakkuk 2:4 along the lines of "the Righteous One", and he maintains that the citation more probably refers to the righteousness of the generic individual who has faith grounded in Christ and the divine saving action enacted in him. In Watson's opinion it is unhelpful, then, to play off an apparently virtuous christocentric reading of Paul's interpretation of Habakkuk 2:4 against a purportedly bad anthropocentric one.

Preston Sprinkle presents the case for a "third view" of the πίστις Χριστοῦ as "Christ-Faith", which is equivalent to the gospel message about Jesus Christ (viz., the gospel and its content). Sprinkle presents an exhaustive survey of proponents of this "third view" and notes the various subtleties of each advocate. This approach takes πίστις Χριστοῦ as a singular entity rather than as two components of "faith" and "Christ". Proponents also identify πίστις Χριστοῦ as something objective to a person's faith in God and Christ. It is Sprinkle's contention that this reading may solve the apparent incongruity of how faith can be the instrument that reveals the "righteousness of God" in Romans 1:17 and 3:21–22. He then proceeds to test this conclusion against the text of Galatians, where he maintains that πίστις Χριστοῦ signifies the "event of the gospel itself". In so doing he also draws attention to some pertinent texts in Ignatius and Origen that might have a bearing on the debate. Sprinkle acknowledges that this "third view" does not account for all of the textual data (e.g., Phil. 3, where he favours an objective genitive) but suggests that it can fill in a sizeable gap in the debate between subjective and objective interpretations of the genitive.

Ardel Caneday analyzes the theme of Christ's faithfulness in the theology of Galatians as indicative of Paul's theology as a whole. He sees ἔργα νόμου and πίστις Χριστοῦ as reflecting Paul's antithetical pairing of Torah and Christ. This polarity means that the contrast is between two distinct covenants – one bounded by Law the other bounded by Christ. According to Caneday, the source of this polarity is an underlying narrative about Israel incurring the curse of the Law for its unfaithfulness to the covenant and those who belong to the "works of the Law" being under the curse of Torah. In contrast, Christ's faithfulness through his curse-bearing death serves to redeem others from the curse of the Torah. The coming of πίστις is the coming of Christ's faithfulness to undo the curse of the Law.

Part IV explores the wider witness of the New Testament in order to see how the concept of Jesus' obedience and faithfulness is expressed in the theology and narrative of the biblical authors outside of the Pauline writings. Peter Bolt brings material from the Synoptic Gospels and Acts into the sphere of the debate and contends that this material not only supports the subjective genitive but also makes it a better option. He examines Mark 11:22 to the effect that Jesus reminds his disciples that they have the faithfulness of God to his promises. Mark 9:23 suggests that Jesus has what the disciples do not have – namely, a faith in God to work miracles. And Matthew 27:43 speaks explicitly of Jesus' entrusting himself to God. Bolt adds that these texts need to be seen in light of a broader Christology of Jesus as the "Servant of the Lord" which provides a serious picture of the faithfulness of Jesus Christ and also provides an additional substructure for the "faith of Christ" in the Pauline sense.

Bill Salier surveys the Fourth Gospel and notes the centrality of the theme of Jesus' dependence upon God and his obedience to the Father throughout. The obedience of the Son is set within the context of a sending-sent relationship where Jesus comes to Israel in order to make the promises of God a reality. In addition, his obedience is also displayed in the "hour" which is the singular moment of his death and resurrection and its redemptive achievement. According to Salier, the Gospel of John provides a fine balance between depicting Jesus as an exemplary model of faithfulness and portraying Jesus as the object of faith.

Bruce Lowe explores the significance of James 2:1 ("My brothers show no partiality as you hold the faith of our Lord Jesus Christ, the Lord of Glory"). He rejects the view of ἡμῶν Ἰησοῦ Χριστοῦ ("our Jesus Christ") as a conjectural emendation and instead locates the phrase as part of the wider rhetorical discourse of James 2:1–13. Lowe argues that "glory" is a cipher for understanding matters in light of honour and that "Jesus' faith" is not a reference to his faithful law-abiding life but more properly denotes confidence in the eschatological reward of God in the midst of suffering.

David deSilva draws attention to the relevance of the book of Revelation for the debate in its representation of faith and faithfulness. He acknowledges the overall significance of the semantic domain of the πιστ-word group and he is cognizant of Barry Matlock's observation that varying uses of nouns and verbs can appear within a single span of text and that less ambiguous constructions should clarify the potentially more ambiguous ones. Here deSilva covers the semantic evocations of the adjective πιστός and the noun πίστις in Revelation (the verb πιστεύω does not appear in the book). In his view, John the Seer's use of the adjectival form places emphasis on the quality of loyalty or faithfulness as part of John's program to promote an ethos of discipleship characterized by fidelity to Jesus and God. Jesus himself is a reliable witness (Rev. 1:5; 3:14), and in deSilva's reckoning this is evocative of the trustworthiness of Jesus' word. He identifies in Revelation 2:19; 13:10 an employment of πίστις as connoting the moral quality of "trust" and "faithfulness", while in Revelation 2:13 and 14:12 πίστις carries the sense of an objective genitive evoking "faithfulness" shown towards Jesus. According to deSilva, John the Seer does not use πίστις / πιστός to evoke the sense of an inner disposition of trust in regard to what is trustworthy. In his view, John casts discipleship in terms of imitating the pattern of Jesus especially with respect to Jesus' own faithfulness – even if the direction and object of that faithfulness (towards God or towards the disciples) is not explicated. For deSilva this is part of John's larger agenda of fostering a Christian witness under trying circumstances.

Part V attempts to push the horizons of the debate wider than usual by taking into account insights from church history and perspectives from systematic theology. Mark Elliott surveys material from the Apostolic Fathers, the church fathers, the medieval period, and even from some modern christological debates about Jesus' faith (done largely in dialogue with Ian Wallis and R.A. Harrisville). He contests the study of Wallis and maintains that the objective genitive seems to have been the norm among the church fathers. However, Elliott does detect in Ignatius of Antioch a more complex relationship between Jesus and "faith" in so far as Jesus is author of faith, and he is faithful in so far as God is faithful. He finds much the same in medieval studies of faith and Jesus, but he notes how the Catholic tradition of modern theology has given more room to accommodate a place for Jesus' own faith (e.g., Balthasar). Elliott concludes that the attempt to reintroduce Jesus' faith/faithfulness into theology is an attempt to emphasize the earthly humanity of Jesus as a factor in salvation. Unfortunately it does so only by going against the grain of Christian tradition and Christian theology.

Benjamin Myers draws attention to Karl Barth's unique contribution to the debate through his conception of God's faithfulness as revealed in the πίστις of Jesus. He detects a pervasive Paulinism, running from Barth's *Römerbrief* to the *Kirchliche Dogmatik*, which places God's operations in the context of cosmic apocalyptic action rather than seeing them as the outcome of salvation-history. Myers shows how Barth regards faith as essentially God's faithfulness revealed in Jesus Christ, and human faith as the obedience that participates in Jesus' own obedience to the Father. Myers also regards the construal of the πίστις Χριστοῦ debate as a contest between "anthropological" and "christological" readings to be a false dichotomy since Barth's own model shows that the human subject need not be erased in order to make room for divine action.

Section I

BACKGROUND OF THE DEBATE

2

Debating the Faithfulness of Jesus Christ in Twentieth-Century Scholarship

DEBBIE HUNN

Πίστις Χριστοῦ, a phrase quiet for centuries, has helped rouse broad theological issues hibernating since the Reformation. Its history, however, has been tame. Prior to the twentieth century, the phrase was almost universally understood to mean faith in Christ.[1] When Roy Harrisville searched the *Thesaurus Linguae Graecae* corpus for forms of the πίστις Χριστοῦ construction in the writings of the early church fathers, he found that the Fathers understood πίστις Χριστοῦ as objective in every case in which they clearly indicated the sense of the genitive.[2]

How soon did alternative interpretations appear? Ian Wallis looked for early allusions to Christ having faith and found that Athanasius countered the Arians by denying that Christ had faith. Apparently faith was considered a creaturely response to God, and Athanasius was concerned to preserve the deity of Christ. Those who followed Athanasius were then silent on the issue.[3] Clearly, therefore, the early church did not understand πίστις Χριστοῦ to mean "faith of Christ". In fact, whether anyone interpreted πίστις Χριστοῦ as either "faith of Christ" or "faithfulness of Christ" before the eighteenth century is unknown at this point.

Today, however, the meaning of πίστις Χριστοῦ is debated rather than assumed. In the nineteenth century, a few scholars commented briefly on πίστις Χριστοῦ as a subjective genitive, but Johannes Haußleiter gave it the first known substantial treatment in 1891. He insisted that πίστις Χριστοῦ was the faith in God that Christ maintained even in the face

---

[1] At least thus far, no other view has been discovered from the time of the early church until well after the Reformation.

[2] Roy A. Harrisville, "ΠΙΣΤΙΣ ΧΡΙΣΤΟΥ: Witness of the Fathers", *NovT* 36 (1994): 233–41.

[3] Ian G. Wallis, *The Faith of Jesus Christ in Early Christian Traditions* (SNTSMS 84; Cambridge and New York: Cambridge University Press, 1995), 202–4, 210.

of the crucifixion.[4] Twentieth-century interest in πίστις Χριστοῦ began with Gerhard Kittel, who was heavily influenced by Haußleiter. Kittel's contention was that Paul nowhere speaks of faith in Christ as justifying anyone.[5] The debate lived and died among the Germans in the early part of the century; but Gabriel Hebert, working independently, resurrected the issue for the English-speaking world in the 1950s. T.F. Torrance immediately took Hebert's side, and after a brief sparring match between Torrance and C.F.D. Moule, James Barr stepped into the ring to deliver the final blow. But the final blow was aimed only at the poor lexical argument of Hebert and Torrance: the broader debate continued gaining momentum. When Markus Barth entered the discussion, he introduced it to its past by bringing Kittel and Haußleiter into the current debate and to its future by predicting the spate of books that would tear down much conventional Pauline scholarship, including its ideas on πίστις Χριστοῦ.[6]

The predicted books began arriving, and the number of people interested in πίστις Χριστοῦ multiplied. In particular, the publication of *The Faith of Jesus Christ* by Richard B. Hays in 1983 led to a debate between Hays and James Dunn, a proponent of the objective genitive, at the SBL conference in 1991. The body of scholarship, however, had already grown too large to take up at a single meeting. And it continues to grow. The arguments scholars offer generally fall into lexical, grammatical/syntactical, and theological categories.

Lexical Arguments

When Hebert and Torrance wrote, their main argument, unlike Kittel's, was lexical. Torrance says, for example:

> The usual translation of *'emeth* in the LXX is *aletheia*, but *aletheia* is not used to signify abstract or metaphysical truth, but what is grounded upon God's faithfulness, *i.e.*, truth not as something static, but as active, efficacious reality, the reality of God in covenant-relationship … There is no doubt that

---

[4] Johannes Haußleiter, "Der Glaube Jesu Christi und der christliche Glaube: Ein Beitrag zur Erklärung des Römerbriefes", *NKZ* 2 (1891): 132–4.

[5] Gerhard Kittel, "Πίστις Ἰησοῦ Χριστοῦ bei Paulus", *TSK* 79 (1906): 420–3.

[6] Markus Barth, "The Kerygma of Galatians", *Int* 21 (1967): 131–46 (134–7); Markus Barth, *Ephesians: Introduction, Translation, and Commentary on Chapters 1–3* (AB 34; Garden City, NY: Doubleday, 1974), 224, n.85.

again and again where we have the words *pistis* and *dikaiosune* in the New Testament we must see behind them the Hebrew words, *'emeth* and *'emunah*, and where in the New Testament we have *aletheia* we must understand that not simply as a Greek word, but in the light of the Biblical inclusion of *pistis* and *dikaiosune* in the concept of truth.[7]

Barr chides Hebert and Torrance:

> The whole argument here presupposes that the sense of words is determined predominantly by their metaphysical or theological usages … What is lacking from this discussion is any idea of a word as a semantic marker, indicating an essential difference from another word and having the ability to mark that differentia in any one of a number of contexts; not becoming intrinsically infected by any particular one of these contexts, and having its sense as a marker sustained and determined not by metaphysical or theological usage but by a general social milieu, in which the language has its life.[8]

Barr follows this with examples from both Greek and Jewish writers to show that "neither Greek metaphysics nor Hebrew conceptions of the reality of God are built into the intrinsic semantic function of the word ἀλήθεια".[9] For Hebert and Torrance, their "whole theology becomes the characteristic semantic marker-function of the word 'truth'".[10] Barr single-handedly turned the argument from one faulty path, but this did not stop the debate. Nor should it have. But after Barr few scholars tried to tie Paul's Greek to the Hebrew of the Old Testament.

Πίστις from the Greek

Unfortunately, understanding the illegitimacy of importing Hebrew meanings into Greek words did not prevent importing the meanings of other Greek words into πίστις. Many have followed Kittel in his attempt to bring faith to encompass obedience in the phrase "obedience

---

[7] T.F. Torrance, "One Aspect of the Biblical Conception of Faith", *ExpTim* 68 (1957): 112.

[8] James Barr, "Faith and Truth: An Examination of Some Linguistic Arguments", in *Semantics of Biblical Language* (London: Oxford University Press, 1961), 161–205 (188).

[9] Barr, "Faith and Truth", 190.

[10] Barr, "Faith and Truth", 191.

of faith" in Romans 1:5.[11] This would allow the obedience of Christ in Romans 5 to be read back into πίστις Χριστοῦ in chapter 3. Still others have tried nearly to equate πίστις with righteousness[12] and even with power.[13] What is lacking here, as Barr said of Torrance's work, "is any idea of a word as a semantic marker, indicating an essential difference from another word".[14]

Other scholars look among legitimate meanings of πίστις to try to understand πίστις Χριστοῦ, the most common choices being "faith" and "faithfulness". But some scholars suggest other definitions. In 1966 Greer Taylor proposed that πίστις in Galatians 3:22 referred to the *fidei commissum* of Roman law. The *fidei commissum* allowed a testator of a will to appoint successive heirs, even as the Abrahamic covenant appointed Abraham and then his seed, Christ.[15]

More than twenty years later, David Hay suggested πίστις be translated "pledge" or "evidence" – a meaning he found common in Philo and Josephus. He argued that in Galatians 3:23, 25 πίστις means "the objective ground of faith" – that is, Jesus – and that this explains why Paul speaks of faith as "coming".[16] Hay's view, like Taylor's, has not received wide acceptance. If "*fidei commissum*" or "pledge/evidence" were legitimate possibilities in Galatians 3, it would not help the reader understand πίστις Χριστοῦ in Romans because in Romans the ideas of two successive heirs and of faith as coming do not appear.

Faith or Faithfulness?

Up to this point in the discussion, most scholars have tacitly assumed that πίστις Χριστοῦ has the same meaning in each epistle and they define

---

[11] Kittel, "Πίστις Ἰησου Χριστοῦ", 423. Others include Markus Barth, "The Faith of the Messiah", *HeyJ* 10 (1969): 366; Richard B. Hays, "ΠΙΣΤΙΣ and Pauline Christology: What Is at Stake?", in *Pauline Theology. IV. Looking Back, Pressing On* (ed. David M. Hay and E. Elizabeth Johnson; Atlanta, GA: Scholars Press, 1997; first published in *SBLSP* 30 [1991]: 714–29), 35–60 (40); J. Louis Martyn in *Galatians*, 276; and Sam K. Williams, *Galatians* (ANTC; Nashville, TN: Abingdon, 1997), 66.

[12] Erwin R. Goodenough and A.T. Kraabel, "Paul and the Hellenization of Christianity", in *Religions in Antiquity: Essays in Memory of Erwin Ramsdell Goodenough* (ed. Jacob Neusner; Leiden: Brill, 1968; repr. 1970), 37.

[13] Hung-Sik Choi, "Πίστις in Galatians 5:5–6: Neglected Evidence for the Faithfulness of Christ", *JBL* 124 (2005): 467–90 (482–3).

[14] Barr, "Faith and Truth", 188.

[15] Greer M. Taylor, "Function of πίστις Χριστοῦ in Galatians", *JBL* 85 (1966): 58–76.

[16] David M. Hay, "*Pistis* as 'Ground for Faith' in Hellenized Judaism and Paul", *JBL* 108 (1989): 461–76 (463, 471).

πίστις by "faith" or "faithfulness". Some scholars argue that πίστις must have both meanings whenever it appears. D.H. van Daalen, for example, concludes that because the Greeks used a single word to mean both "faith" and "faithfulness" they did not distinguish between them.[17] Hays labels it a "semantic fallacy" therefore if we make this distinction.[18] By this argument, however, πίστις would also have to include the meanings "pledge", "evidence", and *"fidei commissum"*, which would make nearly every occurrence of πίστις (not to mention πίστις Χριστοῦ) unintelligible. Moisés Silva points out that intentional ambiguity in a text is rare and that context will usually eliminate multiple meanings.[19]

In trying to decide between the meanings "faith" and "faithfulness", Donald Robinson notes that πίστις probably never means faith in the Septuagint.[20] George Howard looks outside the biblical text to find that πίστις means faithfulness more often than it means trust in Jewish Hellenistic Greek.[21] Although these observations are among the most often cited arguments for πίστις meaning faithfulness, they say little other than that the Old Testament and Jewish Hellenistic Greek literature speak more about the concept of faithfulness than they do of faith.

Context helps more in correctly defining the particular use of a term than general statistics. Along these lines, Moule argues that the use of the verb πιστεύω determines the meaning of the noun πίστις in Galatians 2:16 where both words appear.[22] Advocates of the subjective genitive challenge this argument. Douglas Campbell labels it a fallacy to derive the meaning of πίστις from its cognate verb πιστεύω.[23] Barry Matlock counters, however, that Paul himself substitutes the noun πίστις for the verb πιστεύω when he quotes Genesis 15:6 in Romans 4:9. This is important in determining the meaning of πίστις because πιστεύω has a narrower semantic range, one which does not include "be faithful".[24]

---

[17] D.H. van Daalen, "'Faith' according to Paul", *ExpTim* 87 (1975): 83–5 (84).

[18] Hays, "What Is at Stake?", 58.

[19] Moisés Silva, *Biblical Words and their Meaning: An Introduction to Lexical Semantics* (Grand Rapids, MI: Zondervan, 1983), 149–56. For a test for ambiguity, see R. Barry Matlock, "Detheologizing the ΠΙΣΤΙΣ ΧΡΙΣΤΟΥ Debate: Cautionary Remarks from a Lexical Semantic Perspective", *NovT* 42 (2000): 4.

[20] Donald W.B. Robinson, "'The Faith of Jesus Christ': A New Testament Debate", *RTR* 29 (1970): 76.

[21] George E. Howard, "Romans 3:21–31 and the Inclusion of the Gentiles", *HTR* 63 (1970): 230.

[22] C.F.D. Moule, "The Biblical Conception of 'Faith'", *ExpTim* 68 (1957): 222.

[23] Douglas A. Campbell, "False Presuppositions in the ΠΙΣΤΙΣ ΧΡΙΣΤΟΥ Debate: A Response to Brian Dodd", *JBL* 116 (1997): 715–16.

[24] Matlock, "Detheologizing ΠΙΣΤΙΣ ΧΡΙΣΤΟΥ", 13, 15.

For the objective genitive view, faith is the only possible meaning of πίστις in πίστις Χριστοῦ phrases but, for the subjective genitive, either "faith" or "faithfulness" would make the phrase intelligible. Proponents of the subjective genitive have been vague about the meaning of πίστις Χριστοῦ through much of the discussion. But scholars are working to define the term more precisely, and at this time "faith of Christ" and "faithfulness of Christ" each has its backers. In the nineteenth century, J.P. Lange stood with "the faithfulness of Christ" because "[a]s to his knowledge, Christ of course did not walk by faith but by sight".[25] Hung-Sik Choi and Ardel Caneday take the same stand today but on the grounds that Christ having faith is not a prominent theme in Paul.[26] Advocates of this view often define the faithfulness of Christ specifically as his death for humankind.[27]

"Faith of Christ" has early origins in the debate as well. Kittel wrote that Paul used the name "Jesus" in Romans 3:26 to make it clear that πίστις Χριστοῦ is the faith Jesus had in the days of his flesh.[28] Erwin Goodenough says that Romans 4 compares Christ's faith with Abraham's and that 4:22 assumes that Christ believed in his own resurrection: this is the faith of Christ that brings righteousness.[29] Scholars also turn to the gospels to find examples of Jesus' faith. For example, Paul Pollard, along with others, reasons that since the disciples failed to heal the boy with the demon in Mark 9:14–29 because of their lack of faith, Jesus' success must have been due to his faith. Furthermore, when Jesus cursed the fig tree in Mark 11:12–14, 20–25, his words "have faith in God" imply that he dried up the fig tree by faith and that similar faith can move mountains. Jesus' prayer in Gethsemane was a prayer of faith, and even Jesus' enemies said he trusted (πείθω) in God.[30]

---

[25] Johann P. Lange, *Romans* (trans. Philip Schaff; n.p., 1865; reprint, Grand Rapids, MI: Zondervan, ca. 1950), 129.
[26] Ardel B. Caneday, "Galatians 3:22ff.: A *Crux Interpretum* for ΠΙΣΤΙΣ ΧΡΙΣΤΟΥ in Paul's Thought", (conference paper, Evangelical Theological Society, Philadelphia, 16–18 November 1995), 10; Choi, "Πίστις in Galatians 5:5–6", 471.
[27] Hays, "What Is at Stake?", 48; Morna D. Hooker, "Πίστις Χριστοῦ", in *From Adam to Christ: Essays on Paul* (Cambridge: Cambridge University Press, 1990; first published in *NTS* 35 [1989]: 321–42), 174; Luke Timothy Johnson, "Romans 3:21–26 and the Faith of Jesus", *CBQ* 44 (1982): 80.
[28] Kittel, "Πίστις Ἰησοῦ Χριστοῦ", 426.
[29] Goodenough and Kraabel, "Paul and the Hellenization of Christianity", 49.
[30] Jesse Paul Pollard, "The Problem of the Faith of Christ" (PhD dissertation, Baylor University, 1982), 64, 71, 77, 80.

Advocates of the objective genitive argue against both views. Dunn maintains that the meaning "'the faithfulness of Christ' would require a good deal of unpacking, which Paul never provides".[31] Furthermore, in Romans 4 Paul attacks the Jewish tradition that Abraham was "the archetype of *faithfulness*". Abraham's πίστις meant his faith in God's promises (4:16–22), not his faithfulness. Proponents of the subjective genitive, therefore, who demand that the structurally similar phrases πίστις Χριστοῦ in Romans 3:26 and πίστις Ἀβραάμ in 4:16 correspond in meaning cannot take πίστις Χριστοῦ as "the faithfulness of Christ".[32] To give up the link between 3:26 and 4:16, however, is to give up one of the strongest arguments for the subjective genitive. But to turn to the "faith of Christ" view is difficult to sustain even in the gospels, much less in Paul. These problems may not finally defeat the subjective genitive, but they do suggest that the battle must be fought with more than a lexical sword.

Grammatical Arguments

Arland Hultgren hypothesizes that whenever Paul uses πίστις followed by a subjective genitive, the article is "invariably present" before πίστις. Since πίστις is anarthrous in all πίστις Χριστοῦ formulations, except that in Ephesians 3:12 (which he does not consider Pauline), Hultgren concludes that the genitive in πίστις Χριστοῦ cannot be subjective.[33] Hultgren's theory does not tell the reader whether or not the genitive is subjective if the article is present. It simply says that if the article is absent, then the genitive is not subjective. Therefore, to test Hultgren's theory, we must consider Paul's anarthrous uses of πίστις followed by a genitive. Any subjective uses of the genitive disprove the theory. Aside from the πίστις Χριστοῦ formulations, anarthrous πίστις is rarely followed by a genitive in Paul. However, πίστις Ἀβραάμ in Romans 4:16 hammers the nail into the coffin of Hultgren's grammatical rule. Paul did not consider the article necessary before πίστις followed by Ἀβραάμ as a subjective genitive.[34]

---

[31] James D.G. Dunn, *The Epistle to the Galatians* (BNTC; Peabody, MA: Hendrickson, 1993), 138–9.

[32] James D.G. Dunn, "Once More ΠΙΣΤΙΣ ΧΡΙΣΤΟΥ", in Hay and Johnson, eds., *Looking Back, Pressing On*, 75.

[33] Arland J. Hultgren, "The *Pistis Christou* Formulation in Paul", *NovT* 22 (1980): 253–8.

[34] Contra Dunn, "Once More", 66.

Unfortunately, to verify his theory, Hultgren primarily examines articular uses of πίστις followed by a genitive.[35] When he does deal with Romans 4:16, he does not adequately substantiate why he finds it clear that the genitive is not subjective.[36] Similarly, Sam Williams, in trying to refute Hultgren, considers Romans 3:3 and 4:12, passages where the nouns are articular rather than anarthrous.[37] This instance of confusion in the debate shows more than a momentary slip in the thinking of Hultgren and Williams. Scholars on both sides of the πίστις Χριστοῦ debate cite Williams' argument as decisively disproving Hultgren's hypothesis.

As for the subjective genitive, George Howard led the way down the grammatical/syntactical path. He notes that Paul uses πίστις plus a genitive of person or personal pronoun twenty-four times outside the πίστις Χριστοῦ phrases, and each refers to the faith of that person.[38] He states further that "it was inappropriate to the Hellenistic Jewish mentality to express the object of faith by means of the objective genitive … it does not occur".[39] He also cites Bible versions, such as the Peshitta and the Latin Vulgate, which translate πίστις Χριστοῦ with a phrase equivalent to "faith of Christ" and concludes that Luther appears to be the first to use πίστις Χριστοῦ as an objective genitive.[40]

Unlike Hultgren, Howard has been widely followed by proponents of his view. And as far as I have found, his syntactical claims went unchallenged until Harrisville and Matlock took them on. Harrisville, as mentioned earlier, found the early church fathers (so much as their writings speak on the issue) uniformly to have understood πίστις Χριστοῦ as an objective genitive.[41] He later found that well-known Greek writers and orators expressed an object for πίστις using both objective and subjective genitives.[42]

Matlock replies to Howard that "unless 'God' or 'Christ' is the 'object' in question, the possibility of the objective genitive typically does not

---

[35] Hultgren, "*Pistis Christou* Formulation", 253–8. In fact, each instance of πίστις he lists on p. 253 is articular.

[36] Hultgren, "*Pistis Christou* Formulation", 256–7.

[37] Sam K. Williams, "Again *Pistis Christou*", *CBQ* 49 (1987): 432–3.

[38] George E. Howard, "Notes and Observations on the 'Faith of Christ,'" *HTR* 60 (1967): 459.

[39] George E. Howard, "Faith of Christ", in *ABD* (New York: Doubleday, 1992), 2.758.

[40] Howard, "Notes and Observations", 460–1.

[41] Harrisville, "Witness of the Fathers."

[42] Roy A. Harrisville, "Before ΠΙΣΤΙΣ ΧΡΙΣΤΟΥ: The Objective Genitive as Good Greek", *NovT* 48 (2006): 353–8.

even arise".[43] It is context and not the meaning with the highest count in the literature that must determine the sense of any use of πίστις.[44] Furthermore, translations resembling "faith of Christ" in the Latin Vulgate and Syriac Peshitta cannot be used to determine the translators' understanding because they used a "translation-by-default" and passed on the ambiguity they inherited from Paul without making an exegetical decision.[45]

The main arguments of Hultgren and Howard have been effectively disproven, but grammatical and syntactical arguments still help shape the debate. The most common charge against the objective genitive, for example, is that it creates a redundancy in Romans 3:22; Galatians 2:16; 3:22; and Philippians 3:9.[46] Moule gave the first defense of the redundancy in Galatians 2:16 when he said that the verb πιστεύω determines the meaning of the noun πίστις in the same verse.[47] Regarding Romans 3:22, Dunn states that Paul repeats himself to emphasize "all".[48] Dunn also writes that Paul's Greek in Philippians 3:9 "would scarcely be intelligible" if he meant the first occurrence of πίστις to refer to Christ's faith and the second to human faith.[49] And because the second reference to faith modifies the first, there is a redundancy whether the genitive is subjective or objective.[50] In fact, the twofold occurrence of πίστις Χριστοῦ in Galatians 2:16 and the threefold occurrence of δικαιόω and ἐξ ἔργων νόμου in the same verse show well enough that Paul did not share our aversion to repetition.

Other aspects of Paul's style, such as his use of prepositions, also play a role in the πίστις Χριστοῦ debate. Williams, for example, concludes that Paul never uses πίστις ἐν Χριστῷ "faith in Christ" because for Paul the object of our faith is God, not Christ.[51] However, Veronica Koperski

---

[43] R. Barry Matlock, "'Even the Demons Believe': Paul and πίστις Χριστοῦ", *CBQ* 64 (2002): 304.

[44] Matlock, "Detheologizing ΠΙΣΤΙΣ ΧΡΙΣΤΟΥ", 5.

[45] Matlock, "Even the Demons Believe", 306.

[46] See, e.g., Markus Barth, "Jews and Gentiles: The Social Character of Justification in Paul", *JES* 5 (1968): 241–67 (247); Hays, "What Is at Stake?", 46; R. Longenecker, "The Obedience of Christ", 147, n.1; Peter T. O'Brien, *The Epistle to the Philippians: A Commentary on the Greek Text* (NIGTC; Grand Rapids, MI: Eerdmans, 1991), 249, n.114; Tonstad, "Reading Paul in a New Paradigm", 54, n.71.

[47] Moule, "Biblical Conception of 'Faith'", 222.

[48] Dunn, "Once More", 75.

[49] Dunn, "Once More", 79.

[50] Paul J. Achtemeier, "Apropos the Faith of/in Christ: A Response to Hays and Dunn", in Hay and Johnson, eds., *Looking Back, Pressing On*, 84.

[51] Williams, *Galatians*, 70.

observes that Paul does not use ἐν after πίστις to denote faith in God either.[52] On the other hand, Hultgren concludes that where another writer might use πίστις plus a preposition to say "faith in Christ", Paul uses πίστις Χριστοῦ.[53] However, this assumes that Paul ever wanted to say "faith in Christ". Campbell challenges Hultgren's conclusion, contending that Hultgren bases it on too slim a list of works he considers Pauline.[54] (The same observation could apply to Williams.) Preston Sprinkle, depending upon a larger Pauline corpus, sees Ephesians 1:15 as a point against an objective genitive because Paul's use of πίστις ἐν τῷ κυρίῳ Ἰησοῦ shows that he had an unambiguous phrase with which to say "faith in".[55] However, Paul did not shrink from using more than one expression to state an idea. He uses, for example, two different prepositions in the phrases ἐν τῷ θελήματι τοῦ θεοῦ in Romans 1:10 and διὰ θελήματος θεοῦ in Romans 15:32, when he says that "by the will of God" he wishes to visit the Roman believers.[56] Therefore, to say that Paul said "faith in Christ" with ἐν does not mean he would not say it without. In short, Paul's style has been used to back various claims but ultimately cannot deliver on them.

Scholars also turn to grammatical parallels to decipher πίστις Χριστοῦ. Kittel, for example, observes that ἐκ πίστεως Ἰησοῦ in Romans 3:26 and ἐκ πίστεως Ἀβραάμ in Romans 4:16 are identical except for the person named. Romans 4:16 clearly speaks of the faith Abraham had. Kittel concludes, therefore, that Romans 3:26 speaks of the faith Christ had.[57] Kittel has many followers. Hays, in fact, calls this a "fatal embarrassment" for the objective genitive position, and Howard says that Paul would be "hopelessly confusing his readers" if he intended Romans 3:22, 26 as objective genitives but Romans 3:3 and 4:16 as subjective.[58] On the other hand, Hans Lietzmann finds ἡ πίστις τοῦ εὐαγγελίου in Philippians 1:27 to parallel πίστις Χριστοῦ in Romans

[52] Veronica Koperski, "The Meaning of *Pistis Christou* in Philippians 3:9", *LS* 18 (1993): 202, n.28.

[53] Hultgren, "*Pistis Christou* Formulation", 253–4.

[54] Douglas A. Campbell, *The Rhetoric of Righteousness in Romans 3.21–26* (JSNTSup 65; Sheffield: JSOT Press, 1992), 215.

[55] Preston Sprinkle, "'Two's Company, Three's a Crowd?': Another Option for the '*PISTIS CHRISTOU*' Debate" (conference paper, Far West Region of the Evangelical Theological Society, Sun Valley, CA; 2 May 2003), 25.

[56] Cf. also Paul's use of διά with θέλημα in 1 Cor. 1:1; 2 Cor. 1:1 with his use of κατά with θέλημα in Gal. 1:4.

[57] Kittel, "Πίστις Ἰησοῦ Χριστοῦ", 424.

[58] Hays, "What Is at Stake?", 47; Howard, "Notes and Observations", 459.

3:22 and uses this as evidence for πίστις Χριστοῦ as an objective genitive.[59] Schreiner uses the objective genitive τῆς γνώσεως Χριστοῦ Ἰησοῦ in Philippians 3:8 to conclude that πίστις Χριστοῦ in 3:9 is objective.[60] However, from the parallel between πίστις Χριστοῦ and ἔργα νόμου in Galatians 2:16, Kittel concludes that πίστις Χριστοῦ is subjective and Dennis Lindsay that it is attributive.[61] The real problem with the parallels is not difficulty in pinpointing the type of genitive in the parallel expression. It is that the type of genitive in one expression has no bearing on the genitive in another. In Acts 9:31, for example, Luke sets "the fear of the Lord" beside "the comfort of the Holy Spirit", an objective beside a subjective genitive, which readers clearly understand.[62] Harrisville, in fact, found the early church fathers to understand Romans 4:16 as subjective and Romans 3:26 as objective without confusion or question.[63]

The failure of most grammatical and syntactical arguments to persuade has left a few people in both the subjective and objective camps and a few others in neither. Torrance sees πίστις Χριστοῦ as a "polarized expression", and Morna Hooker views it as a *"concentric expression"*.[64] To read πίστις Χριστοῦ as both subjective and objective, however, means that in each occurrence of the phrase we are to read of both Christians and Christ expressing πίστις and to track these parallel meanings through the text as Paul continues his argument. Overloading a phrase with theology overloads the reader's mind as well.

On the other hand, Hultgren and Williams, although they disagree about who exercises πίστις, agree that the genitive is adjectival in function, rather than purely subjective or objective, and translate the phrase "Christic faith" (Hultgren) or "Christ-faith" (Williams).[65] Caneday argues, however, that the adjectival genitive is "difficult to sustain and more difficult to explain".[66] He notes that Williams' view of

---

[59] Hans Lietzmann, *An die Römer* (HNT; Tübingen: Mohr Siebeck, 1933), 48.

[60] Thomas R. Schreiner, *Paul, Apostle of God's Glory in Christ: A Pauline Theology* (Downers Grove, IL: InterVarsity Press, 2001), 213.

[61] Kittel, "Πίστις Ἰησοῦ Χριστοῦ", 427; Dennis R. Lindsay, "Works of Law, Hearing of Faith and Πίστις Χριστοῦ in Galatians 2:16–3:5", *SCJ* 3 (2000): 87.

[62] Noted by Matlock, "Detheologizing ΠΙΣΤΙΣ ΧΡΙΣΤΟΥ", 16.

[63] Harrisville, "Witness of the Fathers", 236–41.

[64] T.F. Torrance, "The Biblical Conception of 'Faith'," *ExpTim* 68 (1957): 221; Hooker, "Πίστις Χριστοῦ", 184.

[65] Hultgren, *"Pistis Christou* Formulation", 257; Williams, "Again *Pistis Christou*", 437.

[66] Caneday, "Galatians 3:22ff.: A *Crux Interpretum*", 6.

the genitive as adjectival still depends upon the concept of the subjective genitive because the faith belongs to Christ. In this case, therefore, Caneday sees the adjectival and subjective categories as merging.[67] Of course, a similar observation could be made about πίστις Χριστοῦ as an adjectival genitive with believers exercising the faith. The adjectival genitive thus carries some of the objections to the subjective or objective genitive. However, more important objections arise against the adjectival view. What, for example, is "Christic faith"? Williams has in mind a faith "which is given its distinctive character by the absolute trust and unwavering obedience of Jesus".[68] Hultgren describes it as "faith which is in and of [i.e., from] Christ".[69] Seifrid says that with πίστις Χριστοῦ as a "qualifying genitive" (i.e., adjectival) Paul expresses "the basis of faith and therewith its character".[70] Some scholars reject a subjective or objective category because Paul had other, and even clearer, ways to express either idea.[71] But are there not clearer ways (even if wordier) to express the thought of an adjectival genitive? Furthermore, most πίστις Χριστοῦ phrases include the proper name Ἰησοῦς, but proponents of the adjectival genitive have yet to address whether or not the Greek of Paul's time allowed a proper noun to modify πίστις as an adjectival genitive. And, if it did, what did it mean? The definitions cited here are more theological than lexical and could hardly be inherent in the simple phrase.

Although grammatical arguments continue to be important, scholars on all sides of the issue agree that the meaning of πίστις Χριστοῦ will not be determined by grammar alone.[72] Moreover, it is theology, not grammar, that continues to drive the debate.

Theological Arguments

In the 1950s, scholars would state their theological positions. As the debate has progressed, however, they have been more inclined to

---

[67] Caneday, "Galatians 3:22ff.: A *Crux Interpretum*", 6.

[68] Williams, "Again *Pistis Christou*", 446.

[69] Hultgren, "*Pistis Christou* Formulation", 257.

[70] Mark A. Seifrid, *Christ, Our Righteousness: Paul's Theology of Justification* (Downers Grove, IL: InterVarsity Press, 2000), 146.

[71] See, e.g., Seifrid, *Christ, Our Righteousness*, 146; Sprinkle, "Two's Company, Three's a Crowd?", 26.

[72] E.g., Caneday, "Galatians 3:22ff.: A *Crux Interpretum*", 5; Hooker, "Πίστις Χριστοῦ", 165; Schreiner, *Paul*, 213.

accuse others of theological bias than to state their own theological concerns. Certain concerns which *are* stated serve more to distort other interpretations of πίστις Χριστοῦ than to clarify relevant issues. There is thus a need to define plainly the theological issues related to πίστις Χριστοῦ.

Hebert stated one of the first theological issues in the debate when he noted that if Paul put up "simply a personal attitude of 'believing'" against the Jewish claim to righteousness in the early chapters of Romans, he would "have a singularly weak case". Instead Paul sets "the work of God's Righteousness" in opposition to Jewish claims of justification.[73] Many have followed Hebert. Hays, in fact, adds that πίστις Χριστοῦ as an objective genitive "leaves Christ in the passive role of being the object of our justifying faith".[74] Van Daalen disagrees: "[I]f I say that I have faith in someone, I do not mean that I have some wonderful quality called faith, but simply that he or she is someone who can be relied upon; I am not really saying something about myself at all but about the other person."[75] With the translation "faith in Christ", "the emphasis is still on the reliability of the object".[76] A salvation depending wholly upon God is true for πίστις Χριστοῦ as a subjective or objective genitive and therefore cannot be used to distinguish between the two interpretations.

Theological differences also extend to views of the context of πίστις Χριστοῦ verses. Proponents of the subjective genitive usually interpret the context of the πίστις Χριστοῦ phrases as universalistic in scope, whereas proponents of the objective genitive normally apply it to the individual. This fits the fact that "faith in Christ" is exercised by the individual believer, and "the faith/fulness of Christ" is not. The categories are not hard and fast, however, as some advocates of the objective genitive also see Paul arguing from a universalistic position.[77] It is pertinent, then, to ask whether or not the scope of Paul's argument demands a particular view of the genitive. If the thrust of Romans 1–4 or Galatians 2–3 is salvation-historical, must πίστις Χριστοῦ directly name Christ's deed, or may it speak of an individual's involvement in a salvation-historical justification?

---

[73] Gabriel Hebert, "'Faithfulness' and 'Faith'", *RTR* 14 (1955): 33–40 (38–9).

[74] Hays, *The Faith of Jesus Christ*, 121.

[75] van Daalen, "Faith", 84.

[76] van Daalen, "Faith", 84.

[77] See, e.g., Achtemeier, "Apropos the Faith", 85, 91; Ronald Y.K. Fung, *The Epistle to the Galatians* (NICNT; Grand Rapids, MI: Eerdmans, 1988), 168, n.6; Schreiner, *Paul*, 214.

A new view of the Law is often linked to πίστις Χριστοῦ as a subjective genitive as well. The clear contrast between πίστις Χριστοῦ and ἔργα νόμου in Galatians 3, Romans 3, and Philippians 3 should leave it as no surprise that those who differ on the meaning of πίστις Χριστοῦ usually differ on Paul's view of the Law. The traditional position is that Paul contrasts two ways of obtaining righteousness: by faith in Christ or by works of Law. Instead of two human responses, however, proponents of the subjective genitive see a contrast between a human activity and an activity of God or Christ. J.L. Martyn says, for example, that when Paul spoke of πίστις Χριστοῦ, he meant "an act of God carried out in Christ".[78] Campbell, also defending the subjective genitive, observes that since World War II:

> Pauline scholarship has been reorienting its presentation of late Second Temple Jewish soteriology away from a depiction in terms of crabbed legalism … This has in turn necessitated a reorientation of Paul … Paul and Second Temple Judaism now share the principle of individual faith, since it exists at the heart of the covenant relationship. Consequently, it no longer seems necessary for Paul to state, particularly to a Jewish or Jewish-taught audience, that God requires a response of faith … [T]he more distinctive and contentious idea of Christ's messianic faithfulness may be a more appropriate antithesis to the notion of '*torah*-works' when Paul speaks of πίστις.[79]

But surely the contrast between ἔργα νόμου and πίστις Χριστοῦ for the objective view of the genitive is at heart also a work of human beings versus a work of God because "faith in Christ" means a reliance on Christ's work on the cross. The new view of the Law, however, is a true contrast to that of the past, but does the meaning of πίστις Χριστοῦ depend upon it?

Advocates of the subjective genitive often tie new views of justification and salvation to πίστις Χριστοῦ. Williams, for example, acknowledges that δικαιόω was a forensic term used in the law court. However, he says that the notion of relationship was always implicit in the term because one is righteous by fulfilling the covenant that obtains.[80] Hays explains further that justification does not confer a "legal status" on human beings or consist of a declaration of righteousness ("legal fiction") for

---

[78] Martyn, *Galatians*, 270.
[79] Campbell, *Rhetoric of Righteousness*, 61–2.
[80] Williams, *Galatians*, 63.

them. It is rather a "formal inclusion" of people into the community of the "sons of the living God".[81] Douglas Moo's concern is that reading justification by faith as having its "primary focus on the inclusion of the Gentiles" challenges the Reformation doctrine of justification.[82] And Harrisville states that a reduced emphasis on faith causes readers to wonder what connects them to Christ apart from a vague sense of "participationism" in Christ.[83] Hays, however, replies that Romans does not answer the question, "How can I be saved?"[84] And Campbell sees individual appropriation of salvation as a minor theme that seems incongruous with respect to Romans as a whole.[85] Howard writes that the focus of scholarship is turning away from seeing salvation by grace through faith as the solution to the human dilemma under the Law and toward Paul's concern for admitting Gentiles into the kingdom of God. Interpreting πίστις Χριστοῦ as divine faithfulness fits the new emphasis in Pauline theology because it focuses on the faithfulness of God to Jew and Gentile alike.[86] This difference is genuinely related to the translation of πίστις Χριστοῦ because if πίστις Χριστοῦ does not mean "faith in Christ" there are eight fewer references in Paul to the means of appropriating salvation than was previously supposed. But must one who sees πίστις Χριστοῦ as subjective "no longer equate justification by faith with the basis of Paul's gospel"?[87]

Twelve years after Hebert reintroduced the πίστις Χριστοῦ debate, Markus Barth predicted a change in theological outlook that would break the traditional mould on Paul. Strands of some of the theological issues run through the πίστις Χριστοῦ debate. Scholars choose their strands and tie them together in different ways around the phrase. But it has not yet been shown whether most strands are contingent upon a particular interpretation of πίστις Χριστοῦ. That depends upon exegesis, and it is to exegesis that many scholars look today as they continue the debate.

---

[81] Richard B. Hays, "Justification", in *ABD* (New York: Doubleday, 1992), 3:1131.

[82] Douglas J. Moo, *The Epistle to the Romans* (NICNT; Grand Rapids, MI: Eerdmans, 1996), 243.

[83] Harrisville, "Before ΠΙΣΤΙΣ ΧΡΙΣΤΟΥ", 357.

[84] Richard B. Hays, "Psalm 143 and the Logic of Romans 3", *JBL* 99 (1980): 107–15 (112).

[85] Campbell, *Rhetoric of Righteousness*, 206.

[86] Howard, "Notes and Observations", 464–5.

[87] Joseph Plevnik believes this to be the viewpoint of most scholars today. Joseph Plevnik, "The Understanding of God at the Basis of Pauline Theology", *CBQ* 65 (2003): 567.

Conclusion

Because the faithfulness of Christ implies that people can have faith in him and because an injunction to have faith in him assumes that he is faithful, both the faithfulness of Christ and faith in Christ are ideas that fit the context of each passage that uses πίστις Χριστοῦ. This is the primary cause for difficulty in making a strong case for one view against the other. Forgetting this has led to some unfounded concerns, as mentioned previously. It is necessary, however, with many issues, to determine exactly what will stand or fall with a particular view of πίστις Χριστοῦ. Will justification by faith in Christ stand if the genitive is subjective? Will the New Perspective on Paul fall if the genitive is objective? What becomes of participation in Christ? Must different readings of πίστις Χριστοῦ lead to different pictures of the theology of Romans or Galatians? Does the subjective genitive mean that faith is simply the response of those already justified? Does the objective genitive mean that God's act in Christ is simply a response to human faith? Must we confuse means and grounds or hold that faith is another term for obedience? What must we actually conclude if πίστις Χριστοῦ is objective, subjective, adjectival?

Good lexical, grammatical, and syntactical arguments, although necessary to keep the πίστις Χριστοῦ debate on track, have proven inadequate by themselves to answer these questions. Sound exegesis is needed, and scholars are turning to the text. This, too, however, has multiplied the questions: how is πίστις Χριστοῦ related to ὁ δίκαιος in Romans 1:17, to δικαιοσύνη θεοῦ in Romans 1:17 and 3:21, to ὑπακοή in Romans 1:5, to ἐκ πίστεως εἰς πίστιν in Romans 1:17, to ἔργα νόμου in Galatians 2:16? How does τὴν ἐκ θεοῦ δικαιοσύνην in Philippians 3:9 relate to δικαιοσύνη θεοῦ in Romans 3:21, 22? Is Abraham's faith in Romans 4 and Galatians 3 a picture of Christ's faith, the believer's faith, or both?

Concern for exegesis has, unfortunately, also multiplied assumptions, and the assumptions are not always shared even by those on the same side of an issue. Some scholars, for example, redefine "faith", "justification", or "righteousness", ideas clearly related to πίστις Χριστοῦ.[88] Without solid support for changes in definitions, however, the debate will come full circle to the lexical problems of Hebert and Torrance.

---

[88] E.g., Martyn, *Galatians*, 272–3; N.T. Wright, *Paul: In Fresh Perspective* (Minneapolis, MN: Fortress, 2005), 110–22.

Barth's prediction has proven true, but perhaps even Barth would have been surprised at the number of ways Paul has been rewritten. The twentieth century has made progress by asking some questions and by disproving some answers. It is for the twenty-first century to provide careful exegesis; to shore up its arguments; to support or discard its assumptions; to determine the implications of a subjective, objective, or adjectival genitive in πίστις Χριστοῦ; and to place the debate on a sound footing. And so let the debate continue.

3

Πίστις with a Preposition and Genitive Modifier: Lexical, Semantic, and Syntactic Considerations in the πίστις Χριστοῦ Discussion

STANLEY E. PORTER and ANDREW W. PITTS

Introduction

The debate over the meaning of the formulation πίστις Χριστοῦ continues unabated. The traditional view is that this word group consisting of a noun and its modifying genitive constitutes an objective genitive relationship and should be rendered "faith in Christ".[1] Starting about forty years ago, a number of scholars began to question such an interpretation and to argue for the subjective genitive, rendered "faith of Christ" or "Christ's faithfulness".[2] What started as a few protesting voices

---

[1] Most commentators on Romans and Galatians still argue for this position. These include C.E.B. Cranfield, *A Critical and Exegetical Commentary on the Epistle to the Romans*, II (ICC; Edinburgh: T&T Clark, 2004 [1975]), 203; J.D.G. Dunn, *Romans* (WBC 38A, B; Waco, TX: Word, 1988), 1.166–67; J.A. Fitzmyer, *Romans* (AB 33; New York: Doubleday, 1993), 345–6; Moo, *Romans*, 224–5; T. Schreiner, *Romans* (BECNT; Grand Rapids, MI: Baker, 1998), 181–6; R. Jewett, *Romans* (Hermeneia; Minneapolis, MN: Fortress, 2007), 276–8; H.D. Betz, *Galatians* (Hermeneia; Philadelphia, PA: Fortress, 1979), 117–18; F.F. Bruce, *The Epistle to the Galatians* (NIGTC; Grand Rapids, MI: Eerdmans, 1982), 138–9; Dunn, *Galatians*, 138–9. Apart from commentaries, see Hultgren, *"Pistis Christou* Formulation"; Dunn, "Once More, *Pistis Christou*", *SBLSP* 30 (1991): 733–44; Harrisville, "Witness of the Fathers"; B. Dodd, "Romans 1:17: A *Crux Interpretum* for the πίστις Χριστοῦ Debate?" *JBL* 114 (1995): 470–73; C.E.B. Cranfield, "On the Πίστις Χριστοῦ Question", in his *On Romans and Other New Testament Essays* (Edinburgh: T&T Clark, 1998), 81–97; Seifrid, *Christ, our Righteousness*, 139–46.

[2] A few recent commentators on Romans and esp. Galatians argue for this position. These include: K. Barth, *The Epistle to the Romans* (trans. E.C. Hoskyns; Oxford: Oxford University Press, 1933), 41, 96; Richard Longenecker, *Galatians* (WBC 41; Dallas, TX: Word, 1990), 87–8; F.J. Matera, *Galatians* (SP 9; Collegeville, MN: Liturgical Press, 1983), 93–4; L.T. Johnson, *Reading Romans: A Literary and Theological Commentary* (New York: Crossroad, 1997), 58–61; Martyn, *Galatians*, 251, 263–75.

soon became a sizeable body of opinion, and the subjective genitive now commands the support of many, if not most, scholars – though some argue for both, or some broader sense.[3] Although grammatical issues

---

This position had some early proponents: J. Haußleiter, *Der Glaube Jesu Christi und der christliche Glaube: Ein Beitrag zur Erklärung des Römerbriefes* (Erlangen: Deichert, 1891), 109–45; idem, "Der Glaube Jesu",; idem, "Was versteht Paulus unter christlichen Glauben?" in *Theologische Abhandlungen* (Festschrift H. Cremer; Gütersloh: Bertelsmann, 1895), 159–81; Kittel, "Πίστις Ἰησοῦ Χριστοῦ". Revival came with Hebert, "Faithfulness", *Theol* 58 (1955): 373–9; Torrance, "One Aspect" (with responses by C.F.D. Moule, pp. 157, 222 and Torrance, p. 221). Revivalists include: E. Fuchs, "Jesu und der Glaube", *ZTK* 55 (1958): 170–85; P. Valloton, *Le Christ et la foi: Etude de théologie biblique* (Geneva: Labor & Fides, 1960), 47; Richard Longenecker, *Paul, Apostle of Liberty* (New York: Harper & Row, 1964), 149–52; idem, "The Obedience of Christ"; H.J. Ljungman, *Pistis: A Study of its Presuppositions and its Meaning in Pauline Use* (Lund: Gleerup, 1964), 38–40; G. Taylor, "Function of πίστις Χριστοῦ"; Goodenough and Kraabel, "Paul and the Hellenization of Christianity"; K. Kertelge, *Rechtfertigung bei Paulus* (Münster: Aschendorff, 1967), 162–6; Howard, "Notes and Observations"; idem, "Romans 3:21–31"; idem, "The 'Faith of Christ'," *ExpTim* 85 (1973–74): 212–15; idem, *Paul: Crisis in Galatia* (SNTSMS 35; Cambridge: Cambridge University Press, 1979), 57–8; idem, "Faith of Christ"; J. Bligh, "Did Jesus Live by Faith?" *HeyJ* 9 (1968): 414–19 (418–19); M. Barth, "Faith of the Messiah"; Robinson, "The Faith of Jesus Christ"; J.J. O'Rourke, "πίστις", *CBQ* 36 (1973): 188–94; S.K. Williams, "The 'Righteousness of God' in Romans", *JBL* 99 (1980): 272–8; Johnson, "Romans 3:21–26"; Hays, *The Faith of Jesus Christ*, 170–77; idem, "What Is at Stake?"; L. Gaston, *Paul and the Torah* (Vancouver: University of British Columbia Press, 1987), 58; Hooker, "Πίστις Χριστοῦ"; L.E. Keck, "'Jesus' in Romans", *JBL* 108 (1989): 443–60; Campbell, *Rhetoric of Righteousness*, 58–69; idem, "The Meaning of πίστις and νόμος in Paul: A Linguistic and Structural Investigation", *JBL* 111 (1992): 85–97; idem, "False Presuppositions"; idem, "The Story of Jesus in Romans and Galatians", in *Narrative Dynamics in Paul: A Critical Assessment* (ed. Bruce Longenecker; Louisville, KY: Westminster John Knox, 2002), esp. 120–23; idem, *The Quest for Paul's Gospel: A Suggested Strategy* (JSNTSup 274; London: T&T Clark, 2005), esp. 191 (who notes the use of prepositions with "πιστ-phrases" but does not tie this to πίστις Χριστοῦ); Bruce Longenecker, "Πίστις in Romans 3:25: Neglected Evidence for the 'Faithfulness of Christ'?" *NTS* 39 (1993): 478–80; idem, "Defining the Faithful Character of the Covenant Community: Galatians 2.15–21 and Beyond", in *Paul and the Mosaic Law* (ed. J.D.G. Dunn; Tübingen: Mohr Siebeck, 1996), 75–97; S.K. Stowers, *A Rereading of Romans: Justice, Jews, and Gentiles* (New Haven, CT: Yale University Press, 1994), 201; Wallis, *Faith of Jesus Christ*, 65–102; N.T. Wright, "Romans and the Theology of Paul", in *Pauline Theology. III. Romans* (ed. D.M. Hay and E.E. Johnson; Minneapolis, MN: Fortress, 1995), 30–67.

[3] E.g., A. Deißmann, *St. Paul: A Study in Social and Religious History* (trans. L.R.M. Strachan; London: Hodder & Stoughton, 1912), 140–43; Nigel Turner, *Syntax*, III, *A Grammar of New Testament Greek* (ed. J.H. Moulton; Edinburgh: T&T Clark, 1963), 76; S.K. Williams, *Jesus' Death as Saving Event: The Background and Origin of a Concept* (HDR 2; Missoula, MT: Scholars Press, 1975), 48; idem, "Again πίστις Χριστοῦ."

have been raised along the way throughout the debate – such as the meaning of πίστις and its cognate verb πιστεύω, the meanings of the genitive relationship, and criteria for differentiating subjective (and related types) and objective genitives (as well as the issue of translation, not properly a matter of grammar) – most scholars at the end of the day despair of solving the issue linguistically and consign it to a matter of exegesis or even theology. One of the first to make such a pronouncement was none other than J.H. Moulton, who said regarding distinguishing between the objective and subjective genitive: "It is as well to remember that in Greek this question is entirely one of exegesis, not of grammar."[4] More recently, Hans Dieter Betz stated that "Because of the grammatical ambiguity [of the genitive construction] the problem must be decided by context analysis."[5] Morna Hooker insists that the issue "cannot be settled on the basis of appeals to grammatical construction alone", but only by exegesis.[6] Richard Hays thinks that the arguments from grammar are "finally inconclusive".[7] And Francis Watson contends that the issue "may be clarified, not by grammar but by context".[8] A few claim to have reached the point of believing that the terms of the discussion itself might need revisioning, although they usually opt for one or both of the usual solutions.[9] The only genuinely bright spot on the horizon, in so far as those who continue to pursue the issue with linguistic interests in mind, is the work of Barry Matlock. Matlock has provided three studies that have addressed the issue – the first two are concerned with a lexical semantic approach,[10] and the last has addressed the issue of supposed redundancy in theologically sensitive passages (e.g., Gal. 2:16; 3:22; Rom. 3:22; Phil. 3:9).[11] On the basis of his study, Matlock concludes that there are good lexical semantic reasons for maintaining the objective genitive position. However, at the end of his own discussion, Dan Wallace concludes: "Although the issue is not to

---

[4] J.H. Moulton, *Prolegomena*, vol. 1 of *A Grammar of New Testament Greek* (3rd ed.; Edinburgh: T&T Clark, 1908), 72.

[5] Betz, *Galatians*, 118, n.45.

[6] Hooker, "Πίστις Χριστοῦ", *NTS*, 321.

[7] Hays, "Πίστις and Pauline Christology", 716.

[8] F. Watson, *Paul and the Hermeneutics of Faith* (London & New York: T&T Clark, 2004), 76.

[9] E.g., Williams, "Again *Pistis Christou*"; Martyn, *Galatians*, 270; F. Watson, *Paul and the Hermeneutics of Faith*, 73–6; Jewett, *Romans*, 277.

[10] Matlock, "Detheologizing ΠΙΣΤΙΣ ΧΡΙΣΤΟΥ"; idem, "Even the Demons Believe".

[11] R.B. Matlock, "The Rhetoric of πίστις in Paul: Galatians 2:16, 3:22, Romans 3:22, and Philippians 3:9", *JSNT* 30.2 (2007): 173–203.

be solved via grammar, on balance grammatical considerations seem to be in favor of the subjective genitive view."[12] Wallace unfortunately does not offer substantive grammatical arguments for his position. With such conclusions readily at hand, it is not surprising that scholars are looking to exegetical and theological reasons for progress in the discussion.

In what follows we will try to accomplish four tasks: (1) discuss the role of lexical semantics in sense disambiguation; (2) offer a description of the Greek case system; (3) reframe the debate in terms of lexis and case; and then (4) present analysis and results. We conclude that these four considerations illustrate that lexical, grammatical, and syntactical factors are probably more important to the discussion than is usually assumed.

Lexical Semantics and Sense Disambiguation

The controversy over the word group πίστις Χριστοῦ is, in a number of ways, less about the genitive construction and more about disambiguating the meaning of the head term πίστις. Part of the problem with the contemporary discussion rests with the fact that the debate is often driven by determining what kind of genitive is modifying the head term (more will be said about this below). This statement assumes that the selection of a case form determines the lexical meaning of its head term – a supposition that is hard to substantiate linguistically. As we suggest below, the genitive occurs in a modification structure that restricts the meaning of the head term, πίστις. The language user assumes the lexical meaning of the head term and then restricts its meaning through the use of the case system. The case system does not seem to be employed to determine the lexical meaning of its head term, but only modifies the nominal idea expressed by the head term. Initial analysis, therefore, should proceed from an investigation of the lexical meaning of πίστις and how particular sense components are realized by contextual and co-textual features, instead of beginning with an analysis of the word group, such as a genitive construction.

The first issue, therefore, is to determine lexical meaning. In terms of the theoretical discussion, this raises a central linguistic question concerning how language users disambiguate a particular contextual

---

[12] D.B. Wallace, *Greek Grammar beyond the Basics: An Exegetical Syntax of the New Testament* (Grand Rapids, MI: Zondervan, 1996), 116.

meaning from a lexeme's larger semantic domain.[13] From a lexical semantic standpoint, the scholarly discussion is about whether πίστις means faith in the sense of "faithfulness" or in the sense of "belief". A number of linguistic proposals have been put forward in relation to semantic sense disambiguation. Traditional lexica operate under the assumption that words are polysemous, or have multiple meanings. Several current theorists argue, however, that lexemes are monosemous, or realize one essential meaning but have divergent functions based upon the interaction of the lexeme's meaning with its co-text and context. This monosemy is said to exist within circumscribed authorial sets of usage. In order to disambiguate lexemes along these lines, it is necessary to observe how co-textual features realize particular meanings in unambiguous cases in order to develop criteria for assessing cases that are ambiguous. One of the major patterns of lexical usage is that a lexeme appears with its single meaning in a given definable linguistic unit.

Contextual and co-textual disambiguation criteria extend from a given discourse down to syntactical configurations. Perhaps the most promising line of analysis for the present purposes of semantic sense determination is through collocation analysis. Stanley E. Porter and Matthew O'Donnell note,

> In the field of corpus linguistics (see O'Donnell 2005), work on collocation has demonstrated that where a word has a number of different senses, each sense is accompanied by a unique syntactical pattern (Partington 1998). Some structural pattern, for example the combination of two words in a word group with one as the head-term and the other as a qualifier, can be identified and correlated with a specific sense. Equally within a clause specific patterns in terms of structure, transitivity (i.e., a specific word as actor with a certain type of process) or word order can likewise be used to identify a specific sense of a word.[14]

Several of these criteria should be part of the initial analysis of the lexical meaning of πίστις in the debatable instances before moving on

---

[13] This paragraph is based on S.E. Porter and M.B. O'Donnell, "'On the Shoulders of Giants' – The Expansion and Application of the Louw-Nida Lexicon", SBL 2005 Annual Meeting, Biblical Greek Language and Linguistics / Lexicography Sections Joint Session, Philadelphia, 19–22 November 2005. Reference is to M.B. O'Donnell, *Corpus Linguistics and the Greek of the New Testament* (Sheffield: Sheffield Phoenix Press, 2005) and A. Partington, *Patterns and Meanings: Using Corpora for English Language Research and Teaching* (Amsterdam: Benjamins, 1998).

[14] Porter and O'Donnell, "On the Shoulders", 12.

to ask how the case of the modifying term affects the lexical content expressed by πίστις. This is not to minimize the role case plays in determining the meaning of an individual element or of the larger collocational unit. A collocation of πίστις with a particular case may combine with other features to provide precisely the type of disambiguating structure described above. However, the relation of the case of the modifying term to the lexeme is what is under debate so, in this instance, case provides an unsuitable starting point. The case system will, nevertheless, need to be considered, but it is important to understand first what is indicated by the Greek case system and how the respective cases in Hellenistic Greek function in relation to lexical meaning.

Description of the Greek Case System

In order to understand how the genitive modifier functions in πίστις Χριστοῦ, it is necessary to gain an understanding of the Greek case system as a whole and the way the genitive works in relation to the other cases. Previous research on case in Hellenistic Greek has not been entirely successful in treating the semantics either of the Greek case system as a whole or of individual case forms in particular. Traditional grammars typically – apart from a few localist descriptions[15] – do not give an explanation of the case system itself, but seek to provide an exemplary definition in light of distinct usages of individual case forms within different contexts. They rarely provide a definition of either the particular case or what constitutes an interpretive context. The role of implicature or context-constraints in realizing semantic features associated with the case form is not treated. There are hints of what might legitimately be expected in, for example, A.T. Robertson's comments on the genitive[16] and Wallace's remarks on the vocative when he discusses the "unaffected meaning" of a case and the discourse context ("use").[17] A systematic distinction between semantics and pragmatics, or the meaning of the form and what is meant when the form is used (e.g., through implicature), however, is not maintained

---

[15] See S.E. Porter, *Idioms of the Greek New Testament* (2nd ed.; Biblical Language: Greek 2; Sheffield: Sheffield Academic Press, 1994), 80–100.

[16] A.T. Robertson, *A Grammar of the Greek New Testament in the Light of Historical Research* (4th ed.; Nashville, TN: Broadman, 1934), 493.

[17] Wallace, *Greek Grammar*, 37, 67–71.

or elucidated.[18] This seems to be primarily a methodological issue. Traditional approaches often begin their analyses with lists of usage or, in other words, at the pragmatic level of text rather than at the semantic level of linguistic code. This model of analysis seems to blur the line between semantics and pragmatics instead of letting the semantic level of code govern the usage of the form. This procedure results in the imposition of entire contexts onto the meaning of individual case forms. Such an approach also fails to respect authorial status, with regard to what Paul may have been contemplating when he used the genitive. It is highly unlikely that he was working with notions of subjective or objective genitive, or corresponding categories, as he made linguistic choices.[19] These definitional issues are correlated to various linguistic levels (e.g., syntax, semantics, pragmatics, etc.) that, as we have already seen, need to be clearly distinguished. Both traditional and modern linguistically based approaches (i.e., semantic theories) to the study of the issue of the genitive in πίστις Χριστοῦ have failed to do so.

As can be seen from our discussion up to this point, there are two basic notions regarding case that must be discussed. One is case semantics and the other is case function.

Case Semantics

M.A.K. Halliday distinguishes between two kinds of grammatical definitions: encoding definitions and decoding definitions.[20] In ancient Greek linguistics, Halliday points out, technical grammatical terms evolved out of everyday usage. γραμματική, for instance, which meant "writing", later came to be applied as a technical designation for the study of grammar. Similarly, the common term for "fall" (πτῶσις) was applied to the case system, and various other common terms were employed to describe the individual case forms.[21] Halliday explains that initially language users were concerned with identifying certain forms: "How do I recognize a noun when I see it?" This is a question about a particular token. However, this question later led to inquiries

---

18   See S.E. Porter, *Verbal Aspect in the Greek of the New Testament, with Reference to Tense and Mood* (New York: Lang, 1989), 15, citing N.J.C. Gotteri, "A Note on Bulgarian Verb Systems", *JMALS* NS 8 (1983): 49–60, esp. 49.

19   See Matlock, "Detheologizing ΠΙΣΤΙΣ ΧΡΙΣΤΟΥ", 22–3.

20   M.A.K. Halliday, "On the Ineffability of Grammatical Categories", in *Linguistics in Systemic Perspective* (ed. J.D. Benson, M.J. Cummings, and W.S. Greaves; Amsterdam: Benjamins, 1988), 27–51 (28).

21   See M. Butt, *Theories of Case* (Cambridge: Cambridge University Press, 2006), 13.

about the values of such tokens: "What is a noun, in the sense of what function does it serve?" These kinds of questions provided a catalyst for definitions of the noun such as "a person, place, or thing", where a value is assigned to the token, namely "person, place, or thing". This definition is what Halliday calls an encoding definition. Similarly, "the encoding of our experience of processes" is the name given to "transitivity".[22] Encoding definitions involve three steps: (1) a move in rank – a noun inflects case; (2) a move in delicacy – case is nominative, genitive, dative, or accusative; (3) a move in exponence – the accusative ends in -*n*. By contrast, defining a noun as a word that has the inflection characteristics of case and number is what Halliday calls a decoding definition, since it seeks to decode the semantics of the form. The development of decoding definitions is more involved, since "a metalanguage has to be created, and created out of natural language, in order to assign a Value to a Token".[23] But it is hard to develop metalinguistic categories without being tautologous, and various ambiguities result from assigning values to forms – grammatical categories are ineffable – unless language is viewed as a system in which each choice implies a distinct meaning.[24] With grammatical categories such as "noun", which represent an output condition in the grammar (an item that can figure at a particular place in the syntagma), the question "What does it mean?" (e.g., "person, place, or thing") may provide a helpful analytical question that sets one on the course of developing encoding definitions, since the "noun has no direct contact with semantics, other than in this restricted sense of semantics as the commentary on the meaning of forms".[25] "But", Halliday insists, "input categories of the grammar – the systems, such as 'mood'; their features, such as 'indicative'; and the functions, such as 'Subject' – cannot be so readily glossed in this way: they relate directly to the semantic system that is 'above' the grammar, that which interprets the ideologies of culture … and codes them in a wordable form." It is useless, according to Halliday, to ask what these categories mean. Instead, we must ask, "What is encoded in this language, or in this register (functional variety) of the language?" This perspective reverses the historical linguistic model, which understands language

---

[22] M.A.K. Halliday, "The Form of a Functional Grammar", in *Halliday: System and Function in Language* (ed. G. Kress; Oxford: Oxford University Press, 1976), 7–25, esp. 21.

[23] Halliday, "Categories", 32.

[24] Halliday, "Categories", 33–43.

[25] Halliday, "Categories", 43.

first as a system of forms with meanings attached to them that make sense of the forms. On Halliday's understanding, "A language is treated as a system of meanings, with forms attached to express them. Not grammatical paradigms with their interpretation, but semantic paradigms with their realization."[26]

Previous approaches to the Greek case system have confined themselves to decoding definitions, treating case more or less as an inflectional property of nouns rather than as a system of meaningful choices that are realized in case endings.[27] Even more linguistically adept approaches to the case system, like that found in Louw,[28] do not pose this essential and fundamental question: "What semantic value is encoded within the grammatical category 'case'?" It is surprising that previous research has typically failed to provide a definition of case as a semantic/grammatical category. Moreover, the few definitions that have been provided or assumed do not move the discussion significantly forward, since they are decoding definitions and therefore say nothing of the semantic value encoded within case as a system of meanings. If Halliday is right, the Greek case system is in need of much more detailed grammatical and semantic analysis, explicating the system of meaning not only in terms of a decoding value for the system as a whole (mainly at the morphological level) but also in encoding meanings with reference to its features (nominative, accusative, etc.) and its functions (subject, object, etc.).

In Hellenistic Greek, the cases seem to be differentiated semantically through encoding definitions in the following way:

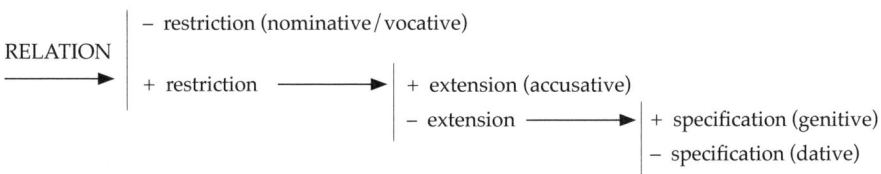

The early commentators on Theodosius's Κανόνες came closest to grasping the values encoded in Greek cases. They suggested "relation" as what we might call the entry condition into the semantics of the Greek

---

[26] Halliday, "Categories", 43.

[27] Cf. J. Lyons, *Introduction to Theoretical Linguistics* (Cambridge: Cambridge University Press, 1968), 289–90.

[28] J.P. Louw, "Linguistic Theory and the Greek Case System", *Acta Classica* 9 (1966): 73–88; Porter, *Idioms*, 80–3.

case system which, for them, only consisted of oblique forms.[29] Most of the description of case after them falls into the trap of repeating the tradition of analysis, instead of attempting to move our understanding of case semantics forward. However, their analysis was extremely underdeveloped and lacked semantic rigor. One obvious flaw was their inability to disambiguate semantically between the dative and the accusative. In terms of meaning and choice, their exclusion of the nominative inhibits their system's ability to function as part of a complete network of forms and therefore limits its ability to communicate meaning. In Hallidayan terminology, its connection to semantics is drastically weakened in that it becomes an independent output rather than being a meaningful choice in terms of the non-nominative cases. So while their approach was a useful starting point, it is far from complete.

Our approach to the Greek cases attempts to re-situate the results of Theodosius and his commentators within a semantically rigorous systemic framework. The semantic category Relation is similar to what the Greek grammarians intended: signifying properly something attendant on or with respect to the essence of the form (ὡς κυρίως μὲν τὰ περὶ τὴν οὐσίαν).[30] Relation is a synthetic semantic category (realized in the forms of case endings) used by the language user to establish the conditions for the expression of the lexical content of the form at the word-group level, and its relation to its co-text, which may function at the clause and clause complex levels, but in certain cases at higher levels of discourse as well.

The nominative is the unmarked case.[31] It is the least marked semantically, cognitively, and formally, and is distributed within non-restricted syntactic contexts and expresses the pure nominal idea [– restriction].[32] The nominative (as well as the vocative), therefore,

---

[29] Theodosius was a significant teacher of grammatical theory in the Greco-Roman world. He lived and taught around the second half of the fourth century and is perhaps best known for his Κανόνες, which amounts to an exposition of morphological, inflectional, and derivational rules for Gk. nouns and verbs, as well as a listing of various possible grammatical forms (the text is found in A. Hilgard, ed., *Grammatici Graeci* [Leipzig: Teubner, 1889–94; repr. Hildesheim: Olms, 1965] 4.1, 4.2, I.1–99).

[30] Hilgard, *Grammatici Graeci*, 4.1, 4.2.

[31] B.J. Blake, *Case* (Cambridge: Cambridge University Press, 1994), 30; Louw, "Theory", 79; Porter, *Idioms*, 84–5.

[32] G.B. Winer, *A Treatise on the Grammar of New Testament Greek* (trans. W.F. Moulton; Edinburgh: T&T Clark, 1882), 226; S.G. Green, *Handbook to the Grammar of the Greek Testament* (London: Religious Tract Society, n.d.), 16; Porter, *Idioms*, 83; Louw, "Theory", 78–9.

is not marked for restriction. It is semantically unrestricted. No bounds or conditions are placed upon the lexical content of the form, nor does it extend restriction to the forms to which it stands in relation. Semantically, it is the most indeterminate of the cases and enters into opposition with the oblique forms. It is also unmarked cognitively in that its meaning is the most conceptually basic of the cases. It is "less definite, unstructured, loosely organised, bound-less".[33] The nominative also exhibits morphological simplicity and regularity. It relates the lexical content of its form to its co-text without semantic restriction. Unrestricted meaning also accounts for its potential to be used in a variety of contexts. Syntactically, it is naturally inclined to function as the subject, since expression of the nominal idea without restriction makes it suitable to function as a head term. This also accounts for its independent function, since the nominative does not restrict the meaning of the form(s) that it stands in relation to. Thus it can function free from syntactic modification while still relating the unrestricted lexical content of the element in the nominative to its co-text. The vocative does not have a full set of inflectional forms (it only occurs in the singular), but it serves to single out participants and make characterizations in a more exclamative and direct, less reserved and formal fashion than the nominative (or accusative – also used for address), which merely expresses the nominal idea.[34]

The oblique forms all *restrict* meaning in some way [+ restriction]. They provide a semantic parameter or condition for the expression of the meaning of the term they stand in relation to. The accusative is prominent in the hierarchy of oblique cases,[35] since it is marked with respect to the nominative but unmarked in opposition to the dative and genitive forms. It is the least semantically determinate of the oblique cases, since the way the accusative enters into semantic relation with its co-text involves restriction through grammaticalizing the semantic feature *extension* [+ extension]. It restricts the extent of the meaning of

---

[33] S. Wallace, "Figure and Ground: The Interrelationships of Linguistic Categories", in *Tense-Aspect: Between Semantics and Pragmatics* (ed. P.J. Hopper; Amsterdam: Benjamins, 1982), 201–23, esp. 212.

[34] Cf. Louw, "Theory", 80.

[35] Cf. Porter, *Idioms*, 82–3; Louw, "Theory", 80–81; A.C. Moorhouse, "The Role of the Accusative Case", in *In the Footsteps of Raphael Kühner* (ed. A. Rijksbaron, H.A. Mulder, and G.C. Wakker; Amsterdam: Gieben, 1988), 209–18, esp. 209–12; see also the scholiast in Hilgard, *Grammatici Graeci*, 1.3, 548.34–549.2.

the lexical item it stands in relation to, usually the verb of a Predicator. It is more semantically dense than the nominative, however, in that it limits meaning and occurs in more syntactically restricted contexts (e.g., in a word group as the complement of a Predicator). The accusative may restrict the extent of the nominal designation of the nominative to a particular object. It may restrict the extent of an action performed with respect to a person or thing, and so on.[36] In all these functions, the accusative case grammaticalizes extension, indicating the extent of the term to which it stands in relation.

The remaining two oblique forms restrict but are opposed in terms of specificity. They constrain or restrict the meaning of words to or within a semantic realm. For example, in the noun phrase πίστις Χριστου τὸ εὐαγγέλιον τοῦ θεοῦ, the genitive restricts "gospel" to the realm of God. Similarly, in εἴτε γὰρ ἐξέστημεν θεῷ the dative restricts the meaning of the verbal form to the realm of benefit or advantage of the participant in the dative. The genitive is the most marked case semantically, since it is marked for *specification* (+ specification; being more rich [i.e., determinate] in meaning than the accusative or dative); formally, through morphological irregularities, especially in the first declension; and distributionally, as it occurs in highly restricted syntactic contexts related to the noun. The genitive grammaticalizes a restricting relation with the semantic feature *specification* in that it specifies, for example, a possessor or a part (partitive), a kind (apposition; epexegetical), or a time (temporal). The genitive consistently restricts meaning through the feature of specification. *What* it specifies is a function realized through its occurrence in a particular context.

The dative is the most versatile of the cases and is unmarked with respect to the genitive, but marked in relation to the other oblique cases and the nominative, since it realizes a restricted relation but *without* the feature of extension or specification [– specification]. From a diachronic linguistic perspective (viewing Hellenistic Greek in terms of the phenomena of grammaticalization), the reason appears to be that the dative became less determinate in its meaning and was on its way out of use by the Hellenistic period, slowly being replaced by the accusative until we get to modern Greek, where there is no dative. The function of the dative is especially apparent in various instrumental uses. The dative often limits a relation (e.g., it grammaticalizes, at times, a local relation), but this is gained

---

[36] Cf. Porter, *Idioms*, 89.

through various implicatures and is not inherent in the meaning of the case form. When the dative specifies or extends, this feature is gained solely from context and therefore is not part of its semantic meaning. For example, prepositions are typically used to support goal, instrumental, and local distinctions of the dative case. As Moulton comments regarding the extension in the meaning of ἐν, "It seems certainly to imply a growing lack of clearness in the simple dative, resulting in an unwillingness to trust it to express meaning without further definition."[37] Therefore, while the dative has the semantic feature restriction, it is unspecified and unextended in terms of the kind of relation it enters into, and so is in need of further contextual determination. This accounts for both its semantic versatility and its contextual specificity.

Case Functions

The functions of the cases are accounted for in terms of syntactical relations and pragmatic usage. Their interaction within particular lexical and syntactic contexts (i.e., frames) limits the semantics of the case forms within particular contexts. These frames function as levels of implicature, causing particular meanings to be activated at the syntactic and pragmatic levels through an interaction with the relational semantic component of the case form.[38] In this section, we illustrate how the relational content of case forms functions within particular frames to realize various levels of functionality.

   1. *Lexical Frames.* Lexis is the most significant factor in creating implicatures for case forms, since the fundamental role of case is to relate the lexical content of the inflected element to its co-text, and since the relation that is created often involves constricting the lexical content of the inflected element. Lexis is fundamental because it influences the function of a case within syntactic frames. For example, the lexical meaning of a pronoun will typically specify a possessive relation in restricting the meaning of its head term when it occurs in the genitive. Lexical frames or contexts are initially realized at the group level through the semantic interplay of the lexical content of the head term with the lexical content and case forms of the words in its modification structure. This interaction between the essential semantic feature of the case form and the lexical items within its contextual frame often

---

[37] Moulton, *Prolegomena*, 62.

[38] See W. Croft and D.A. Cruse, *Cognitive Linguistics* (Cambridge: Cambridge University Press, 2004), for information on frames – lexical and otherwise.

activates additional semantic features. The frames are in this sense *lexico-semantic*.

The most obvious type of lexical frame is perhaps formed through the creation of so-called prepositional phrases. Mainstream syntactic theory suggests that, in a prepositional phrase, the preposition functions as the head term with the object of the preposition (taking the case form) as the dependant. In Greek, however, it is difficult to understand the preposition as the head term of the object. At the syntactical level, prepositions mark a specifying relation to the inflected element, which functions as the head term of the word group. Semantically, the lexical content of the preposition enters into relation with its inflected element, forming a lexical frame for the case form.

Componential analysis provides an important tool for understanding lexical frames. Prepositions have broad ranges of componential meaning and depend heavily upon contextual determination. The genitive realizes an intrinsic restricting relation with specification. When the genitive has the sense component +Animate or +Location, it activates the semantic notion of Separation or Origin/Source – that is, an ablative genitive. Disambiguation between Separation and Origin occurs within the co-textual frame. For example, at the word group and lexical level ἀπὸ ἀνατολῶν (Matt. 2:1) could mean "away from or separated from the East" (Separation) or "comes from the East" (Origin). Relations of the prepositional word group at the clausal co-textual level, specifically the relation of ἀπὸ ἀνατολῶν to the verb (παρεγένοντο), realize the semantic feature of Origin. The genitive restricts the lexical content of ἀνατολή with specification and the contextual frame specifies the precise nature of the relation (i.e., the function of the case form) – in this case the point of origin for the magi.

2. *Syntactic Frames.* Syntactic frames or contexts are formed at the word group and clausal levels through the syntactic relation of the case form to the word group or clausal structure. The syntactic requirements of a transitive verb, for example, may activate the direct object function of the accusative (the accusative word group being used as a complement). Specialized constructions are also realized through the occurrence of a case form within a specific syntactic frame. The genitive absolute, for example, is formed on the basis of its having a circumstantial participle as one of its constituent elements. While there is a significant amount of overlap with the syntactic level of case analysis when dealing with syntactic frames, separate treatment of syntactic frames is warranted at the level of pragmatics in order to specify the precise role of syntactic frames in realizing particular contextual functions.

Reframing the Debate: Lexis and Case

Much of the lack of clarity and the ambiguity in discussion of the Greek case system appear to be the result of imprecision in the scholarly discussion of the language, rather than there being a lack of clarity and ambiguity in the language itself, as many, whom we have noted, have insisted. As noted above in our brief description of lexical semantics (and as is now clear from our analysis of the Greek case system), oblique cases restrict the meaning of the head term but they do not determine it. Yet the contemporary discussion of issues related to case does not reflect sensitivity to this issue. The traditional discussion proceeds almost entirely in light of the function of the genitive construction. Yet, if possible, the lexis of the head term should be disambiguated before asking how the genitive modifies its head term. This is seen, for example, in the unofficial description of the discussion ("the πίστις Χριστοῦ debate" or something along these lines) indicated by numerous articles with πίστις Χριστοῦ in their title. This is itself potentially misleading because it extracts the head term and its genitive modifier from its word group, which always has a prepositional specifier. In other words, centring the discussion upon πίστις Χριστοῦ has in many cases moved the analysis away from the relevant lexical and syntactic contexts for the structure.

Another issue is the lack of precision in descriptive terminology. The objective/subjective dichotomy is inadequate as it does not accurately reflect the nature of the relations that are being described by the case system, and by the genitive case in particular.[39] "Subject" and "object" refer to clause-level phenomena, usually dealing with the relation of a syntactic constituent to a Predicator. The πίστις Χριστοῦ construction, however, functions at the word-group level where subject-object relations are not grammaticalized. The word groups in which the constructions are found usually occur in an adjunct, not as a syntactic object or subject (i.e., as a complement or subject). The labels unwarrantedly move the discussion to the clause level, treating πίστις as a Predicator and Χριστοῦ as a subject or object, when the relations are strictly nominal (occurring in the modification structure of a word group). Although particular lexemes may function in some ways like verbs, in πίστις Χριστοῦ we are still dealing with a noun group and need to assess it accordingly. Framing the discussion in this way further confuses the syntactic and

---

[39] Matlock, "Rhetoric", 174, n.1, notes others who have questioned the labels.

semantic functions of the forms. There seems to be an attempt to describe the semantic relations ("faithfulness of Christ" or "faith in Christ") through syntactic categories (subjective or objective), which distorts the issue – quite apart from the fact that the syntactic categories being used are inaccurate. These labels also fail to reflect authorial intentionality, and the question that really seems to be driving the discussion is this: Did Paul intend to use a subjective or objective genitive, and how do we find out? However, the reality is that this question – or a corresponding first-century version of it – probably never crossed Paul's mind.

When Paul used the genitive he merely intended to restrict the meaning of the head term through specification, using the context to determine what he was specifying. We may talk about the question at the semantic level in this way in terms of case semantics. What is Paul specifying through the genitive in relation to its head term? As far as lexical semantics goes, it will be important to disambiguate the meaning of πίστις in order to clarify how its meaning is being specified by the genitive. Again, case semantics may play a role in such a determination in certain instances, but this is an inappropriate starting point in the πίστις Χριστοῦ conversation because this is precisely what is under debate. At the syntactic level, the questions do not have as much to do with subjects and objects – at least not in terms of the construction itself – as they do with various forms of modification and their relation to πίστις as the head term, which we address below.

Once the structure is treated at the word-group level, various considerations at the clause and clause complex levels will be appropriate. Analyzing the πίστις Χριστοῦ structure in terms of its lexical and case semantic relations and syntactic configurations at the word-group, clause, and clause complex levels will help avoid the prevailing tendencies to confuse semantic and syntactic categories, treat case relations apart from lexis, and unwarrantedly cross syntactic boundaries between the group, clause, and/or clause complex levels of language.

Analysis and Results

There are seven or eight Pauline uses of πίστις Χριστοῦ in six or seven verses (Gal. 2:16, 20; 3:22; Rom. 3:22, 26; Phil. 3:9; and some bring in Eph. 3:12) that have occupied the current discussion. To consider the lexical semantics of πίστις in this construction, it will finally be necessary to consider the entire word group common to all seven or eight occurrences, variations of: preposition-πίστις Χριστοῦ. In general terms, then, we have a prepositional specifier with πίστις as the head term and a nominal modifier. We are initially concerned, however, with the lexical semantics and function of πίστις. The major considerations at the group level are collocations in terms of word order, the role of pronominal and/or nominal modifiers, and the function of prepositions with and without the article. There are only six occurrences of premodification word order (where the modifier precedes the head term) and, with the exception of Jude 20, these are all numerative modifiers.[40] Pronominal modifiers often modify πίστις, but they do so far less frequently within word groups utilizing a preposition. But since the modifiers in the πίστις Χριστου constructions are nominal, pronominal modification has less relevance to our purposes. The insights gained from studying the role of prepositions in establishing the semantic function of πίστις are more helpful.

Prepositions and *πίστις*

There are three major collocational patterns with a preceding prepositional specifier that restricts the meaning of πίστις: (1) instances with the article; (2) instances without the article; and (3) πίστις as a relator. There are 55 word groups (excluding the 8 debated instances) with πίστις as the head term, with a preceding prepositional specifier – 22 have an intervening article modifying the head term, 33 do not.

(1) In constructions with the article, one of three senses is possible: (a) a possessive meaning with a pronoun – for example, "your faith" (Matt. 9:29; Rom. 1:12; 1 Thess. 3:2, 7; Heb. 11:39; 2 Pet. 1:5); (b) a doctrinal meaning, "the faith" (Acts 13:8; 24:24; 1 Cor. 16:13; 2 Cor. 13:5; Gal. 3:23; 1 Tim. 1:19; 6:10, 21; Titus 1:13); and (c) an abstract meaning with (Acts 3:16; Eph. 3:17; Col. 2:12) or without (Rom. 3:30, 31; Gal. 3:14, 26) specifying the designation for the faith – for example, "through faith in Christ" (with) or "through faith" (without). What is important to note is that what may be called an ethical usage ("faithfulness") is not present when the preposition is used with an intervening article modifying the head term. The article seems to have

---

[40] All searches are done using the OpenText.org database in the Logos 3.0d platform. OpenText.org terminology is used in the descriptions.

various functions within these categories of usage. It may resume the anaphoric introduction of faith earlier in the co-text, help connect faith with a particular participant, specify faith as a system of tradition and belief, or help support various other anaphoric relations.

(2) In constructions without the article, all 33 of the instances have the abstract meaning, both with (1 Tim. 3:13; 2 Tim. 3:15) and without (e.g., Rom. 1:17 [3×]; 3:30; 4:16; 5:1; 9:32; 14:23 [2×]; 2 Cor. 5:7; Gal. 3:8, 11, 12, 24; 5:5; Eph. 2:8; 6:23; 1 Tim. 1:14; 2:7, 15; 4:12; 2 Tim. 1:13; Titus 3:15; Heb. 6:12, 10:38, 11:6, 13, 33; Jas. 1:6; 2:24; 1 Pet 1:5) specifying the designation for the faith.

(3) πίστις can also be used as a relator with a preposition, as it is twice in Philippians 3:9. Of the 15 undebated occurrences of the construction with πίστις as a relator with or without a prepositional specifier, only one occurrence is a doctrinal usage (with the article in 2 Tim. 3:8). The other instances are anarthrous and realize an abstract sense (Acts 26:18; Rom. 3:25 [note the textual variant], 26; 4:12; 9:30; 10:6; Gal. 3:7, 9; 1 Tim. 1:2, 4; Titus 1:1, 4; Heb. 11:7; Jas. 2:5). The instances in Philippians 3:9 are arguably either abstract or doctrinal. There is also one instance of πίστις as a relator with a possessive meaning (Rom. 4:16) – an example that may be subjective.[41]

A significant conclusion that must be noted is that in all 33 instances of the anarthrous usage of πίστις as a head term with a prepositional specifier (a parallel structure to that found in the theologically debated instances), and in all 14 clear instances of the anarthrous use of πίστις as a relator, the abstract meaning is invoked. This abstract sense, furthermore, is never stated in direct connection with a participant in the discourse (the faith of *x* or *x*'s faith), but always as an abstract conceptual notion unconnected to a particular individual. When a connection with an individual needs to be established, an article is typically employed to establish a referential connection. According to the collocation criterion for disambiguating semantic senses based upon consistently occurring grammatical structures, there seems to be good lexical semantic grounds for understanding the collocation of a prepositional specifier with πίστις

---

[41] This example is problematized by the fact that the modifier, Ἀβραάμ, is undeclined. The fact that it is undeclinable makes the choice of the genitive constrained and, therefore, such an example cannot yield substantial weight in the discussion.

as an indicator of the abstract function of the lexeme. When an author wants to add to this a referential relation or specify a larger body of tradition, he employs the article to focus the meaning further.

Analysis of the πίστις Χριστου structure is less complicated in this respect since, of the debated passages, only the instance in Ephesians 3:12 employs the article. All of the others are anarthrous with the preposition. This syntactical association is solidified by the fact that none of the unambiguous so-called subjective uses of πίστις with the post-modified genitive are introduced by a preposition or used as a relator, and all have the article (e.g., Rom. 3:3; Phil. 1:27; Rev. 13:10; cf. also Rom. 14:22 without the article). At the lexical semantic level – at least within the word-group level – the prepositions that specify all seven anarthrous πίστις head terms appear to help support the semantic selection of the abstract meaning, unconnected to a particular participant (i.e., not someone's faith), rather than the ethical sense of πίστις.

How should the question regarding the genitive, then, be framed in terms of case semantics? Is the genitive restricting the meaning of πίστις by specifying a person's faith (Christ's faith/faithfulness) or by specifying the appropriate realm of faith (Christ) as an abstract notion? Most who opt for the former view do not want to suggest that Paul thought a person was justified in some way by Christ's exercise of faith. Instead, they usually insist that the lexical sense in this context is "faithfulness". However, this is difficult to accept on lexical semantic grounds. Every time πίστις functions as an anarthrous head term preceded by a prepositional specifier, it has an abstract function unrelated (possessively) to an explicit participant in the discourse. Furthermore, the fact that the article is not present in instances of the structure under consideration probably indicates that a specific person's faith (Christ's) is not in view. The lexical frame for the genitive Χριστοῦ, then, seems to restrict the appropriate realm of faith to the specific figure Christ rather than specifying Christ's faith.

Further Linguistic Considerations

After offering some initial suggestions on some of the important semantic issues, we may now consider several other syntactic con-figurations. In our analysis of lexical semantics, we considered the function of the πίστις Χριστοῦ construction at the word-group level. At the clause level, πίστις Χριστου constructions function as prepositional adjuncts, indicating the circumstances under which justification is to take place. As prepositions function with lexical items to help realize differing functions of the genitive at the word-group level, a Predicator may have a similar function at the clause level. For example, in Mark 11:22 Jesus says: ἔχετε πίστιν θεοῦ (cf. Jas. 2:1). The Predicator signals the function of the genitive to specify the appropriate object (in a semantic [i.e., not syntactic] sense) of faith. At the word-group level, structures with πίστις as a head term preceded by a specifying preposition can be further modified by prepositional structures that may give additional insight into less clear instances. Four datives with the preposition ἐν following πίστις may be considered:

Galatians 3:26: διὰ τῆς πίστεως ἐν Χριστῷ Ἰησοῦ
Romans 3:25: διὰ τῆς πίστεως, ἐν τῷ αὐτοῦ αἵματι
1 Timothy 3:13: ἐν πίστει τῇ ἐν Χριστῷ Ἰησοῦ
2 Timothy 3:15: διὰ πίστεως τῆς ἐν Χριστῷ Ἰησοῦ

In each instance, the dative following πίστις is introduced by ἐν. On the theory of case outlined above the dative is unspecified and, therefore, in need of co-textual semantic determination. Syntactically these structures are similar in every respect to the πίστις Χριστοῦ constructions, except that they have a dative modifier with a preposition instead of a genitive modifier. It is interesting that, each time the dative is used, the preposition ἐν is employed. The result is that faith is seen here to be the proper realm of faith. This is similar to what the scribe of Codex Alexandrinus did at Romans 3:22. Rather than διὰ πίστεως Ἰησοῦ Χριστοῦ, the scribe wrote διὰ πίστεως ἐν Χριστῷ Ἰησοῦ. This appears to have been a conscious change on the part of the scribe to indicate Christ Jesus (note the change in word order here to emphasize Christ) as the realm of faith.[42] When the dative case (the case without semantic specification) is used in this construction, the author uses the context, including the preposition, to indicate Christ as the appropriate realm of faith in each instance. Why, then, would the author in other contexts not use the dative with the preposition instead of the genitive Χριστοῦ if it was less ambiguous? It might not have been less ambiguous. Perhaps considerations such as those suggested above would have helped the

---

[42] See S.E. Porter, "The Rhetorical Scribe: Textual Variants in Romans and their Possible Rhetorical Purpose", in *Rhetorical Criticism and the Bible* (ed. S.E. Porter and D.L. Stamps; JSNTSup 195; London: Sheffield Academic Press, 2002), 403–19, esp. 416–17; cited favorably by Jewett, *Romans*, 268. Reasoner (*Romans*, 39) wonders in his history of discussion (pp. 38–40, and the rest of the chapter) why Paul did not use the preposition ἐν.

original hearer / reader determine the meaning. The genitive also would have created a more marked construction in contexts of justification, where the author wanted to lay special emphasis upon Christ as the proper object of faith.

Conclusion

We cannot hope to solve such a delicate and sensitive issue as the meaning of the phrase πίστις Χριστοῦ *simply* by means of Greek linguistics, because there is more at stake – including exegesis and theology. Nevertheless, discussion should never hope to proceed without at least considering linguistic issues. And, as it turns out, grammatical analysis appears to have a lot more to offer than is typically assumed. Much of the previous and traditional discussion of the Greek case system has utilized a decoding approach which has attempted to extrapolate meanings from the forms. The approach that we have taken has utilized a systemic-functional approach to lexis and semantics. The semantic system has been used to encode the meanings of the forms. When we consider the lexis and larger word group – including the entire collocation of preposition-πίστις Χριστοῦ – we see a number of interesting results. The use of πίστις as a head term with a prepositional specifier, without an intervening article and followed by an element in the genitive, provides further evidence that, at least from a linguistic standpoint, when Paul used the phrase πίστις Χριστοῦ he was indicating that Christ was the proper object of faith.

Section II

PAULINE TEXTS IN CONTENTION

4

The Faithfulness of Jesus Christ in Romans 3:22

DOUGLAS A. CAMPBELL

This question is highly contested, so I will focus here on the strongest arguments for the subjective construal of [διὰ] πίστεως Ἰησοῦ Χριστοῦ in Romans 3:22.[1] A quick survey of all the relevant texts in Romans and Galatians would probably accomplish little that is decisive, and a powerful treatment of the key material in Galatians already exists that ought to receive continued attention.[2] We will build toward a subjective construal of the disputed genitive construction in Romans 3:22 in several steps, beginning in a way that might seem counter-intuitive. But this oblique approach should ultimately generate some decisive conclusions. We will in fact start by addressing Romans 1:17, relying on an argument I first made in 1992 and 1994 that still seems valid.[3] In this famous sentence – that by some accounts launched the Reformation – Paul states:

[17a] δικαιοσύνη γὰρ Θεοῦ ἐν αὐτῷ ἀποκαλύπτεται

ἐκ πίστεως εἰς πίστιν

[17b] καθὼς γέγραπται

Ὁ δὲ δίκαιος ἐκ πίστεως ζήσεται.

We will build from this text in seven stages to a particular configuration of the relevant data, at which point we will turn to consider our key question.

---

[1] The following is drawn, in the main, from my study *The Deliverance of God: An Apocalyptic Rereading of Justification in Paul* (Grand Rapids, MI: Eerdmans, 2009), esp. chs. 11, 15, and 16. All the other contested genitives receive detailed treatment there as well – the Galatian issues in ch. 20.

[2] See Hays, *The Faith of Jesus Christ*.

[3] To my knowledge, no cogent rejoinders or refutations have yet been made to it. See my studies, "Meaning"; and "Romans 1:17 – A *Crux Interpretum* for the ΠΙΣΤΙΣ ΧΡΙΣΤΟΥ Dispute", *JBL* 113 (1994): 265–85.

(1) The prepositional series ἐκ πίστεως εἰς πίστιν in verse 17a is famously problematic,[4] but is followed immediately by the citation of Habakkuk 2:4 (slightly modified[5]), which contains the phrase ἐκ πίστεως as well. In view of this proximity it is difficult to avoid the conclusion that Paul has quoted Habakkuk 2:4 in verse 17b to resume, define, and affirm his use of its central phrase in the immediately preceding series in verse 17a, regardless of the phrase's precise meaning. It seems to follow, moreover, that these two textual units should be interpreted in parallel. It is implausible to supply a reading for ἐκ πίστεως in the prepositional series in 1:17a that Habakkuk 2:4 cannot match in 1:17b (and vice versa).

(2) Further investigation reveals that Paul uses the phrase ἐκ πίστεως frequently in Romans and Galatians, where it occurs 21 times,[6] *but nowhere else in his corpus*. The distinctive distribution of the prepositional phrase therefore correlates exactly with the quotation of Habakkuk 2:4, which is only cited in Romans and Galatians – a correlation that is too marked to be mere coincidence. This all suggests that the citation of Habakkuk 2:4 in Romans 1:17b does indeed underlie Paul's use of the phrase ἐκ πίστεως in the series in 1:17a.

(3) But this perfect correlation suggests that Habakkuk 2:4 is probably related closely to Paul's use of the phrase ἐκ πίστεως everywhere else as well. The parallelism between the citation and the phrase therefore extends well beyond Romans 1:17 through many other texts in Romans and Galatians, asking for this entire data set to be mutually interpreted. We ought to interpret that text and this phrase in the same way. But the data set is not yet complete.

---

[4] Cranfield gives a succinct account of the difficulties in *Romans*, I, 98–100.

[5] The personal pronoun μου has been dropped, which is positioned in slightly different locations in different Lxx MS traditions. But these issues have little bearing on our current question.

[6] Including the citations of Hab. 2:4 in this total. More specifically, it occurs in Romans 12 times, in Galatians nine times, and elsewhere in the NT only in Heb. 10:37–38, which cites Hab. 2:3–4, and in Jas. 2:24. The first study to notice this strange set of correlations was, to my knowledge, Bruno Corsani, "Ἐκ πίστεως in the Letters of Paul", in *The New Testament Age: Essays in Honor of Bo Reicke* (ed. W.C. Weinrich; Macon, GA: Mercer University Press, 1984), 87–93.

(4) In several passages employing ἐκ πίστεως Paul seems to use a stylistic variation developed with διά instead. This parallelism is apparent in Romans 3:30–31 and Galatians 2:16, but it is also apparent, in a slightly more diffuse way, in Romans 3:21–26, 4:13–16, and (arguably) 5:1–2, as well as in Galatians 3:7–14 and 3:21–26. It is really impossible to detect a significant shift in meaning between the prepositional variations used in these passages.[7] They seem mere stylistic flourishes supplied to avoid needless repetition. These further instances marginally increase the data in play, adding Paul's διά πίστεως phrases to the set.

(5) These additional phrases now supply useful information about the function of ἐκ in the statistically dominant phrase ἐκ πίστεως. Paul's parallel use of διά in the genitive indicates that ἐκ is functioning *instrumentally* (and most probably in terms of instrumentality by an agent; impersonal agency tends to use the dative, if not the preposition ἐν). This is the only plausible semantic overlap between the two prepositional constructions. Hence, the programmatic phrase ἐκ πίστεως seems to mean "through …" or "by means of πίστις".[8]

(6) We should note now that the πίστις Χριστοῦ debate has been significantly recontextualized. The disputed genitives in Romans and Galatians all lie within the boundaries of this broader data set that is composed of a set of thirty-odd short prepositional

---

[7] Which is also to suggest that such a shift would have to be demonstrated. Stanley K. Stowers has made the most perceptive and plausible such attempt in relation to Rom. 3:30, but no one – not surprisingly! – has attempted this in relation to Gal. 2:16, which undermines the case in Romans. (The case also has other problems.) See Stowers, "ἐκ πίστεως and διὰ τῆς πίστεως in Romans 3.30", *JBL* 108 (1989): 665–74.

[8] See BDAG, meanings 3 and 4, 224–25 (here, in due course, 4, i.e., agency); and see esp., in Paul, Rom. 1:8; 2:16; 7:25; 1 Cor. 8:6; Gal. 1:1; 3:19; see also Col. 1:16, 20; 3:17. Meaning 1 – "through" – looks unlikely, partly on the grounds of parallels in context (esp. the dative constructions), and partly on grounds of contradiction. If an essentially spatial notion of passing "through" is intended, then in key texts like Rom. 1:17a faith functions *simultaneously* as both a way-station and a goal on that journey – an obvious contradiction. Paul is not asserting with these series the theological equivalent of the statement, "I passed through Durham on the way to Durham". For the overlap with ἐκ see BDAG, meanings 3d–f, 296–7 – to denote effective cause, so "by, because of" (2 Cor. 7:9), reason, so "by reason of, as a result of, because of" (Rom. 3:20, 30; 4:2; 11:6; 12:18 [?]; 2 Cor. 13:4; Gal. 2:16; 3:2, 5, 24), or means in relation to a definite purpose, so "with, by means of" (Lk. 16:9).

phrases using πίστις, a half dozen of which are expanded by christological material in genitive relations (i.e., Rom. 3:22, 26; Gal. 2:16 [2×], 20; and 3:22). But, in addition, this entire data set bears a significant and presumably generative relation to one of Paul's key scriptural intertexts – Habakkuk 2:4. All this material should be interpreted in mutual relation. That is to say, an *integrated* explanation really needs to be supplied for it.[9]

(7) We do not need to address all this material in its contexts immediately, however; it will suffice for now to note one further specific connection within it, between Romans 1:17 and 3:21–22. These seem to be sibling texts, if not twins. Both deploy δικαιοσύνη Θεοῦ in the position of subject and then construct the predicate from a verb of revelation – ἀποκαλύπτω in 1:17 and φανερόω in 3:21 and 22.[10] This clause is then expanded with the addition of what we can now recognize as identical prepositional phrases in semantic terms – ἐκ πίστεως in 1:17a (echoed by 3:26) and διὰ πίστεως in 3:22 (which probably recurs in v. 25.) A purposive εἰς construction using πιστ-terms is also present in both texts (see also 1:16). And the attestation of the Scriptures features prominently in both texts, with the citation of Habakkuk 2:4 in 1:17b, and the claim in 3:21 that the disclosure of δικαιοσύνη Θεοῦ is witnessed to by the Law and the Prophets, followed by the echo of Habakkuk 2:4 in verse 22 (as well as v. 26). These are *five* points of explicit overlap. Clearly, then, the interpretation of Romans 1:17 (presumably following on from v. 16) and 3:22 (presumably extending from v. 21 through to v. 26) belong together. These texts and their key concerns should be interpreted in parallel.

We come now to the crucial step in the argument, although it is worth recalling the correlations that have been established in the data thus far. Essentially, a πίστις discourse is now apparent in Romans and Galatians that asks for some plausible integrated explanation. (Note that it does not cover *all* Paul's "faith" language, but only a part of it.) It is composed primarily of short prepositional phrases that speak in some

---

[9]   Francis Watson agrees with my analysis up to this point: see *Paul and the Hermeneutics of Faith*, 43–53.

[10] These verbs have received some discussion. I am convinced that for Paul they were largely interchangeable. See Jewett, *Romans*, 142–3, 273 (esp. n.37).

sense of instrumentality or means – ἐκ or διὰ πίστεως. These phrases seem deliberately designed, moreover, to echo a scriptural intertext, Habakkuk 2:4, so the discourse is introduced overtly in Romans in 1:17. Some of its phrases also have an appended christological marker in a genitive construction, Ἰησου and/or Χριστοῦ – see especially Romans 3:22. Finally, Romans 1:17 and 3:21–22 lock all of these motifs together in a further, richer parallelism supplying the additional information that this discourse reveals (the) δικαιοσύνη Θεοῦ.

Thus we possess several interpretative controls in relation to our crucial question – a number of interlocking features of the data that require mutual explanation. And we should now simply ask what the meaning of the christological genitive in Romans 3:22 is – as well as, by implication, the meaning of the discourse as a whole, and of Paul's deployment of Habakkuk 2:4, bearing in mind the motif's revelatory and instrumental functions. There are two main options:

I. The construction is christocentric (i.e., it refers to the faith[fulness] *of* Christ – a subjective construal of the genitive in question)

II. It is anthropocentric (i.e., it refers to faith *in* Christ undertaken by the individual, the ἄνθρωπος – an objective construal)

I suggest in what follows that only option I – a subjective construal of the genitive relating the πίστις to Christ himself – can answer this question satisfactorily, resolving all the correlations in the data, and yet it does so without difficulty. An anthropocentric, objective reading is falsified by the data at certain key points.[11]

---

[11] I have excluded two further possible options immediately given present space constraints – what we might dub option III: "theocentric" (i.e., a reference to the faithfulness of God "the Father"); and option IV: "evidentiary" (i.e., πίστις in the sense of "proof" or "demonstration").

Option III is sometimes suggested as a resolution of the difficulties in the πιστ-series in 1:17a (i.e., allowing a translation "from [God's] faithfulness to the faith [of humanity]", or some such). Intriguingly, this is a rare point of agreement between Richard B. Hays ("What Is at Stake?") and J.D.G. Dunn ("Once More"). O'Rourke's study also emphasizes this reading throughout the Romans data: "πίστις".

But it is an awkward reading of Hab. 2:4 in Rom. 1:17b (and impossible when that text is cited in Gal. 3:11), and it is also impossible in relation to the πίστις Χριστοῦ genitives themselves – here in 3:22. So it will not be tabulated and addressed in detail here. (Note, these are the principal problems in recent studies of Rom. 1:17 by Charles Quarles, "From Faith to Faith: A Fresh Examination of the Prepositional Series in Romans 1:17", *NovT* 45 [2003]: 1–21; and John W. Taylor, "From Faith to

When πίστις is related directly to Christ, the exact sense of Romans 3:22 is completed nicely: "the δικαιοσύνη Θεου is disclosed or revealed by means of the πίστις of Jesus Christ".

We should remind ourselves at this point of certain lexicographical distinctions – that πίστις can signify, among other notions, "belief", "trust", and "faithfulness", all of which are related but subtly different actions. Literature contemporary to Paul is replete with these distinctions – not to mention with shifts between them – and it is worth noting in particular that both Josephus and the LXX attest repeatedly to the notion of πίστις as "fidelity."[12]

We should also recall that Paul frequently refers to a story of Christ's passion metonymically (or, as Hays puts it, metaleptically) – that is to say, by mentioning only one element within it that serves to evoke the entire narrative, a claim that is often misunderstood.

It is clear that Paul knows and uses a passion narrative.[13] He mentions the night of Jesus' last supper, establishment of the Eucharist, and betrayal, when he was "handed over" to his enemies. Paul knows as well that Jesus submitted to the humiliation of an execution by crucifixion, endured that form of death, shed his blood, and died. Jesus was then buried and, "on the third day", raised and enthroned, receiving at that point the acclamation of lordship. But more often than not, Paul alludes to this story metonymically rather than by way of longer syntactical

---

Faith: Romans 1:17 in the Light of Greek Idiom", *NTS* 50 [2004]: 337–48.) This is not to exclude the notion of God's faithfulness from either Romans or Paul's thinking as a whole; clearly, it has a role to play there (see esp. Rom. 3:3). However, it *is* to point out that this theme cannot be signified by the prepositional πιστ-phrases and their associated texts that are being considered here.

Option IV is infrequently but cogently suggested in resolution of the revelatory and instrumental implications of πίστις Χριστου in 3:22 – the "proof that is Christ" (i.e., a genitive of content or hendiadys). See David Hay, *"Pistis"*; the case has been made more generally by James L. Kinneavy, *The Greek Rhetorical Origins of Christian Faith* (Oxford: Oxford University Press, 1987) – and it is Philo's most frequent usage. But it is impossible in relation to the πιστ-series in 1:17a *and* the Habakkuk quotation in v. 17b! So it will also be discarded from this point onward.

[12] Existing surveys of the Koiné data can be misleading, as Matlock points out in "Detheologizing ΠΙΣΤΙΣ ΧΡΙΣΤΟΥ". The actual data is well summarized in *TDNT*, although Rudolf Bultmann's conclusions are of course slanted: see (with Artur Weiser), "πιστεύω [κ.τ.λ.]", in *TDNT* 6:174–228. The divisions within BDAG must be treated with caution (818–20). I make some recommendations concerning more accurate categories in *Quest*, ch. 9, esp. 178–88, arguing there principally in relation to Philo, Josephus, and Paul.

[13] See Hays, *The Faith of Jesus Christ*; and my essay, "The Story of Jesus in Romans".

units and fuller descriptions, and doubtless because his early Christian audiences already knew it fairly well. So a single motif can denote the presence of the entire narrative, or of one of its main trajectories, within the Apostle's developing arguments: "obedience", "blood", "death", "cross", "crucifixion", and so on. It is important to emphasize that not one of these motifs is functioning in strict isolation. No one seriously suggests that when Paul refers to the blood of Christ he is referring *only* to the important oxygen-carrying liquid that ran in his veins and then spilled out to a degree during his suffering and execution, thereby ignoring the rest of Christ himself – his body, his actions, and the rest of his passion. Similarly, any reference to Christ's death by Paul involves far more than a reference to the actual moment at which Christ expired. So the claim that the phrase "the fidelity of Christ" could denote Jesus' passion more broadly is quite consistent with Paul's usual practice.

Indeed, the notion of fidelity fits smoothly into the downward martyrological trajectory in the story of Jesus' passion. It is largely self-evident that fidelity is an ingredient within any essentially martyrological story. Martyrs faithfully endure suffering and death (if not a horrible execution); the story of martyrdom thus encodes its heroes with the quality of fidelity in view of their endurance and steadfastness within these unfolding stories.[14] And numerous martyrologies mention fidelity explicitly (see 4 Macc. 15:24; 16:22; 17:2).[15] So it seems appropriate to suggest that Paul's account of Jesus' death – an essentially martyrological story – could include the element of faithfulness.[16]

This broader evidence confirms the plausibility of the suggestion that Paul is speaking in Romans 3:22 of the definitive disclosure of the δικαιοσύνη Θεοῦ "by means of the faithfulness of Jesus Christ". He means by this, in immediate terms, only that Jesus' death – followed

---

[14] This quality is discernible in both militantly violent and pacifist narratives of martyrdom: see Daniel; Wisdom of Solomon; 2 Maccabees 6 and 7; 3 and 4 Maccabees. But pagan and Christian martyrologies make this point as well: see H.A. Musurillo, ed., *The Acts of the Pagan Martyrs* (Oxford: Acta Alexandrinorum, 1954); and idem, *The Acts of the Christian Martyrs* (Oxford: Acta Alexandrinorum, 1972).

[15] See also 1 Macc. 2:52 (the cognate adjective), 59 (cognate verb); 2 Macc. 1:2 (adjective); and 4 Macc. 7:19, 21 (verbs).

[16] Hence it also seems significant that ὑπακοή is used as a strategic summary of Christ's saving activity – of his passion – in Rom. 5:19, where it functions opposite the first Adam's παρακοή, the context then articulating these paradigmatic actions in terms of broader narratives of life and death (5:12–21): see Hooker, "Πίστις Χριστοῦ", 182–3.

presumably by his resurrection – *discloses* or *reveals* God's δικαιοσύνη – a reading that makes sense *irrespective of the precise meaning of the latter controversial phrase.*[17] Whether the δικαιοσύνη in question comes from God, is valid before him, or is an attribute and activity intrinsic to God himself, Jesus' passion, alluded to here metonymically in terms of his "faithfulness", can function to disclose it. And we thereby explain two of the critical aspects of the relevant data – the instrumentality of the πίστις phrase, conveyed here by the preposition διά, and the entire phrase's function in 1:17a and 3:22 to disclose something. But can this reading explain the remaining key correlation in the data set – namely, the reading's extension to 1:17b and the citation there of Habakkuk 2:4?

In fact, it is becoming increasingly difficult to deny the possibility that Habakkuk 2:4 is functioning as a messianic proof-text for Paul;[18] much research has created this interpretative option.[19]

(1) Paul often uses arthrous constructions to denote Christ, and especially in Romans;[20] (2) ὁ δίκαιος is an attested christological title apparent in other parts of the New Testament;[21] (3) the citation of

---

[17] Fuller discussion of this phrase can be found in *Deliverance of God*, ch. 17, §3.

[18] An early advocate of the messianic construal of Hab. 2:4 in Rom. 1:17 is A.T. Hanson, *Studies in Paul's Technique and Theology* (Grand Rapids, MI: Eerdmans, 1974), 39–45; further advocates are referenced in my *Rhetoric of Righteousness*, 211, n.1. Most recently see Heliso, *Pistis and the Righteous One*.

[19] Note I am not suggesting the *necessity* that Hab. 2:4 is functioning in this way, considered in its own immediate locations in either Rom. 1:17b or Gal. 3:11, but at this stage we do not need a watertight case in relation to this data; we only need a plausible possibility that can integrate with the christological indications and reading already given in context, thereby extending a plausible interpretation to the data set as a whole.

[20] Merely in Romans itself, Paul seems to refer to Christ frequently in this way: see, e.g., ὁ υἱός (1:3, 4, 9; 5:10; 8:3, 29, 32); ὁ Χριστός (9:3, 5; 14:18; 15:3, 7, 19; also 16:16); ὁ εἷς (5:15, 17, 18, 19); and probably also ὁ ἀποθανών (6:7; 8:34). R. Scroggs, "Rom. 6.7 ὁ γὰρ ἀποθανὼν δεδικαίωται ἀπὸ τῆς ἁμαρτίας", *NTS* 10 (1963): 104–8.

[21] The arthrous form is also found in Acts 7:52 (an explicitly martyrological setting) and 22:14 (here on the lips of Paul), and possibly also in Jas. 5:6 and Matt. 27:19. Also relevant are several anarthrous occurrences – Acts 3:14; 1 Pet. 3:18; and 1 Jn. 1:9; 2:1, 29; and 3:7; and possibly also Lk. 23:47. (My thanks to Matt Easter for this last suggestion, and other helpful comments on this study.) This was noted some time ago by Richard Longenecker in *The Christology of Early Jewish Christianity* (London: SCM Press, 1970) and canvassed recently by Larry W. Hurtado, *Lord Jesus Christ: Devotion to Jesus in Earliest Christianity* (Grand Rapids, MI: Eerdmans, 2003), 189–90.

Habakkuk 2:4 in Hebrews 10:38 is quite possibly messianic;[22] (4) a messianic reading would accord neatly with the story of the suffering, executed, and resurrected "righteous one" spoken of in Wisdom 2:12–20 (see also 3:1–9; 4:7–16; and 5:1 and 15), a story most likely read by the early church in relation to Jesus, and a text deeply implicated in the argumentation of Romans;[23] (5) this would align in addition with the early church's frequent use of Isaiah 53 to explain Jesus' passion, a text from which the title [ὁ] δίκαιος may well have been drawn;[24] (6) this fulfils the expectations set in motion by Romans 1:2–4, where Paul's gospel is said to centre on a prophetically attested messiah who is declared to be the "son of God" by his resurrection – and Habakkuk 2:4 is the first scriptural text explicitly cited after this set of claims;[25] and (7) Paul's scriptural citations are often demonstrably christological.[26] So it seems that a messianic construal of Habakkuk 2:4 in Romans 1:17b is far from being an impediment to our developing reading; numerous considerations suggest that it is entirely appropriate.

Indeed, in the light of my earlier argument concerning 3:22, Romans 1:17b is best understood as affirming that "the righteous one (i.e., Jesus)

Other intertexts are also very important in relation to this question: see esp. Isa 3:10; 53:11; 57:1; various motifs in the Similitudes of *1 Enoch* – 38:2; 53:6, and also possibly 47:1 and 4; Justin, *Dialogue with Trypho*, 13:7; 16:4, 5; 17:1–3; 86:4 (2×); 119:3; 133:2; 136:2; see also 110:6. Richard B. Hays, "'The Righteous One' as Eschatological Deliverer: A Case Study in Paul's Apocalyptic Hermeneutics", in *Apocalyptic and the New Testament: Essays in Honour of J. Louis Martyn* (ed. J. Marcus and M. Soards; Sheffield: JSOT, 1988), 191–215, provides a useful discussion of the Enochic evidence, and is usefully supplemented by James C. Vanderkam, "Righteous One, Messiah, Chosen One, and Son of Man in 1 Enoch 37–71", in *The Messiah: Developments in Earliest Judaism and Christianity* (ed. James H. Charlesworth; Minneapolis, MN: Fortress, 1992), 169–91.

[22] As Hays observes, a messianic reading of the quotation of Hab. 2:3–4 in Heb. 10:37–39 "is by no means an unreasonable one" since "the LXX translators produced a text that is readily susceptible to messianic interpretation" (*The Faith of Jesus Christ*, 136, 135).

[23] See esp. M.J. Suggs, "Wisdom 2:10–5: A Homily Based on the Fourth Servant Song", *JBL* 76 (1957): 26–53; see also *Deliverance of God*, esp. chs. 14 and 19.

[24] See esp. Donald H. Juel, *Messianic Exegesis: Christological Interpretation in the Old Testament and Early Christianity* (2nd ed.; Minneapolis, MN: Augsburg Fortress, 1998 [1988]); Joel Marcus, *The Way of the Lord: Christological Exegesis of the Old Testament in the Gospel of Mark* (Louisville, KY: Westminster John Knox, 1992); and Richard Bauckham, *God Crucified: Monotheism and Christology in the New Testament* (Carlisle: Paternoster, 1998), esp. 51–3, 56–61.

[25] See *Deliverance of God*, ch. 18.

[26] E.g., 1 Cor. 10:4; 2 Cor. 1:20; 4:4–6 (etc.).

by means of his faithfulness (i.e., to the point of death) will live (i.e., be resurrected)". And God's δικαιοσύνη is therefore disclosed by Jesus' faithfulness (so 1:17a and 3:21–22). Christ's passion is the extraordinary set of events where God's decisive saving act on behalf of humanity is revealed – the events of which Paul's gospel speaks so proudly, and to which certain key texts from the Scriptures attest – here Habakkuk 2:4 (properly read, of course!). Moreover, the important instrumental πίστις phrases that echo Habakkuk 2:4, including the disputed πίστις Χριστοῦ genitives, can all plausibly be viewed as continuing to speak of Christ's death and resurrection. (It can hardly be offensive to suggest that Paul speaks frequently in his gospel of the importance of the death and resurrection of Christ to God's saving act!) All of which is to observe that a subjective construal of the contested πίστις Χριστοῦ genitive in Romans 3:22, coupled with a messianic construal of Habakkuk 2:4 in Romans 1:17b, explains the entire data set with all its subtle correlations in an integrated and plausible manner.[27] We should now consider that it is the only interpretation that can do so (assuming, in addition, that all objections to this reading are invalid[28]).

---

[27] Note that I have not made use of any argument in terms of tautology or redundancy in Rom. 3:22, principally because it is a bad argument, as Matlock has recently emphasized: see "Rhetoric". Although I used this argument in 1992, in *Rhetoric of Righteousness* (62–3), I have not done so since and acknowledged its weakness in print in 2005 (see *Quest*, 221–2, n.19; see also *Deliverance of God*, ch. 15, n.15, and ch. 20, n.25).

Neither have I emphasized any considerations in relation to the perfect tense, used in 3:21 and elided from 3:22, or in relation to δικαιοσύνη Θεοῦ. In the latter relation: if this much-debated phrase is read in the broadly eschatological terms advocated by (i.a.) Käsemann, then the considerations apparent in relation to the revelatory argument are reproduced and reinforced. (See Ernst Käsemann, "The Righteousness of God in Paul", in *New Testament Questions of Today* [London: SCM Press, 1969 (1965)], 168–93.) However, I prefer to settle the interpretation of this phrase *after* the πίστις Χριστοῦ issue has been decided – see *Deliverance of God*, chs. 15–17. (My "*Crux Interpretum*" tends to confuse these distinguishable considerations together.)

[28] Critics of the reading tend to beg the question, so direct criticisms of the subjective genitive approach are rare. Those that are made tend to be weak, and so they need not detain us beyond the following comments.

The most frequent objection is couched in terms of the presence or absence of the definite article. A subjective construal ought to be fully arthrous, in accordance with Apollonius's ancient dictum, the objection runs (see, i.e., Dunn, "Once More", 61–81). Since 3:22 is not, it follows that it probably is not subjective. However, the disputed phrase reproduces *a scriptural text*, which is anarthrous, and then appends a *name*, which usually does not take the definite article in Koiné. To make matters

Interpretation II – the anthropocentric, objective reading – although much advocated, actually fails upon closer examination.

The conventional reading of the broader context of Romans 1:17 and 3:22 – Romans 1–4, along with its associated soteriology of justification – tends to attribute "faith" monolithically to the Christian.[29] It is of course the act by which non-Christians grasp salvation and, as such, it plays a critical role in the unfolding theory of salvation that these texts are usually held to describe. Conventional readers therefore expect Paul to speak in these thesis paragraphs in Romans of salvation sola fides – in terms of the saving faith of the Christian.[30] But what the conventional reading cannot explain is a "faith" that discloses or reveals the "righteousness of God" in instrumental terms. "Faith" simply does not function as the means by which something moves from a position of invisibility to one of visibility, from the unknown to the known, and to affirm that it does is to make a basic

---

worse, Rom. 4:16 is clearly both anarthrous and subjective and is paralleled exactly by Rom. 3:26. So this objection clearly does not hold. The actual data falsifies it at several points.

Another putative difficulty is the absence of any supposed attestation in Paul to Jesus as the subject of the cognate verb, πιστεύω. However, this objection founders as well on numerous grounds. In the first instance, 2 Cor. 4:13 probably *is* evidence that Jesus is the subject of the verb: see Thomas Stegman, "Ἐπίστευσα διὸ ἐλάλησα (2 Corinthians 4:13): Paul's Christological Reading of Psalm 115:1a LXX", *CBQ* 69 (2007): 725–45. But, second, it does not follow that every subjective construction in Paul must have an attested parallel instance using the cognate verb. We are never told, for instance, that Jesus "bled", thereby justifying the reading "the blood *of* Jesus", or that Jesus "was sacrificed", justifying the reading "the sacrifice *of* Jesus", and so on. Third, this objection misunderstands the reading it seeks to refute. It interprets Jesus' πίστις in terms of an *objective* reading – as his (justifying?!) belief or trust. But the subjective advocate prefers the connotation of fidelity, which is appropriate to the narrative in play, *and to which no cognate verb actually exists.*

Sometimes broader appeals are made to Paul's use of Abraham and/or faith in general. These are too complex to assess here, but they receive a detailed treatment in *Deliverance of God*, esp. chs. 11 and 19. Suffice it to say that, at every point, further difficulties *for* the objective approach tend to arise!

[29] See *Quest*, 146–77; and *Deliverance of God*, ch. 1. Not all advocates of the objective approach endorse a traditional broader interpretation in terms of justification, but if they do not then they do need to supply their own alternative overarching construal – a difficult task.

[30] Douglas Moo asserts this – e.g., *Romans*, 218, 224. Cranfield disavows the conditionality of faith explicitly (90), citing Barth (*CD* IV.1 608–42, 740–49), but then interprets it conditionally! (See *Romans* I, 98, 100, 203 ("received by means of faith"), 210, 214.)

semantic error – to assert something meaningless or ungrammatical. "Faith" tends to affirm something already known as true, which is of course the way that it functions in justification, in response to Christian preaching and the gospel. *The gospel*, when preached, makes God's saving act in Christ known or "visible". And "faith" then *responds* to that prior disclosure as an act of affirmation, *and not the act of disclosure itself*.

In clarification of this important but frequently overlooked distinction, consider how an act of belief cannot itself disclose what is hidden inside a locked safe. People can have beliefs about what is hidden there, but these may be right or wrong; they will not *reveal* what is hidden – something that can only be done by opening the safe and scrutinizing what is inside (or some such), at which point people might then find their beliefs confirmed or disconfirmed. Hence, to press human faith into the role of active disclosure is to commit a semantic mistake. "Faith" does not *mean* this, and so these texts, which speak explicitly and unavoidably of disclosure, should not be read in this way. *Paul has to be talking about something else here when he uses this phrase.* (This is of course not to exclude Christian faith from Paul's thinking more broadly; it is only to suggest that this is not what he is trying to articulate here. Paul's purposive εἰς constructions in 1:16b, 17a and 3:22 clearly denote Christian faith in some sense, presumably as the goal or end of this process of disclosure.)

In fact, most commentators fall back on inaccurate paraphrases to avoid this difficulty in Paul's texts. For example, Douglas Moo states: "Paul highlights [in 3:22a, resuming a 'key theme' from 1:17] faith as the means by which *God's justifying work becomes applicable* to individuals."[31] Of course, Paul doesn't actually *say* this. Verse 22 does not contain the verb δικαιόω, the process of "applicability", or an individual (except arguably as an implication of "faith in Christ"; the second, uncontested reference to faith is plural – πάντας τοὺς πιστεύοντας). The apostle speaks of faith as the "means by which" God's righteousness is disclosed, which is rather a different thing.

It should also be noted how the addition of a further process that faith can function meaningfully in relation to – usually by way of a participle – begs the question at the critical point. So Moo speaks of justification "becoming applicable". But this begs the question that this is in fact what Paul is talking about; it is an essentially anthropocentric interpretation

---

[31] *Romans*, 224, emphases added.

that christocentric advocates might want to challenge. Perhaps Paul wishes to speak of God's right actions rather than a process of justification, and of Christ rather than of what an individual purportedly has to do in order to be saved. Moo's additions, moreover, now fail to complete what Paul *does* say – that an extraordinary soteriological disclosure has already taken place. "Where?" one is tempted to ask, since the focus of the text has been interpretatively shifted toward the question of how to appropriate or apply this disclosure. In short, such tendentious additions to the text must clearly be resisted, and doubly so when it is recalled that we already have a reading that does not need to supply them.

The only interpretative alternative that I am aware of within this basic option that tries to address this difficulty shifts the verb presupposed by 3:22 away from the disclosure spoken of explicitly in 3:21; this then avoids the need for "faith" in verse 22 to speak of anything instrumental in relation to revelation. This was the perceptive suggestion of Adolf Schlatter, who was doubtless aware of the πίστις Χριστοῦ issue because it was being discussed in Germany at the time he was writing.[32] However, this suggestion is implausible:

(1) There is no reason, in view of the repeated subject and the formulaic contrasting instrumental constructions (i.e., not by "works" but by "faith"), to suppose that the elided verb in verse 22 *is* different from the verb supplied in verse 21. (2) The parallel text 1:17, which uses πιστ-terms overtly, affirms the centrality of disclosure to Paul's claims in relation to πίστις with the verb ἀποκαλύπτω. And (3) the supplied verb begs the question in the manner just noted.[33] Hence, we really ought

---

[32] Schlatter tries to resolve the issue by reading the instrumental prepositional phrase attributively, then supplying a further appropriate implicit verbal notion. Indeed, he concedes that if the phrase is read adverbially, then it must refer to Christ's fidelity! However, he views this reading as unlikely *because of his conventional construal of the preceding argument*: "the urgent question is what kind of behavior is able to bring the individual into that relationship intended by God … how the individual may obtain God's pleasure": see *Romans: The Righteousness of God* (trans. S. Schatzmann; Peabody, MA: Hendrickson, 1995 [1935]), 94; see also 93–5. Of course, his resolution is consequently only as good as this preceding construal, which must be strong enough to override the explicit indications in 3:21–22. Suffice it to say that this broader reading also begs the key question, besides possessing additional difficulties (see *Deliverance of God*, ch. 11). A good survey of the early debate is provided by Hays in *The Faith of Jesus Christ*, 121–4, 42–7.

[33] Schlatter's attributival suggestion is also undermined by the function of the many parallel πίστις phrases elsewhere in Paul adverbially (and specifically instrumentally) – see esp. 1:17a. But with the supply of the right verb in v. 22 – like

to supply the verb of revelation found in verse 21 to 3:22 unless strong reasons to the contrary are adduced (and I know of none that are cogent), at which point the original difficulty faced by the anthropocentric approach remains – the instrumentality in the data that is correlated with a process of revelation. Human faith cannot function to disclose something. Hence, although the popular anthropocentric approach can explain Paul's use of Habakkuk 2:4,[34] along with his frequent emphasis on the motif of "faith", it runs afoul of the further correlations set up by the actual prepositions and their associated verbs of revelation in 1:17 and 3:21–22 (and in fact this approach also struggles to account for the prepositional series in verse 17a, which raises similar issues[35]).

It can be seen by this point, then, that the complex data set we are seeking to explain here can only be comprehended by a christocentric approach in general that construes the contested πίστις Χριστοῦ genitive in Romans 3:22 subjectively, relating the fidelity in question to Christ himself. The anthropocentric reading fails to account for key aspects of the relevant data (as do the theocentric and evidentiary approaches). Furthermore, there are no good reasons *not* to read any of the other contested genitives – or, for that matter, any of the shorter πίστις phrases elsewhere in Paul – in the same way, although I am aware that this claim concerning sustainability ideally ought to receive much more detailed consideration.[36] It seems nevertheless that a reasonably decisive interpretative conclusion has been reached in relation to Romans 1:17 and 3:22.

These important if not programmatic texts state that the faithfulness of Christ – in the broader sense of his obedience, death, and resurrection – has revealed the saving righteousness of God. Moreover, this event is attested by the Prophets, meaning specifically at this point in Romans

---

"appropriated" – he *could* read the πίστις phrase there coherently and adverbially, so this difficulty will not be pressed here. The illegitimacy of the supplied verb, which differs from the overtly supplied verb in v. 21, is the main problem.

[34] Although here it does also arguably struggle with the exact rendering of the text. A broadly anthropocentric approach fits best with an adjectival construal of the key phrase ἐκ πίστεως. But an adverbial function seems more likely: see esp. see D. Moody Smith, "Ο ΔΕ ΔΙΚΑΙΟΣ ΕΚ ΠΙΣΤΕΩΣ ΖΗΣΕΤΑΙ", in *Studies in the History and Text of the New Testament in Honor of Kenneth Willis Clark* (ed. Boyd L. Daniels and M. Jack Suggs; Salt Lake City, UT: University of Utah, 1967), 13–25. Smith assembles 7 contentions, the combined weight of which is overwhelming.

[35] My principal argumentative point in the 1992 and 1994 studies ("Meaning" and "*Crux Interpretum*").

[36] See *Deliverance of God*, esp. chs. 11, 15–16, and 19–21.

Habakkuk 2:4, which declares that "the righteous one by means of faithfulness will live".[37]

---

[37] Unfortunately, there is insufficient space to include analysis even of 3:25 and 3:26 here, but see B. Longenecker, "Πίστις in Romans 3:25". R. Barry Matlock objects in "Πίστις in Galatians 3:26: Neglected Evidence for 'Faith in Christ'?", *NTS* 49 (2003): 433–9; but he is insufficiently sensitive to the likelihood that the key prepositional phrases in both Rom. 3:25 and Gal. 3:26 are coordinate, not consecutive, constructions. He also overestimates the cogency of the variations in 𝔭⁴⁶. For 3:26 see Keck, "'Jesus' in Romans", 443–6. (These texts are assessed in detail in *Deliverance of God*, chs. 16 and 20.)

5

Saving Faith: The Rhetoric and Semantics of πίστις in Paul

R. BARRY MATLOCK

The question of πίστις Χριστοῦ in Paul has been persistently pressed now for a generation, having arisen intermittently throughout the last century. It has proved as difficult to resolve as it is impossible to avoid. What accounts for the apparent intractability of this problem? It is not as though there is anything mysterious about the ambiguity between an objective and a subjective reading (or what have you) posed by these Pauline phrases.[1] English usage offers a number of analogues: possessives like "the President's murder" and "of" phrases like "the love of a woman" pose the same objective/subjective ambiguity (absent a disambiguating context, that is). Or take the participial phrase "saving faith" in my title. Without a context, "faith" would probably be read as the subject, "faith saves". In fact, it is the object: I am "saving faith", that is, saving the reading "faith in Christ" from its many foes! Of course, Paul is not here to parse his own phrases. But he left behind his contexts. Is that enough?

In Paul's absence the stakes have run high. According to J.L. Martyn, the interpretive choice posed by πίστις Χριστοῦ represents "a matter of life and death" for Paul himself and is make-or-break for Paul's interpreters.[2] It is no exaggeration to say that two accounts of Paul, and indeed of Christian theology as a whole, are often at war here: a

---

[1] I use the conventional terms "objective" versus "subjective" genitive as convenient shorthand for the most basic consideration of whether the πίστις in question is that of Christ or of "believers"; I leave open the question whether in either case other labels might be preferred. At points below I write of Christ as the "focus" of πίστις, in recognition of the fact that, in Paul, "faith in Christ" is inclusive of "God" and "the gospel" – that is, πίστις in Paul is directed toward "(the [message of the] saving action of God in) Christ" (see Rom. 9:30–10:21). As far as labels go, for my part this directionality is adequately indicated by the term "objective genitive".

[2] J. Louis Martyn, "The Apocalyptic Gospel in Galatians", *Int* 54 (2000): 250.

corporate, participationist reading and an individual, forensic one. To that extent, the debate over πίστις Χριστοῦ is a proxy war, and this, more than anything, accounts for its persistence. It is in this context that I have previously called for a "detheologizing" of this debate.[3] This has been taken as a polemic against theological interpretation as such.[4] It is not.[5] That wider campaign will not be won or lost over πίστις Χριστοῦ; conversely, much can be done here by way of exchanging reasons for our positions without predetermining the other. To "detheologize" the debate (however felicitous the term) is precisely to keep it in "the space of reasons", rather than allowing it to be forced to the level of a wholesale choice between these two Pauls.[6]

I have also previously recommended "reconceptualizing" the debate along linguistic semantic lines.[7] This is a matter of the kind of reasons that are particularly called for. Patently, two very basic lexical semantic questions are posed by the πίστις Χριστοῦ phrases: the sense of πίστις; and the relation between πίστις and Χριστοῦ as conjoined by the genitive. As to the first question, I have argued that πίστις is a polysemous word, two of whose conventional senses are at issue here: either "believing, trusting, having faith", or "being trustworthy, dependable, reliable", depending on context. As to the second question, I have pointed out that the relation between any two nominals linked together by the genitive will be given by context and/or convention. Our own language constantly presents us with polysemous words and nominals that stand in some or other implicit relation to one another, and we consider English neither reckless nor irresponsible for allowing such manifold potential for confusion: for ambiguity has free rein only in the

---

[3] Matlock, "Detheologizing ΠΙΣΤΙΣ ΧΡΙΣΤΟΥ"; "Even the Demons Believe", 309–14.

[4] Hays, *The Faith of Jesus Christ*, lxvi–lxvii.

[5] R. Barry Matlock, "Afterword" to "The Arrow and the Web: Critical Reflections on a Narrative Approach to Paul", in *Narrative Dynamics* (ed. B. Longenecker; Louisville, KY: Westminster John Knox Press, 2002), 54–7; cf. Francis Watson, *Paul, Judaism, and the Gentiles: Beyond the New Perspective* (2nd ed.; Grand Rapids, MI: Eerdmans, 2007), 243, n.54.

[6] On the epistemology implicit in these remarks, see R. Barry Matlock, "Beyond the Great Divide? History, Theology, and the Secular Academy", in *Moving Beyond New Testament Theology? Essays in Conversation with Heikki Räisänen* (ed. Todd Penner and Caroline Vander Stichele; Publications of the Finnish Exegetical Society 88; Göttingen: Vandenhoeck & Ruprecht, 2005), 369–99; contrast the implicit relativism of Douglas Campbell in *Quest*.

[7] Matlock, "Detheologizing ΠΙΣΤΙΣ ΧΡΙΣΤΟΥ"; "Even the Demons Believe", 314–17.

absence of context. The same holds for Hellenistic Greek. The least that we should expect Paul's contexts to do for us, quite simply, is to select the sense of πίστις ("faith" or "faithfulness", or whatever) and define the relation of Χριστός to πίστις ("subject" or "object", or whatever). These contexts seem to have done this very well for early Greek readers, who appear to have been unanimous in reading the objective genitive (more on this below). Indeed, context worked in the way it usually does in such cases: silently. These early readers, native speakers of Hellenistic Greek, appear entirely unaware of this debate that has vexed us so. How could that be? Here I offer a selective sketch of how the πίστις Χριστοῦ contexts do their requisite work. I focus on those four πίστις Χριστοῦ verses where there is an additional verb or noun phrase employing πιστεύω or πίστις: Galatians 2:16, 3:22, Romans 3:22, and Philippians 3:9. Proponents of the subjective genitive reading have typically blamed the objective reading for creating a suspicious redundancy in these verses, duly removed by the subjective reading, while proponents of the objective reading have countered that the repetition in these verses is a simple matter of emphasis.[8] This phenomenon of the reduplication of πίστις / πιστεύω phrases is, of course, a question of *rhetoric* (or "style", or "structure"). But it is also a *semantic* question.[9] What semantic force do these additional phrases exert upon Paul's πίστις Χριστοῦ phrases? Do they suggest a relation of contrast or of identity? Here I will consider these four texts in reverse order.[10]

Philippians 3:9

We begin, then, with the long participial clause of Philippians 3:9, μὴ ἔχων ἐμὴν δικαιοσύνην τὴν ἐκ νόμου ἀλλὰ τὴν διὰ πίστεως Χριστοῦ,

---

[8] See Matlock, "Rhetoric", 175–7.

[9] My analysis here draws prominently on Matlock, "Rhetoric". There the question of "redundancy" was to the fore and the semantic aspect more implicit, while here the reverse. Another, related dimension of analysis, partly brought into play below, is "intertextuality", where the leading works are by Francis Watson – *Paul and the Hermeneutics of Faith* and *Paul, Judaism, and the Gentiles* (cf. his contribution to the present volume). While differences of nuance may exist between our two approaches to πίστις Χριστοῦ, I regard them as complementary. Indeed I regard Watson's two recent works as presently among the most significant in the field.

[10] While my remit here is to consider πίστις Χριστοῦ in Galatians and Romans, my particular approach to this debate involves me in matters ably dealt with by others in this volume (including linguistic semantics, the evidence of Philippians, and patristic interpretation of πίστις Χριστοῦ).

τὴν ἐκ θεοῦ δικαιοσύνην ἐπὶ τῇ πίστει, "not having a righteousness of my own that comes from the Law, but one that comes through faith in Christ, the righteousness from God based on faith". The rhetoric of this clause is based on antithesis, parallelism, and repetition. I would analyze the pattern of salient parallels and contrasts in Philippians 3:9 as follows:

I	μὴ ἔχων		ἐμὴν	δικαιοσύνην	τὴν	ἐκ νόμου
	<u>ἀλλα</u>				τὴν	διὰ πίστεως Χριστοῦ,
II		τὴν ἐκ θεοῦ	δικαιοσύνην			ἐπὶ τῇ πίστει

The second line (II) parallels the first (I). The first formulation is more complex: formally an antithesis (not …, but rather …), it thus includes both negative and positive elements. The second is formally simpler, including only positive elements. There is movement between the two lines. The second formulation amplifies the first, adding the final missing element, the counterpart to "my own", namely "from God"; and it reiterates the instrumental element, "by (this) faith", omitting the negative "by Law". Each formulation thus characterizes δικαιοσύνη both upstream ("my own" / "from God") and downstream ("by Law" / "by faith"), as it were. The first δικαιοσύνη is characterized in one go, the second in two stages. This analysis falls out clearly and precisely from the syntax and word order of Philippians 3:9, as the four articles handily indicate: the first two articles function much like relative pronouns, pointing back to the first occurrence of δικαιοσύνη and qualifying it with two prepositional phrases in the third attributive position (ἐκ νόμου, διὰ πίστεως Χριστοῦ); the third article introduces the second δικαιοσύνη, enclosing a third prepositional phrase (ἐκ θεοῦ) in the first attributive position, the same position as ἐμήν; the fourth article (τῇ πίστει) is anaphoric, pointing back to the first occurrence of πίστις.

On my analysis, "my own" stands opposed to "from God". This may be justified not only in terms of syntax and word order, but also by appeal to the similar wording of Romans 10:3 (τὴν τοῦ θεοῦ δικαιοσύνην καὶ τὴν ἰδίαν [δικαιοσύνην]), with which Philippians 3:9 is often compared. And on this analysis, "by Law" belongs together with "through πίστις Χριστοῦ" and "on the basis of faith" in the same structural position. Again, this may be justified not only in terms of syntax and word order, but also by appeal to wider Pauline usage. In a striking recurrent pattern, Paul sets πίστις and νόμος in antithesis, with instrumental ἐκ or διά (or occasional stylistic variants), where the middle term is δικαιόω or δικαιοσύνη (and variations):

With ἐκ: Gal. 2:16; 3:2, 5, 7, 8, 9, 10, 11, 12, 18, 21, 22, 24; 5:5; Rom. 3:20, 26, 30; 4:2, 14, 16; 5:1; 9:30, 32; 10:5, 6; Phil. 3:9

With διά: Gal. 2:16, 19, 21; 3:14, 26; Rom. 3:20, 22, 25, 27, 30, 31; 4:13; Phil. 3:9

Other: Gal. 2:20; 3:11; 5:4 (ἐν); Rom. 3:28 (simple dative); Rom. 3:21, 28; 4:6 (χωρίς); Rom. 4:11, 13 (simple genitive); Phil. 3:9 (ἐπί)

My structural analysis of Philippians 3:9 thus takes account of its conformity to an antithetical rhetorical pattern encompassing all the πίστις Χριστοῦ contexts. Notice finally that Paul could have drawn his πίστις / νόμος contrast here around a single use of δικαιοσύνη. What is implicit in his initial, antithetical formulation is made explicit in the second: there are *two righteousnesses* in question. That is to say, the repetition in Philippians 3:9 is as much about δικαιοσύνη as it is about πίστις: πίστις is initially bound grammatically to the first (supposed) δικαιοσύνη, but is immediately reassigned to the second (true) δικαιοσύνη, to which it properly belongs. This graphically highlights the qualitative shift from the first to the second "righteousness", and implicitly denies that πίστις is a matter of "one's own righteousness" (whatever one takes this to be). Paul's very rhetoric rings the changes on "righteousness" in Christ.

So far, this analysis equates the two πίστις phrases without yet fully explicating them. To that end, there are in Philippians at least three clear contextual indications of the sense of πίστις in Philippians 3:9: the corresponding verb, πιστεύω, "believe, have faith, trust" (1:29); the synonym πεποίθησις, "confidence" (3:4); and the (spatially and semantically) contiguous γνῶσις, γινώσκω, "knowledge", "know" (3:8, 10). And there are at least three clear contextual indications of the relation between πίστις and Χριστός in Philippians 3:9: τὸ εἰς αὐτὸν πιστεύειν, "believing in him (Christ)" (1:29); πεποίθησις ἐν σαρκί, "confidence in the flesh" (3:4; cf. v. 3); and τῆς γνώσεως Χριστοῦ Ἰησοῦ, τοῦ γνῶναι αὐτόν, "the knowledge of Christ Jesus", "that I might know him" (3:8, 10). If we inquire into the relation between πίστις and Χριστοῦ in Philippians 3:9, then Philippians 1:29 immediately comes to our attention as the only other verse in the letter to relate πίστις or πιστεύω and Χριστός. But there is more than just this to connect the two texts. The parallel between Philippians 1:29 and 3:9–10 is too striking to be coincidental: ὅτι ὑμῖν ἐχαρίσθη τὸ ὑπὲρ Χριστοῦ, οὐ μόνον τὸ εἰς αὐτὸν πιστεύειν ἀλλὰ καὶ τὸ ὑπὲρ αὐτοῦ πάσχειν, "For he [God, v. 28] has graciously granted you the privilege not only of believing in Christ (τὸ εἰς αὐτὸν πιστεύειν), but of suffering (πάσχω) for him as well" (1:29); now compare Philippians 3:9–10, where Paul again juxtaposes "faith" and "suffering", proceeding immediately from talk of his having a righteousness "that comes through faith in Christ (διὰ πίστεως Χριστοῦ), the righteousness from God based on faith (ἐπὶ τῇ πίστει)" to "I want to know Christ and the power of his resurrection and the sharing of his sufferings (πάθημα) by becoming like him in his death" (cf. 1:30). Philippians 1:29 clearly anticipates 3:9–10, and the latter harks back to the former: πιστεύειν εἰς Χριστόν and πίστις Χριστοῦ are thus shown to be parallel constructions (just as in Gal. 2:16, on which see below). This speaks both to the sense of πίστις and the nature of the genitive Χριστοῦ ("faith in Christ", not "Christ's faithfulness"). The second set of contextual factors is nearer to hand: Paul puts no confidence in the flesh (πεποίθησις ἐν σαρκί, 3:4), but rather he boasts in Christ (οἱ ... καυχώμενοι ἐν Χριστῷ Ἰησοῦ καὶ οὐκ ἐν σαρκὶ πεποιθότες, 3:3) and he places his trust in Christ (πίστις Χριστοῦ, 3:9). Again, the sense, the subject, and the object of πίστις are thus contextually selected as according to the objective reading. Nearest to hand, we find that πίστις Χριστοῦ is flanked on either side by talk of "knowing Christ", τῆς γνώσεως Χριστοῦ Ἰησοῦ (objective genitive), in verse 8, and, following immediately on from ἐπὶ τῇ πίστει, "knowing him", τοῦ γνῶναι αὐτόν, in verse 10 (with the antecedent of αὐτόν understood from πίστις Χριστοῦ). The presence of γνῶσις, γινώσκω further contributes to the selection of the semantically contiguous sense of πίστις ("belief, faith, trust", not "faithfulness"). As to the relationship between πίστις and Χριστοῦ, the fourfold repetition of "knowing", "believing", "believing", "knowing *Christ*" selects the appropriate subject and object of πίστις. Thus *each* of these three contextual parallels (1:29; 3:3–4; 3:8, 10) provides semantic evidence *both* for the sense of πίστις in 3:9 ("belief, faith, trust") *and* for the relation of πίστις to Χριστοῦ (the direction or focus of "faith" is "Christ"); and because they do so *tacitly*, and in three quite *different* ways, their cumulative weight in favour of the objective genitive reading is even greater than the sum of their parts.

Romans 3:22

In the case of Romans 3:22, δικαιοσύνη δὲ θεοῦ διὰ πίστεως Ἰησοῦ Χριστοῦ εἰς πάντας τοὺς πιστεύοντας, "the righteousness of God through faith in Jesus Christ for all who believe", it is generally acknowledged that Paul's emphasis on "all" (πᾶς) might provide an (at least partial) explanation for the reduplication of πίστις / πιστεύω phrases. Well should this much, at least, be conceded. After all, πᾶς is a thematic word in Romans (1:5, 16; 2:9–10; 3:9, 19–20, 22–23; 4:11, 16; 5:12, 18; 10:4, 11–13; 11:26, 32); it keeps some interesting company with πιστεύω (in addition to 3:22, we have παντὶ τῷ πιστεύοντι, 1:16; πάντων τῶν πιστευόντων, 4:11; παντὶ τῷ πιστεύοντι, 10:4; and πᾶς ὁ πιστεύων, 10:11); and it is a matter of emphasis at this precise point in Paul's argument: οὐ γάρ ἐστιν διαστολή, πάντες γὰρ ἥμαρτον καὶ ὑστεροῦνται τῆς δόξης τοῦ θεοῦ, "For there is no distinction, since all have sinned and fall short of the glory of God" (3:23, the fifth repetition of πᾶς in as many verses). If the repetition is found nevertheless still to be troubling, how would we propose to improve upon Paul's formulation? To recommend that he drop the πίστις Χριστοῦ phrase would be to ask him to dispense with his signal counterpart to ἔργα νόμου (Rom. 3:20; cf. Gal. 2:16), while the verb phrase clearly stands in service of πᾶς (which only appears with the verb: again, 1:16; 3:22; 4:11; 10:4, 11). Such rhetorical and syntactical considerations readily account for Paul's noun and verb formulations in Romans 3:22. And a closer look leads us to further contextual and intertextual considerations yielding yet more semantic information regarding πίστις Χριστοῦ.

Among those five phrases in Romans combining πᾶς and πιστεύω, Romans 10:11 fairly leaps to our attention: πᾶς ὁ πιστεύων ἐπ' αὐτῷ, "everyone who believes on him". Naturally enough, Romans 10:11 has sometimes been invoked in the πίστις Χριστοῦ debate as general evidence that Christ is an "object of faith" in Paul. But this text has not received the attention it merits, and when we take a closer look we find that it has much more than just this general bearing on 3:22. Romans 10:11 in full runs thus: λέγει γὰρ ἡ γραφή· πᾶς ὁ πιστεύων ἐπ' αὐτῷ οὐ καταισχυνθήσεται, "The scripture says, 'No one who believes in him will be put to shame'." That Paul is quoting Scripture is thus prominently signaled; compare 9:33, where this same biblical text (Isa. 28:16) is quoted. This time Paul himself adds πᾶς to the beginning of the quotation, which he now amplifies thus: οὐ γάρ ἐστιν διαστολή Ἰουδαίου τε καὶ Ἕλληνος, "For there is no distinction between Jew and Greek" (10:12a). Who is this on whom (ἐπ' αὐτῷ) one believes?

He is the one whom (αὐτόν) God raised from the dead, namely κύριος Ἰησοῦς (10:9). Of this same one it is further said: ὁ γὰρ αὐτὸς κύριος πάντων, πλουτῶν εἰς πάντας τοὺς ἐπικαλουμένους αὐτόν· πᾶς γὰρ ὃς ἂν ἐπικαλέσηται τὸ ὄνομα κυρίου σωθήσεται, "the same Lord is Lord of all and is generous to all who call on him. For, 'Everyone who calls on the name of the Lord shall be saved'" (10:12b–13). This latter quotation of Joel 3:5 justifies Paul's addition of πᾶς to Isaiah 28:16 (providing the fourth occurrence of πᾶς in three verses, a concentration paralleled in 3:19–23). The two biblical quotations of verses 11 and 13 correspond to the "believing" and "confessing" of verses 9–10, which expand in turn upon the "heart" and "mouth" of verse 8 (Deut. 30:14). Together, these verses _explicitly_ name "Jesus" (v. 9) as the one on whose name one calls, as the risen "Lord" who is the focus of "faith".[11] He is the one "heralded" and "proclaimed" (κηρύσσω, εὐαγγελίζω) in Paul's "gospel" (εὐαγγέλιον), "the word of faith" (τὸ ῥῆμα τῆς πίστεως), the "word of Christ" (ῥῆμα Χριστοῦ), the one in whom (εἰς ὄν, v. 14) "faith" (πίστις / πιστεύω) is to be placed (vv. 8, 14–17). What does it mean that no one who believes in him will be "put to shame" (καταισχυνθήσομαι, 10:11)? This is not Paul's usual term but is lent him by Isaiah; nevertheless, it serves well enough as a place-holder for δικαιοσύνη and δικαιόω, σωτηρία, and σῴζω (9:30–31, 10:1, 3, 4, 5, 6, 9, 10, 13). There is another important intertextual dimension to Paul's πᾶς ὁ πιστεύων formulations in Romans: in Romans 4:11, Abraham is said to be the "father" of "all who believe" (πάντων τῶν πιστευόντων), to whom "righteousness" (δικαιοσύνη) is likewise "reckoned" (λογίζομαι), echoing Genesis 15:6 (cf. 4:3, 5, 6, 9, 11, 22, 24). Here in Romans 10, verses 4 and 11 echo Romans 3–4 in the association of πᾶς and πιστεύω, and verses 4 and 10 echo Genesis 15:6 specifically in the combination of πιστεύω and εἰς δικαιοσύνην (cf. 4:3, 5, 9, 22). Returning to Romans 10:11: by adding πᾶς to the quotation of Isaiah 28:16 and by continuing with precisely the same wording as 3:22 (οὐ γάρ ἐστιν διαστολή), Paul makes 10:11 the closest parallel to 3:22 outside 1:16–17, which latter Romans 10:11–13 also echoes (ἐπαισχύνομαι, σωτηρία παντὶ τῷ πιστεύοντι, Ἰουδαῖος τε καὶ Ἕλλην). _For Paul, Isaiah 28:16 as emended and quoted in Romans 10:11 is point-for-point the biblical counterpart to Romans 3:22._ Together, Romans 1:16–17, 3:22, and 10:11 form a mutually interpreting trio, offering the cumulative voice of "the Law and the

---

[11] On dissenting views as to the identity of the αὐτῷ ("him / it") of Isa. 26:18 as cited in Rom. 9:33 (and to a lesser extent in 10:11), see further Matlock, "Rhetoric", 186, n.16.

prophets" (3:21) – most particularly Habakkuk 2:4 and Genesis 15:6 – regarding πίστις Χριστοῦ. And these contextual and intertextual factors serve to select the sense ("faith"), the subject ("all"), and the object ("Christ") of πίστις as according to the objective genitive reading.

Galatians 3:22

We turn now to Galatians 3:22, ἀλλὰ συνέκλεισεν ἡ γραφὴ τὰ πάντα ὑπὸ ἁμαρτίαν, ἵνα ἡ ἐπαγγελία ἐκ πίστεως Ἰησοῦ Χριστοῦ δοθῇ τοῖς πιστεύουσιν, "But the scripture has imprisoned all things under the power of sin, so that what was promised through faith in Jesus Christ might be given to those who believe". Here the structural/rhetorical question is not simply the reduplication of πίστις/πιστεύω phrases but the relationship between the several elements of 3:22b (ἐπαγγελία, ἐκ πίστεως Ἰησοῦ Χριστοῦ, δοθῇ, and τοῖς πιστεύουσιν). According to Richard Hays, the NRSV translation (above) reflects

> the awkwardness of attempting to interpret ἐκ πίστεως Ἰησοῦ Χριστοῦ to mean "through faith in Jesus Christ." The NRSV reads the phrase as a modifier of the noun "promise" (ἐπαγγελία), producing the peculiar rendering, "what was promised through faith in Jesus Christ." This makes no sense, since neither the Genesis text nor Paul's exposition of it has referred to anything being promised through faith in Jesus Christ.[12]

Hays thus takes it as read that there is no "faith in Christ" in Genesis.

To determine whether or not this is so, we will start with Galatians 3:22 and work back, tracing the threads that Paul ties together here. The problem with the NRSV rendering cannot be that it "makes no sense" in and of itself. It follows the word order of Galatians 3:22 exactly, without any question of redundancy; and the assertion that the terms of the promise have not changed, that the promise is now being kept on the same terms as were in view when it was first made, is precisely the point that Paul labours to make in Galatians 3:6–21. Paul emphatically insists that the-coming-four-hundred-and-thirty-years-later-law (ὁ μετὰ τετρακόσια καὶ τριάκοντα ἔτη γεγονὼς νόμος) cannot and does not alter the promise (3:17–18, 21); nor has he, Paul, altered the terms, but rather

---

[12] Richard B. Hays, "The Letter to the Galatians: Introduction, Commentary, and Reflections" (*NIB* 11; Nashville, TN: Abingdon, 2000), 181–348 (269).

his adversaries in Galatia are attempting to do so (1:6–9; 5:7). One can easily see why Paul, as a matter of some urgency, would maintain that "what was promised through faith in Jesus Christ [should] be given to those who believe" (3:22b): some would now have it be given rather to those who observe the Law, placing the Galatians (the "believers" most immediately in view) outside the promise unless they comply. For Paul, this is a matter of the integrity of the gospel (2:5, 14), the integrity of Paul himself as apostle to the Gentiles (1:16, 2:1–10), and, most importantly, the integrity of God in making and keeping his promises (3:15–18).

But Hays does not explore the sense that such a reading *might* make, because for him it is a complete non-starter. Why? Again, the only reason he offers is that "neither the Genesis text nor Paul's exposition of it has referred to anything being promised through faith in Jesus Christ". We need not wonder that Genesis should fail to speak of "anything being promised through faith in Jesus Christ" as such. But what about Paul's exposition of it? In Galatians, three times ἡ γραφή, "the Scripture", actively speaks: at 3:8, 3:22, and 4:30. In the first and third of these instances, a specific word of Scripture is meant: Genesis 12:3 (with 18:18) at Galatians 3:8, and Genesis 21:10 at Galatians 4:30. In Galatians 3:22a, "but the scripture has imprisoned all things under the power of sin", the particular speech-action of "the Scripture" effecting this "imprisonment" is the curse pronounced by Deuteronomy 27:26 on "everyone who does not observe and obey all the things written in the book of the Law" (Gal. 3:10), while the "promise" in question in Galatians 3:22b is the blessing pronounced by Genesis 12:3/18:18, the first speech-action of "the Scripture" in Galatians (Gal. 3:8). There, the promise, spoken to Abraham (τῷ Ἀβραάμ), is that "all the Gentiles shall be blessed in you" (ἐνευλογηθήσονται ἐν σοὶ πάντα τὰ ἔθνη). In speaking thus, ἡ γραφή "declared the gospel beforehand" (προευηγγελίσατο) to Abraham. It was able to do so because it commanded a view from which it could be seen "that God would justify the Gentiles by faith" (προϊδοῦσα ... ὅτι ἐκ πίστεως δικαιοῖ τὰ ἔθνη ὁ θεός). *That is to say, "the Scripture" foresaw Paul's very mission and proclaimed beforehand Paul's gospel.* Paul moves directly from talk of this "blessing" to the "curse" pronounced by the Law on its transgressor (3:10–14). But through Christ's death, the outworking of the Law's "curse" is, paradoxically, that the promised blessing has been received ἐν Χριστῷ Ἰησοῦ, διὰ τῆς πίστεως (3:14). This outcome was anticipated in both particulars: the promised blessing is that of being "justified" ἐκ πίστεως (3:8), and the promise was spoken not *just* to Abraham, but to Abraham *and to his seed* (τῷ Ἀβραάμ ... καὶ τῷ σπέρματι αὐτοῦ), namely, "Christ" (3:16; cf. v. 19) – for Paul, ἐν σοί

(3:8) already includes ἐν Χριστῷ. The Law could not alter the terms of the promise (3:17, 18). Nor does it even attempt to: the Law is not against (κατά) God's promises – emphatically not (μὴ γένοιτο) – they are not true rivals: εἰ γὰρ ἐδόθη νόμος ὁ δυνάμενος ζῳοποιῆσαι, ὄντως ἐκ νόμου ἂν ἦν ἡ δικαιοσύνη, "For if a law had been given that could make alive, then righteousness would indeed come through the Law" (3:21). God has promised that "in/through Christ" he will "justify" (δικαιόω) the Gentiles ἐκ πίστεως (3:8, 14, 16). The promised δικαιοσύνη cannot be ἐκ νόμου (3:21). By juxtaposing Deuteronomy 27:26 and Genesis 12:3/18:18 in Galatians 3:22, Paul brings to a single point the argument he has been running since 3:6: *the Law subserves the promise.* The terms of the promise have not changed – and not despite the Law, but rather the Law has played its own (paradoxical) role in this very outcome. The Law actually enforces the original terms of the promise: "But the scripture has imprisoned all things under the power of sin, so that what was promised through faith in Jesus Christ might be given to those who believe" (3:22). By Paul's lights, God has been true to his word as given (despite the attempt of some of his would-be spokespersons in Galatia to break his word for him). And if in Galatians 3:22 Paul asserts that the promise has been kept on the same terms as were in view from the beginning, this means that the two πίστις/πιστεύω phrases *must* be equivalent, by the very contextual and intertextual logic of Paul's argument. And in that case, ἐκ πίστεως Ἰησοῦ Χριστοῦ and τοῖς πιστεύουσιν both speak of the πίστις of "believers": which is to say, the sense, the subject, and the object of πίστις are selected as according to the objective genitive reading.

Galatians 2:16

As we turn finally to Galatians 2:16, the first rhetorical feature to notice, obvious on even a cursory glance at the verse, is the threefold repetition of contrasting νόμος and πίστις/πιστεύω phrases (underlined): εἰδότες [δὲ] ὅτι οὐ δικαιοῦται ἄνθρωπος ἐξ ἔργων <u>νόμου</u> ἐὰν μὴ διὰ <u>πίστεως</u> Ἰησοῦ Χριστοῦ, καὶ ἡμεῖς εἰς Χριστὸν Ἰησοῦν ἐπιστεύσαμεν, ἵνα δικαιωθῶμεν ἐκ <u>πίστεως</u> Χριστοῦ καὶ οὐκ ἐξ ἔργων <u>νόμου</u>, ὅτι ἐξ ἔργων <u>νόμου</u> οὐ δικαιωθήσεται πᾶσα σάρξ, "yet we know that a person is justified not by the works of the Law but through faith in Jesus Christ. And we have come to believe in Christ Jesus, so that we might be justified by faith in Christ, and not by doing the works of the Law, because no one will be justified by the works of the Law." Here the structural / rhetorical question is that of the interrelation of, and the movement between, these six phrases.

Although this case is quite different in detail from that of Philippians 3:9, I propose that the rhetoric of Galatians 2:16 is likewise based on antithesis, parallelism, and repetition:

εἰδότες [δὲ] ὅτι   A   B

Ia   οὐ δικαιοῦται ἄνθρωπος ἐξ ἔργων νόμου ἐὰν μὴ διὰ πίστεως Ἰησοῦ Χριστοῦ,

                                              B
Ib   καὶ ἡμεῖς εἰς Χριστὸν Ἰησοῦν ἐπιστεύσαμεν,

                                              B   A
IIa   ἵνα δικαιωθῶμεν ἐκ πίστεως Χριστοῦ καὶ οὐκ ἐξ ἔργων νόμου,

            A
IIb   ὅτι ἐξ ἔργων νόμου οὐ δικαιωθήσεται πᾶσα σάρξ.

This two-part structure is built around two antitheses: Ia and IIa. These are simply inverse formulations of the same antithesis: *not* ἔργα νόμου, *but rather* πίστις Χριστοῦ; πίστις Χριστοῦ, *and not* ἔργα νόμου.[13] In each case, the final element of the antithesis is reiterated in an amplifying clause: Ib and IIb. In the first instance, Paul affirms "faith in Christ" on the part of "we (Ἰουδαῖοι)" (cf. v. 15); in the second instance, he denies "works of Law" on behalf of "all flesh". The pattern of repetition (broken up by the NRSV translation, above) is ABB // BAA. While not strictly speaking a chiasm, II is thus the inverse of I. Notice that this structure in and of itself selects the objective genitive reading of πίστις Χριστοῦ: Ib and IIb reiterate and amplify the final member of the antithesis stated in Ia and IIa, which establishes the equivalence of διὰ πίστεως Ἰησοῦ Χριστοῦ and ἡμεῖς εἰς Χριστὸν Ἰησοῦν ἐπιστεύσαμεν. In general terms, the parallel between these two formulations has long been held to argue in favour of the objective reading, an argument typically cancelled out by the subjective reading by appeal to redundancy. On this analysis, that stalemate is broken.

There is one final dimension to the structure of Galatians 2:16 to be observed, which brings the rationale for Paul's rhetoric more clearly into view:

---

[13] On dissenting views regarding ἐὰν μή, see further Matlock, "Rhetoric", 197-8, n.25.

εἰδότες [δὲ] ὅτι   **A**   **B**   Antithesis,
Ia   οὐ δικαιοῦται ἄνθρωπος ἐξ ἔργων νόμου ἐὰν μὴ διὰ πίστεως Ἰησοῦ Χριστοῦ,   Generic

                                 B   Amplification,
Ib   καὶ ἡμεῖς εἰς Χριστὸν Ἰησοῦν ἐπιστεύσαμεν,   Personal

                   B   **A**   Antithesis,
IIa   ἵνα δικαιωθῶμεν ἐκ πίστεως Χριστοῦ καὶ οὐκ ἐξ ἔργων νόμου,   Personal

                   A   Amplification,
IIb   ὅτι ἐξ ἔργων νόμου οὐ δικαιωθήσεται πᾶσα σάρξ.   Generic

The first antithesis (Ia) is formulated in generic or impersonal terms:
the subject is ἄνθρωπος. It is amplified (Ib) in specific or personal
terms: the subject is ἡμεῖς. The second antithesis (IIa) is personal: the
subject ἡμεῖς is continued in the first-person plural form of δικαιόω.
Its amplification (IIb) is generic: the subject is πᾶσα σάρξ. Notice that
this dimension reveals another inversion in the order of the repetition.
The verse moves from impersonal to personal, then from personal
to impersonal, a movement reflected in the three named subjects,
ἄνθρωπος, ἡμεῖς, and πᾶσα σάρξ. With this final dimension of Galatians
2:16 in view, its carefully-wrought structure is on full display and we
see that every piece is integral to the complete thought. Thus contextual
pressure is simultaneously exerted from a number of directions to
read the objective genitive. Fear of redundancy and tautology is
utterly misplaced. But notice now that if we manipulate this structure,
combining the generic and the personal clauses (Ia with IIb, IIa with Ib),
we can *induce* tautology and redundancy: "we know that a person is
not justified by works of Law but through faith in Christ, since no one
will be justified by works of Law; in order that we might be justified
by faith in Christ and not by works of Law, even we have believed in
Christ Jesus". In this hypothetical case, there would indeed be no clear
reason for the repetition other than perhaps to create the appearance of
argument. This helps us pinpoint the actual argumentative movement
of the verse: here the Jewish Christian experience of the gospel is placed
within a common human narrative. The repetition serves not merely for
the sake of emphasis but to make a point of this Jewish experience for
the benefit of a non-Jewish audience: "in seeking to be justified in Christ
[cf. v. 17], we Jews have implicitly acknowledged our place alongside,
not above, the gentiles where righteousness is concerned". "Even we"

take our place, literally, between ἄνθρωπος and πᾶσα σάρξ. Once again, Paul's very rhetoric rings the changes on "righteousness" in Christ.

In this all-too-brief examination of these four πίστις Χριστοῦ texts, we have worked from what on the traditional dating is the latest, Philippians 3:9, to what on any view is the earliest, Galatians 2:16. In these two cases, the semantic information afforded by our rhetorical analysis weighs decisively in favour of the objective genitive reading. In between these two, Galatians 3:22 is directly impacted by Galatians 2:16 and was thus never really in any doubt; and in that case, the contextual and intertextual factors highlighted above were operating under a considerable tailwind. Alas, Galatians 2:16 could not have assisted the first readers of Romans 3:22 as it does us, but equally strong contextual and intertextual forces exert themselves in Romans as well. From beginning to end, then, the objective genitive reading of πίστις Χριστοῦ has been confirmed.

Early Greek Readers of πίστις Χριστοῦ

I return finally to the question of Paul's early Greek readers. The semantic value, in principle, of evidence from native speakers of Hellenistic Greek is obvious – though, as with the question of redundancy in the πίστις Χριστοῦ texts, one has to ask a semantic question to get a semantic answer. Two analyses of the patristic evidence, by Roy Harrisville and Ian Wallis, simultaneously entered the recent debate over πίστις Χριστοῦ and draw opposite conclusions, in favour of the objective genitive and the subjective genitive, respectively.[14] Is the evidence finely balanced, then? Hardly. Our concern here is less with the details than with how such evidence is evaluated. Harrisville's evidence focuses on early Greek commentary specifically on Paul's πίστις Χριστοῦ phrases. His search uncovers no debate on πίστις Χριστοῦ, but in the only instances found where a paraphrase reveals the commentator's interpretation (a number of examples from Origen and Chrysostom), the objective genitive is read; no instance of the subjective genitive reading is found.[15] In contrast,

---

[14] Harrisville, "Witness of the Fathers"; Wallis, *Faith of Jesus Christ*, 175–212.

[15] Harrisville, "Witness of the Fathers", 238–9: in commenting on Rom. 3:26, Origen twice glosses Paul's genitive phrase with πιστεύειν εἰς Ἰησοῦν and with an allusion to Gen. 15:6/Rom. 4:3 (Origen, *Commentarii ad Romanos*); in commenting on Gal. 2:16, Chrysostom twice glosses its πίστις/πιστεύω formulations with πίστις εἰς Χριστόν/αὐτόν (Chrysostom, *In Epistulam ad Galatas*). To Harrisville's evidence

Wallis does not attend specifically to early readings of Paul's πίστις Χριστοῦ phrases but searches more generally for texts that associate the language (or concept) of "faith" with Christ.[16] The two investigations thus overlap very little but nevertheless share an important result: neither finds an example of the subjective genitive reading of πίστις Χριστοῦ on the part of any early Greek reader, *nor indeed any discussion of the matter.* Nevertheless, Richard Hays pronounces Harrisville's evidence "surprisingly slight" and prefers instead Wallis's account of the evidence, from which Hays infers that the subjective genitive would have been the normal reading of πίστις Χριστοῦ until fourth-century christological controversies made it appear unorthodox to speak of Christ as having "faith" – Athanasius is the key witness here for Wallis and Hays.[17] But, on the evidence, this cannot be right. Remember, no instance of the subjective genitive reading is found and, more important methodologically, no debate on the πίστις Χριστοῦ phrases is found. It is not that the subjective genitive reading is explicitly rejected among early Greek readers (on theological grounds that Wallis and Hays might then find suspect), but rather that no awareness is shown of this option nor indeed of any problem, and so the objective genitive is read without polemic or apology.[18]

Silence can be very eloquent, and here it fairly sings. When Origen and Chrysostom read the objective genitive they do not argue the point, nor indeed do they make a point of it at all. If Wallis and Hays were right, they would have to. And because they do not, they bear tacit witness not to a private opinion but to the commonplace understanding of πίστις Χριστοῦ, as far as we can see. But that is not all. It is true that Athanasius bridles at the Arian suggestion that the use of πιστός of Christ in Hebrews 3:2 implies a (mere) creaturely figure. But in response, Athanasius brings to bear precisely the semantic distinction made above with respect to πίστις: there are, he says, two senses of πιστός in question, "believing" (πιστεύων) and "trustworthy" (ἀξιόπιστος); thus, he explains, the word is used of Christ not as one having faith in

---

should be added Chrysostom's paraphrase of Gal. 2:20, τὴν εἰς Χριστόν μοι πίστιν, "my faith in Christ" (PG 61.646; *NPNF*[1] 13:22). For both Origen and Chrysostom, the πίστις in question is the "faith" of "believers", directed toward or focused through "Christ".

16 Wallis, *Faith of Jesus Christ*, 181–200.

17 Hays, *The Faith of Jesus Christ*, xlvii–lii; cf. Wallis, *Faith of Jesus Christ*, 200–12.

18 See further Matlock, "Detheologizing ΠΙΣΤΙΣ ΧΡΙΣΤΟΥ", 18, n.55; "Even the Demons Believe", 305–7; "Πίστις in Galatians 3:26", 437–8.

someone else (εἴς τινα πιστεύων) but as one who ought to be believed (πιστεύεσθαι ὀφείλων).[19] Athanasius thus confirms, though in a different context, a feature of the πίστις Χριστοῦ contexts that on my analysis helped silently to select the objective genitive reading among early Greek readers (semantic evidence that was before the eyes of Wallis and Hays, but not evaluated as such). Notice finally that Athanasius is perfectly happy to attribute "trustworthiness" to Christ – what Christian, "orthodox" *or* "heterodox", wouldn't be? – and that the Arians, who apparently were ideologically eager to attribute πίστις to Christ, evidently did so on the basis of πιστός in Hebrews 3:2 and not πίστις Χριστοῦ in Paul. In explaining the supposed demise of the original subjective genitive reading of πίστις Χριστοῦ, Wallis and Hays seem to think that in Athanasius they have found the proverbial "smoking gun". In fact they found the dog that didn't bark.

Conclusion

This brief and selective examination of these four πίστις Χριστοῦ texts inevitably leaves much untouched. It is simply an effort to expose some of the linguistic machinery bearing on πίστις Χριστοῦ. One does not *have* to look under the bonnet to enjoy a drive in the car. But sometimes it becomes necessary, and it can even enhance the enjoyment. The conventional wisdom of the πίστις Χριστοῦ debate seems to be that the objective and subjective genitive readings are both equally legitimate linguistically. But this is only a half-truth – and it leaves off the half that really counts. Both readings are equally possible *in the abstract*. But what about *in context*? What linguistic-contextual factors might serve to disambiguate πίστις Χριστοῦ? What evidence of this sort has each reading in its favour? (Another proposal that is also becoming commonplace is that maybe some sort of combined reading should be preferred – suggested to some, perhaps, by the very inconclusiveness of the debate thus far, as though there must be something to *both* readings. Here it must suffice to say that any such combined reading needs just as much linguistic-contextual support as either of the other two, and does not prevail simply by virtue of our finding it difficult or loathsome to choose.) This "linguistic machinery" is simply a matter of the effect of

---

[19] Athanasius, *Orationes contra Arianos* II.6, 9, cited in Wallis, *Faith of Jesus Christ*, 203–5.

Paul's words upon one another. These four instances of repetition are but part of a much wider pattern of repetition of πίστις / πιστεύω in Galatians and Romans, rooted in Genesis 15:6 (πιστεύειν εἰς δικαιοσύνην) and Habakkuk 2:4 (δίκαιος ἐκ πίστεως): see Galatians 2:16, 20; 3:2, 5, 6, 7, 8, 9, 11, 12, 14, 22, 23, 24, 25, 26; Romans 1:16, 17 // 3:22, 25, 26, 27, 28, 30, 31; 4:3, 5, 9, 11, 12, 13, 14, 16, 17, 18, 19, 20, 24; 5:1 // 9:30, 32, 33; 10:4, 6, 8, 9, 10, 11, 14, 16, 17! The effect of these (and associated) words upon each other, in the particular case of πίστις Χριστοῦ, is such as clearly to select the sense, the subject, and the object of πίστις as according to the objective genitive reading. In arguing thus, I have offered what proponents of the subjective genitive reading have not (and I suspect cannot): concrete linguistic-contextual evidence, precisely of the requisite sort.

6

Πίστις Χριστοῦ Terminology in Philippians and Ephesians

PAUL FOSTER

What Is at Stake and What Is Not?

It is sometimes suggested that one of the main reasons for adopting the subjective genitive reading of the πίστις Χριστοῦ phrase is that it provides a theologically richer understanding of the role of Christ in the soteriological plan of God. Such a theological approach insists that even the very act of faith (or faithfulness) required to restore right relations between humans and the deity does not belong to humanity, either individually or corporately, but in fact is itself a divine gift provided through the πίστις of Christ. Thus, Mark Reasoner can suggest that "the best arguments for the subjective genitive seem to be its theological utility, not the lexical or syntactical difficulties of the objective genitive".[1] The "theological utility" in question according to Reasoner is that emphasis will be placed on Christ's salvific act rather than on "individual(istic) conversion", that participatory perspectives of "being in Christ" are enlarged and that a false dichotomy in Paul's thinking between works and faith is torn down.[2] While each of these points might offer a more attractive theology (although that is another debate), they should at best be seen at "pay-offs" or consequences of adopting the subjective genitive reading. To use them as reasons for accepting this reading is logically unsound.

In order to judge the correctness of proposals concerning the type of genitive construction intended it is necessary to engage in close grammatical and syntactical analysis which can be combined with exegetical arguments about how either reading coheres with Paul's overall theological scheme. It might indeed be the case that such

---

[1] Reasoner, *Romans*, 39.
[2] Reasoner, *Romans*, 39–40.

an investigation leads one to suggest that Paul's choice of genitive construction does not result in as theologically rich a reading as alternative grammatical constructions. If that is the case, so be it. Exegesis is not an exercise in "rescuing" ancient authors to make them more palatable to modern taste. Rather, its goal is to understand the thought of an author within an original context – even with the possible limitations of that specific culture. While such a statement may seem to have taken little on board from the postmodern agenda (although it recognizes that recovering the author's original meaning is no easy task and that the attempt to reconstruct the thought world of a figure in the first century cannot be done in total neutrality from the investigator's own context), it does seek to prevent the notion of "theological pay-off" controlling the detailed work of textual and exegetical analysis.

Also it should be recognized that the debate concerns the nature of the set of genitive constructions that links the word Χριστοῦ with πίστις language, and this should not be cast as a litmus test of orthodoxy or otherwise. Biblical scholars are engaged in a contested debate about the meaning of certain Pauline phrases and their implications for understanding Paul's own soteriology. While such questions are important for understanding Pauline conceptions of the salvific process, no official church statement requires adherence to one interpretation as opposed to its alternatives. It may be the case that if biblical scholars are able to bring some clarity to the debate, or to show that certain options should be excluded, then official formulations may be redrafted to include such perspectives. In the meantime, the work of New Testament scholars is prior to such considerations. Thus, scholars are engaged in the common collaborative task of seeking a clearer understanding of such texts. This often involves robust dialogue among those with differing points of view, but such strong debates often clarify competing positions. Nevertheless, it needs to be repeated that the activity in question has the goal of clarifying the text, not adjudging doctrinal orthodoxy.

Related to this issue is the idea (often not fully articulated) that the subjective genitive interpretation rescues Paul from the charge of "semi-" or "proto-Pelagianism". The objective reading can be (mis)represented as implying that one's own faith is a "work" or responsive action that activates the salvific efficacy of Christ's atoning sacrifice. By contrast, in order to make it appear more attractive and theologically sound than the alternative, the subjective reading can be represented as ensuring that the recipients of Christ's grace do not even bring their own faith as the means that makes salvation effectual. Instead it is Christ's act of faithfulness in enduring the cross and displaying obedience to the

Father's will that creates the context in which the community of the redeemed can participate in the salvific age which Jesus himself has inaugurated. This can be seen as safeguarding against any possibility of "a works-based righteousness". Apart from the theological problem of how such a reading actually dispenses with the responsorial aspect of believing found elsewhere in Paul's writings, it also sets up an anachronistic and in some ways paternalistic attitude to the ancients, which sees them as in need of rescue from their own potential theological faux pas. Instead, without applying such inappropriate categories as "Pelagian", Paul's theology should be discussed in the terms that he uses while being fully cognizant of all its *aporias*, its less than fully developed ideas, and even its inconsistencies.

Philippians 3:9

The approach adopted here consists of initially studying each case of πίστις Χριστοῦ language separately. Furthermore, there is no reason to assume beforehand that the same type of genitive construction is used in each instance. Only after the individual cases have been considered can it be seen whether a clear and consistent picture emerges in Paul's thinking. The use of this phraseology in Philippians occurs in a context in which Paul mixes autobiographical reflection (Phil. 3:4–6) with a discussion of theocentric righteousness imputing soteriology (Phil. 3:9), anti-circumcision polemic (Phil. 3:2–3), and thoroughgoing participatory language (Phil. 3:7–11).[3] The single specific example of πίστις Χριστοῦ language that occurs in Philippians is found in 3:9, where Paul states:

> καὶ εὑρεθῶ ἐν αὐτῷ μὴ ἔχων ἐμὴν δικαιοσύνην τὴν ἐκ νόμου ἀλλὰ τὴν διὰ πίστεως Χριστοῦ τὴν ἐκ θεοῦ δικαιοσύνην ἐπὶ τῇ πίστει

> and I might be found in him, not having a righteousness of my own, based on law, but that which is through πίστεως Χριστοῦ, the righteousness from God that depends on faith

Here the key Greek phrase has been left untranslated so as not to prejudge the related issues of its translation, interpretation, and force.

---

[3] Bockmeuhl notes that this section is introduced without any syntactical markers. He observes that the introductory statement relies on "sharp contrasts to make its rhetorical points". M. Bockmuehl, *The Epistle to the Philippians* (BNTC; London: A&C Black, 1998), 182.

As an objective genitive the construction would read "but that which is through faith in Christ", while a subjective genitive would result in a translation along the lines of "but that which is through Christ's faith".[4]

Grammatically either construction is possible, and stock examples can be paraded that show similar syntactical units functioning in different contexts unambiguously as objective or subjective genitives. Thus the phrase in Mark 11:22, ἔχετε πίστιν θεοῦ, is almost certainly an objective genitive: "have faith in God" (to read "have the faith of God" seems both forced and foreign to the context).[5] By contrast, there are a number of texts in which subjective genitive constructions exhibit the same syntactical structure as we find in Philippians 3:9 and the other key texts in the discussion (i.e., Rom. 3:3, μὴ ἡ ἀπιστία αὐτῶν τὴν πίστιν τοῦ θεοῦ καταργήσει, "does their faithlessness nullify the faithfulness of God?"; or Rom. 4:16, ἀλλὰ καὶ τῷ ἐκ πίστεως Ἀβραάμ, "but also to the one who is from the faith of Abraham").[6]

Unlike the other texts usually discussed as part of the core group of seven examples from the genuine Pauline use of πίστις Χριστοῦ terminology, Philippians 3:9 stands in greater isolation.[7] Of the other six examples, four occur in chapters 2 and 3 of Galatians and the remaining two both occur in Romans 3. In some ways this makes the task of interpreting Philippians 3:9 somewhat more difficult, since there are not cross-checks for the use of this phrase in the same epistle. This means that one is left having to rely primarily on exegetical considerations based on the flow of Pauline rhetoric in this passage to determine the probable sense of this expression.

---

[4] O'Brien rearranges some of the Gk. clauses to produce the following translation: "but that righteousness which comes from God through the faithfulness of Christ and is based on faith" (*Philippians*, 382).

[5] Among commentators this interpretation appears to be predominant. See V. Taylor, *The Gospel according to St. Mark* (2nd ed.; London: Macmillan, 1966), 466; W.L. Lane, *The Gospel of Mark* (Grand Rapids, MI: Eerdmans, 1974), 408–10. Although Lane appears to support an objective reading he does entertain the possibility of a subjective construction: "It is possible that it should be understood as an encouragement rather than an exhortation: you have the faithfulness of God (cf. Hab. 2:4)." M.D. Hooker, *The Gospel according to Saint Mark* (London: A&C Black, 1991), 269; C.A. Evans, *Mark 8:27–16:20* (WBC 34B; Nashville, TN: Thomas Nelson, 2001), 186.

[6] See Dunn, *Romans*, 132, 216; Fitzmyer, *Romans*, 327, 385; Jewett, *Romans*, 244, 331.

[7] The seven examples that constitute this group are to be found in Rom. 3:22, 26; Gal. 2:16 (2×), 20; 3:22; Phil. 3:9.

Commentators in favour of objective readings often see the righteousness of which Paul speaks as having divine origin, whereas the faith is an expression of response which accepts the gift of divinely imputed righteousness. Thus Hawthorne can suggest, "he [Paul] has in mind a righteousness that has its origin in God (ἐκ θεοῦ) and that is humbly appropriated by a person through faith *in* Christ (διὰ πίστεως Χριστοῦ)".[8] Using different arguments, Silva also supports an objective reading. First he suggests that linguistic arguments can help resolve the question of interpretation. "Ambiguous grammatical forms should be interpreted in light of unambiguous ones, and the very repetition of Gal. 2:16 ('faith in Christ' twice; 'we believe in Christ Jesus' once) supports the traditional understanding."[9] Although Silva concedes that the classic counter-examples of Romans 3:3 and 4:12 are subjective genitives, it is not entirely clear how his discussion of the disputed reading in Galatians 2:16 actually removes the ambiguity of πίστις Χριστοῦ language. By contrast, those who prefer adopting a subjective genitive, while also making use of arguments based upon identifying a coherent exegesis of the passage, see that coherence established by different factors. Bockmuehl notes that there is an obvious contrast between status based on Torah observance or human achievements and the righteousness that comes as a divine gift.[10] On this point his argument broadly aligns with Hawthorne. Thus they suggest that, in order to make the argument consistent concerning Paul's rejection of his own striving after righteousness on the basis of Torah observance, the means of acquiring such righteousness cannot be derived from one's own faith but rather through the faith of Christ which makes such righteousness accessible. Consequently, Bockmuehl states,

> This righteousness "through the faith of Christ" is further defined as being from God on the basis of faith, in contrast to that which was from the Torah. God is its source and "the faith of Christ" is the means by which it is revealed.[11]

Thurston perhaps makes this point even more forcefully when she notes the repudiation of human status encapsulated in the wider context of Philippians 3:2–11. Therefore she comments that,

---

[8] G.F. Hawthorne, *Philippians* (WBC 43; Waco, TX: 1983), 141–2.

[9] M. Silva, *Philippians* (BECNT; 2nd ed.; Grand Rapids, MI: Baker, 2005), 161.

[10] Markus Bockmuehl, *The Epistle to the Philippians* (BNTC; Peabody, MA: Hendrickson, 1998), 210.

[11] Bockmuehl, *Philippians*, 212.

In view of the context I think it is Christ's faith (subjective genitive) that is in view here. Paul's righteousness comes as a gift by means of Christ's faithfulness (another possible translation of *pistis*), his obedient sacrifice (for another view see Fee, *Philippians*, 324–6). The whole point of this passage is repudiation of human (even theological or spiritual) accomplishment. What Christ did makes personal relationship with God possible.[12]

Hence one key aspect of the argument in favour of the subjective genitive is based on consistency of the logical contrast between Paul's own experience of his inability to gain righteousness through Torah observance or human accomplishments and his new perspective that true righteousness is a divinely imputed gift which does not depend on any human act, but rather derives from a christocentric act of faithfulness.

Arguments for reading a subjective genitive in Philippians 3:9 have not centred entirely upon exegetical considerations. Bockmuehl and, to a greater extent, O'Brien and Howard have utilized grammatical and lexical considerations. Howard notes the following statistic about the 24 cases in the Pauline corpus where πίστις is followed by either a name or a pronoun (apart from those examples involving πίστις Χριστοῦ):

> Twenty of these refer to the faith of Christians (either individually or collectively), one to the πίστις of God (Rom. 3:3), two to the faith(fulness) of Abraham (Rom. 4:12, 16), and one to the person whose faith is reckoned as righteousness (Rom. 4:5). In every case reference is made to the faith of an individual, never to faith in an individual.[13]

This appears to be a strong argument for seeing such genitive constructions with a personal name in the Pauline corpus as subjective genitives.

Lexical discussions focusing on the semantic range of the term πίστις have also been prominent in arguments about the meaning of the πίστις Χριστοῦ phrases. Drawing primarily on the suggestions of Robinson, certain commentators have noted that the word πίστις encompasses ideas of "fidelity", "firmness", or "fixity". They have made this determination by looking at the word's use in the LXX and wider literature of the Hellenistic period. Robinson himself thinks that, at

---

[12] B.B. Thurston and J.M. Ryan, *Philippians and Philemon* (SP 10; Collegeville, MN: Liturgical Press, 2005), 124.

[13] Howard, "Notes and Observations", and cited in O'Brien, *Philippians*, 398.

least in part, the problem of misunderstanding the meaning of the term πίστις arises from a simplistic attempt to map modern semantic ranges of certain terms onto Greek words as though there existed a one-to-one correspondence. He says:

> where we think we see a distinction through applying a test based on our own language and its distinctions, none existed for the native user of *pistis*. In this event, *pistis* did not convey to Paul either precisely what we mean by "faith" or precisely what we mean by "fidelity", but something else, a tertium quid, some notion, say, of fixity or firmness, which was suitable for use in a variety of contexts, but which did not, as a constant semantic marker, require any differentiation in significance.[14]

Admittedly, much of the discussion that has been carried out pertains to the seven examples of πίστις Χριστοῦ collectively, and not to the specific formulation in Philippians 3:9. Although the bulk of the discussion has focused on the examples in Romans and Galatians, when attention has been directed towards Paul's construction in Philippians a further piece of evidence is brought into the discussion.

There are actually two occurrences of the term πίστις in Philippians 3:9. Apart from the disputed πίστις Χριστοῦ phrase, at the end of the verse Paul declares that the righteousness that is of significance is τὴν ἐκ θεοῦ δικαιοσύνην ἐπὶ τῇ πίστει. There is virtually uniform agreement among all commentators that the last three words – a preposition and a dative construction – designate an act of human response.[15] For Hawthorne and others advocating an objective construction, the fact that believers' faith is most likely referenced here should then become the controlling interpretation when deciding on the sense of πίστις a few words earlier. Thus he comments that "the phrase, 'the righteousness of God based on faith' in v. 9c is simply added for clarification and emphasis without any concern for being tautological, and just because such emphatic redundancy is in keeping with Paul's style of writing".[16] Diametrically opposed to this train of thought, supporters of the subjective genitive see the phrase not as redundant but as the necessary complement and contrasting description of the responsive aspect of

---

[14] Robinson, "The Faith of Jesus Christ".

[15] Using somewhat androcentric language, O'Brien (*Philippians*, 400) states that "it specifies man's answering response, with ἐπί, indicative 'of that upon which a state of being, an action, or a result is based' (cf. Acts 3:16)".

[16] Hawthorne, *Philippians*, 142.

believers' faith which is predicated upon the very faithfulness of Christ. Discussing this distinction at some length Bockmuehl argues that

> Like Rom. 3.22 and Gal. 2.16, then, Phil. 3.9 is best understood as referring to *two* kinds of faithfulness in relation to God's righteousness revealed in Christ: the instrumental faithfulness *of* Christ in his self-humbling death on the Cross (*dia pisteôs Christou*), and the responding faithfulness of the believer (on the basis of faith, *epi té pistei*; cf. Rom. 3.22 "for all believers", *eis pantas tous pisteuontas*; Gal. 2.16 "and we have believed", *kai hémeis episteusamen*). This distinction allows one to specify *both* the objective ground of righteousness and the subjective mode of its acceptance, while removing what otherwise seems a surprising and possibly redundant *second* reference to human faith.[17]

These opposing interpretations show that the second reference to πίστις contained in Philippians 3:9, which is widely accepted as denoting human faith, can be read as offering corroborative evidence for either a subjective or objective reading of the first reference to faith in the same verse.

It is apparent that proponents of both subjective and objective genitive constructions in Philippians 3:9 have managed to build cumulative arguments in favour of their respective positions based on a combination of lexical, grammatical, and exegetical factors. Therefore, those in support of an objective genitive highlight the necessity of a consistent approach, whereby the linguistic factors govern interpretation. Thus, in Galatians 2:16 the action of "believing in Christ" (καὶ ἡμεῖς εἰς Χριστὸν Ἰησοῦν ἐπιστεύσαμεν), which is obviously an action of believers, controls the interpretation of πίστις Χριστοῦ language elsewhere in the Pauline corpus.[18] Apart from such linguistic consistency, advocates of an objective genitive reading also call for exegetical consistency in the use of "faith" language in Philippians 3:9. If this plea is followed, then the widely accepted understanding of the second use of πίστις terminology in the verse as a reference to human faith becomes determinative for the interpretation of the first occurrence of this word in the same verse. One false caricature, either implicit or explicit, of the opposing position that is

---

17 Bockmuehl, *Philippians*, 211–12.
18 Silva reiterates his earlier arguments at greater length in his essay "Faith versus Works of Law in Galatians", in *Justification and Variegated Nomism*, II, *The Paradoxes of Paul* (ed. D.A. Carson, P.T. O'Brien, and M.A. Seifred; WUNT 2.181; Tübingen: Mohr Siebeck, 2004), 247.

sometimes suggested by those who hold to this objective reading is that proponents of the subjective genitive fail to take seriously Paul's broader statements about the faith that believers express towards Christ.[19] In this regard we need to restate that what is under discussion is only the interpretation of a set of texts linking the significant terms πίστις and the genitive Χριστοῦ or its equivalent. There is no suggestion on the part of those who support a subjective reading that the notion of believers expressing their faith in Christ is an unimportant idea for Paul.[20]

Similarly, the argument for a subjective genitive is based upon a cumulative argument. First it is noted that, grammatically, when πίστις is followed by a name or pronoun in the Pauline corpus (and we exclude here the disputed texts under investigation), such constructions consistently and unambiguously refer to that individual's faith and not to the act of placing faith in such an individual.[21] Secondly, lexical studies have shown that the semantic range of the term πίστις was indeed broad during the Hellenistic period and that the primary or most widespread meaning of the term encompassed notions of fidelity, firmness, and faithfulness. Thirdly, the double occurrence of πίστις in Philippians 3:9 is not a case of Paul being formally redundant or using repetition for the purpose of emphasis. Rather, it is suggested that Paul is consciously emphasizing two aspects of his understanding of faith in the salvific scheme of God. Initially, and in line with his primary thesis that he could not obtain righteousness on the basis of his own merit or Torah observance, he emphasizes the fact that the freely given divine righteousness is imputed on the basis of Christ's act of fidelity. Then in the final part of the verse he highlights the obverse of this understanding, which is the need for the responsive faith of believers. Another false representation of the opposing position by supporters of a subjective reading is that those who hold to the objective construction are not open to the richer theological perspectives of the subjective genitive. As has been noted above, correct interpretation should not be predicated on "theological pay-off", and those who continue to argue for an objective reading are right to insist that this is an invalid argument that cannot be used to determine the nature of the genitive constructions under discussion.

---

[19] See Silva, "Faith versus Works", 230–32.

[20] Thus Wallis clearly states: "As we shall see, it is possible that Jesus' faith is referred to in conjunction with the faithfulness of God or the faith of believers." (*Faith of Jesus Christ*), 65, n.5.

[21] In particular see, e.g., Rom. 3:3; 4:5, 16.

These competing perspectives that have be constructed around the respective coherent interpretations make it difficult to offer a conclusive determination about the most plausible interpretation of the phrase διὰ πίστεως Χριστοῦ in Philippians 3:9. Initially, the point that the two usages of πίστις should be interpreted consistently appears compelling. However, the wider Pauline writings show that he was able to use both nuances of the term. The observation made by Silva, that the repetition of πίστις language in Galatians 2:16 is coupled with the description of "believing in Christ", may initially seem supportive of an objective reading.[22] However, the evidence marshalled by Howard and others shows that when Paul combines πίστις language with either a name or a pronoun in the genitive case he is referring to the faith of the individual in question.[23] For this reason, while acknowledging the finely balanced nature of the evidence in relation to Philippians 3:9, there appears to be a stronger combination of arguments in favour of reading the text as a subjective genitive construction which speaks of Christ's faithfulness as the means by which divine righteousness is given to those who respond with faith. This interpretation aligns with Paul's main point in the passage, which is that his attempt to obtain righteousness on the basis of his own merit was doomed to failure.

Ephesians 3:12

The πίστις Χριστοῦ terminology in Ephesians 3:12 raises a number of problems not encountered with the other texts containing this phrase.[24] The result is that scholars tend to speak of a core of seven texts and, more often than not, exlude Ephesians from the discussion.[25] The reasons for the omission are varied. Perhaps the most significant has arisen from the fairly widespread doubts concerning the Pauline authorship of Ephesians.[26] Presumably those who question Pauline authorship think

---

[22] Silva, *Philippians*, 161.

[23] Howard, "Notes and Observations", 459–60.

[24] For a more detailed discussion of this passage in relation to the πίστις Χριστοῦ debate see my earlier article, P. Foster, "The First Contribution to the πίστις Χριστοῦ Debate: A Study of Ephesians 3:12", *JSNT* 85 (2002): 75–96.

[25] Hultgren states, e.g., "Paul uses the πίστις Χριστοῦ formulation in seven instances". See "*Pistis Christou* Formulation", 254.

[26] Raymond Brown, in his *Introduction to the New Testament* (ABRL; New York: Doubleday, 1997), comments that "A fair estimate might be that *at the present moment about 80 percent of critical scholarship holds that Paul did not write Ephesians*" (620).

that such a deutero-Pauline text offers little by way of clarification of the intended meaning of this phrase in the genuine Pauline epistles. And those who support the Pauline authorship of Ephesians often have omitted this text because basing an argument on such a highly contested piece of evidence would leave any conclusion drawn from it susceptible to criticism. A second reason Ephesians 3:12 is often left out of consideration is because, unlike the seven core texts, it does not directly link πίστις terminology with either the genitive form of the name Ἰησοῦ or the titular name Χριστοῦ. Instead it employs a pronoun – which does, nevertheless, unambiguously refer back to Christ Jesus in the previous verse.

κατὰ πρόθεσιν τῶν αἰώνων ἣν ἐποίησεν ἐν τῷ Χριστῷ Ἰησοῦ τῷ κυρίῳ ἡμῶν, ἐν ᾧ ἔχομεν τὴν παρρησίαν καὶ προσαγωγὴν ἐν πεποιθήσει διὰ τῆς πίστεως αὐτοῦ. (Eph. 3:11–12)

According to the eternal purpose which was accomplished in Christ Jesus our Lord, in whom we have the boldness and access in confidence through τῆς πίστεως αὐτοῦ. (Eph. 3:11–12)

Finally, another possible reason why this text has been omitted from the debate may relate to the slightly different grammatical structure. Specifically, unlike the seven key texts which have anarthrous forms of the genitive phrase, the example in Ephesians is formulated with a definite article before the noun πίστις.

Much ink has been spent on discussing the grammatical force of the definite article in this construction, and more widely in relation to the whole πίστις Χριστοῦ question. Expressing the view that the presence of a definite article is important for signalling a subjective genitive, Burton states in relation to genitival clauses involving πίστις,

Those in which πίστις is accompanied by a subjective genitive or equivalent phrase indicating by whom the faith is exercised. The article in this case is almost invariably present. The object of faith is usually indicated, more or less definitely, by the context, but occasionally directly expressed.[27]

Burton finds overwhelming support for this syntactical pattern. In fact, he cites only one example of a subjective genitive without an article –

---

[27] E.D. Burton, *A Critical and Exegetical Commentary on the Epistle to the Galatians* (ICC; New York: Scribner's Sons, 1920; Edinburgh: T&T Clark, 1921), 482.

Titus 1:1.[28] The conclusions that Burton drew from the syntactical data he considered have been hotly contested.[29] While Burton noted that when a subjective genitive was intended an article was usually present, he was more cautious about formulating a rule for the objective genitive. Discussing cases where "the object of the faith is distinctly expressed by an objective genitive or prepositional phrase", he states, "[t]he article is sometimes prefixed and the faith is definitely identified as the faith in Christ Jesus or towards God".[30] Hultgren, however, produces a stronger two-way test, whereby anarthrous forms are objective genitives and the presence of the article provides decisive evidence for a subjective genitive. He confidently argues that "on the basis of such usage elsewhere in Paul, one can expect that Paul would have supplied the article (so ἡ πίστις τοῦ Χριστοῦ) if he had intended to speak of the (subjective) faithfulness of Christ, but that is precisely what he does not do".[31] Dunn takes a slightly different approach and restates the argument expressed by Burton so that greater emphasis falls on the identification of objective genitives. Consequently, an anarthrous form provides strong evidence for an objective genitive – however, little can be determined when the article is present.[32] The inconclusive significance of the presence of the article is then used to exclude Ephesians 3:12 as an example of a subjective genitive.

The force of such grammatical arguments has been strongly questioned. Silva has gone so far as to categorically state that "the presence or absence of the definite article is of no help whatever in determining the force of the genitival construction".[33] The number of exceptions to the rules propounded by scholars such as Burton and Hultgren makes one sympathetic to Silva's statement. Such grammatical rules, however, may still have some use as a very broad "rule of thumb". In fact, examples such as Romans 3:3 and 4:16 may show that the greater problem is using anarthrous forms to identify the objective genitive. However, while the presence of a definite article may lead to the expectation that a genitival construction is subjective, this can only be

---

[28] Burton, *Galatians*, 482.

[29] For a much fuller discussion of the debate surrounding the grammatical and syntactical force of the presence or absence of the definite article see my "First Contribution", esp. 80–3.

[30] Burton, *Galatians*, 482.

[31] Hultgren, *"Pistis Christou Formulation"*, 253.

[32] See Dunn, "Once More", section 2.2 *The absence of the definite article*, 64–6.

[33] Silva, "Faith versus Works", 227, n.27.

determined with any confidence by looking at the grammatical features of individual examples and considering the exegetical ramifications of such a reading.

We need to briefly address the Pauline authorship of Ephesians before considering the exegetical sense of Ephesians 3:12. As we have said, it appears that the majority of critical scholarship questions whether this epistle is a genuine Pauline writing. Regardless of the stance taken on this issue, one must defend the legitimacy of using a possibly non-Pauline text as evidence in a debate that relates to the meaning intended by the genuine Pauline uses of the phrase πίστις Χριστοῦ. Obviously one potential strategy would be to mount a stronger case for the Pauline authorship of Ephesians. However, without some fresh evidence or the ability to better account for the obvious stylistic deviation between Ephesians and the generally accepted genuine epistles, there seems little to be gained by such an approach. Another potentially more productive approach is to see that even if the epistle does not come from the hand of Paul himself, it definitely comes from a person who was in some sense a disciple or devotee of Paul. Consequently such a person may have been attuned to the Apostle's intended meaning while also being at home with the use of Hellenistic Greek. Therefore, by closely analyzing the meaning of Ephesians 3:12 both in terms of its specific sense and also in terms of its wider exegetical links to the surrounding ideas in the epistle, it may be possible to cast further light on the wider meaning of πίστις Χριστοῦ terminology in Paul's thinking, even if the epistle did not come directly from his own hand.

Within the immediate context of Ephesians 3:1–12, the author has Paul declare himself to be a possessor of the mysteries of Christ (3:3–4), a minister of the gospel (3:7), and appointed to preach to the Gentiles (3:8). Lincoln notes that this section is a digression from the intercessory prayer which begins in verse 1. In this digression it is noted that "the apostolic ministry is linked with the making known of the mystery of Christ, and … this mystery has its focus in the church".[34] The mystery that Paul makes known to his readers is contained in verse 6: εἶναι τὰ ἔθνη συγκληρονόμα καὶ σύσσωμα καὶ συμμέτοχα τῆς ἐπαγγελίας ἐν Χριστω Ἰησοῦ διὰ τοῦ εὐαγγελίου ("the Gentiles are fellow-heirs and fellow-members and fellow-sharers of the promise in Christ Jesus through the gospel"). Here there is a strong emphasis on participatory language with συν-type prefixes and "in Christ"

---

[34]   A.T. Lincoln, *Ephesians* (WBC 42; Dallas, TX: Word, 1990), 193.

phraseology. This focus on Christ remains in the foreground in verses 8–13 with its emphasis upon how the once-hidden mystery is now revealed to Gentiles in Christ. Although the author does not fully explain the process by which the revelation of this mystery results in the new-found "boldness and access" (3:12), there does appear to be an allusion to this process in verse 8. In that verse τὸ ἀνεξιχνίαστον πλοῦτος τοῦ Χριστου ("the unsearchable riches of Christ") aligns with the description in Philippians 2:6–11 of the wealth and status bestowed on Christ because of his obedience to the Father's will. This implies some kind of participatory process by which believers become partakers of the riches that have been given to Christ because of his faithfulness. This point is recognized by O'Brien, who suggests that "[h]ere in Ephesians 3:8, however, Paul uses rhetorical language to show that his proclamation is about the wealth of divine grace and glory which Christ possesses in himself and which he lavishly gives to others".[35] Hence, there is a partially developed train of thought in this section of the epistle which first announces that the mystery is the ability of Gentiles to become partakers of the promise of Christ (3:6). This is achieved by making believers benefactors of the riches of Christ (3:8), and the consequence of this participation is confident boldness and access obtained by Christ's obedience to the divine plan.[36] Thus as Hoehner observes commenting on verse 12, "[t]he preposition with the relative pronoun ἐν ᾧ, 'in whom', relates back to Christ as the sphere in whom we have access to the Father".[37]

Ephesians 3:8–12 stresses what Christ has achieved on behalf of Gentiles, and it is this "mystery" which Paul makes known. Therefore, the key theme is the revelation of the divine plan which is linked implicitly to Christ's own obedience to the Father's will through faithfully accepting death on the cross. Such obedience results in the bestowal of riches, which in turn believers share and through which they obtain boldness and access by participating in this divinely inaugurated order.[38]

---

[35] P.T. O'Brien, *The Letter to the Ephesians* (PNTC; Grand Rapids, MI: Eerdmans, 1999), 241.

[36] Again, see O'Brien, who sees such obedience to the will of the Father as "the means by which this marvellous privilege of coming to the throne of grace is provided" (*Ephesians*, 249).

[37] H.W. Hoehner, *Ephesians: An Exegetical Commentary* (Grand Rapids, MI: Baker, 2002), 465.

[38] For a more detailed discussion of the exegesis of this passage see my "First Contribution", 84–9.

Within the wider context of the epistle there are two significant statements that help to clarify the meaning of Ephesians 3:12. The first, which occurs in Ephesians 2:18, provides a strong structural parallel utilizing similar vocabulary.

Eph. 2:18a ὅτι δι᾿ αὐτοῦ ἔχομεν τὴν προσαγωγὴν
Eph. 3:12a ἐν ᾧ ἔχομεν τὴν παρρησίαν καὶ προσαγωγὴν

Eph. 2:18a "because through him we have the access"
Eph. 3:12a "in whom we have the confidence and access"

As is common in Ephesians, the author here uses the technique of repetition of key words and concepts. There are some differences, such as the coordination of the term παρρησίαν ("confidence") in Ephesians 3:12 with the word προσαγωγήν ("access"), which occurs both in Ephesians 2:18 and 3:12. Also, in Ephesians 2:18a the prepositional phrase ὅτι δι᾿ αὐτοῦ ("because through him") is required since the subject, Christ, has not been explicitly mentioned since verse 13. Having highlighted this parallel it is interesting to consider the basis of the access in the two passages – since the understandings in these thematically related passages might inform one another. As has been noted in Ephesians 3:12, the disputed phrase διὰ τῆς πίστεως αὐτοῦ states the grounds for access. In Ephesians 2:11–22, the basis on which believers have such access to the Father is stated in the discussion that precedes Paul's declaration of this privileged status. Paralleling the concerns in Ephesians 3:6 and following, Paul clearly articulates that his discussion is an explanation of how formerly estranged Gentiles have been reconciled to God. The actual process which has brought about this reconciliation and enabled access to the divine presence is stated initially in verse 13. Here the author says:

νυνὶ δὲ ἐν Χριστῷ Ἰησοῦ ὑμεῖς οἱ ὄντες μακρὰν ἐγενήθητε ἐγγὺς ἐν τῷ αἵματι τοῦ Χριστοῦ. (Eph. 2:13)

But now in Christ Jesus you who once were far off have been brought near in the blood of Christ. (Eph. 2:13)

The sense of this verse, which is fairly clear, is described by Schnackenburg in the following terms. "The separation from God of the former heathen is first overcome 'in Christ Jesus' or, more exactly, through 'the blood of Christ'."[39] The language in verse 13 of being "far

---

[39] R. Schnackenburg, *The Epistle to the Ephesians: A Commentary* (Edinburgh: T&T Clark, 1991), 110.

off" forms a striking (and probably intentional) contrast with the new-found access of verse 18. In fact, Schnackenburg notes this relationship between verse 13 and verse 18 when discussing the equality of status that the author describes for both Gentiles and Israel. "Both groups have won a common approach to the Father through Christ (v. 18)."[40] The reference to Christ's blood is a vivid metaphor describing sacrificial death on the cross. This is apparent both through the reference to the cross that follows in this passage, which speaks of Christ reconciling people to the Father through the cross (v. 16), and the thematically related phrase in Colossians 1:20 which speaks of reconciliation through "the blood of the cross".[41] Furthermore, Christ's death is seen as tearing down "the barrier of the dividing wall" (v. 14) that separated the Gentiles from Israel. Again this removal of a barrier is another metaphor that relates to the access given to Gentiles through Christ's death. Thus, in the closely argued discussion of Ephesians 2:13–18, the author states that the access to the divine presence which Gentiles now enjoy comes about through Christ's death. This is an important indication of the meaning of the phrase διὰ τῆς πίστεως αὐτοῦ in Ephesians 3:12, which is also the basis of access to the Father. If the author has been consistent in his understanding of that basis of access, then πίστεως αὐτοῦ would refer to Christ's faithfulness and obedience in undergoing a death that provides Gentiles with the privileged access described both in Ephesians 2:18 and 3:12.

The second significant statement that helps to clarify the meaning of Ephesians 3:12 is the comment about πίστις in Ephesians 2:8.

Τῇ γὰρ χάριτί ἐστε σεσῳσμένοι διὰ πίστεως καὶ τοῦτο οὐκ ἐξ ὑμῶν, θεοῦ τὸ δῶρον (Eph. 2:8)

For by grace you have been saved through faith; and this is from you, it is the gift of God (Eph. 2:8)

Like the seven texts from the undisputed Pauline epistles that form the basis of the πίστις Χριστοῦ debate, πίστις is used here anarthrously but without any qualifying genitive. There has been debate about whether this reference is to be understood objectively or subjectively. Preferring the former option, Lincoln states, "Faith is a human activity but a specific kind of activity, a response that allows salvation to

---

40 Schnackenburg, *Ephesians*, 110.
41 See the comments of Lincoln, *Ephesians*, 139.

become operative, but receives what has already been accomplished by God in Christ."[42] It is interesting to note that Lincoln closely links the human response to what has been achieved by Christ. Yet such an interpretation faces the difficulty that the author explicitly states: that the grace that comes by faith "is not from you, it is the gift of God".[43] Thus, in opposition to the view that the faith in question is a human activity, one must ask how such an interpretation can give due force to the emphatic declaration that "this is not from you", which seems to be intended to counter the very type of claims that are being suggested by those who attribute this reference to πίστις to a human action. Rather, the reading suggested by Barth seems to be more attuned to the sense of the passage:

> If Paul calls "faith" a "gift of God" at all, he cannot intend to overlook the fact that the God who gives faith is himself faithful and proves his total loyalty to the covenant by the gift of his beloved, obedient and loving son ... The "faith" by which you are saved would be no good if it were not first shown by God himself and thus begun and completed on earth by Jesus Christ.[44]

Hence, the supporting evidence provided by Ephesians 2:8 and 2:18 lends further weight to the case for understanding the phrase διὰ τῆς πίστεως αὐτοῦ contained in Ephesians 3:12 as a subjective genitive which denotes Christ's act of faithful obedience in undergoing a death that enables previously alienated Gentiles to have access to God.

Conclusions

It would be churlish to suggest that the arguments proposed here in support of reading πίστις Χριστοῦ in Philippians 3:9 and Ephesians 3:12 as subjective genitives have established the case beyond all doubt. The debate has been so disputed and intense precisely because the evidence is ambiguous and because solid arguments can be put forward for either case. I have attempted to show here that a more plausible cumulative

---

[42] Lincoln, *Ephesians*, 111.
[43] See Best's arguments supporting the notion that human faith is in view. E. Best, *A Critical and Exegetical Commentary on Ephesians* (ICC; Edinburgh: T&T Clark, 1998), 273.
[44] M. Barth, *Ephesians*, 273.

case based on a combination of lexical, grammatical, and exegetical considerations can be put forward for reading two texts (Phil. 3:9 and Eph. 3:12) as subjective genitives referring to Christ's own faithfulness, rather than as objective genitives denoting believers' faith in Christ.

Other options are also possible, and these should be considered in future debates. It has been suggested that the genitives in question are "plenary genitives" – specifically, that they encapsulate both the subjective and objective senses. Robinson anticipated this line of thinking in part when he noted that distinctions based on a modern non-Greek language should not be regarded as significant in determining the semantic range of terms current in Koiné Greek of the first century.[45] The suggestion of a plenary genitive seems to be an attempt to allow a primarily objective genitive construction to accommodate the meaning of a subjective genitive concurrently. More grammatical work is required here to see whether such a construction can be shown to have occurred during the period under question.[46] A second consideration that does not seem to have been addressed is whether Pauline thinking itself was clear concerning this distinction between the meanings of different types of genitive constructions. Rhetorical flourishes often appear to overtake clear logical progression in Paul's thinking, and a favourite phrase is sometimes used without close attention to its sense or "fit" in an overall argument. Perhaps this alternative is a last resort and it is best to first consider whether a meaningful and coherent interpretation can be found.

Operating from this starting point, the current discussion has attempted to show that a subjective genitive construction makes better sense in the two passages under discussion. The case of Philippians 3:9 seems finely balanced, although Howard's observations about πίστις language combined with either a name or pronoun in the genitive case referring to the faith of the individual in question is a significant consideration.[47] More compelling were exegetical considerations. The entire argument of Philippians 3:2–11 seems to be predicated upon Paul's rejection of his own quest to find righteous status on the basis of Torah or his own achievements. Instead, he declares that righteousness can only be gained through the gracious gift of God. In line with this argument, a subjective genitive reading of the phrase διὰ πίστεως Χριστοῦ

---

45   Robinson, "The Faith of Jesus Christ", 76.
46   Seifrid, *Christ our Righteousness*; F. Watson, *Paul and the Hermeneutics of Faith*, 73–6.
47   Howard, "Notes and Observations", 459–60.

which sees the whole process as dependent on the obedience of Christ seems to provide the more coherent reading of the passage. It needs to be acknowledged that the second reference to πίστις in Philippians 3:9 certainly denotes the responsive aspect of human faith. This is something that Paul affirms many times in his writings, and adopting a subjective genitive for the disputed phrases in no way constitutes a rejection of the important Pauline notion of human response to God's grace. Ephesians 3:12 appears to offer a stronger case for an intentional subjective genitive. The presence of the definite article may offer some grammatical support, though caution is needed.[48] More importantly, the line of argument in Ephesians 3:1–13 seems to require understanding the phrase διὰ τῆς πίστεως αὐτοῦ as a reference to Christ's faithfulness in undergoing a sacrificial death that obtains equal access for Gentiles to the divine presence. This line of interpretation is strongly supported by the related statements that Paul makes about πίστις (Eph. 2:8) and the basis of the new-found access (Eph. 2:13–18), which is attained through "the blood of Christ". These considerations make it likely that the author of Ephesians interpreted Paul's πίστις Χριστοῦ language in a subjective sense. As an early devotee of Paul who moved in a similar linguistic community to that inhabited by the Apostle, his perspectives deserve due consideration.

---

[48] Silva, "Faith versus Works", 227, n.27.

7

Faith in Christ: Some Exegetical and Theological Reflections on Philippians 3:9 and Ephesians 3:12

RICHARD H. BELL

In my contribution I will discuss the meaning of διὰ πίστεως Χριστοῦ in Philippians 3:9 and διὰ τῆς πίστεως αὐτοῦ in Ephesians 3:12, arguing for the objective genitive "through faith in Christ" and "through faith in him" respectively. In the limited space available I will focus primarily on exegetical and theological issues.

Philippians 3:9

In Philippians 3:9 Paul speaks of "being found in [Christ], not having a righteousness of my own that comes by Law, but one that comes through faith in Christ, the righteousness from God based on faith". Paul writes of two types of righteousness which are related to two "attitudes" or "dispositions" which he sets forward in Philippians 3:2–11; an understanding of these may to some extent help to determine whether I am correct to translate διὰ πίστεως Χριστοῦ as "through faith in Christ" rather than "through Christ's faith/faithfulness". The first disposition is that of his Jewish Christian opponents and of the pre-Christian Paul. His opponents, whom I understand to be Judaizers,[1] are considered by Paul as "the dogs", "the evil workers" and "the mutilation" (v. 2). Such opponents, like those in Galatians, were essentially arguing that one is justified not only by faith in Christ but also by keeping the Law of Moses. Paul reacted with vigour because such teaching had devastating consequences not only for justification but also for Christology; and so in Galatians and Philippians 3 he emphasizes that justification is

---

[1] See Richard H. Bell, *The Irrevocable Call of God: An Inquiry into Paul's Theology of Israel* (WUNT 184; Tübingen: Mohr Siebeck, 2005), 180–1.

"through faith in Christ" and not "by works of Law" (Gal. 2:16) or by
one's own righteousness that comes by Law (Phil. 3:9). Paul writes that
his opponents' stance leads to confidence in the flesh (v. 3). This is a
reference not only to circumcision ("mutilation") but also to the whole
system of fulfilling the Law.[2] And such confidence in the flesh leads to
the sin of "self-righteousness".[3] Paul to a large extent identifies their
situation with that of his life before he came to know Christ. The obvious
difference is that, whereas his opponents did believe in Christ (probably
having a low Christology), Paul, the Pharisee, did not. But there are
common elements and Paul thinks that by recalling his former life he
can outdo his opponents as far as "confidence in the flesh" is concerned.
And so in verses 5–6 he sets out seven of his Jewish credentials. The first
three are related to his birth: circumcised on the eighth day, a member
of the people of Israel, of the tribe of Benjamin. The fourth credential is
partly related to what was given but also includes an element of what
he did: he is a Hebrew born of Hebrews (i.e., he is a Hebrew-speaking
Jew of Hebrew-speaking parents).[4] This then leads to the final three
"performances" in keeping the Law which are attributed to himself
alone: as to the Law, a Pharisee; as to zeal, a persecutor of the church; as
to righteousness under the Law, blameless. In one sense Paul obviously
considered himself a "successful Pharisee" and the aorist γενόμενος
in verse 6, I suggest, is to be understood as an ingressive aorist. This
suggests that Paul reached a point in his life as a Pharisee where he
considered that he had *become blameless*. This righteousness "in the Law"
is equated to what Paul describes as "a righteousness of my own that
comes by Law" in verse 9.

Paul then describes how he turned his back on such "righteousness".
In language which alludes to his conversion, he speaks of coming to
know Christ (vv. 8, 10). Many have taken the line that Paul thought that
the things of his pre-Christian life were good, but that, by comparison to
knowing Christ, he *considered* them loss. Indeed Paul uses such language
in verse 7: "Yet whatever gains I had, these I have come to regard as

---

[2] Rudolf Bultmann, *Theology of the New Testament* (trans. K. Grobel; 2 vols.; London:
SCM Press, 1955), I:240: "To the category of conduct 'according to the flesh' belongs
above all zealous fulfillment of the Torah; it does so because a man supposes one
can thereby achieve righteousness before God by his own strength." This view is
confirmed by the fact that Paul, in saying he has more confidence in the flesh, lists
not only circumcision but also other performance in keeping the Law (3:5–6).

[3] So verse 3 contrasts his "boasting in Christ" to the "confidence in the flesh" of the
Judaizers.

[4] See Bell, *Irrevocable Call*, 14–15.

loss because of Christ" (NRSV). Some have even drawn a comparison between Paul *considering* these things as nothing and Christ laying aside his pre-existent glory (note the use of ἡγέομαι in Phil. 2:6 and then again in 3:7, 8 [2×]). Such a "parallel" has been used, as we shall see, to support the subjective genitive in 3:9.[5] But Paul clearly views the righteousness according to the Law as negative. It is a righteousness that not only led to "confidence in the flesh" but also was associated with his zeal in persecuting the church of Christ (cf. Gal. 1:14; Acts 7:54–8:1a). In Philippians 3:2–11, Paul is playing his opponents at their own game – as verse 4 makes clear.

In verses 8 and 10 the language of "knowing Christ" comes to the fore. In verse 8 Paul speaks of the surpassing value of knowing Christ Jesus his Lord (τὸ ὑπερέχον τῆς γνώσεως Χριστοῦ Ἰησοῦ). The first genitive is one of apposition (the surpassing worth *is* the knowledge of Christ).[6] The second, γνῶσις Χριστοῦ Ἰησοῦ, I take to be an objective genitive: Paul speaks of his knowing Christ, not Christ's own knowledge. This is the natural way to take the expression, since he speaks of "gaining Christ" (v. 8) and being "found in him" (v. 9).[7] We now come to our crucial verse which Matlock[8] sets out as follows:

Καὶ εὑρεθῶ ἐν αὐτῷ,
(I) μὴ ἔχων ἐμὴν δικαιοσύνην τὴν ἐκ νόμου
ἀλλὰ τὴν διὰ πίστεως Χριστοῦ,
(II) τὴν ἐκ θεοῦ δικαιοσύνην ἐπὶ τῇ πίστει

Paul, as indicated earlier, sets forth two forms of righteousness. In (I) he contrasts a human righteousness that is based on Law with the righteousness that is based on faith in Christ. In (II) he then further defines this as a righteousness which is "from God" and which depends on faith. This analysis of 3:9 suggests the objective genitive. So "my

---

[5] See, e.g., Hooker, "Πίστις Χριστοῦ", 175–6. I return to this below.

[6] Cf. O'Brien, *Philippians*, 387.

[7] R.A. Lipsius, "Die Briefe an die Galater, Römer, Philipper", in *Hand-Commentar zum Neuen Testament, Band 2.2* (ed. H.J. Holtzmann, et al.; Freiburg: Mohr Siebeck, 1891), 219, writes: καὶ εὑρεθῶ ἐν αὐτῷ is closely fixed to Χριστὸν κερδήσω "und bestimmt dieses 'Christum Gewinnen' näher als ein Erfundenwerden in ihm, d.h. in seiner (mystischen) Gemeinschaft". O'Brien, *Philippians*, 392, argues that the aorist subjunctives suggest "Paul is looking forward to the day of Christ". However, it is more likely that Paul is speaking of the present and through to the future (see Joachim Gnilka, *Der Philipperbrief* [HTKNT 10.3; Freiburg/Basel/Wien: Herder, 1987 {1968}], 193–4).

[8] Matlock, "Rhetoric", 180.

own" stands over against "from God". A similar pattern is found in Romans 10:3.[9] In both texts Paul contrasts the righteousness gained by one's own righteousness to that which comes from God. Further, in Philippians 3:9 "by Law" (ἐκ νόμου) and "by faith" (διὰ πίστεως) are in antithesis.[10] Matlock argues that Paul could have distinguished between righteousness ἐκ νόμου and διὰ πίστεως with a single use of δικαιοσύνη as he does in (I). But then Paul clarifies that there are in fact two sorts of righteousness. So "the repetition in Philippians 3:9 is as much about δικαιοσύνη as it is about πίστις".[11] The "redundancy problem" therefore seems to be no problem at all in view of this analysis.

Briefly, there are three further reasons for supporting the objective genitive. First, πίστις Χριστοῦ parallels "knowledge of Christ" in verse 8. Secondly, the use of the article before the second reference to faith (ἐπὶ τῇ πίστει) suggests that the faith referred to here is the same as that in the previous clause.[12] Thirdly, the only other verse in the letter which relates faith and Christ, Philippians 1:29, is a striking parallel to 3:9–10 if the objective genitive is assumed: "For [God] has graciously granted you the privilege not only of believing in Christ (τὸ εἰς αὐτὸν πιστεύειν) but of suffering for him as well."[13]

I think that such an understanding of the passage, adopting the objective genitive in verse 9, makes perfect sense and is supported by no less a theologian than John Chrysostom.[14] In "On the Incomprehensible

---

[9] I remain convinced that Paul is referring to Israel's "works righteousness" in both of these texts. On Rom. 10:3 see Richard H. Bell, *Provoked to Jealousy: The Origin and Purpose of the Jealousy Motif in Romans 9–11* (WUNT 2.63; Tübingen: Mohr Siebeck, 1994), 186–91.

[10] Contrast Bockmuehl, *Philippians*, 209, who, in supporting the subjective genitive "through the faith *of* Christ" (διὰ πίστεως Χριστοῦ), finds an antithetical parallelism between (as he translates) "derived from Torah" (ἐκ νόμου) and "derived from God on the basis of faith" (ἐκ θεοῦ ἐπὶ τῇ πίστει). As Matlock, "Rhetoric", 180, argues, although there is a verbal parallel, there is no conceptual parallel. Instead, "by Law" (ἐκ νόμου) stands over against "through faith in Christ" (διὰ πίστεως Χριστοῦ). This corresponds to Paul's wider usage, where πίστις and νόμος are in antithesis with instrumental ἐκ or διά and with δικαιοῦν or δικαιοσύνη as a middle term (Matlock, "Rhetoric", 181).

[11] Matlock, "Rhetoric", 182.

[12] Dunn, "Once More", 78–9: "His Greek would be scarcely intelligible if he meant the first πίστις to refer to Christ's faith and the second πίστις to 'justifying faith'." Of course another possibility is that both occurrences of πίστις refer to Christ's faith, but this is a view which poses additional problems.

[13] Matlock, "Rhetoric", 183.

[14] Harrisville, "Witness of the Fathers", 238–9.

Nature of God" he quotes Philippians 3:7–9 and then explains the meaning of διὰ πίστεως Χριστοῦ: "He means the faith 'of knowing him and the power of his resurrection and the sharing in his sufferings'."[15] The evidence of Chrysostom is powerful since, as a native Greek speaker, he assumes the objective genitive.[16]

Despite the support of a native Greek speaker such as Chrysostom, the objective genitive has been attacked. One of the most frequent objections is that of "redundancy".[17] However, Philippians 3:7–9 is characterized by repetition. Regarding Philippians 3:7–8, Lightfoot writes: "The earnest reiteration of St. Paul's language here expresses the intensity of his desire to produce conviction."[18] It is striking that the repetition found in Philippians 3:9 is found also in Galatians 2:16, and both texts "maintain that there are two opposing human attitudes; one of these attitudes leads to (godly) righteousness and one does not".[19] And in Galatians 2:16 the threefold repetition of "by works of Law" (ἐξ ἔργων νόμου) and "to justify" (δικαιοῦν) could be said to *demand* a threefold repetition of "faith of Christ".[20] In such texts some may find "redundancy"; I find emphasis.[21] Hays, admitting that "redundancy" is found elsewhere in Paul, may feel that "[his] writing would benefit from the judicious application of a red pencil",[22] but we must accept that this is how Paul wrote and that all language to some extent has an intrinsic "redundancy".[23]

---

[15] Paul W. Harkins (ed.), *St. John Chrysostom: On the Incomprehensible Nature of God* (FC 72; Washington, DC: Catholic University of America, 1982), 88.

[16] Silva, *Philippians* (WEC, 1988), 29: "If … [Chrysostom] fails to address a possible ambiguity, his silence is of the greatest value in helping us determinine how Paul's first readers were likely to have interpreted the text."

[17] Hooker, "Πίστις Χριστοῦ", 173, writes: "Paul is perfectly capable of using redundant phrases" but adds: "this argument is only significant because the same phenomenon occurs almost every time the phrase is used: this fact does give some support to the subjective genitive interpretation". In fact, the cases where there is a possible "problem of redundancy" are Rom. 3:22; Gal. 2:16; 3:22; Phil. 3:9 (but not Rom. 3:26, Gal. 2:20 and not, in my view, Eph. 3:12).

[18] Joseph B. Lightfoot, *St. Paul's Epistle to the Philippians* (Peabody, MA: Hendrickson, 1993 [1868]), 149.

[19] Koperski, "Meaning", 214.

[20] Matlock, "Even the Demons Believe", 307.

[21] As Matlock, "Even the Demons Believe", 307, observes, "one person's 'redundancy' might be another's 'emphasis'".

[22] Hays, *The Faith of Jesus Christ*, 184, n.80.

[23] Silva, *Philippians* (1988), 187, n.31, writes: "When we are faced with a linguistic unit whose meaning is uncertain, that meaning should be preferred that adds least to the total meaning of the passage." In *Biblical Words*, 153–4, Silva points to the "rule

I now look again at Philippians 3:9 and ask whether the subjective genitive offers a satisfactory alternative understanding. Some proponents of "Christ's faith" wish to understand the "knowledge of Christ Jesus" in verse 8 as a subjective genitive also,[24] thereby giving a parallel between the "knowledge of Christ" in verse 8 and the "faith of Christ" in verse 9. But it is difficult to understand what "Christ's knowledge" could mean in the context and most commentators, including many who read "faith/ faithfulness of Christ" in verse 9, rightly reject such a view.[25]

If the subjective genitive "faith/faithfulness of Christ" is assumed, verse 9 could be understood something like this. Because Christ was faithful, as exemplified in Philippians 2 and as expressed in 3:9 (according to the subjective genitive view), there is a righteousness through Christ's own faith/faithfulness (διὰ πίστεως Χριστοῦ) and we share this righteousness that depends on faith (ἐπὶ τῇ πίστει). But how is Christ's faith/faithfulness related to ours? Attempting to relate them gives rise to two sets of problems. The first set regards the meaning of πίστις in relation to Christ and in relation to the Christian. I consider three possible ways in which this could be conceived.[26]

1. Taking πίστις to refer to the "faithfulness" of Christ and the "faith-fulness" of Christians, one could possibly argue that our faithfulness is derived from Christ's faithfulness. So Hooker comments generally on the πίστις Χριστοῦ issue: "mankind's faithfulness must depend on [Christ's], for how else can one have faith at all?"[27] Applying this to 3:9 one could then say that the two uses of πίστις do carry the same sense. But there are two problems. First, it is difficult to find other texts in Paul which refer specifically to Christ's faithfulness (I return to this in the conclusion). Secondly, Paul never elsewhere speaks of our being justified by "faithfulness".

---

of maximal redundancy" of Martin Joos: "The best meaning is the least meaning." He suggests that this is supported by the way language naturally has a certain redundancy (e.g., we are generally able to understand a sentence even if there is a missing word).

[24] Wallis, *Faith of Jesus Christ*, 123, understands the phrase to mean "Christ's knowledge of Paul".

[25] O'Brien, *Philippians*, 387–8, takes it as an objective genitive even though he understands the subjective genitive for πίστις Χριστοῦ in v. 9 (398–9).

[26] I am excluding the idea of Christ's faith in God since there are no possible contextual indicators that Paul is speaking of this in Philippians.

[27] Hooker, "Πίστις Χριστοῦ", 182.

2. We could modify solution (1) and say that Christ's faithfulness leads to our faith. The meaning of πίστις then changes in one verse. This is possible[28] but I think it is unlikely because of the presence of the article with the second use of πίστις. I noted above the problem this article raises for the view that the first occurrence refers to Christ's πίστις and the second to the believer's πίστις. This problem is intensified if, in addition, one claims that the meaning of πίστις itself changes.

3. A third possibility is to refuse to make a distinction between faith and faithfulness, leaving πίστις to carry both ideas.[29] I wonder, though, whether this really helps in a text such as Philippians 3:9, and there are two problems. First, in taking this view we are approaching the "illegitimate totality transfer"[30] in that it is assumed that since πίστις can mean both faith and faithfulness, then whenever the word occurs it encompasses both.[31] Secondly, πίστις takes on a number of fairly well-defined meanings in the New Testament, the meaning being dependent on the context.[32]

The second set of problems with the subjective genitive regards the *relation* of Christ's faith/faithfulness to ours. Two basic routes are possible: imitation and participation. The former has been supported by pointing to "parallels" between Philippians 2 and 3. So Hooker writes that in Philippians 3 Paul "becomes poor" (cf. 2 Cor. 8:9) "in imitation of Christ's *kenosis*", and echoes of Philippians 2 in Philippians 3:2–11 suggest that διὰ πίστεως Χριστοῦ "ought to refer to the obedient self-surrender of Christ, that is, to his faithfulness".[33] However, as indicated above, there are no genuine parallels between Christ's becoming poor and Paul's rejection of his Jewish credentials. Christ

---

[28] Cf. Rom. 3:21, where the word νόμος changes meaning from "law" to "Pentateuch".

[29] Hays, "What Is at Stake?", 58, challenges Dunn (who, I think rightly, makes a distinction between "faith" and "faithfulness") "to show that it was semantically possible in Hellenistic Greek to make such a conceptual distinction. The single word πίστις carries both connotations".

[30] James Barr, *The Semantics of Biblical Language* (Oxford: Oxford University Press, 1961), 218, 222.

[31] In this connection see Torrance, "One Aspect", 113 and Barr's critique in *Semantics*, 203–4.

[32] See Matlock, "Detheologizing ΠΙΣΤΙΣ ΧΡΙΣΤΟΥ", 8–9.

[33] Hooker, "Πίστις Χριστοῦ", 176.

gave up his pre-existent glory;[34] Paul gave up something he considered "dung" (σκύβαλα, 3:8). One can hardly say Paul is showing "humility", following the pattern of Christ in Philippians 2:6–8. He is rather saying how he "moved up" and now has the surpassing worth of knowing Christ (3:8).[35] So circumcision "is not a privilege Paul lays aside, but a decisive direction that he wants his followers in Philippi to eschew at all costs, a 'mutilation'".[36] Paul is decisively rejecting the works-righteousness of his Jewish Pharisaic past as something positively bad![37]

If there are problems with such "imitation", what about "participation"? This, it is claimed, provides an understanding for relating Christ's faith to our faith.[38] But nowhere does Paul suggest that faith comes about as a *result* of participation. Faith could be understood as the *means* of participation, but not the *result*. If one works with a temporal scheme the order appears to be faith, union, and then justification!

Now when Paul speaks of *coming to faith* he does not use ideas of participation in the *reconciling act* – that is, the death and resurrection of Christ.[39] Rather, he speaks of an encounter with the *reconciling*

---

[34] I am here assuming that Phil. 2:6–7 refers to Christ's pre-existence. See, e.g., Otfried Hofius, *Der Christushymnus Philipper 2,6–11: Untersuchungen zu Gestalt und Aussage eines urchristlichen Psalms* (WUNT 17; Tübingen: Mohr Siebeck, 1991 [1976]), 114–22.

[35] Such a "knowing Christ" has parallels to 2 Cor. 4:6 and Gal. 1:11–12, 15–16 (Otfried Hofius, "Wort Gottes und Glaube bei Paulus", in *Paulusstudien* [WUNT 51; Tübingen: Mohr Siebeck, 1989], 162, n.101).

[36] Brian J. Dodd, "The Story of Christ and the Imitation of Paul in Philippians 2–3", in *Where Christology Began: Essays on Philippians 2* (ed. Ralph P. Martin and Brian J. Dodd; Louisville, KY: Westminster John Knox, 1998), 154–61 (156).

[37] Contrast N.T. Wright, "Jesus Christ is Lord: Philippians 2:5–11", in *The Climax of the Covenant: Christ and Law in Pauline Theology* (Edinburgh: T&T Clark, 1991; Minneapolis, MN: Fortress, 1994), 88. C.F.D. Moule, "Further Reflections on Philippians 2:5–11", in *Apostolic History and the Gospel* (ed. W. Ward Gasque and Ralph P. Martin; Exeter: Paternoster, 1970), 274–5, rightly rejects any close parallels between Phil. 2 and 3. He admits that the threefold ἡγέομαι is striking. "Paul had flung away what had formerly seemed precious, and, in exchange, had received something incomparably better … But the passage in Ch. 2 would be an exact analogy to this only if Christ had been said to have deemed equality with God sheer loss and to have flung it away."

[38] See Hooker, "Πίστις Χριστοῦ", 181–3. In fact, she comes to prefer participation to imitation (183).

[39] Cf. Richard H. Bell, *Deliver Us from Evil: Interpreting the Redemption from the Power of Satan in New Testament Theology* (WUNT 216; Tübingen: Mohr Siebeck, 2007), 257.

word.[40] Whereas the reconciling act is concerned with sacrifice/ participation (Rom. 3:25; 2 Cor. 5:19a), the reconciling word is concerned with a system of word/faith/justification (e.g., Rom. 1:16–17). Faith comes about not by participating in Christ but by encountering the reconciling word which creates faith in the hearer (or, to be more precise, creates faith in chosen hearers [2 Cor. 2:15–16]). Paul uses the terms "gospel" (εὐαγγέλιον) and "word" (λόγος; ῥῆμα) for this reconciling word, and these are to be distinguished from the "preaching" (ἀκοή).[41] Faith can only come about through the "word" which is delivered in the "preaching".[42] According to Romans 10:17 (ἄρα ἡ πίστις ἐξ ἀκοῆς, ἡ δὲ ἀκοὴ διὰ ῥήματος Χριστοῦ), faith comes from ἀκοή – hearing, that is, the apostolic preaching (see also Gal. 3:2: ἐξ ἀκοῆς πίστεως), and the "hearing" issues out of the word.[43] Another way of viewing the relationship is to say that the preaching witnesses to the ῥῆμα Χριστοῦ and it is this ῥῆμα which produces faith.[44]

Preaching that has the gospel and Christ as its content can lead to faith (1 Cor. 15:11: οὕτως κηρύσσομεν καὶ οὕτως ἐπιστεύσατε);[45] and the sobering possibility exists that either preaching can be vacuous or there is no basis for claims made in the preaching – both leading to a correspondingly vacuous or non-existent faith (cf. 1 Cor. 15:14). Now in

---

[40] The reconciling act and reconciling word can be considered as a dual but integrated activity of God. Cf. Georg Eichholz, *Die Theologie des Paulus im Umriß* (Neukirchen-Vluyn: Neukirchener, 1985 [1972]), 200, who writes: "nach 2. Kor 5 müssen das Christusgeschehen und das Zeugnis von diesem Geschehen als einheitliches, aber zweifältiges Handeln Gottes begriffen werden".

[41] Hofius, "Wort Gottes", 150–1.

[42] Eberhard Jüngel, *Das Evangelium von der Rechtfertigung des Gottlosen als Zentrum des christlichen Glaubens. Eine theologische Studie in ökumenischer Absicht* (Tübingen: Mohr Siebeck, 1999 [1998]), 216: "Der Glaube kommt aus dem Hören und nur aus dem Hören. Ohne die Exklusivpartikel *solo verbo* hinge die Exklusivpartikel *sola fide* in der Luft – so wie das *solo verbo* ohne das *solus Christus* in der Luft hinge."

[43] Heinrich Schlier, *Der Römerbrief* (HTKNT 6; Freiburg/Basel/Wien: Herder, 1987 [1977]), 318, writes that the ῥῆμα Χριστοῦ is "die Quelle der ἀκοή und somit der πίστις". On the relationship of λόγος to ἀκοή, see also 1 Thess. 2:13, λόγος ἀκοῆς παρ᾽ ἡμῶν τοῦ θεοῦ, translated by Hermann Menge as "das von uns gepredigte Gotteswort" (*Die Heilige Schrift des Alten und Neuen Testaments* [11th ed.; Stuttgart: Württembergische Bibelanstalt, 1949]).

[44] So τὸ ῥῆμα τῆς πίστεως of Rom. 10:8 refers to the word which creates faith (Hofius, "Wort Gottes", 160).

[45] And so Paul can speak of "speaking the word" (τὸν λόγον λαλεῖν, Phil. 1:14) and correspondingly proclaiming Christ (Χριστὸν κηρύσσειν, 1:15; Χριστὸν καταγγέλλειν, 1:17–18).

the expression "gospel of Christ" (τὸ εὐαγγέλιον τοῦ Χριστοῦ, e.g., Phil. 1:27; Rom. 15:19, etc.), "the gospel *concerning Christ*",[46] "Christ" stands as an abbreviation for the person and work of Jesus Christ. The content of the gospel as "the word of the cross" (ὁ λόγος ὁ τοῦ σταυροῦ, 1 Cor. 1:18) and "the word of reconciliation" (ὁ λόγος τῆς καταλλαγῆς, 2 Cor. 5:19) is both Christology and soteriology.[47] The crucial point for our purposes is that the gospel concerning Christ has as its correlate "faith *in Christ*." "Faith in Christ" therefore encompasses all that the gospel says of Christ, *both his work and person.* So Romans 10:10 and following makes clear that "faith in Christ" involves believing in Christ as Lord[48] and calling on his name. In view of this I refute the claim of Williams that "the person of Christ is not faith's object".[49]

Such an understanding of preaching, word, and faith, which can underpin the objective genitive understanding, brings to nought any suggestion that this approach has a tendency "to reduce the gospel to an account of individual religious experience, or even to turn faith into a bizarre sort of work, in which Christians jump through the entranceway of salvation by cultivating the right sort of spiritual disposition".[50] So long as one emphasizes that faith is the work and gift of God, that it is the mode of salvation rather than a condition of salvation, there is no danger of soft-pedalling the grace of God.

Ephesians 3:12

This brings me to a study of Ephesians 3:12: ἐν ᾧ ἔχομεν τὴν παρρησίαν καὶ προσαγωγὴν ἐν πεποιθήσει διὰ τῆς πίστεως αὐτοῦ. I translate this as "in whom (i.e., Christ) we have boldness and confident access [to God] through faith in him".[51] Again I translate using the

---

[46] Hofius, "Wort Gottes", 152, n.31, understands the genitive of content. But Moisés Silva, *God, Language and Scripture: Reading the Bible in the Light of General Linguistics* (FCI 4; Leicester: Apollos, 1990), 109, argues for the vagueness of such an expression in Phil. 1:27.

[47] Hofius, "Wort Gottes", 152.

[48] As Koperski, "Meaning", 212, writes, "[t]he confession *Jesus is Lord* is inseparable from the belief which justifies".

[49] Williams, "Again *Pistis Christou*", 434.

[50] Hays, "What Is at Stake?", 56.

[51] Lincoln, *Ephesians*, 189–90, argues that since "boldness" and "access" are governed by one article, there may well be a hendiadys – "bold access" – and this is bolstered further by "in confidence", giving the sense "the boldness of confident access".

objective genitive. It gives an excellent sense to Ephesians 3:11–12[52] and can be supported by two parallels. First, Romans 5:1–2 not only has key words and ideas taken up in Ephesians as a whole (e.g., peace with God), but it also specifically speaks of our being justified by faith (ἐκ πίστεως) and having access (προσαγωγή) to God's grace through faith (τῇ πίστει).[53] Secondly, Ephesians 3:12 has a parallel in Ephesians 4:13: "Until all of us come to the unity of the faith *and of the knowledge of the Son of God* (καὶ τῆς ἐπιγνώσεως τοῦ υἱοῦ τοῦ θεοῦ), to maturity, to the measure of the full stature of Christ." Note, however, that although "the Son of God" is the object of "knowledge", "faith" in this context is the content of the faith rather than the exercise of faith (cf. 4:5).[54] Nevertheless, this faith still has as its content Jesus Christ as the divine Son of God.

However, Markus Barth, one of the early supporters of the subjective genitive, renders Ephesians 3:12 as: "In him and because of his faithfulness, confidently we make use of our free access [to God]."[55] It is at this point that I must raise certain issues of syntax. It has been claimed that normally the lack of articles suggests an objective genitive and their presence the subjective genitive.[56] This generally is Paul's usage in the case of πίστις Χριστοῦ.[57] In particular (this is important for Eph. 3:12) it

---

[52] Any accusation that the objective genitive gives rise to "redundancy" in view of the word "confidence" seems to be rather hollow since the author argues that it is through faith in Christ that we have confident access to God.

[53] Note the repetition (or redundancy!) of faith. C. Leslie Mitton, *The Epistle to the Ephesians: Its Authorship, Origin and Purpose* (Oxford: Clarendon, 1951), 122, has a useful table comparing Rom. 5:1–2 and Eph. 3:11–12.

[54] Lincoln, *Ephesians*, 255–6.

[55] M. Barth, *Ephesians*, 326. Regarding 4:13, Barth, 488, understands this to refer to "the faith held 'by' the Son of God, and to the knowledge which he possesses". Best, *Ephesians*, 400, rightly rejects this. Faith here, as in Phil. 3:8–10, is related to knowledge, but this knowledge does not have to refer to the "objective content of what is believed" although this may be the case (cf. v. 5).

[56] Hultgren, "*Pistis Christou* Formulation".

[57] Hultgren, "*Pistis Christou* Formulation". I have refrained from using such an argument above since there are a number of exceptions to this rule which have been widely discussed in relation to "faith of Christ". So πίστις Ἀβραάμ is a subjective genitive even though the article is missing. Conversely, "by faith in his name" (ἐπὶ τῇ πίστει τοῦ ὀνόματος αὐτοῦ) in Acts 3:16 is an objective genitive even with the articles. Similar variation is found regarding the disposition of "fear". The objective genitive "fear of God" in 2 Cor. 7:1 lacks the article (φόβος θεοῦ); but the objective genitives "the fear of the Jews" (ὁ φόβος τῶν Ἰουδαίων) in John 7:13; 19:38; 20:19 and "the fear of the Lord" (ὁ φόβος τοῦ κυρίου) in Acts 9:31 and 2 Cor. 5:11 all have them.

is claimed that in pronominal phrases the presence of the article suggests a subjective genitive. In this regard Foster argues that the presence of the article before πίστεως in the pronominal phrase in Ephesians 3:12 (διὰ τῆς πίστεως αὐτοῦ) suggests a subjective genitive.[58] One problem with this argument is that although there are numerous examples where this is the case,[59] Ephesians 3:12 is the only case where the pronoun with πίστις could possibly refer to Christ and therefore comparison is difficult. Also, if pressed, this grammatical rule on pronominal phrases could lead to some problems. So even where the article is employed there is a clear objective genitive in 1 Peter 3:14, "do not fear them" (τὸν δὲ φόβον αὐτῶν μὴ φοβηθῆτε)[60] and in Matthew 28:4, "For fear of him (the angel) the guards shook and became like dead men" (ἀπὸ δὲ τοῦ φόβου αὐτοῦ ἐσείσθησαν οἱ τηροῦντες καὶ ἐγενήθησαν ὡς νεκροί). It has been wisely suggested that grammatical concerns alone cannot alone settle the argument concerning the objective / subjective genitive.[61] The key is exegesis and here, in Ephesians 3:12, the context clearly speaks for the objective genitive. I turn now to considering some of the exegetical problems of the subjective genitive approach.

The first is that although proponents wish to understand the "faithfulness of Christ" in 3:12, the author does not explicitly speak of "faithfulness" or "obedience" of Christ in Ephesians 3, a point recognized by subjective genitive supporters.[62] However, Foster argues that the idea of the obedience of Christ is *implied* in this section. He writes that "references to the cross (1:7; 2:16) or Christ's blood (2:13) … connote the idea of a self-surrendering, an act of entrusting himself to God's eternal purposes, which by its very nature entails obedience or, better still, faithfulness."[63] This, I feel, is a misreading of Ephesians. This letter, like the "genuine" Pauline letters, maintains not so much an "obedient" Son over against the Father but rather a unity

---

[58] Foster, "First Contribution", 81.

[59] So in Paul we have ἡ πίστις ὑμῶν in Rom. 1:8, 12; 1 Cor. 2:5; 15:14, 17; 2 Cor. 10:15 (cf. 2 Cor. 1:24); Phil. 2:17; 1 Thess. 1:8; 3:2, 5, 6, 10 (cf. 3:7); ἡ πίστις αὐτοῦ in Rom. 4:5; ἡ πίστις σου in Phlm 6. Cf. ἡ πίστις ὑμῶν ἐν Χριστῷ in Col 1:4 and ἡ εἰς Χριστὸν πίστις ὑμῶν in 2:5.

[60] See Leonhard Goppelt, *A Commentary on I Peter* (ET; Grand Rapids, MI: Eerdmans, 1993), 242, n.19. Literally the phrase means "do not fear the fear of them", but the sense is clearly "do not fear them". This is a quotation from Isa. 8:12 but αὐτοῦ is changed to αὐτῶν.

[61] Hooker, "Πίστις Χριστοῦ", 165.

[62] Foster, "First Contribution", 86.

[63] Foster, "First Contribution", 86.

of action.[64] This goes also for the "sacrificial overtones" in the letter (e.g., Eph. 1:7). The author saw Christ's death as a "fragrant offering and sacrifice to God" (5:2) but, as in Paul, the emphasis is that God was acting in Christ (4:32) to reconcile us to himself (2 Cor. 5:19). I am not convinced that there are "sacrificial overtones" in 3:12 itself,[65] but even if such overtones are there, the whole idea in the sacrifice of Christ is the gift of God's grace and *not* the obedience of the Son over against the Father. Contrast Foster who speaks of Jesus' "mediatorial role" being stressed "for it is through his *achievements* that the addressees of the epistle can claim both the boldness and access to God".[66] He concludes then that "the emphasis in verses 8–12 falls on Christ's *achievement* on behalf of the Gentiles".[67] But does the author really wish to speak of Christ's "achievements"? It is striking that even in a passage such as Romans 5:18–19, which does speak of the "obedience" of Christ, the whole emphasis is on the "free gift" of the grace of God in Christ (5:15–17)! Precisely the same emphasis is to be found in Ephesians (e.g., 2:8–9).

Turning to Ephesians 2:8, Foster argues that Ephesians 2:8 refers to Christ's faith,[68] a view entertained by Markus Barth[69] and P.T. O'Brien.[70] However, the wording suggests that the author is writing of the faith of the believer. First he writes in verse 8a: "For by grace you have been saved through faith" (τῇ γὰρ χάριτι ἐστε σεσῳσμένοι διὰ πίστεως). The demonstrative τοῦτο in the next phrase probably refers back to verse 8a as a whole rather than to "faith":[71] "and this is not of your own doing;

---

[64] Richard H. Bell, "Sacrifice and Christology in Paul", *JTS* 53 (2002): 1–27 (22–7).

[65] Foster, "First Contribution", 90, points to προσαγωγή in 3:12 as a cultic metaphor (note the use of προσάγω in Lev 1:3; 3:3; 4:14). Best, *Ephesians*, 329, however, may be right in understanding προσαγωγή in relation to access in prayer (see Eph. 3:14). Foster, "First Contribution", 86, noting the sacrifical idea of blood in 1:7 and the "riches of his grace" writes that "it is not implausible to suggest that when the notion of 'riches' is again present in 3:8, the idea of Christ's sacrificial death is also in the author's mind".

[66] Foster, "First Contribution", 88 (my emphasis).

[67] Foster, "First Contribution", 88 (my emphasis).

[68] Foster, "First Contribution", 91–4.

[69] M. Barth, *Ephesians*, 225, suggests three possible meanings for faith in 2:8: God's faithfulness, Christ's faithfulness, faith of believers. He writes: "It is impossible to exclude any one of these three senses from the interpretation of the word 'faith' in Eph. 2:8."

[70] O'Brien, *Ephesians*, 175. He also reads the subjective genitive in 3:12.

[71] See, e.g., Lincoln, *Ephesians*, 111–12. Hoehner, *Ephesians*, 343, points out that there are several instances in Ephesians where τοῦτο refers back to the preceding section (1:15; 3:1; 3:14). There are obvious problems in relating τοῦτο (neuter) back to the immediately preceding noun πίστις (feminine).

it is the gift of God" (καὶ τοῦτο οὐκ ἐξ ὑμῶν, θεοῦ τὸ δῶρον). Then in verse 9 he adds, "it is not by works lest anyone should boast" (οὐκ ἐξ ἔργων, ἵνα μὴ τις καυχήσηται). By saying that salvation is by grace through faith and not of one's own doing lest one should boast, the author is following Paul's idea that the "principle of faith" excludes "boasting" (Rom. 3:27–4.2). Even if, as seems probable, τοῦτο in Ephesians 2:8 does not refer back to "faith", the author is nevertheless making it clear that the whole process of salvation, including faith itself, is the gift of God (cf. Rom. 3:24–25). Again one suspects that those supporting the subjective genitive fail to recognize that being saved through faith is *not* a human act. When the author writes "by grace you are saved", the correlate is "through faith in Christ".[72] In no way can one argue that the apparent equivalence of the two expressions "lends weight to the suggestion that Christ's faithfulness is understood as its mechanism".[73]

Conclusions

Hays, defending his "christological interpretation" of πίστις Ἰησοῦ Χριστοῦ, writes that "we are saved by Jesus' faithfulness, not by our own cognitive disposition or confessional orthodoxy".[74] These comments highlight two crucial issues – "Jesus' faithfulness" and what "faith in Christ" may mean.

Like it or not, faith in Christ for Paul *does* involve believing certain things to be true. Christians believe that Jesus died and was raised (1 Thess. 4:14) and in faith confess that Jesus is Lord (Rom. 10:9). Those who deny such assertions are not considered Christians. The Christian therefore accepts what the gospel says of Christ's person and work as true. Faith involves this rational element.[75] But this rationality is decidedly "anti-Cartesian" and it is personal. In Philippians 3:10 Paul tells of his intention to know Christ (cf. v. 8)[76] using an ingressive aorist (τοῦ γνῶναι αὐτόν);[77] thereby he speaks of coming to know Christ.

---

[72] Note that salvation in both Paul and Ephesians is *per fidem*, not *propter fidem*.

[73] Foster, "First Contribution", 92.

[74] Hays, "What Is at Stake?", 55.

[75] See Hofius, "Wort Gottes", 155–7.

[76] O'Brien, *Philippians*, 400–1, takes the genitive articular infinitive as expressing purpose.

[77] Hawthorne, *Philippians*, 143. F.W. Beare, *A Commentary on the Epistle to the Philippians* (BNTC; London: A&C Black, 1959), 123, seems to prefer an "effective" aorist.

Knowing Christ means knowing the power of Christ's resurrection and the sharing in his sufferings.[78] Coming to know Christ in this way corresponds to "gaining Christ" (ἵνα Χριστὸν κερδήσω [v. 8]) and "being found in him" ([ἵνα] εὑρεθῶ ἐν αὐτῷ [v. 9]).

One of the most powerful aspects of Paul's theology (and of Ephesians) is that in coming to faith in Christ, by encountering the word of God, we undergo an existential displacement (cf. 2 Cor. 5:17; Eph. 2:6). This is something absent in Hebrews (and in James). Hebrews rather has the idea of Jesus, the faithful one, who is obedient to his Father, leading his brothers on to glory (Heb. 12:1–2). Christ is our forerunner and, if we share his faith, we also will end up where he has gone. One of the mistakes often made by the subjective genitive proponents is that this idea of Hebrews is simply read into Paul. For example, Hooker writes of *Paul*: "even the believer's initial response – his faith – is a sharing in the obedient, faithful response of Christ himself".[79] But Paul has a quite different pattern of salvation to that of Hebrews;[80] and can it be any surprise that it is precisely in works such as Hebrews,[81] where the addressees are in danger of apostacizing, or in Revelation,[82] which reflects a time of persecution, that Christ becomes the "faithful one" (ὁ πιστός),[83] being a model for those who may be tempted to fall away in trying circumstances?

---

[78] Many commentators take the καί of 3:10 as epexegetic (e.g., O'Brien, *Philippians*, 402): τοῦ γνῶναι αὐτὸν καὶ τὴν δύναμιν τῆς ἀναστάσεως αὐτοῦ καὶ [τὴν] κοινωνίαν [τῶν] παθημάτων αὐτοῦ, συμμορφιζόμενος τῷ θανάτῳ αὐτοῦ.

[79] Hooker, "Πίστις Χριστοῦ", 185. See also Williams, "Again *Pistis Christou*", 438: "I think that Paul would easily have agreed with the author of Hebrews that Jesus is the 'originator and completer of faith'."

[80] See Bell, *Deliver Us from Evil*, 311–15, for a discussion of the quite different patterns of redemption in Paul and Hebrews.

[81] See recently Still, "*Christos* as *Pistos*". It is telling that when Wallis, *Faith of Jesus Christ*, turns to "patristic evidence" for the faith *of* Christ, he is able to find much relevant patristic comment on Hebrews and struggles to find anything on Paul.

[82] See esp. Rev. 14:12, which is a case where the subjective genitive really does occur: "Here is a call for the endurance of the saints, those who keep the commandments of God and hold fast to the faith of Jesus (οἱ τηροῦντες δὰς ἐντολὰς τοῦ θεοῦ καὶ τὴν πίστιν Ἰησοῦ)". The subjective genitive is also probably to be read in Jas. 2:1: "My brothers, with your acts of favouritism, do you really hold the faith which our glorious Lord Jesus Christ displayed? (τὴν πίστιν τοῦ κυρίου ἡμῶν Ἰησοῦ Χριστοῦ τῆς δόξης)".

[83] Heb. 2:17; 3:2; 5:7–8; 12:2; Rev. 1:5; 3:14; 19:11.

Section III

PAULINE EXEGESIS, HERMENEUTICS, AND THEOLOGY: MEDIATING PROPOSALS AND FRESH APPROACHES

8

The Faith of Christ

MARK A. SEIFRID

What does it mean to believe in Jesus Christ? At root, the revival of exegetical interest in Paul's use of the expression "faith of Christ" has to do with this simple and fundamental question. Isolated from a given context, the meaning of the expression is elastic and elusive. Within its various contexts, it has become a signal and summary of competing readings of Paul which either revise traditional interpretation of the Apostle or reassert it. For the near future at least, the debate appears to have no end. The exegetical decisions entailed in these readings represent the acceptance in varying measures of one of two readings of Paul. Does "the faith of Christ" signify what Jesus has done toward God in faith(fulness) in obedience and suffering? Or does it signify our faith in what God has done in Christ – and therefore in what Christ has done for us – not merely in Christ's obedience and suffering, but also in his death and resurrection? There remains a third option, actively discussed in earlier debate, which recent scholarship largely has ignored. Can it be – and this will be our thesis – that the expression "faith of Christ" (in its various forms) describes Christ as the author and source of faith? In this case, the genitive defines the unique character of faith as the work of God in Christ that creates us anew. It is not our place here to speculate on the theological currents which have lent fresh attractiveness to the "subjectivist" reading over against the traditional one. It is fair to say, however, that to whatever extent interpreters have taken up this interpretation, they reflect a concern to show the connection between faith and life, between "doctrine" and "doing" – and that with a decided emphasis on the "doing". Likewise, to the extent that "objectivists" reaffirm reading the contested expression as "faith in Christ", they are concerned to preserve doctrine that they understand to be connected with "doing", even if they have left the nature of that connection with life unexplored. Can it be that Paul himself expresses the connection between faith and life in this contested expression, and that in a way that the "subjectivists" have misunderstood?

Preliminary Considerations

We may begin with the meaning of πίστις. It is not clear that the "subjectivists" sufficiently have taken into account the radical shift in usage of the term πίστις from "faithfulness" to "faith" that appears in the New Testament writings, the Apostolic Fathers, and beyond.[1] That is the case not only over against Hellenistic literature in general, but also over against Hellenistic Jewish writers – even Philo – and the Septuagint itself. This observation by no means discounts the religious usage of the term in the Hellenistic world on the one hand, nor, on the other, the roots of the New Testament usage which reach back through early Judaism to the Hebrew Scriptures. The use of the term πίστις to signify "faith" is not unique to the New Testament and early Christianity. What is new is the way in which faith – *fides specialis* – becomes decisive and determinative in the human relation to God. Exegetical debates cannot, of course, be decided by this observation. The use of πίστις to signify "faithfulness" continues in the New Testament.[2] Each context must be assessed on its own. Nevertheless, unless otherwise marked by context, the predominance of "faith" in the New Testament creates the expectation that Paul uses the term πίστις to speak of believing and not of acting in faithfulness.

Secondly, both "subjectivists" and "objectivists", by virtue of the categories they defend, assume that we should read the noun πίστις in a verbal sense. Whether it signifies Christ's faithfulness or our believing, πίστις is thought to function as a *nomen actionis*.[3] It is not at all clear that this assumption is valid. In the first place, in the New Testament the noun πίστις does not serve as an appellative, but as an absolute.[4]

---

[1] Against, e.g., Morna D. Hooker, "Glaube. III. Neues Testament", in *Religion in Geschichte und Gegenwart* (ed. Hans D. Betz et al.; 8 vols.; Tübingen: Mohr Siebeck, 4th ed.; 1998–2007), 3:947, who presupposes that the Septuagintal usage had a large impact on that of the NT.

[2] Attempts to merge the concepts of "faithfulness" and "faith" are equivalent to fusing subject and object, and thus lead only to confusion.

[3] Naturally, in one manner or another, both sides understand that "faith" has an object or content. They simply locate it elsewhere, whether in Paul's use of the verb πιστεύω or in the assumptions underlying his statements.

[4] As Ulrichs rightly notes in *Christusglaube*, 28–9.

Pronominal modifiers notwithstanding, there are not differing "faiths", but only one faith "measured out" variously (see Rom. 12:3). Paul thus speaks of "faith" in the opening of Romans, without further definition, in terms of "the obedience of faith" (Rom. 1:5). "Faith" here is categorical. Likewise, when in the same context Paul gives thanks that the faith of the Roman believers is "proclaimed in the whole world", he can hardly be referring merely to their act of believing (Rom. 1:8). The proclamation of their faith includes the message that they received. He thus hopes to be "encouraged together" with the Roman believers – he by their faith, they by his (Rom. 1:12). That exchange involves the verbal communication of content, as is clear from Romans itself, which serves – in place of Paul's personal presence – as the fulfilment of one dimension of his desire.[5] Similarly, unless one is ready to sever Romans 1:17 from Romans 1:16, it is clear that the three occurrences of the term πίστις in verse 17 in one way or another reflect the content of the gospel. Here again "faith" bears particular content and yet has universal validity. The list of examples could be extended easily. In most contexts it is more or less evident that when Paul speaks of faith he does not merely have in view an action (much less a quality) of a person (or persons), but rather the word and message which are believed. In fact, it is not clear that πίστις appears in *any* instance in Paul's letters as a merely verbal noun.[6]

Secondly, a nominal sense of πίστις likewise is present where Paul speaks of faith as a gift and work of God in Christ. Our preceding observations notwithstanding, it is clearly not the case that the Pauline usage of πίστις may be characterized as signifying nothing other than *fides quae creditur*. His usage of πίστις often includes both the act of believing and the content of faith.[7] This remarkable conjunction is clear, for example, in the text we have just considered, Romans 1:12, where Paul attaches personal pronouns to faith ("your faith" and "my faith").[8] How can it be that Paul attributes πίστις to persons (as a *nomen actionis*) while at the same time uses it to signify content (as a so-to-speak "*nomen materiae*")? A number of Paul's statements in Romans and Galatians shed

---

[5] See Rom. 15:14–16.

[6] While each occurrence must be examined, the very frequency of the noun πίστις over against the verb πιστεύω (96× versus 46× in the undisputed Pauline writings) suggests that in it Paul regularly has in view the content of faith.

[7] We should hasten to affirm that this linguistic phenomenon requires no new lexical or grammatical categories, even if it demands a new theological perspective.

[8] See likewise Rom. 4:5; 1 Cor. 15:14, 17; 1 Thess. 1:8; 3:2, 5–7, 10.

light on this question. In Romans 6:17, he describes the conversion of the Roman Christians as a new obedience, and thus implicitly as their coming to faith.[9] Here he also strikingly inverts the expected locution. Rather than speaking of conversion in terms of "a pattern of teaching which was handed over" to the Roman Christians, he speaks of their "being handed over to a pattern of teaching". The unexpected inversion serves to underscore the change of lordship worked by the gospel in which the human being is made new. The act of obedience that is faith is by no means excluded. It is encompassed within the work of the gospel, which creates the human being afresh.[10] Paul's personification of "the righteousness of faith" in Romans 10:6 bears similar significance. As is clear from the larger context, it is the Apostle who proclaims Christ and who thus stands in contrast to Moses and the Law (Rom. 10:8, 14–15). Yet Paul alters the expected wording in verse 6 so that it is not he who speaks, but the "righteousness of faith" (or, as in the following context, "word of faith" and the "word of Christ") that speaks in him (Rom. 10:8, 17). Another voice, that of God, speaks in and through the Apostle. Here again, faith implies the presence of a new person. Likewise, in Galatians 1:23, Paul indicates that the churches of Judea reported his proclaiming (εὐαγγελίζεται) the faith *which once he persecuted*. He identifies the churches and their faith (Gal. 1:13, 23).[11] In the closing of Galatians, Paul speaks yet again of "faith" as the whole person: in Christ Jesus, nothing has force except "faith working through love" (Gal. 5:6). Of course, he also speaks of persons *having faith* (Rom. 14:22; 1 Cor. 13:2; Phlm. 5) and of persons *believing* and thus acting. One must not overlook or overrun this usage. But we likewise dare not overlook the way in which Paul understands faith to *transcend* the individual person, and in fact to make them new.[12] According to the Apostle, Christ in his saving work *communicates himself* to the fallen human being in the gospel by means of faith.

The lexical evidence then brings us afresh to the question as to how we ought to characterize the genitive relation in the various forms of the expression "faith of Christ". The genitive case marks one noun so

---

[9] For the Apostle, faith is obedience. And true obedience can be nothing other than faith. See Rom. 1:5; 10:16; 15:18; 16:19, 26.

[10] See Rom. 6:4–5.

[11] See also the discussion of Gal. 3:22–25 below.

[12] See K. Haacker's discussion of Hermann Binder in "Glaube II: Altes und Neues Testament", in *Theologische Realenzyklopädie* (ed. G. Krause and G. Müller; Berlin: Walter de Gruyter, 1997–), 13:291.

that it *restricts* the meaning of another.[13] At the same time, the genitive is exceedingly "open" semantically.[14] The meaning of the case obviously is bound up closely with the significance of the terms that make up the genitive construct.[15] It is this dynamic, of course, which has given rise to the current debate over πίστις Χριστοῦ. In earlier discussion it fostered the tendency to develop a special category for the interpretation of πίστις Χριστοῦ. Taken to its extreme, the sense of the genitive may be so tightly bound to the meaning of the terms of a particular construct that the usage determines the "category" of the genitive. That is essentially what takes place in Adolf Deißmann's *genetivus mysticus*.[16] The semantic significance of the genitive is so diminished that if the approach were universalized there would be as many categories of the genitive as there are genitive constructs. Otto Schmitz thus distances himself somewhat from Deißmann, his teacher, by describing the usage as a "generally characterizing genitive". Schmitz thereby intends to create a category which approximates the adjectival genitive yet differs in that the *nomen regens* also comes under modification.[17] The particular meaning of such expressions lies in "the logical relation between the terms".[18] Nevertheless, while Schmitz rightly sees that πίστις Χριστοῦ (in its various forms) appears within a special class of usage that is difficult to categorize and interpret (e.g., ὁ πατὴρ τῶν οἰκτιρμῶν, πνεῦμα ζωῆς,

---

[13] It is not clear that the threefold division of genitive usage that Hoffmann and Siebenthal offer is the most appropriate (*genetivus pertinentiae* [including *genetivus subiectivus* and *genetivus obiectivus*], *genetivus partivus, genetivus temporis*). E.G. Hoffmann and H. v. Siebenthal, *Griechische Grammatik zum Neuen Testament* (Riehen, Schweiz: Immanuel-Verlag, 1990), 229. There is much to be said for Delbrück's earlier division of the genitive into the genitive with "*Dingwörtern*" and the genitive with "*Tätigkeitswörtern*", in which the subjective and objective genitives fall into their own basic category. One need only add the qualification that in theological contexts "*Tätigkeitswörter*" may sometimes appear as "*Dingwörter*", where human activity is presented as God's work. See O. Schmitz, *Die Christus-Gemeinschaft des Paulus im Lichte seines Genetivgebrauchs* (NTF 1. Reihe. Paulusstudien 2; Gütersloh: C. Bertelsmann, 1924), 21.

[14] For this reason, the genitive case readily facilitates connotation and wordplay.

[15] At least part of the spectrum of usage of the genitive – including πίστις Χριστοῦ – is therefore exceedingly difficult to characterize.

[16] A. Deißmann, *Paulus: Eine Kultur- und Religionsgeschichtliche Skizze* (2nd ed.; Tübingen: Mohr Siebeck, 1925), 126–7.

[17] Schmitz, *Christus-Gemeinschaft*, 229–37. Regardless of what one might think of Schmitz's category, further definition of the adjectival genitive is certainly worth considering.

[18] Schmitz, *Christus-Gemeinschaft*, 233.

σῶμα ἁμαρτίας), his proposal again unhappily renders the significance of the case negligible over against the meaning of the terms.[19]

Without imagining that it is possible or even desirable to eliminate all ambiguity from the genitive usage in the expression πίστις Χριστοῦ, it would appear to be possible to define it further without reducing its semantic weight. We return to the simple observation that Paul's usage of πίστις often, if not always, includes its content or object (*fides quae creditur*) and that he clearly views faith as a gift and work of God. That being the case, one cannot limit the possible categories of interpretation of πίστις Χριστοῦ (in its various forms) to the "subjective" and "objective" genitive.[20] Nominal categories such as quality, possession, and source also must come into view. In any context in which "faith" (or, for that matter, "hope" or "love") is presented as a divine gift – no matter that it may also serve as a *nomen actionis* – these nominal categories are in play. Discussion of the meaning of the expression, both in the earlier period and presently, has suffered confusion as the result of the failure to consider these categories. Adolf Schlatter, for example, who characterizes the usage of πίστις (Ἰησοῦ) Χριστοῦ as an objective genitive throughout the New Testament, must immediately qualify his judgment. In such usage, the objective genitive expresses the idea that "one concept is bound up with the other and is regarded as belonging to it". The Pauline genitive was called forth by the fulness of the apostolic understanding of faith, which includes its source, content, and result.[21] Johannes Haußleiter, appreciative of Schlatter's interpretation, freely speaks of Christ as the author and the "normative principle" of faith (as the Law is of works), without expressly appealing to the category of *genetivus auctoris*.[22] They

---

[19] He cites with approval a statement by Blaß – later omitted by Debrunner – that in the NT the relation between a genitive and a noun is often a matter of theological understanding that grammar cannot teach. Schmitz, *Christus-Gemeinschaft*, 21.

[20] Already in the earlier debate, Otto Schmitz recognized that, precisely because πίστις functions as something more than a purely verbal noun for Paul, it is necessary to consider categories other than the subjective and objective genitive (Schmitz, *Christus-Gemeinschaft*, 21–2). Consequently, as Karl Friedrich Ulrichs has observed, "the subjective-objective-genitive dichotomy is philologically a somewhat naive alternative", the assumption of which has weakened the whole of the recent debate. See Ulrichs, *Christusglaube*, 21, n.123.

[21] A. Schlatter, *Der Glaube im Neuen Testament* (3rd ed.; Calv/Stuttgart: Vereinsbuchhandlung, 1905 [1885]), 588.

[22] Haußleiter, "Der Glaube Jesu Christi", 230. Not many have been willing to follow Haußleiter's distinction between "the faith of Jesus" (a subjective genitive: Jesus' faith and obedience) and "the faith of Christ" (an objective genitive).

both approximate Adolf Deißmann's reading of it as a *genetivus mysticus* and Schmitz's "generally characterizing genitive". The categorization of the genitive here starts to become superfluous to interpretation. As a result, the exegetical conclusions lose some measure of clarity and persuasiveness. As is especially evident in Schlatter's comments, his confusion is due to his classifying the usage as an objective genitive – thus presupposing that πίστις functions as a verbal noun – while interpreting the expression so as to include meanings that represent a nominal function.[23] With Paul, we may suggest, the genitive categories associated with a nominal interpretation of πίστις more aptly describe the meaning of the expression "faith of Christ". This simple clarification does not remove the inherent "openness" of the genitive – it only marks some of its limits.[24]

While Paul's understanding of faith as creating and determining the new person is qualitatively different from the following examples from Josephus and Philo, we nevertheless find in them something of a parallel to his thought. To that extent, the usage here anticipates Paul's various references to "the faith of Christ". The two following examples, which Schlatter offers as examples of the objective genitive, better fit nominal categories of the genitive:

δεικνύειν ἄρχεται Μωυσῆς ἃ προυδιδάχθη τέρατα, νομίσας τοὺς θεασομένους ἐκ τῆς ἐπεχούσης ἀπιστίας εἰς πίστιν τῶν λεγομένων μεταβαλεῖν (Philo, *Mos.* 1.90.5). Moses began to show the signs which he had been taught beforehand, intending to bring over those whose beheld (the signs) from the unbelief which held (them) to the faith of the things that were said.

ὡς καίπερ φιλαδελφότατον ὄντα τὸν ΄Ηρώδην εἰς πίστιν ὑπαχθῆναι τῶν λεγομένων καὶ δέος (Josephus, *B.J.* 1.485.3–4). Although he was a most affectionate brother, Herod was led over to the faith of what was said (about the plots of Pheroras) and feared.

Philo and Josephus here present the subjects of faith as passive, persuaded by another to a certain belief. It is thus unlikely that we

---

[23] Schlatter, *Glaube*, 588, is formally correct when he argues that "the genitive in itself alone says nothing". But the genitive case appears only in actual word usage, where in one way or another it may be categorized.

[24] On the semantic "openness" of the genitive see, e.g., R. Kühner and B. Gerth, *Ausführliche Grammatik der griechischen Sprache* (Hannover/Leipzig: Hahn, 1898; Darmstadt, 1966), 1:334; F. Blass, A. Debrunner and F. Rehkopf, *Grammatik des neutestamentlichen Griechisch* (15. durchges. Aufl.; Göttingen: Vandenhoeck & Ruprecht, 1979 [1896]), 134.

should read πίστις as the act of believing and τῶν λεγομένων as its object. Persons *are moved* to a new state of mind. Πίστις expresses that state, as is especially apparent in Philo's statement that unbelief "restrained" Israel. The genitive τῶν λεγομένων describes the content of that state – yet not as an objective genitive, but rather again as a sort of *"genetivus materiae"*.

The usage of πίστις Χριστοῦ in the Apostolic Fathers obviously is more relevant to our concern. It is relatively easy to find usages here that have been classed as objective genitives, when it is arguable that one nominal category or another is more appropriate.[25] Ignatius, for example, warns against the corruption of "the faith of God" (ἐὰν πίστιν θεοῦ ἐν κακῇ διδασκαλίᾳ φθείρῃ ... *Eph.* 16:2) with false teaching.[26] Not only the contrast of "faith" with heresy, but also its connection with the work of Christ and Ignatius' concluding description of it as a gift, suggest a *genetivus auctoris* or a *genetivus qualitatis*. Likewise, when Ignatius describes the "economy" of "the new human being, Jesus Christ", as ἐν τῇ αὐτοῦ πίστει καὶ ἐν τῇ αὐτοῦ ἀγάπῃ, ἐν πάθει αὐτοῦ καὶ ἀναστάσει, he speaks of a new reality in which he hopes the Ephesians share (*Eph.* 20:1). Here "faith" and "love" (and even Christ's passion and resurrection, in which Ignatius himself hopes to share fully) appear as gifts of salvation. That is also likely the case in the opening of the letter to the Magnesians, where Ignatius rejoices to speak to them "in the faith of Jesus Christ" (ἐν πίστει Ἰησοῦ Χριστου; *Mag.* 1:2).[27] Polycarp urges the instruction of widows "concerning the faith of the Lord" (περὶ τὴν τοῦ κυρίου πίστιν; *Phil.* 4:3), having twice spoken in context of "the faith given to us" (*Phil.* 3:2; 4:2). In all probability we find here again a *genetivus auctoris*. Hermas speaks of the apostles and teachers who have fallen asleep, "in the power and faith of the Son of God" (κοιμηθέντες ἐν δυνάμει καὶ πίστει τοῦ υἱοῦ τοῦ θεοῦ; *Sim.* 9.16.5).[28]

---

[25] The conclusions of Harrisville, "Witness of the Fathers", are therefore to be revised.

[26] See also the translation of Henning Paulsen in A. Lindemann and H. Paulsen, eds. and trans., *Die Apostolischen Väter griechisch-deutsche Parallelausgabe auf der Grundlage der Ausgaben von Franz Xaver Funk/Karl Bihlmeyer und Molly Whittaker* (Tübingen: Mohr Siebeck, 1992), 189.

[27] See again also Paulsen in Lindemann and Paulsen, eds. and trans., *Die Apostolischen Väter*, 193.

[28] See also Herm. *Vis.* 6.1.8; *Sim.* 6.1.2; 6.3.6; *Mand.* 11.4, 11.9 ([πίστις] θείου πνεύματος).

Within the New Testament itself we find a clear example of the expression "faith of Christ" used in the sense of a genitive of source (or perhaps a *genetivus auctoris*). Not only does it represent the first use of the term πίστις in Acts (and thus arguably serves a definitive function for Luke), but Luke in fact elaborates it in such a way that its meaning is unequivocal. Within the report of Acts, Peter explains the healing of the lame man in the temple as follows:

16a καὶ ἐπὶ τῇ πίστει τοῦ ὀνόματος αὐτοῦ τοῦτον ὃν θεωρεῖτε καὶ οἴδατε,

16b ἐστερέωσεν τὸ ὄνομα αὐτοῦ,

16c καὶ ἡ πίστις ἡ δι᾽ αὐτοῦ ἔδωκεν αὐτῷ τὴν ὁλοκληρίαν ταύτην ἀπέναντι πάντων ὑμῶν. (Acts 3:16)

The "faith of (Jesus') name" brought healing to the one who was lame. As the break in the grammar shows – the opening clause is not complete (v. 16a) – the emphasis rests on the name of Jesus, which gave the lame one strength (v. 16b). The third clause (v. 16c) then summarizes the first two. It was "the faith *which is through him* (Christ)" which worked the wholeness of the lame one. The third clause obviously elaborates the sense of the genitive in the first clause. There are very good reasons, then, to consider nominal categories such as source, authorship, possession, and quality when we interpret "the faith of Christ" in Paul's letters.

Exegetical Observations

Paul's use of πίστις Χριστοῦ (in its various forms) is not evenly distributed in his letters. It is clustered in several brief passages where fundamental themes of his theology appear in remarkable concentration: sin and righteousness, the Law and works, Jews and Gentiles, Christ's crucifixion and the resurrection, life and death (Rom. 3:21–26; Gal. 2:15–21; 3:19–22; Phil. 3:2–11).[29] These connections clearly suggest that

---

[29] We may leave Eph. 3:1–21 and the reference in Eph. 3:12 (πίστις αὐτοῦ) aside. Although the terminology differs, the same themes are at work here. The wide variety of references to Christ which Paul employs given the limited number of texts is remarkable: "Jesus Christ" (Rom. 3:22; Gal. 2:16b; 3:22); "Jesus" (Rom. 3:26); "Christ" (Gal. 2:16c; Phil. 3:9); "the Son of God" (Gal. 2:20). One need not adopt Haußleiter's distinction between "the faith of Jesus" (subjective genitive) and "the faith of Christ" (objective genitive) to see that Paul's emphasis shifts from context to context.

it is expressive of a significant dimension of his gospel. It is no wonder that it has caught the attention of interpreters. We shall here give our attention primarily to Paul's statements in Romans and briefly discuss the texts from Galatians and Philippians at the conclusion.

Romans 1:16–17

Before we turn to the passages in which πίστις Χριστοῦ appears, it is necessary to give some attention to Paul's opening declaration in Romans 1:16–17. Basic elements of his understanding of faith come to expression in this text, so it is only natural that it has been drawn into the debate.

Paul's calling as an apostle remains the primary theme of the declaration, just as it is in the letter-opening which precedes it.[30] His affirmation that he is "not ashamed of the gospel" elaborates (γάρ) his eagerness to "proclaim the good news" in Rome (Rom. 1:15–16). As this biblically formed language indicates, Paul's proclamation of the gospel is nothing other than an act and expression of faith.[31] By means of this letter he already is fulfilling his aim of "encouraging" the believers in Rome *by his faith* (Rom. 1:12). In verse 17, then, the paired phrases ἐκ πίστεως εἰς πίστιν may be understood to describe the apostolic proclamation and its effect.[32] It is *in the gospel* that the righteousness of God is revealed. The locus of revelation implies proclamation. Out of the faith of the Apostle who announces the gospel, God's righteousness is revealed in the gospel, effecting faith in the fallen world.

As Paul makes clear, the revelation of God's righteousness is no mere informational event, no mere dispensing of knowledge about the kind of righteousness which God favours.[33] It renders the gospel God's

---

[30] See Rom. 1:1, 5–7; 9–15. As Paul's interjected self-references make clear, it remains a primary theme throughout the letter. See Rom. 2:16; 3:8–9, 27–21; 9:1–5; 10:1–21; 11:13–14; 15:14–33.

[31] The references to faith which appear in Paul's three final statements (1:16b, 17a, 17b) are the expression of the apostolic calling of which he speaks in this opening statement (1:16a).

[32] The phrasing of v. 17 may well recall the effecting of the obedience of faith among the nations, which is Paul's calling as apostle (εἰς ὑπακοὴν πίστεως; Rom. 1:5; 16:26). Elsewhere he uses similar pairings of prepositions to speak of cause and effect, or source and result (Rom. 5:16 [2×]; see also 2 Cor. 3:18), including the effect of his apostolic ministry (2 Cor. 2:16 [2×]).

[33] Unfortunately, Francis Watson misses this point and rather badly misreads the passage in a number of ways. See F. Watson, *Paul and the Hermeneutics of Faith*, 47–51.

saving power and effects faith in the one who hears (ἀποκαλύπτεται ... εἰς πίστιν).[34] As becomes clear in Paul's shift from his reference to "the righteousness of God" to "the righteous one who lives",[35] God's righteousness is a communicative righteousness. The righteousness of God *makes righteous* and thus *imparts life*, as a speech-act that takes place in the proclamation of the gospel.[36]

The revelation of this saving, communicative righteousness takes place *"by faith"* – that is, by the faith of the Apostle who speaks "for faith" (v. 17a). Is then the revelation of God's saving righteousness finally grounded in the faith of the Apostle? The reading which we are offering here may seem to suggest the thought. But the problem is only apparent. Paul's appeal to the text of Habakkuk points in an entirely different direction. As the tiny particle "δε" indicates, he reads the passage in context and points his readers to that context as well. Furthermore, he does not merely reproduce the text; he interprets it. That is immediately apparent in his speaking of "faith" rather than "faithfulness", varying from both the LXX and the underlying Hebrew text. This transposition is characteristic of the massive shift in usage that appears in the New Testament and which must have been typical of earliest Christianity, as we have noted already.[37] Here it presents difficulties for interpreters, as may be seen in the almost universal tendency of English translations to give אֱמוּנָה in Habakkuk 2:4 the impossible rendering "faith". The resolution of the problem lies elsewhere. In all likelihood, the antecedent of the pronominal suffix of בֶּאֱמוּנָתוֹ is חָזוֹן – the promissory vision given to the prophet that is *personified* in Habakkuk 2:2. By implication, it is the faithfulness of Yahweh which is at stake in Habakkuk 2:4. Whether by accidental misreading of the *waw* as a *yod*, or by its own interpretive

---

[34] As Paul later makes clear, the revelation of God's righteousness is a saving act of judgment in which the Creator triumphs over and (thus!) saves the fallen human being (Rom. 3:26).

[35] See Rom. 3:22. The claim that the "righteous one" is somehow a messianic title fails. In Habakkuk, the contrast between "the righteous one" and "the proud one" corresponds to the opening lament that the wicked person besieges the righteous (Hab. 1:5). The prophetic complaint finds its answer in the promise of deliverance through disaster. It is not "the righteous one" but the coming vision of salvation, understood as the coming of the Lord himself, which takes on messianic overtones in the tradition – as Heb. 10:38 attests. In Romans, Paul's focus rests on the salvation of the one who believes the gospel. The form of the citation from Habakkuk corresponds to this concern: the righteous one lives by faith.

[36] This implication is present so long as one sees something more than the conveying of information in the revelation of God's righteousness!

[37] See Heb. 10:38!

move, the LXX captures this sense in its rendering "the righteous one shall live by *my* faithfulness" – the faithfulness of the Lord. To live by God's faithfulness to his promise is to live by faith. Just as the prophet formerly was commissioned to write the vision and make it plain for a messenger to read, run, and announce it, so the Apostle now announces the word of Christ that he has received. The faith of the Apostle as well as that of the prophet before him is created and sustained by the concrete promises of salvation given to them. Both of them live and speak out of the message they received.[38] Faith has its source in the faithfulness of the God who promises and fulfils. In citing Habakkuk 2:4, Paul recalls this setting and draws out its theological significance. The context of the citation thus explains why the prior double phrase ἐκ πίστεως εἰς πίστιν in verse 17a is folded into the single phrase ἐκ πίστεως in verse 17b. There is no distinction between the Lord's messengers and those who receive their message. Prophet and Apostle themselves are called to faith in the promise they are commissioned to bear. They themselves live out of that promise. As one already effectively called by the crucified and risen Christ (Rom. 1:15), the Apostle stands alongside all those who hear him. As the God who promises and fulfils comes into view through the citation of Habakkuk 2:4 in verse 17b, the two phrases shift to one: the righteous one lives by faith.

Romans 3:21–26

It is the righteousness of God which becomes the primary theme of Romans 3:21–26, as the four bracketing references make clear. The

---

[38] There is a significant connection between Rom. 1:16–17 and 10:14–17. The gospel is a "report" (ἡ ἀκοή) with specific content – a message heard, received, and announced anew to others (Rom. 10:16). This "report" is a *message heard* and then announced to others, and thus it is not ultimate. The "report" comes about through "the word of Christ" (διὰ ῥήματος Χριστοῦ; Rom. 10:17). With this phrase, Paul clearly recalls his preceding allusion to Deut. 30:14 in Rom. 10:6–8. Just as the Law was once present as "word" in the mouth and heart of Israel, so now the incarnate, crucified, and risen Christ is present as "word" in the mouths and in the hearts of those who believe: ἐγγύς σου τὸ ῥῆμά ἐστιν (Rom. 10:8). The speaking work of God in Christ so addresses and transforms human beings. They no longer inquire vainly about what they must do. They now proclaim what God has done. The "word" is thus the "word of faith" that the Apostle proclaims (τὸ ῥῆμα τῆς πίστεως [*genetivus qualitatis* or *materiae*] ὃ κηρύσσομεν; Rom. 10:9). Behind and before the message of the Apostle is the "word of Christ" which is the source of his own faith and preaching (Rom. 10:17). God *first* speaks in his work in Christ. The Apostle merely reports and hands on the divine speech (Rom. 10:18).

opening language of "the revelation of God's righteousness", with its more immediate noetic overtones, shifts to the visual (φανερόω) and demonstrative (ἔνδειξις). It is the *event* of the manifestation of God's righteousness within human history which stands at the centre of Paul's interest here. As is already clear from Romans 1:16–17, *this event itself is an effective act of divine speech*, in which God communicates himself savingly to the rebellious human creature.[39] Precisely for this reason, reference to the apostolic calling and mission retreat into the background (cf. Rom. 3:27–31). Paul here presents the foundational speech-act of God from which the apostolic mission arises.

The theocentric thrust of the text, which is characteristic of the letter as a whole, creates problems for both the "subjectivist" and "objectivist" readings of πίστις Χριστοῦ. It is not Jesus who acts here, but God who acts in Jesus. That is explicitly the case in verse 25 (God purposed Jesus as mercy-seat) and implicitly the case everywhere else in these verses. Indeed, Paul does not speak of Christ's work in Romans without speaking of him acting as *resurrected Lord and God*.[40] It is therefore highly unlikely that Paul refers to Christ's faithfulness in verses 22 and 26 in the expression πίστις Ἰησοῦ (Χριστοῦ). That is especially clear in that God's justifying work entails God's raising Jesus from the dead. Both the "redemption that is in Christ Jesus" (v. 24) and Jesus' appointment as God's "mercy-seat" (v. 25) imply that Jesus' resurrection is integral to the saving event. The "subjectivist" reading, with its focus on *Jesus' faithfulness*, simply leaves the resurrection out of view.

Similar difficulties arise for the attempt to find objective genitives in the references to πίστις Ἰησοῦ (Χριστοῦ). If God is the subject who works salvation, it is properly *God* who is the object of saving faith. In this context, all attention is focused on the God who savingly manifests his righteousness to fallen human beings. Paul's description of the saving event in terms of the exodus and the tabernacle ("redemption"

---

[39] Consequently the apostolic words are not a mere interpretation of a mute historical event, but rather the faithful bearing of a message received. See the note above; also O. Bayer, *Schöpfung als Anrede: Zu einer Hermeneutik der Schöpfung* (Tübingen: Mohr Siebeck, 1990), 9–32; Otfried Hofius, "'Die Wahrheit des Evangeliums'", in *Paulusstudien II* (Tübingen: Mohr Siebeck, 2002), 17–37.

[40] See esp. Rom. 1:1–4, the series of summary statements in Rom. 4:25; 5:21; 6:23; 7:25; 8:39; and Rom. 10:9–13. Rom. 5:15–19 is no exception: the grace of God is coterminous with the gift and grace of the one human being, Jesus Christ (Rom. 5:15). The obedience of Christ is no generic human faith(fulness), but obedience to the concrete will of God for *this one* (Rom. 5:19; cf. Rom. 8:32).

and "mercy-seat") is directed toward God, as is his reference to God's passing over of sins. It is natural to suppose, then, that it is *God* who is the implicit object of faith – especially in verse 25 where faith is connected to *God's* purposing Jesus as "mercy-seat". We may remind ourselves that Paul generally uses πίστις as something more than a verbal noun. The content of faith is implied in the term and signalled by the context. This context provides strong indications that it is God – in his saving action in Jesus – whom Paul presents as the object of faith here. In the following chapter of Romans, Paul defines Christian faith in precisely this manner. We believe, in the pattern of Abraham's faith, in the One who raised Jesus, our Lord, from the dead (Rom. 4:24–25).[41]

That God is the object of faith in this context already is an indication that with the expression πίστις Ἰησοῦ (Χριστοῦ) Paul identifies Jesus as the *source* of faith. Paul speaks here of the righteousness of God that is communicated to human beings through the faith *which comes from Jesus Christ* (Rom. 3:22). The righteous God justifies the one who is of the faith *that comes from Jesus* (Rom. 3:26).[42] As we have seen, Paul's citation of Habakkuk 2:4 in Romans 1:17 points to God's ultimacy in salvation as the Creator who through his promissory word effects faith, righteousness, and life. What was implicit in the earlier citation now becomes open and emphatic in Romans 3:21–26, as Paul moves from the gospel to the speech-act of God in Jesus Christ that the gospel announces. Verse 24 is of particular significance, since here Paul summarizes the whole of God's saving work without reference to faith. Sinful and perverted human beings are "justified as a gift by his grace through the redemption that is in Christ Jesus". As in the following verse 25, in verse 24 it is the crucified and risen Christ who mediates the past event of salvation to the present. Justifying redemption is present *in him*. This final phrase not only spans the gap of time, it also marks the location of justification, which is present as a comprehensive whole – both accomplished and applied – solely *in Christ Jesus*. Even in verse 25, where Paul again speaks of faith as the means by which God's atoning work comes to the human being, God's work in Christ remains ultimate, appearing in emphatic, final position: God purposed

---

[41] He uses similar language in Rom. 10:9, where he speaks of confessing Jesus as Lord and believing that God raised him from the dead. This ascription of deity to the crucified and risen Jesus does not set aside the affirmation of God's work in him.

[42] The thought approximates that of Rom. 5:1, where Paul affirms that "having been justified by faith, we have peace with God through our Lord, Jesus Christ". The second statement describes the more fundamental reality that underlies the first.

Christ as mercy-seat, through faith, *by his blood*. The genitive of source consequently is also definitive. Paul speaks of "(Jesus-)Christ-faith".[43] To read the genitive references to Christ in verses 22 and 26 as expressing the source of faith and of justification corresponds to Paul's central description of God's justifying work in verse 24. As a counterpart to his announcement of the gospel in Romans 1:16–17, Paul here locates the source of faith (and thus of proclamation) in God's justifying work in Jesus, crucified and risen.[44] Faith is "of Jesus". God's gift and work of justification in Jesus Christ creates its own reception within the fallen human being.[45]

Galatians and Philippians

Again in Galatians the various forms of "faith of Christ" call for a reading that allows for a nominal interpretation of πίστις. In context, "faith" bears a dimension that transcends the action of the human being, so that the genitive relation cannot be reduced to the subjective or objective genitive. The structural parallelism in Galatians 2:16 suggests a semantic parallelism that entails reading "πίστις (Ἰησοῦ) Χριστοῦ" as a *genetivus auctoris*. Just as works arise from the Law, so faith arises from Christ. Similarly, in Galatians 2:17 Paul locates justification in its entirety "in Christ". To believe in Christ is "to seek to be justified in Christ". As Paul's continuing analysis makes clear, he does more than describe the disposition of the believer here. He provides a theological

---

[43] Here we are using the expression in a somewhat different manner from Hultgren, "*Pistis Christou* Formulation", and radically differently from Williams, "Again *Pistis Christou*", 437.

[44] Most likely for this reason, the name "Jesus" receives priority in v. 22, and in v. 26 "Christ" (with its titular overtones) falls away. In contrast, in v. 24, where Paul underscores the presence of salvation, he speaks of "Christ Jesus".

[45] Paul's references to "the faith of Abraham" in Rom. 4:12, 16 in a certain respect correspond to his usage of the "the faith of Jesus" here. While in Rom. 4:12 his attention is focused on the pattern of obedience which Abraham provides, it is hardly the case that he thinks merely of Abraham's action. Everything is contingent on the promise given to Abraham, which performs its work through him. Abraham is thus "our father". The "one of the faith of Abraham" in Rom. 4:16 is, of course, the Gentile who believes. Here, however, the act of faith is not primary. Attention has shifted to the effective promise of God. To be "of the faith of Abraham" is to have Abraham as father, to be born of his faith and of the Creator who gave him the word of promise. In both instances the "faith of Abraham" may well entail a *genetivus possessoris*.

characterization of faith that is thus found "in Christ". Its source and origin are located in him. Finally, and most significantly, Paul makes the personal confession "I live by the faith of "the Son of God, who loved me and gave himself up for me" (Gal. 2:20b). As he has just made clear, this "living" is no longer his life, but the life of another: "I have been crucified with Christ. I live, but no longer I. Christ lives in me." Paul's statement on faith proceeds from this confession. Christ, the Son of God, is the source of his new life and therefore of his very faith.[46] Christ is thus something more than the object of faith. He is the agent of salvation in all its dimensions, as is already the case in Galatians 1:4.[47] In his self-giving, the grace of God is at work (Gal. 2:21). We most likely find, then, a *genetivus auctoris* in each of the three references to "the faith of Christ". The localizing language which appears in Galatians 2:17a again suggests that the expressions bear defining dimension. We seek to be justified *in Christ*: justification is found in this definite place, and no other. As the author of faith, Christ defines faith. In that sense, again in Galatians Paul speaks of a "Christ-faith".

In Galatians 3:19–29 the "trans-subjective" dimension of faith becomes prominent. Christ now appears as the recipient of the promise to Abraham. Through him that promise is distributed to all the nations. The promise is thus "of the faith of Jesus Christ" (Gal. 3:22). Faith – which was already present with Abraham – arrives only with the coming of Christ, who alone is the "seed" to whom the promise was given (Gal. 3:16, 23–25). Faith is present "in Christ Jesus" and makes us all "sons of God" (Gal. 3:26). Baptism is a baptism into Christ, a being clothed with Christ (Gal. 3:27). Those who are "of Christ", who thus share in him and belong to him – a genitive appears here as well – are Abraham's seed (as Christ alone is!) and heirs "according to the promise". Faith is the new reality "in Christ Jesus" (Gal. 3:26), given through him and found in him alone. The "faith of Christ" again appears as a genitive of source and again bears overtones of definition and exclusivity. In this sense once again, Paul speaks of a "Christ-faith".

In Philippians 3:9, the interpretation of the expression "faith of Christ" depends on whether Paul here uses πίστις purely as a *nomen actionis* or if he speaks of it as a gift and presupposes content within the term itself. Paul's voicing of his desire to know Christ in verse 10, which clearly resumes his reference to "the knowledge of Christ" in verse

---

[46] We should not forget that Paul personifies faith – the new person – in Gal. 5:6.

[47] On this passage see Seifrid, *Christ, Our Righteousness*, 139–46; idem, "Paul, Luther, and Justification in Galatians 2:15–21", *WTJ* 65 (2003): 215–30.

8, seems at first sight to favour reading "faith of Christ" as "faith in Christ".[48] Paul in fact speaks of "believing in Christ" earlier in the letter (Phil. 1:29; τὸ εἰς αὐτὸν πιστεύειν). Nevertheless, there are reasons why reading the expression in terms of a genitive of source or author may be more appropriate. Knowing Christ for Paul is clearly experiential and transcends the intellectual comprehension of an object: to know Christ is to know the power of his resurrection and participation in his sufferings (v. 10). Likewise, when Paul speaks of "believing in Christ" in Philippians 1:29, he speaks of it as a gift granted to the Philippians. In the present context, Paul describes the knowledge of Christ in a twofold way ("gaining him" and "being found in him") in which action and passivity are joined (vv. 8–9). Paul takes up the action of "gaining Christ" (v. 8) again in verse 10, where he describes it in synthetic relation to his passivity. In verse 9, Paul appears in a passive role. With obvious anticipation of the final judgment, he desires "to be found in [Christ]". He elaborates this desire in the following three-part participial clause, in which the first and third adjectival phrases stand in parallel. Being "found in Christ" means *not* having one's own righteousness from the Law. It means having a righteousness that God works on and for faith. The second phrase anticipates and elaborates what Paul says in the decisive third phrase. The righteousness that comes from God, which God effects upon and for "faith", is a righteousness given "through the faith of Christ". To be found in Christ is to have a righteousness already given and effected through the faith of Christ. Both the passivity of Paul's person as well as the participatory thrust of the entire passage suggest that "the faith of Christ" signifies faith which comes as a gift from Christ. The righteousness from God that Paul desires is the righteousness that God effects through the faith which comes from Christ. In this way – and only in this way – the righteousness that Paul desires is not Paul's own (v. 8), but "the righteousness that is *from God*" (v. 10) given through Christ Jesus, Paul's Lord.

Conclusion

We return to our opening question. What does it mean to believe in Jesus Christ? The recent revival of interest in interpreting "the faith

---

[48] The "subjectivist" reading again essentially excludes itself here in that the resurrection of Christ, and not merely his suffering, is directly included within "the faith (and knowledge) of Christ". See Phil. 3:8 ("Christ Jesus, my *Lord*") and 3:10–11.

of Christ" in terms of a subjective genitive takes its bearing from the humanity of Jesus. He is the faithful human being doing his best before God for the whole of the human race. In so far as Christ's resurrection comes into view, it does so only as an event *facilitated* by a faithful human being. The failure to account for Christ's present rule as risen Lord remains an obvious and fatal shortcoming for the "subjectivist" interpretation of Pauline faith. The same is true of Christ's cross itself. For the representatives of this view, in so far as they see that Christ acts as God – and although Paul sees him so, they rarely do – Christ's deity and lordship become so deeply buried within his humanity that they are no longer alive and active. Other theological problems for this view are mere concomitants of this fundamental flaw. How might Jesus' faith(fulness) be thought to work our salvation? It is no accident that the answer to this question remains vague among the "subjectivists". By its very nature, the "subjectivist" reading bears an inherent tendency to find in Jesus nothing more than a model for our faith(fulness). Despite its legitimate concern to articulate afresh the connection between doctrine and doing, this approach to Paul has to be judged an exegetical and theological failure.

In his various uses of the expression "faith of Christ", Paul does not describe a human being doing his best before God but rather – to borrow the words of P.T. Forsyth – God doing God's best for humanity. The shortcomings of the traditional reading of the expression as an objective genitive are slight, and generally compensated for by what Paul says expressly elsewhere. Nevertheless, the recognition that in the expression "faith of Christ" Paul speaks of Christ as the source and author of faith brings to light a fundamental theological dimension of his theology. For the Apostle, to believe in Jesus Christ is not first to act, but rather to be acted upon by God in his work in Jesus Christ. It is to know that our faith is the work of another. It is to know that the crucified and risen One is our Lord. Here lies the connection between doctrine and doing that the "subjectivists" have sought but failed to find. Here our "doing" is not our own doing, but the doing and work of another, given to us in the apostolic proclamation of the gospel.

9

By Faith (of Christ): An Exegetical Dilemma and its Scriptural Solution

FRANCIS WATSON

To many Pauline scholars, it now seems clear that in a small number of passages – crucially important ones, no doubt – the Apostle Paul speaks of "the faith of Christ" as the grounds of our justification or salvation. If so, Christ himself is the subject of the faith or faithfulness whereby we are justified; the "faith" in question is in the first instance not ours but his.[1] To translate the Pauline ἐκ πίστεως Χριστοῦ as "by faith *in* Christ" is therefore a serious error, which exemplifies the objectionable anthropocentrism and individualism of so much western theology since the Reformation. In correcting our exegesis, it is said, we may also renew our theology. We (or those of us who are Protestants) will find ourselves transported "beyond Protestantism".[2]

That there are significant shortcomings in traditional readings of Paul is beyond doubt. As I have argued elsewhere, it has been widely overlooked that, in the discussion in Romans and Galatians of matters of faith and Law, Paul is engaged throughout in *scriptural exegesis and hermeneutics*. His so-called "doctrine of justification by faith" is actually his interpretation of certain scriptural texts, and of Scripture as a whole in the light of those texts. His denial that righteousness is "by works of Law" refers us to the Jewish way of life as codified in the Torah, and not to some more pervasive and universal error in the way humans seek to relate to God.[3] As for "faith in Christ", it is quite proper to ask whether

---

[1] On this view, "faithfulness" is often preferred to "faith" as a translation of πίστις. In retaining the traditional rendering, I am not pre-empting the translation question but merely seeking to avoid awkward formulations such as "faith/faithfulness", or "faith(fulness)".

[2] So Douglas Harink, *Paul among the Postliberals: Pauline Theology beyond Christendom and Modernity* (Grand Rapids, MI: Brazos, 2003), 25–65.

[3] These two points are developed, respectively, in my *Paul and the Hermeneutics of Faith* and *Paul, Judaism and the Gentiles*.

this is really an appropriate translation of Paul's open-ended genitive formulations. "By faith of Christ" might be understood in various ways, of which "by faith *in* Christ" is only one.[4]

So there is no reason why old assumptions about Paul should not be challenged, and there is every reason to venture the attempt to understand him better. A venture is a risk, however, and some risky undertakings will succeed while others fail. A proposed new reading of Paul should not be adopted just because it is new, nor because it represents a consensus of respected scholars, nor because it confirms our prejudices about conventional Protestantism, nor because it promises theological renewal. A new reading of Paul must be subjected to rigorous exegetical scrutiny. If exegesis is truly to *serve* theology, rather than merely reflecting it, exegetical debate must not be allowed to degenerate into allegations about "theological presuppositions".[5]

In what follows I shall argue that Paul's "by faith of Christ" formulations all derive from Habakkuk 2:4. As cited by Paul, this text states *either* that "the one who is righteous by faith will live", *or* that "the Righteous One will live by faith". A decision about the "faith of Christ" formulations resolves itself into a decision about this specific translation issue. The discussion will focus on the precise form of the Pauline phraseology. Paul never speaks of "*the* faith of Christ", as he speaks of "the faith of our father Abraham" (Rom. 4:12). The substitution of the definite article for the Pauline preposition ("by" or "through") means that "the faith of Christ" is isolated from its natural context within Paul's repeated use of prepositional phrases involving πίστις (ἐκ πίστεως, διὰ [τῆς] πίστεως). Paul does not speak of "the faith of Christ", but he does say that we are justified ἐκ πίστεως or ἐκ πίστεως Χριστοῦ. If we are to understand Paul's language, we must not neglect his prepositions. Since διὰ [τῆς] πίστεως is simply a variant of ἐκ πίστεως, and since the

---

[4] On this issue see also *Paul and the Hermeneutics of Faith*, 47–53, 73–6; *Paul, Judaism and the Gentiles*, 238–45. In these three sections, I argue: (1) that Rom. 1:17a is an introductory gloss on Hab. 2:4, cited in v. 17b, and that this precludes a reference to Christ's own faith; (2) that in Paul's faith-of-Christ formulations the relationship between the two substantives remains under-defined, so that "faith *in* Christ" may be too restrictive an interpretation (see note 8, p. 150); and (3) that Paul's treatment of his key faith-related Scripture citations (Hab. 2:4; Gen. 15:6; Isa. 28:16) shows that for him πίστις and πιστεύειν are interchangeable.

[5] For an incisive critique of the subordination of exegesis to theology in this area of Pauline studies, see Matlock, "Detheologizing ΠΙΣΤΙΣ ΧΡΙΣΤΟΥ". To "detheologize" this debate does not, of course, mean that the relevant texts are permanently removed from the sphere of theological reflection.

latter phrase is clearly and explicitly derived from Habakkuk 2:4, the argument will further support the claim that Paul speaks of "justification by faith" in the context of his interpretation of Scripture, and not as a free-standing "doctrine" developed by himself or revealed on the Damascus Road.[6]

More specifically, I shall argue (1) that the relevant antithetical constructions all derive from the ἐκ πίστεως of Paul's Habakkuk citation; (2) that there is no non-Pauline evidence that this text was read christologically, as a reference to "the Righteous One"; and (3) that this negative result is confirmed by Paul, who finds in his Habakkuk text an assertion about a generic individual (the one-who-is-righteous-by-faith) rather than about Christ (the Righteous One). *If the scriptural citation underlies and generates all the relevant antithetical constructions, including the faith-of-Christ ones, and if for Paul the citation speaks of a generic individual and not of Christ, there is no room for the christological, subjective genitive interpretation of this phraseology.* On these largely formal grounds, and (on this occasion) without recourse to wider theological considerations, I propose to *solve* the exegetical problem by *refuting* the interpretative option that is currently so widely championed, at least in English-language scholarship.[7]

(1) Antithetical Constructs and their Scriptural Origin

The relevant prepositional formulations first occur in Galatians 2:16, where it is said that "a person [ἄνθρωπος] is justified not by works of Law [ἐξ ἔργων νόμου] but through faith of Jesus Christ [διὰ πίστεως Ἰησοῦ Χριστοῦ]". In a remarkable example of Paul's use of redundancy for the sake of emphasis, the general statement is immediately repeated in first-person plural form: *we* are justified "by faith of Christ [ἐκ πίστεως Χριστοῦ] and not by works of Law [ἐξ ἔργων νόμου]". The two slightly different "by faith of Christ" formulations balance "not by

---

[6] My argument is indebted to Douglas Campbell's observation that Paul uses the phrase ἐκ πίστεως only in the two letters where he cites Hab. 2:4, and that this text should therefore be seen as the root of Paul's ἐκ/διά phrases, including those that refer to πίστις Χριστοῦ ("*Crux Interpretum*", 268). Campbell draws the opposite conclusion to mine from this observation because he does not see that Paul draws from Habakkuk not only ἐκ πίστεως but also δικαίος ἐκ πίστεως.

[7] The largely English-speaking character of this debate is noted by Klaus Haacker (*Der Brief des Paulus an die Römer* [THKNT; 3rd ed.; Leipzig: Evangelische Verlagsanstalt, 2006], 94–5).

works of Law". In both cases, similarly constructed phrases make use of a preposition (*by, through*) together with paired genitives (*works, Law; faith, Christ*) that together create a double antithesis (*works/faith; Law/ Christ*). The faith-formulations are apparently modelled on the Law ones. In both cases, the second genitive substantive serves to delimit the scope of the first: the works in question are specifically "works of Law", the faith in question is specifically "faith of Christ". In spite of this delimitation, however, the precise relationship between the paired substantives on both sides of the antithesis is left under-defined. It is left to the reader to determine whether "works of Law" refers to actions *prescribed* by the Law or *performed* by it; and it is similarly left to the reader to decide whether "faith of Christ" refers to the faith *oriented* towards Christ, or *mandated* by him, or *exemplified* in him.[8] Finally, we note that the (three) references to "works of Law" are identical, whereas the "faith of Christ" references vary slightly. "Works of [the] Law" or *ma'aśê [ha-]Tōrah* appears to be already established phraseology which provides the template for Paul's "faith of [Jesus] Christ".[9]

---

[8] Note, however, Barry Matlock's brilliant analysis of Gal. 2:16, which seeks to show on purely structural grounds that καὶ ἡμεῖς εἰς Χριστὸν Ἰησοῦν ἐπιστεύσαμεν must determine the sense of the ἐκ πίστεως Χριστοῦ formulations ("Rhetoric", 197–9). Matlock also finds similar correspondences between Phil. 3:9 and 1:29 (182–4), and between Rom. 3:22 and 10:11 (184–7). While Matlock has shown conclusively that πιστεύειν εἰς (Gal. 2:16; Phil. 1:9; Rom. 10:14) or ἐπί (Rom. 10:11) is integral and fundamental to πίστις Χριστοῦ, the latter phrase is in my view too open-ended to be simply *reducible* to the former. Had Paul wanted an *exact* equivalent of πιστεύειν εἰς or ἐπί, one might have expected a preposition following πίστις (cf. Phlm. 5: πίστις πρός), instead of the remarkably consistent use of the genitive wherever "faith" and "Christ" are correlated. Like Matlock, however, I too believe that the "faith" in question is that of Paul's Christian readers, and that the subjective genitive reading is *demonstrably* mistaken.

[9] The author of 4QMMT summarizes the content of his letter as "a selection of the works of the law" [מקצת מעשי התורה] (C 27). 4Q *Florilegium* states that the community exists to be "a human temple, so that in it they may offer up before him works of law [מעשי תורה]" (4Q174 1 i 6–7). (For the reading תורה rather than תודה ["praise"], see J.A. Fitzmyer, "Paul's Jewish Background and the Deeds of the Law", in his *According to Paul: Studies in the Theology of the Apostle* [New York: Paulist Press, 1993], 19–35 [20–21].) 1Q *Pesher Habakkuk* speaks repeatedly of those "observing the law" [עושי התורה] (1QpHab. 7.11; 8.1; cf. 12.4–5). For detailed analysis of this material, see Jacqueline de Roo, *Works of Law at Qumran and in Paul* (Sheffield: Sheffield Phoenix, 2007). For the scriptural background to this terminology, see the brief but helpful analysis in Simon Gathercole, *Where Is Boasting? Early Jewish Soteriology and Paul's Response in Romans 1–5* (Grand Rapids, MI: Eerdmans, 2002), 92–3.

We encounter similar balanced antithetical formulations as we read on into Galatians 3. In verses 3 and 5, ἐξ ἔργων νόμου again remains constant and is balanced by a new double genitive prepositional construction, ἐξ ἀκοῆς πίστεως. We received the Spirit "not by works of Law" but "by hearing of faith", and the second phrase is again constructed on the template provided by the first. We also note that the preposition ἐκ (ἐξ) has been used in preference to διά in eight of the nine formulations we have so far considered, in all five references to "works of Law" and in three of the four references to faith.

In Galatians 3:6–29, ἐξ ἔργων νόμου recurs only in verse 10, where it is said that "those who are of works of Law are under a curse". A shorter version of the phrase occurs in 3:18, 21 (ἐκ νόμου; cf. διὰ νόμου, 2:19, 21). Similarly, the διά-form of the faith phrase (διὰ πίστεως Ἰησοῦ Χριστοῦ, Gal. 2:16) also recurs in shorter versions. We received the promise of the Spirit through faith (διὰ τῆς πίστεως, v. 14), and we are sons of God through faith (διὰ πίστεως, v. 26). The prepositional phrases relating to both Law and faith occur in longer and shorter forms. Are the longer versions extensions of the shorter ones, or are the shorter versions abbreviations of the longer ones? In the sequence of Paul's argument, the longer versions are prior (Gal. 2:16; 3:2, 5, 10). Yet, as we shall see, it is the short version of the faith-phrase in its ἐκ-form that underlies and generates this antithetical machinery in its entirety.

We have noted that there are two alternative longer versions of this phrase: ἐκ πίστεως Χριστοῦ (Gal. 2:16), and ἐξ ἀκοῆς πίστεως (3:2, 5). The double genitive formulations serve in each case to balance "by works of Law". In 3:6–29, however, a short version of the phrase (ἐκ πίστεως) occurs six times – together with one final occurrence in 5:5. This formulation is used in a variety of ways that defy consistent translation. The children of Abraham are twice described as οἱ ἐκ πίστεως (3:7, 9). Scripture foresaw that God would justify the Gentiles ἐκ πίστεως (3:8). It is said that the Law does not justify because (as Scripture states), "the one who is righteous by faith [ἐκ πίστεως] will live" – or, as Paul's Habakkuk citation should possibly be translated, "the Righteous One will live by faith" (3:11). The Law, however, is not ἐκ πίστεως (3:12). The first form of the longer version recurs in 3:22, where it is said that the promise, ἐκ πίστεως Ἰησοῦ Χριστοῦ, is to be given to those who believe. The short form returns where it is said that the Law is our παιδαγωγός until Christ, so that we might be justified ἐκ πίστεως (3:24). Lastly it is said that, through the Spirit and ἐκ πίστεως, we await the hope of righteousness (5:5). In the letter as a whole, the ἐκ-form of the faith-phrase occurs four times in longer versions (2:16; 3:2, 5, 22) and seven times in the short version (3:7, 8, 9, 11, 12, 24; 5:5). Since long and short διά-phrases occur only three times (2:16; 3:14, 26), in contrast to the eleven occurrences of ἐκ-phrases, the διά-formulations may be seen as variants of the ἐκ-ones. The priority of ἐκ/ἐξ over διά is confirmed by the prepositional formulations relating to the Law, where ἐκ/ἐξ occurs eight times (2:16 [3×]; 3:2, 5, 10, 18, 21) and διά only twice (2:19, 21). Overall figures, then, are nineteen for ἐκ/ἐξ and five for διά. The possibility of a subtle semantic distinction between ἐκ and διά is already excluded in 2:16, where the two forms are used interchangeably. There is one final statistical observation which will prove to be crucial to the argument: the ἐκ/ἐξ-formulations are closely correlated with righteousness terminology on eight occasions – with the verb δικαιοῦν (2:16 [3×]; 3:8, 11, 24), the adjective δίκαιος (3:11), and the substantive δικαιοσύνη (5:5).

This analysis shows how misleading it is to isolate "the faith of Christ" from this network of prepositional formulations. It also raises the question of priority. Are we to conclude that ἐκ πίστεως Χριστοῦ is the basic formulation, which is then abbreviated to ἐκ πίστεως, as the sequence of the letter might lead us to suppose? Or is ἐκ πίστεως the basic formulation, which is extended into double genitive formulations (ἐκ πίστεως Χριστοῦ, ἐξ ἀκοῆς πίστεως) in order to balance ἐξ ἔργων νόμου? For several reasons, this second explanation seems preferable:

(i) ἐκ πίστεως is the common denominator of the otherwise divergent longer formulations (ἐκ πίστεως [Ἰησοῦ] Χριστοῦ, ἐκ/ ἐξ ἀκοῆς πίστεως). This suggests that it is the origin of both.

(ii) While the phrase "works of [the] Law" is attested outside Paul, ἐξ ἔργων νόμου is not. This formulation may have been constructed on the model of ἐκ πίστεως, which was then itself extended into symmetrical double genitival constructions (2:16; 3:2, 5).

(iii) We have already seen that the διά-formulations are secondary variants of the more numerous ἐκ-formulations. In conjunction with the two preceding points, this means that the short ἐκ πίστεως formulation can account for *all* the other formulations discussed here.

(iv) ἐκ πίστεως originates not from Paul but from Habakkuk 2:4b.[10] This text is cited in Galatians 3:11, in conjunction with righteousness terminology that Paul also exploits: ὁ δίκαιος ἐκ πίστεως ζήσεται. Paul's prepositional phrases have been

---

10 Rightly noted by Hays, *The Faith of Jesus Christ*, 150.

shaped by this scriptural text from the outset (2:16). If, as noted above, the ἐκ πίστεως formulation can account for all the other formulations, then their common origin lies in the terminology of Scripture.

(v) This scriptural derivation of Paul's terminology is confirmed by the citation of Habakkuk 2:4 at the outset of the main theological argument of Romans. Here Paul states that in the gospel "the righteousness of God is revealed, by faith, for faith – as it is written, 'The one who is righteous by faith will live'" (Rom. 1:17). The antecedent to the citation ("... in it the righteousness of God is revealed, by faith, for faith") is already a paraphrase of the citation itself (cf. Rom. 9:32b–33 for a parallel case). The Habakkuk text also underlies the preliminary account of righteousness by faith in Romans 3:21–31, where the range of prepositional phrases corresponds closely to that of Galatians.[11]

It is quite wrong to assume that Paul already believed that righteousness is "by faith" independently of Scripture, and that he subsequently came across a scriptural passage that happened to coincide with his thinking. Where Paul's own terminology coincides with the scriptural texts he cites, it is because his own assertions *derive* from these texts. It is from Scripture that he learns that in Abraham the Gentiles are blessed, and that Christ died under the Law's curse (Gal. 3:8–10, 13). In addition to Habakkuk 2:4, Genesis 15:6 is also a crucial source for Paul's righteousness-by-faith language; in Galatians, however, Paul draws three times on Habakkuk's ἐκ πίστεως formulation even as he interprets the Genesis text (Gal. 3:7, 8, 9).

The common scriptural derivation of Paul's varying prepositional formulations confirms that they are essentially of a piece. The longer formulations cannot be isolated from the shorter ones. While Paul's usage is flexible, so that each occurrence will possess its own contextual nuance, it is unlikely that "by faith of Christ" will mean something quite different from "by hearing of faith" or simply "by faith". The longer formulations *elaborate* the shorter one, but the shared structure means that they are unlikely to *deviate* from it. If "faith" is in the first instance "the faith of Christ" (that is, Christ's own faith or faithfulness), then this

---

[11] διὰ πίστεως Ἰησου Χριστοῦ, τὸν ἐκ πίστεως Ἰησοῦ (Rom. 3:22, 26; cf. Gal. 2:16, 3:22); διὰ [τῆς] πίστεως (Rom. 3:25, 30b, 31; cf. Gal. 3:26); ἐκ πίστεως (Rom. 1:17 [2×]; 3:30a; 4:16 [2×]; 5:1; 9:30, 32; 10:6; 14:23; cf. Gal. 3:7, etc.). This gives a total of 11 occurrences of ἐκ πίστεως for Romans as a whole (10 short, one extended).

will be the case throughout. If so, Paul must understand the Habakkuk citation christologically: Christ is the promised "Righteous One" who "will live by faith" (3:11). Other occurrences of "by faith" will also refer to the faith of Christ; thus, it is those who participate in *Christ's* faith who are Abraham's children, justified and blessed alongside him (Gal. 3:7–9). The Habakkuk citation would apply in the first instance to Christ, and only secondarily to those who are "in Christ" and who thereby participate in *his* faith (cf. 2:17; 3:14, 26, 28).

Thus, *the sense we assign to Paul's disputed "faith of Christ" formulations is dependent on our interpretation of Habakkuk 2:4 as cited by Paul.* These formulations may be taken to refer to Christ's own faith or faithfulness *if and only if* Paul reads Habakkuk 2:4 messianically. If for Paul the Habakkuk text speaks of a generic person rather than a specific individual, the subjective genitive interpretation of the faith of Christ formulations cannot be correct.

As we have already noted, the two interpretative possibilities correspond to two alternative translations. The ambiguity arises from Paul's omission of the pronoun that occurs in all other early versions of this text. According to the Masoretic text, "the righteous one by *his* faith/faithfulness will live". According to most Septuagint manuscripts, "the righteous one by *my* faith/faithfulness will live".[12] The divergence probably arises from a confusion between Hebrew *waw* and *yod*.[13] Where either pronoun is present, the prepositional phrase must be connected to the verb rather than to the subject. In the absence of the pronoun, however, the alternative connection becomes possible. In consequence, Paul may take his text to mean *either*:

(1) The Righteous One will live by faith.

or:

(2) The one-who-is-righteous-by-faith will live.

The first translation takes ὁ δίκαιος as a christological title and detaches it from ἐκ πίστεως, which now qualifies the verb. The second translation

---

[12] However, A and C read: ὁ δὲ δίκαιός μου ἐκ πίστεως ζήσεται. This reading probably derives from Heb. 10:38, where the shift in the position of the pronoun is motivated by the contextual need for a reference to human faith rather than divine faithfulness.

[13] See my *Paul and the Hermeneutics of Faith*, 86–7, where the alternative Gk. translation from Nahal Heber is also discussed. This reads: [καὶ δί] καιος ἐν πίστει αὐτοῦ ζήσετ[αι] (8HebXIIgr xvii 30). Along with 1QpHab. 8.1–3, this passage supports the originality of MT here.

understands ὁ δίκαιος generically and links it directly to ἐκ πίστεως.[14] The subject of this cryptic sentence is ὁ δίκαιος ἐκ πίστεως, and the compound subject rules out the possibility of a christological title. The two translations cannot both be correct. The question is which is to be preferred.[15]

This question is best addressed by asking, first, whether the evidence of ὁ δίκαιος as a christological title is relevant to Paul's citation from Habakkuk and, second, by asking whether Paul connects ἐκ πίστεως to ζήσεται or to ὁ δίκαιος. If there is little or no evidence that anyone else read Habakkuk 2:4 christologically, and if Paul derives from this text a connection between the faith and righteousness of the generic individual, then both external and internal factors combine to exclude the christological interpretation of Paul's by-faith-of-Christ formulations.

(2) Jesus Christ as "the Righteous One"?

Understood christologically, and as cited by Paul, Habakkuk 2:4b might be translated: "The Righteous One will live by faith." If that is what this text means for Paul, then the subjective genitive interpretation of his faith-of-Christ formulations must be correct. An argument for this interpretation of the Habakkuk text will naturally appeal to non-Pauline evidence that "the Righteous One" was an established messianic title both in early Judaism and in early Christianity.[16] Such an argument

---

14 For generic use of [ὁ] δίκαιος in the sg., see Matt. 10:41; Rom. 5:7; 1 Tim. 1:9; Jas. 5:6 (?); 1 Pet. 4:18; Rev. 22:11. It should also be noted that the translation, "the righteous one will live by faith", can be taken generically rather than christologically: so Fitzmyer, *Romans*, 265, arguing that "the-one-righteous-by-faith" would require a citation in the form, ὁ δὲ ἐκ πίστεως δίκαιος (cf. ἡ δὲ ἐκ πίστεως δικαιοσύνη, Rom. 10:6). Arguably, however, the parallel from Rom. 10 actually confirms that Paul could take ὁ δίκαιος ἐκ πίστεως as equivalent to ὁ ἐκ πίστεως δίκαιος without modifying the word order of his citation.

15 Commentators on Gal. 3:11 and Rom. 1:17 have generally discussed the translation issue without reference to the christological possibility (see, e.g., Cranfield, *Romans*, 101–2; U. Wilckens, *Der Brief an die Römer* [EKKNT VI/1, Zurich/Neukirchen-Vluyn: Benziger Verlag/Neukirchener Verlag, 1978], 89–90). Both commentators rightly argue that Paul's linkage of righteousness and faith elsewhere is the key to his understanding of his Habakkuk citation.

16 See Richard Hays, "Apocalyptic Hermeneutics: Habakkuk Proclaims 'the Righteous One'", in his *The Conversion of the Imagination: Paul as Interpreter of Israel's Scriptures* (Grand Rapids, MI: Eerdmans, 2005), 119–42. Outside the NT, Hays finds evidence in the "Similitudes of Enoch" (*1 Enoch* 37–71) for "a Jewish tradition that identified

would be most persuasive if it could be shown not only that this is an established title but that it is actually *derived* from Habakkuk 2:4 (as "Lord" may have derived primarily from Ps. 110:1, or "Son of man" from Dan. 7:13). Jesus would then be "the Righteous One" *on the basis of* the scriptural claim that "the Righteous One will live by faith". If the christological title has some other scriptural source, however, it would still be possible to argue that this identification is carried over into the interpretation of the Habakkuk text – if Paul's own usage appears to warrant this.

Christian evidence for "the Righteous One" as a christological title is limited. The main passages that have been discussed in this connection are Acts 3:14; 7:52; 22:14; 1 Peter 3:18; and 1 John 2:1. It is striking that allusions to the "Fourth Servant Song" (Isa. 52:13–53:12) occur in close proximity to several of these passages. This would suggest that "the Righteous One" as a christological title may derive from Isaiah 53:10–11 LXX, which tells how God willed

to remove the suffering of his soul, to show him light and to form understanding, to justify the Righteous One who serves many well [δικαιῶσαι δίκαιον εὖ δουλεύοντα πολλοῖς] – and he shall bear their sins.

In spite of the indefinite δίκαιον (rather than τὸν δίκαιον), it is clear that the translator saw here a reference to the Servant, ὁ παῖς μου (52:13).[17]

The Isaianic passage is reflected in at least three of the five references to Jesus as "the Righteous One" listed above:

(1) In Acts 3:14, Peter reminds his hearers of how they "denied the Holy and Righteous One [τὸν ἅγιον καὶ δίκαιον] and asked for a murderer ..." Peter's speech at the Beautiful Gate of the Temple has opened by recounting how the God of the fathers "glorified

---

the expected eschatological deliverer as 'the Righteous One'" (123). It is a problem for Hays that, even if such a tradition existed, it is *not* reflected in the most significant pre-Christian interpretation of Hab. 2:4 itself. The pesherist comments on the three main components of Hab. 2:4b ([1] the righteous one [2] by his faith [3] will live), as follows: "This concerns [1] all who observe the law in the house of Judah, [3] whom God will deliver from the house of judgment [2] on account of their faith in the Teacher of righteousness" (1QpHab. 8.1–3). On this passage, see my *Paul and the Hermeneutics of Faith*, 119–26, where the translation "faith in ..." is defended.

17 Compare Wisdom 2:12–20, where ὁ δίκαιος (vv. 12, 18) understands himself as παῖς κυρίου (v. 13) and is persecuted for his claim. This passage is probably dependent on Isa. 53 and was later understood christologically.

his Servant" (ἐδόξασεν τὸν παῖδα αὐτοῦ, v. 13). The language is obviously derived from the opening of the Fourth Servant Song: "Behold, my Servant shall understand and shall be exalted and greatly glorified" (ἰδοὺ συνήσει ὁ παῖς μου καὶ ὑψωθήσεται καὶ δοξασθήσεται σφόδρα, Isa. 52:13).[18]

(2) In Acts 7:52, Stephen claims that "your fathers ... killed those who spoke beforehand about the coming of the Righteous One [περὶ τῆς ἐλεύσεως τοῦ δικαίου], whom you have now betrayed and murdered".[19] If the reference to the Righteous One is Isaianic, there may be an allusion here to the tradition about the death of Isaiah, sawn in two at the order of King Manasseh.[20] In a Christian addition to the *Martyrdom of Isaiah*, Isaiah is put to death on account of his visions (5:1), which recount in advance the entire sequence of events from incarnation to eschaton (3:13–4:18). The Acts passage may similarly reflect an early Christian appropriation of a prior Jewish tradition of prophetic martyrdoms, such as was later embodied in the *Lives of the Prophets* (where the death of Isaiah retains its pre-eminence).[21] In a Christian context, the fate of the prophet Isaiah now foreshadows the fate of the Righteous One whose coming he announces. In Acts 8:26–35, the central role of Isaiah 53 in

---

[18] Although Hays states that the Isaianic connection here is "much disputed" ("Apocalyptic Hermeneutics", 124), the derivation from Isa. 52:13 could hardly be clearer.

[19] According to Hays, περὶ τῆς ἐλεύσεως τοῦ δικαίου in Acts 7:52 "may echo a well-established tradition of reading Hab. 2:3–4 as a messianic prophecy" ("Apocalyptic Hermeneutics", 125). Hays suggests that the Baptist's reference to Jesus as ὁ ἐρχόμενος (Lk. 7:19) may indicate Luke's familiarity with such a tradition. But ὁ ἐρχόμενος here derives from Ps. 117:26 (ὁ ἐρχόμενος ἐν ὀνόματι κυρίου) rather than Hab. 2:3 (ὅτι ἐρχόμενος ἥξει); cf. Lk. 19:38 and parallels (Mk. 11:9; Matt. 21:9; Jn. 12:13). Hays is quite unable to demonstrate either that non-Pauline references to "the Righteous One" have anything to do with Habakkuk (124–31), or that non-Pauline interpretation of Hab. 2:4b understands this text messianically (131–5, discussing 1QpHab. and Heb.).

[20] Justin, *Dialogue with Trypho*, 120.5; *Martyrdom of Isaiah*, 5.1–16; *Lives of the Prophets*, 1.1. Heb. 11:37 ("they were stoned, they were sawn in two ...") indicates that the tradition of Isaiah's death was extant in the first century. For translations of the prophetic legends, with introductions, see J.H. Charlesworth, ed., *Old Testament Pseudepigrapha* II (London: Darton, Longman & Todd, 1985), 143–76, 379–99.

[21] For this possibility see C.K. Barrett, *The Acts of the Apostles* I (ICC; Edinburgh: T&T Clark, 1994), 376–7. In the *Lives of the Prophets* violent deaths are attributed to Isaiah, Jeremiah, Ezekiel, Micah, Amos, and Zechariah son of Jehoiada.

the encounter between Philip and the Ethiopian confirms its significance for Luke. It should also be noted that, in Acts 7:52 as in 3:14, the reference to Jesus as "the Righteous One" occurs in connection with his death (cf. Lk. 22:47). It is the *suffering* Jesus who is "the Righteous One".

(3) In 1 Peter 3:18, it is said that "Christ suffered once for sins, the righteous for the unrighteous [δίκαιος ὑπὲρ ἀδίκων], so that he might bring us to God". The absence of the article recalls Isaiah 53:11 (δικαιῶσαι δίκαιον); compare also the reference in 1 John 2:1 to Ἰησοῦν Χριστὸν δίκαιον ("Jesus Christ the righteous", or "Jesus Christ Righteous One"). Once again, Jesus is identified as δίκαιον in connection with his death. The possibility of a derivation from Isaiah 53 is strengthened by the extensive use of material from that chapter in 1 Peter 2:21–25. Here we learn that Christ "did not commit sin, nor was deceit found in his mouth" (v. 22), that "he bore our sins" (v. 24), that "by his chastisement you were healed" (v. 24), and that "you were straying like sheep" (v. 25) – a series of almost *verbatim* allusions to Isaiah 53:9, 4 (12), 5, 6. Since the author seeks to apply a broad selection of material from Isaiah 53 to Jesus, the likelihood is that he continues to do so in referring to Jesus as δίκαιον precisely in connection with his death.

The (limited) evidence for "the Righteous One" as a christological title strongly implies a derivation from Isaiah 53:11. There is no indication in these or other relevant passages that [ὁ] δίκαιος is drawn from Habakkuk 2:4 or is influenced by it in any way. If Paul does read this passage christologically, he has done so either on the basis of Isaiah 53:11 or independently. Either the christological reference has been read out of one text into another, or Paul and Luke find different scriptural bases for their identification of Jesus as "the Righteous One". Paul does indeed employ lexical items drawn from Isaiah 53. As I have argued elsewhere, his conviction that Christ died "for us" or "for our sins", and that he was "given up" by God, are dependent on the Fourth Servant Song in its Septuagintal guise. An identification of Jesus as the δίκαιον of Isaiah 53:11 is quite conceivable for Paul. Yet, even if there were any direct evidence for this unsubstantiated possibility, that would not mean that Paul read the *Habakkuk* text messianically. He might have understood Isaiah to refer to the suffering Jesus while still taking Habakkuk to refer to a generic individual who is righteous by faith. To appeal to a hypothetical reading of Isaiah to interpret an actual reading of Habakkuk would do nothing to advance the debate.

(3) "Righteous by faith" or "... will live by faith"?

If Paul reads Habakkuk 2:4 as asserting that "the Righteous One will live by faith", then his "by faith of Christ" formulations must refer to Jesus himself as the exemplar and embodiment of faith, and as such the source of our own righteousness before God. Alternatively, if Paul takes this text to mean that "the-one-who-is-righteous-by-faith will live", then "by faith of Christ" will indicate that faith constitutes the righteousness of the generic individual only insofar as it is oriented towards and grounded in Christ and the saving divine action enacted in him. The reference to Christ is absolutely fundamental in *both* cases, and it is disingenuous to play off a (virtuous) "christocentric" reading against a (bad, protestant) "anthropocentric" one. It is simply a matter of exegesis.[22]

As we have seen, there is no evidence that a prior messianic or christological reading of Habakkuk 2:4 was available to Paul. If he read this text christologically, he was the first to do so; it is the internal evidence of his own usage that must decide. We have to determine at what point Paul *divides* his Habakkuk citation. Does he find one sense-unit in ὁ δίκαιος and another in ἐκ πίστεως ζήσεται? Or does he construe ὁ δίκαιος ἐκ πίστεως as a single sense-unit and treat ζήσεται as an absolute, without object or adverbial qualification? In other words, does ἐκ πίστεως point back to δίκαιος or forward to ζήσεται?[23] The entire

---

[22] It is now customary to answer Bultmann's question, "Is there such a thing as a presuppositionless exegesis?" with a resounding negative, perhaps throwing in a disparaging remark or two about those who are so hermeneutically naïve as to think otherwise. In my view, it is *sometimes* possible and useful to trace an exegetical conclusion back to a prior theological commitment, but by no means *always*. Even where an exegetical conclusion is closely correlated with a theological commitment, it can be as uncertain which led to which as in the well-known case of the chicken and the egg. In the case of the faith-of-Christ formulations, it seems unhelpful to speculate about the "grounds" or "doctrinal presuppositions" on which "resistance to the notion of 'the faith of Jesus' is based" (Johnson, "Romans 3:21–26", 80–1).

[23] The latter reading is found in Heb. 10:38a, where Hab. 2:4b is cited in the form, ὁ δὲ δίκαιός μου ἐκ πίστεως ζήσεται – an adaptation of LXX's ὁ δὲ δίκαιος ἐκ πίστεως μου ζήσεται. In Hebrews, the transposition of the pronoun is intended to secure the reference to the faith or faithfulness of the righteous person rather than of God, in

exegetical debate about the faith-of-Christ formulations is encapsulated in this question.

To answer the question we must turn again to the Pauline usage based on this citation, to see whether Paul associates the phrase ἐκ πίστεως and its derivatives with righteousness or with life. (In a number of cases, of course, the phrase is associated with neither.) And we discover that ἐκ πίστεως is *never* associated with life, yet it is *repeatedly* associated with righteousness or being made righteous. Paul consistently replaces the adjective δίκαιος with the cognate sustantive δικαιοσύνη or the verb δικαιοῦν, yet the basic structure of ὁ δίκαιος ἐκ πίστεως is almost invariably preserved. Cases where the substantive or verb follows the prepositional phrase, thereby diverging from the scriptural order, are indicated below with an asterisk. Underlining is intended to highlight the role of the prophetic δίκαιος ἐκ πίστεως as the template for a range of Pauline locutions:

> ... ἵνα δικαιωθῶμεν ἐκ πίστεως Χριστοῦ (Gal. 2:16b)
>
> * ... ὅτι ἐκ πίστεως δικαιοῖ τὰ ἔθνη ὁ θεός (Gal. 3:8)
>
> * ... ἵνα ἐκ πίστεως δικαιωθῶμεν (Gal. 3:24)
>
> * ... ἐκ πίστεως ἐλπίδα δικαιοσυνης ἀπεκδεχόμεθα (Gal. 5:5)
>
> ... δικαιοσύνη γὰρ θεοῦ ἐν αὐτῷ ἀποκαλύπτεται ἐκ πίστεως εἰς πίστιν (Rom. 1:17)
>
> ... καὶ δικαιουντα τὸν ἐκ πίστεως Ἰησοῦ (Rom. 3:26)
>
> ... ὅς δικαιώσει περιτομὴν ἐκ πίστεως ... (Rom. 3:30)
>
> ... Δικαιωθέντες οὖν ἐκ πίστεως ... (Rom. 5:1)
>
> ... κατέλαβεν δικαιοσύνην, δικαιοσύνην δὲ τὴν ἐκ πίστεως ... (Rom. 9:30)
>
> * ... ἡ δὲ ἐκ πίστεως δικαιοσύνη οὕτως λέγει ... (Rom. 10:6)

On three occasions, the scriptural δίκαιος ἐκ πίστεως also provides the template for statements incorporating διά-formulations:

> ... οὐ δικαιοῦται ἄνθρωπος ἐξ ἔργων νόμου ἐὰν μὴ διὰ πίστεως Ἰησοῦ Χριστοῦ (Gal. 2:16a)

---

preparation for ch. 11. "My righteous one" cannot be understood messianically, since the faith in question is oriented towards "the Coming One" and so cannot be Christ's own faith (Heb. 10:37b = Hab. 2:3b); note also the reference to the possibility of failure ("If he draws back ...", v. 38b), which cannot be referred to Christ. In these text-forms, it is clearly stated that "[my] faith/faithfulness" is the means whereby "[my] righteous one will live". It is precisely Paul's omission of any pronoun that makes it possible that he took his citation to refer to "the one who is righteous by faith".

... μὴ ἔχων ἐμὴν δικαιοσύνην τὴν ἐκ νόμου ἀλλὰ τὴν διὰ πίστεως Χριστοῦ ... (Phil. 3:9)

... δικαιοσύνη δὲ θεοῦ διὰ πίστεως Ἰησοῦ Χριστοῦ ... (Rom. 3:22)

All three cases include longer formulations referring to [Jesus] Christ. In the first two cases, Paul probably selects διά for the faith-formulation because he has already used ἐκ/ἐξ in the Law-formulation. The distinction is purely stylistic (cf. Rom. 3:30); the διὰ πίστεως statements are no less shaped by Habakkuk 2:4 than the ἐκ πίστεως ones.[24] Together, these statements provide a total of thirteen cases, distributed over three letters, in which the prepositional phrase is closely associated with righteousness terminology. In nine of the thirteen cases, even the word order follows the scriptural precedent, with the reference to righteousness or being made righteous preceding the reference to faith. This order is strictly maintained in six of the seven passages from Romans, in keeping perhaps with the formal citation of Habakkuk 2:4 at the outset of the letter. It is also maintained in all five of the relevant "faith of Christ" passages. This remarkable conformity to the Habakkuk text is all the more striking in view of the fact that no two of Paul's own formulations are exactly the same. There are *no* counter-examples in which ἐκ πίστεως is associated with life-terminology rather than with righteousness.[25] And that means there is no evidence that Paul found the assertion that "the Righteous One will live by faith" in Habakkuk, in contrast to overwhelming evidence that he read there that "the-one-who-is-righteous-by-faith will live". As we have seen, the entire debate about Paul's faith-of-Christ formulations hangs on this translation issue.

If further confirmation is needed, it may be found in the very sentence in Galatians 3 in which the Habakkuk citation is embedded:

> But it is clear that by the Law no-one is justified [ἐν νόμῳ οὐδεὶς δικαιοῦται] with God, for "the one who is righteous by faith will live". (Gal. 3:11)

Paul's own negative formulation is constructed on the basis of the positive scriptural formulation as he understands it. ὁ δίκαιος corresponds to οὐδεὶς δικαιοῦται, and ἐκ πίστεως corresponds to ἐν νόμῳ. No one is justified by the Law, for (according to Scripture) it is the person righteous

---

[24] See Campbell, "Meaning", 93–6.

[25] An argument for this might perhaps appeal to (1) ἐν πίστει ζῶ τῇ τοῦ υἱοῦ τοῦ θεοῦ ... (Gal. 2:20); (2) ... ζήσεται ἐν αὐτοῖς (Gal. 3:12). But these passages offer only weak support for "... will live by faith".

by faith who will live. The precision of the antithetical construction recalls the formulations of Galatians 2:16. On the alternative translation of the Habakkuk citation, the antitheses lose their precision. No one is justified by the Law, for (according to Scripture) the Righteous One will live by faith. The symmetry of "justified by Law" and "righteous by faith" has been lost. The immediate context of the citation confirms the evidence of Pauline usage as a whole.

Conclusion

In Galatians as also in Romans, Paul's prepositional faith-formulations all derive from the ἐκ πίστεως of Habakkuk 2:4 which also occurs in variant and extended forms. The extended forms include the disputed faith-of-Christ passages, and the solution to the exegetical disagreement is to be found in the correct translation and interpretation of the Habakkuk citation as Paul understands it. The crucial question is whether to connect "by faith" to "righteous" or to "will live". The latter option results in a christological interpretation according to which "the Righteous One will live by faith". Yet the relevance of the marginal christological title "the Righteous One" is doubtful; it appears to be derived exclusively from Isaiah 53:11 LXX, and there is no evidence that anyone linked it to Habakkuk. Paul's use of the Habakkuk text as the template for his own varied formulations makes it overwhelmingly probable that he reads the text as affirming that "the one who is righteous by faith will live".

In view of these findings, can the subjective genitive reading of the faith-of-Christ formulations still be maintained? It is unlikely that anyone will wish to venture a further translation, according to which "the One who is righteous by faith will live". The only possibility left open is to argue that Habakkuk 2:4 underlies Paul's usage but does not control the substance of his thought. Formally adhering to the scriptural template, his theological ideas take him far beyond it, reaching their most developed form in the faith-of-Christ formulations. While that is not impossible, it is hard to see why Paul remains bound by the formal structure of Habakkuk 2:4 if it no longer serves his theological purpose. This text's fundamental significance in Galatians is retrospectively confirmed by Paul's decision to place it at the head of the theological argument of Romans.

It seems that Paul does *not* argue that we are justified by Christ's own faith or faithful conduct. The claim that he does so argue is based on a mistaken exegesis, supported too often by unsubstantiated claims of theological superiority. There is no reason to suppose that a focus on "our" faith rather than Christ's will inevitably issue in theological disaster. This is a faith that has its origin and content in God's reconciling act in the incarnate, crucified, and risen Jesus – an act whose scope is extended to us through the agency of the Holy Spirit in the proclaimed word and the communal and individual acknowledgment it evokes. Pauline faith is not self-generated or self-sufficient; it is not a "condition" of salvation; it is not a mere mental disposition; it is not a sanctuary for the solitary individual. It has to do with the human participation intended in the divine reconciling act, which does not reduce its objects to passivity but reconstitutes them as agents and subjects within the overarching, all-embracing sphere of grace.

10

Πίστις Χριστοῦ as an Eschatological Event

PRESTON M. SPRINKLE

Introduction: Reflections on a Journey through the Πίστις Χριστοῦ Debate

I was first introduced to the πίστις Χριστοῦ debate a number of years ago when I was searching for a topic for my master's thesis. Πίστις Χριστοῦ: Are we justified by "faith in Christ" or by "Christ's (own) faith(fulness)"? I initially swung from an objective genitive position, "faith *in* Christ", to a subjective genitive position, "faith *of* Christ", primarily because of its christological emphasis. However, I began to see some problems with this view. While I resonated (and still resonate) with its accent on divine agency in justification, I struggled with some of the exegetical implications. In particular, it seems that if you take ἐκ/ διὰ πίστεως Χριστοῦ as referring to Christ's faith, then to be consistent you would have to take the more abbreviated ἐκ πίστεως phrases as referring to Christ's faith as well (Gal. 3:7, 8, 9, 11, 12, 24). But this only created more problems than solutions. Furthermore, the christological reading seemed to require that Habakkuk's "Righteous One" who "lives ἐκ πίστεως" (Hab. 2:4) is Jesus. But again, despite the fascinating studies by Doug Campbell and Richard Hays,[1] I was not convinced.

And so I swung back to the other side. Πίστεως Χριστοῦ, then, must be interpreted as an objective genitive, referring to a person's faith in Christ. But here I faced an even greater problem. In Romans 1:17 and 3:21–22, πίστεως and πίστεως Χριστοῦ are the means, or grounds, of the eschatological manifestation of God's righteousness. So, for instance, Paul says in Romans 3:21–22:

---

[1] Campbell, *"Crux Interpretum"*; Hays, "Righteous One"; see also the recent work by Heliso, *Pistis and the Righteous One*.

But now at the turn of the ages (νυνὶ δέ) ... the righteousness of God (δικαιοσύνη θεοῦ) has been manifested (πεφανέρωται) ... by means of a person's faith in Jesus Christ (διὰ πίστεως Ἰησοῦ Χριστοῦ) unto all who believe in Jesus. (Rom. 3:21–22, my paraphrase)

With most interpreters of the post-Käsemann era I agreed that δικαιοσύνη θεοῦ meant something like God's saving power,[2] and so the glaring questing was this: Is a person's faith the means through which God's saving power is apocalyptically revealed? Does faith in Jesus manifest God's saving power, here at the turn of the ages (νυνὶ δέ, Rom. 3:21)? While some of course say "yes",[3] I thought (and still think) that this puts a tremendous amount of stress on the human agent in the event of God's cosmic act of redemption.

While frustrated at my stalemate position between the subjective and objective genitive views, apparently the only two options, I came across the following footnote in an article by Sam Williams:

For those readers who cannot accept the view that *pistis Christou* means Christ's own faith but who recognize the weaknesses of the traditional translation "faith in Christ", I offer an alternative: when Paul wishes to stress that even the capacity to accept the grace of God coming finally, from beyond man's own power of willing and doing, he speaks of the source of eschatological faith, *pistis Christou*, which might be rendered "Christ-faith".[4]

Although I did not quite understand what Williams was talking about, I clung to the hope that there was perhaps "another option to the πίστις Χριστοῦ debate".[5]

Having now returned to this debate a few years later, I am very happy to see that a number of good scholars have taken a view along the lines of Williams' suggestion – and many of them actually proposed it long

---

[2] See recently Michael F. Bird, *The Saving Righteousness of God: Studies on Paul, Justification, and the New Perspective* (Carlisle: Paternoster, 2007), 6–39.

[3] See the response in Matlock, "Detheologizing ΠΙΣΤΙΣ ΧΡΙΣΤΟΥ", 22; cf. Taylor, "From Faith to Faith".

[4] Williams, "Righteousness of God", 266, n.111.

[5] I have since presented two papers with this title: "Another Option to the *Pistis Chistou* Debate" – the first at the regional ETS meeting in Sun Valley, CA (April 2002), and the second at the Tyndale Fellowship meeting in Cambridge, England (June 2004). Neither paper, however, proved to be very convincing to my hearers!

before Williams. What is really quite remarkable is that this "third view" has gone virtually unnoticed in the πίστις Χριστοῦ debate.[6] This may be because most of the "third view" advocates have written in German (or Japanese), while the vast majority of πίστις Χριστοῦ discussions have been in English. In any case, I would like to introduce this "third view" to the discussion and suggest that it is a view worthy of consideration in the πίστις Χριστοῦ debate.

Survey of the "Third View"

Ernst Lohmeyer[7]

Lohmeyer was the first to assert a "third view" of πίστις Χριστοῦ, though his main concern is with πίστις and not primarily the πίστις Χριστοῦ construction. He argues that πίστις in Paul does not refer to the believing experience of the individual but to the objective events upon which this believing experience is directed.[8] Faith is primarily a metaphysical principle, or an objective and transcendent power, and only secondarily the experience of believers. The πίστις Χριστοῦ construction itself is used to speak of faith in its primary sense of a principle that first exists outside humankind.[9] This is why, says Lohmeyer, "faith" and "Christ" are brought together in the πίστις Χριστοῦ construction. Πίστις Χριστοῦ "is not only the faith which Christ has, also not only

---

[6] In using the term "third view" I do not include those who say that πίστις Χριστοῦ refers to *both* Christ's faith and ours (e.g., Morna Hooker; and Sam Williams, to some extent), nor those, following A. Deißmann, who argue for a "mystical genitive". The common ground among "third view" advocates is that they understand πίστις Χριστοῦ to refer to an event (Christ-event) or entity (gospel message) that is outside the subjective genitive or objective genitive options.

[7] *Grundlagen paulinischer Theologie* (BHT 1; Tübingen: Mohr Siebeck, 1929).

[8] "... das Wort [i.e., *pistis*] weniger die Fülle des Erlebens bezeichnet ... , sondern starker einen gegenständlichen Sachverhalt, auf den das gläubige Ich sich richtet und in dem es sich gründet, daß es ein Prinzip des gläubigen Erlebens, nicht so sehr die monadisch erfüllte Tat dieses Erlebens meint" (*Grundlagen*, 116). Lohmeyer bases this on the fact that the noun, πίστις, is used twice as often (96×) as the verb, πιστεύειν, in Paul (40×), and that the noun is never attached to personal pronouns such as "my" or "our". Moreover, the phrase "I believe" in the Lutheran sense is never found in Paul (see further, *Grundlagen*, 115–16; cf. Wolfgang Schenk, "Die Gerechtigkeit Gottes und der Glaube Christi", *TLZ* 97 [1972]: 161–74 [171]).

[9] *Grundlagen*, 117–18.

that which he gives, but, above all, the faith which *is himself*".[10] Faith is revelation in the same way that Christ is revelation, and both – Christ and faith – are gifts of God.[11]

While Lohmeyer underscored Paul's understanding of faith as an objective event (see esp. Gal. 3:23–25), his description of πίστις Χριστοῦ lacks exegetical precision and his depiction of πίστις Χριστοῦ in modern philosophical terms (metaphysical principle) has been criticized.[12] But it is his study of πίστις that will lay the groundwork for later "third view" proponents.

Fritz Neugebauer[13]

Fritz Neugebauer follows Lohmeyer in his view of πίστις in Paul and argues, against Bultmann, that faith is primarily an objective eschatological event, not a subjective anthropological decision.[14] Paul does not say, for example, "have faith", but "stand firm in the faith".[15] Neugebauer's main contribution is his analysis of Paul's "in Christ" formula in relation to πίστις. He sees no essential difference in Paul's use of ἐκ πίστεως and his use of ἐν Χριστῷ. "ἐκ πίστεως and διὰ πίστεως correspond entirely to the ἐν Χριστῷ [formula], and οἱ ἐκ πίστεως means nothing other than οἱ ἐν Χριστῷ."[16]

Neugebauer actually speaks very little about the πίστις Χριστοῦ construction in particular, but his view of Pauline πίστις has implications

---

[10] "Es ist nicht nur der Glaube, den Christus hat, auch nicht nur der, den er gibt, sondern vor allem der Glaube, der *er selber ist*" (*Grundlagen*, 121, emphasis mine).

[11] Lohmeyer points to passages in Paul where "faith" and "Christ" are used as virtual synonyms (e.g., Rom. 1:12; 15:30; 2 Cor. 1:5; Rom. 10:8, 17; Lohmeyer, *Grundlagen*, 121, n.2).

[12] Cf. Fritz Neugebauer: "Man muß E. Lohmeyer hier besser verstehen, als er sich ausgedrückt hat. So darf ich vorausschicken, daß man das, was E. Lohmeyer mit „metaphysischem Prinzip" sagen will, besser als eschatologiesches Geschehen bezeichnet, sofern es in diesem Zusammenhang darum geht, daß der Glaube kommt und geoffenbart wird" (Neugebauer, *In Christus = En Christoi: Eine Untersuchung zum paulinischen Glaubenverständnis* [Göttingen: Vandenhoeck & Ruprecht, 1961], 156). See also Schließer, *Abraham's Faith*, 48–9.

[13] *In Christus*.

[14] *In Christus*, 164, 167; against Bultmann, see 157–71.

[15] "Es ist typisch für Paulus, daß er nie sagt: πιστεύετε!, sondern daß er den Korinthern höchstens zurufen kann: στήκετε ἐν τῇ πίστει, ἐν παντὶ περισσεύετε, πίστει καὶ λόγῳ und ἑαυτοὺς πειράζετε εἰ ἐστὲ ἐν τῇ πίστει" (Neugebauer, *In Christus*, 167).

[16] "ἐκ πίστεως und διὰ πίστεως entsprechen also völlig dem ἐν Χριστῷ, und οἱ ἐκ πίστεως bedeutet nichts anderes als οἱ ἐν Χριστῷ" (Neugebauer, *In Christus*, 172).

for it. He critiques the subjective genitive view[17] in passing and suggests that πίστις Χριστοῦ corresponds to the πιστεύειν εἰς construction.[18] This would seem to suggest that he holds to an objective genitive view. However, he believes that πίστις is directly related to the Christ-event and even endorses Lohmeyer's view of πίστις Χριστοῦ – faith is Christ himself. In another passage he says that the πίστις Χριστοῦ construction, like the shorter ἐκ πίστεως construction, essentially corresponds to ἐν Χριστῷ. Πίστις Χριστοῦ, then, is the event through which the promises of God are confirmed (Gal. 3:22; 2 Cor. 1:20)[19] and the sphere in which the benefits of this event are bestowed.

Hermann Binder[20]

Hermann Binder's reading of πίστις Χριστοῦ comes close to that of Lohmeyer, though he failed to draw upon Lohmeyer's work.[21] Binder conceives of πίστις as a new salvific reality that involves both God and humans disclosed in the history of salvation through the Christ-event. It is "the event coming from God in the new covenant, which has the character of a transsubjective power, of a divine objective event".[22] With regard to πίστις Χριστοῦ in particular, Binder renders the phrase as a *genetivus identificationis;*[23] πίστις Χριστοῦ is Paul's shorthand description of the Christ-event.

Wolfgang Schenk[24]

Wolfgang Schenk's reading of πίστις Χριστοῦ draws heavily on the studies of Binder and Lohmeyer. He argues with exegetical vigour for

---

[17] Neugebauer, *In Christus*, 168, n.69.

[18] Neugebauer, *In Christus*, 167–8; cf. 172.

[19] Neugebauer, *In Christus*, 172.

[20] *Der Glaube bei Paulus* (Berlin: Evangelische Verlagsanstalt, 1968). I have been unable to locate a copy of Binder's book – either in the UK or here in Ohio. The following brief analysis will rely on other scholars who have summed up his thesis.

[21] See also Schenk, "Die Gerechtigkeit Gottes", 163; Schließer, *Abraham's Faith*, 50, n.327.

[22] "Πίστις ist bei Paulus ... das von Gott herkommende Geschehen im Neuen Bund, das den Charakter einer transsubjektiven Größe, einer göttlichen Geschehenswirklichkeit hat" (Binder, *Glaube*, 5, quoted in Schenk, "Die Gerechtigkeit Gottes", 163).

[23] Binder, *Glaube*, 61, 63, cited in Schließer, *Abraham's Faith*, 52, n.345.

[24] "Die Gerechtigkeit Gottes", 161–74; idem, *Die Philipperbriefe des Paulus* (Stuttgart: Kohlhammer, 1984), 310–14.

a "third view" of the phrase, examining three passages in Romans – 1:5, 1:16–17, and, most significant for our discussion, 3:22 (πίστις Χριστοῦ). He agrees with Lohmeyer and Binder that πίστις Χριστοῦ is conceived primarily as an objective reality, but he states more precisely that it refers to the gospel message and its content. "Πίστις in the Genitive (resp. Dative) is the faith-message, whose content is Christ. Πίστις Χριστοῦ is the gospel of Christ as the message which demands recognition."[25] So Schenk renders Χριστοῦ as an epexegetical genitive – the gospel of faith, which is Christ.[26] The exegetical foundation for this reading comes from Romans 1:16–17. Here the gospel, as the power of God, reveals the righteousness of God to believers. This revelation is underscored by the cryptic phrase ἐκ πίστεως εἰς πίστιν. The righteousness of God is revealed ἐκ πίστεως – "by the gospel" – εἰς πίστιν – "unto all believers". This same structure is repeated in Romans 3:21–22, where the righteousness of God is revealed ἐκ πίστεως Χριστοῦ (= ἐκ πίστεως, 1:17) εἰς πάντας τοὺς πιστεύοντας. Πίστις Χριστοῦ, as the gospel, is the means by which God's eschatological saving power is revealed to believers.[27]

David Hay [28]

David Hay argues that ancient Greek, Jewish, and Christian literature often uses πίστις "in the sense of 'pledge' or 'evidence' on which subjective confidence or belief may appropriately be based".[29] According to Hay, Philo uses πίστις as "pledge" 7.1% (11×) and "evidence" 52.6% (82×) of the time. Josephus uses the term as "pledge" 29.7% (58×) and as "evidence" 10.3% (20×) of the time.[30] Hay says that while "scholars

---

[25] "Πίστις im Genitiv (bzw. Dativ) ist die Glaubensbotschaft, deren Inhalt Christus ist. πίστις Χριστοῦ ist das Evangelium Christi als die Anerkennung heischende Botschaft" ("Die Gerechtigkeit Gottes", 168; cf. 170).

[26] In his Philippians commentary, Schenk states perhaps more clearly that the πίστις Χριστοῦ construction refers to both the gospel message and its content (*Die Philipperbriefe*, 312).

[27] He paraphrases Rom. 3:22: "Die auf seine ganze Schöpfung zielende Heilsmacht Gottes, die uns total Unqualifizierte in diesen Dienst einbezieht und dafür qualifiziert, wird geschichtlich wirksam auf Grund der eröffnenden glaubensstiftenden Christusbotschaft für alle, die auf diese Botschaft hörend eingehen" ("Die Gerechtigkeit Gottes", 171).

[28] "*Pistis*".

[29] Hay, "*Pistis*", 461.

[30] Hay, "*Pistis*", 463.

remarked that Philo can use πίστις to mean 'evidence' or 'proof', the sheer frequency of this sense of the term in his writings seems to have escaped notice".[31] He then proposes that we should understand Paul's use of πίστις in the same purview as Philo (along with ancient Greek literature and Josephus). Jesus, according to Paul, is the objective grounds, or pledge, upon which human subjective faith is based and made possible.[32]

In understanding πίστις as the "ground for faith", Hay interprets πίστις Χριστοῦ as a genitive of apposition – faith which is Christ. So, for instance, he translates Galatians 3:22, "... in order that the promise that depends on the *ground for faith* (ἐκ πίστεως) that is Jesus Christ (Χριστοῦ) might be given to those who believe".[33] In Galatians 3:22; 2:20, and elsewhere in Paul, the emphasis "is on faith not as a general human capacity but as a reaction made possible 'from outside' believers by the disclosure of a crucified Messiah".[34]

Charles H. Cosgrove [35]

Charles Cosgrove argues for a reading of πίστις Χριστοῦ that is similar to that of many of the interpreters above, though he gives no indication that he has read any of them. Cosgrove suggests that Paul uses the πίστις Χριστοῦ construction i in Galatians 2:16 and 3:22 "to refer to the whole of the eschatological reality of salvation inaugurated by God in Jesus Christ".[36] The terms "faith" and "Christ" are joined to describe "a single eschatological reality"[37] and serve as a "metonymy for God's act in Jesus Christ seen as a whole",[38] a reading that

---

[31] Hay, *"Pistis"*, 464.

[32] Hay, *"Pistis"*, 472. A similar understanding is suggested by Albert Vanhoye, "Πίστις Χριστοῦ: Fede in Christo o affidabilità di Cristo", *Bib* 80 (1999): 1–21 (cited in Hung-Sik Choi, "Πίστις in Galatians 5:5–6", 469).

[33] Hay, *"Pistis"*, 475; cf. his interpretation of Gal. 2:20.

[34] Hay, *"Pistis"*, 475.

[35] *The Cross and the Spirit: A Study in the Argument and Theology of Galatians* (Macon, GA: Mercer University Press, 1988).

[36] Cosgrove, *The Cross*, 56. Don Garlington takes a similar view, though he only states it in passing: *"The Obedience of Faith:" A Pauline Phrase in Historical Context* (WUNT II.38; Tübingen: Mohr Siebeck, 1991), 256, n.5; idem, *Faith, Obedience, and Perseverance: Aspects of Paul's Letter to the Romans* (WUNT II.79; Tübingen: Mohr Siebeck, 1994), 19, n.48; idem, "Role Reversal and Paul's Use of Scripture in Galatians 3:10–13", *JSNT* (1997): 85–121 (89, 112).

[37] Cosgrove, *The Cross*, 56.

[38] Cosgrove, *The Cross*, 57.

corresponds with the views of Binder and Schenk, above. Cosgrove assumes this reading throughout his book, but he fails to wrestle with any of the grammatical or exegetical issues which surround the πίστις Χριστοῦ debate.[39]

Shuji Ota [40]

Shuji Ota – a Japenese scholar who brings a refreshing non-western perspective to the πίστις Χριστοῦ debate – has written four articles on πίστις Χριστοῦ (three of which are in Japanese and one in English).[41] Ota is influenced heavily by David Hay's study mentioned above. With Hay, Ota argues for an objective sense of πίστις connoting "an *objective dispensation or system of salvation by God*", "a superindividual/ collective-communal reality rather than individual faith of the believer", or, in its most comprehensive sense, "a collective communal reality of God's grace that consists of (the faith of) believers, (the faithfulness) of believed Christ/God, and the word of proclamation that creates their relationship".[42]

With regard to πίστις Χριστοῦ, Ota interprets πίστις Χριστοῦ as a subjective genitive, but his understanding is different from previous subjective genitive proposals. Πίστις refers to Christ's faithfulness – not in relation to God, but in relation to human beings. Πίστις Χριστοῦ "refers to *Christ's faithfulness to humanity*, i.e., in the sense of Christ's being steadfast, truthful, and trustworthy as God's Christ". "By the expression πίστις Χριστοῦ Paul placed Christ on the believed or God's side."[43] As I understand Ota's view, πίστις does not refer to Christ's *personal* faithfulness (i.e., unto death, etc.) but to Christ, or the Christ-event, as the objective grounds, which proves God's faithfulness to humanity. As Christians believe in this event, they believe in πίστις Χριστοῦ – God's faithful act toward humanity.

---

[39] Cosgrove, *The Cross*, 56–8.

[40] "Absolute Use of *ΠΙΣΤΙΣ* and *ΠΙΣΤΙΣ ΧΡΙΣΤΟΥ* in Paul", *AJBI* 23 (1997): 64–82.

[41] The three articles in Japanese are: "πίστις Ἰησοῦ Χριστοῦ – Consideration Based on Survey of Uses of πίστις and πιστεύειν in LXX, OT Pseudepigrapha, and Philo", *Seishogakuu Ronshu* 26 (1993): 132–63; idem, "*Pistis* of Jesus Christ in Galatians", *Nihon-no-Sishogaku* 1 (1995): 123–46; idem, "Structure of Pauline *Pistis*", *Shinyakagaku Kenkyu* 24 (1996): 1–12.

[42] Ota, "Absolute Use", 76. Πίστις "indicates a superindividual, collective-communal reality which works as a new dispensation for salvation" ("Absolute Use", 78).

[43] Ota, "Absolute Use", 80.

Karl Friedrich Ulrichs [44]

The most recent and comprehensive treatment of πίστις Χριστοῦ is by Karl Ulrichs, who argues that neither the subjective genitive nor the objective genitive view can rightly account for Paul's meaning. By examining all the πίστις Χριστοῦ references in Paul – including the neglected 1 Thessalonians 1:3[45] – Ulrichs underscores the close connection between πίστις Χριστοῦ and Paul's participatory soteriology. Paul often describes the relationship between Christ and the believer as "in Christ" (ἐν Χριστῷ), and then subsequently develops his thought with πίστις terminology. It is understandable, then, that the complex and compact πίστις Χριστοῦ phrase corresponds to the believer's participation in Christ.[46] With πίστις Χριστοῦ, Paul brings together different soteriological models (justification by faith, participation in Christ) in one compact phrase to refer to the believer's existence in Christ.

Benjamin Schließer [47]

Another important recent work, published just prior to Ulrichs' book, is Benny Schließer's dissertation from Fuller Seminary. Schließer also wants to understand πίστις Χριστοῦ as an objective event within the purview of Lohmeyer, Binder, Schenk, and others above. For instance, he endorses the general direction of Lohmeyer but does not like the term "metaphysical principle" as a description of πίστις.[48] Instead, he suggests other categories: ἐκ πίστεως refers to a "universal-eschatological sphere of power, new salvation historical reality, and new ground and possibility of existence".[49] With regard to πίστις Χριστοῦ, he says:

> [T]he alternatives "objective" or "subjective" cannot convey satisfactorily the complexity of the Greek genitive in the phrase in question. Πίστις Χριστοῦ is "subjective" in that faith has its origin in Christ, in what God has

---

[44] *Christusglaube.*
[45] Μνημονεύοντες ὑμῶν τοῦ ἔργου τῆς πίστεως καὶ τοῦ κόπου τῆς ἀγάπης καὶ τῆς ὑπομονῆς τῆς ἐλπίδος τοῦ κυρίου ἡμῶν Ἰησοῦ Χριστοῦ; see Ulrichs, *Christusglaube*, 71–93.
[46] *Christusglaube*, 251.
[47] *Abraham's Faith.*
[48] *Abraham's Faith*, 245.
[49] *Abraham's Faith*, 245, specifically in reference to Rom. 1:17.

done in Christ, and so belongs to Christ – but not in its denoting Christ's character. It is "objective" in that it has its goal in Christ, in what God has done in Christ pro nobis, and so also belongs to Christ – but not in signifying Christ as a motionless, disposable object.[50]

In terms of grammatical categories, *genetivus relationis* is perhaps best: "Faith relates to Christ insofar as it only exists in relation to Christ – faith came with Christ, and it establishes a relation to Christ – we come to faith."[51] Christ is the "origin, content, and goal of faith".[52] "[T]he concept πίστις Χριστοῦ describes not only Christ's bringing about faith in his coming, but also the resultant state of those who receive that faith and are called 'believers'."[53]

Schließer develops this understanding of πίστις exegetically from Romans 1:17 and 3:21–4:25. The enigmatic ἐκ πίστεως εἰς πίστιν serves as a template for "the salvation-historical event of faith" – ἐκ πίστεως – and the appropriation of this event by all who believe – εἰς πίστιν.[54] Paul develops this structure in Romans 3:21–22 (cf. Schenk), and in Romans 3:21–4:25. God apocalyptically reveals his righteousness ἐκ πίστεως (Rom. 3:21–22a) and it is this revelation that is appropriated εἰς πίστιν (Rom. 3:22b, εἰς πάντες τοὺς πιστεύοντας; 4:1–25).[55]

Summary

The two commonalities I see among "third view" interpreters are: (1) they all view πίστις Χριστοῦ as a *singular entity* rather than focusing on the individual lexemes πίστις and Χριστοῦ; and (2) they all view πίστις Χριστοῦ as something objective – that is, something that is outside (though not wholly unrelated to) the realm of a person's response to God – whether that person be a believer or Jesus. While all proponents of the "third view" agree on these, we can probably distinguish the following three variations in their understanding of πίστις Χριστοῦ:

---

[50] *Abraham's Faith*, 263, following Käsemann.
[51] *Abraham's Faith*, 263; cf. 277. Schließer understands the phrase "righteousness of God" along the same lines. "[B]oth 'God-righteousness' and 'Christ-faith' are salvation-historical realities having power-character, but both also contain within themselves the dimensions of individual participation and appropriation, hence having gift-character" (*Abraham's Faith*, 277).
[52] *Abraham's Faith*, 415.
[53] *Abraham's Faith*, 277.
[54] *Abraham's Faith*, 246.
[55] *Abraham's Faith*, 247–8.

1. Πίστις Χριστοῦ = content of the gospel (the Christ-event)
2. Πίστις Χριστοῦ = the preached gospel (the message about the Christ-event)
3. Πίστις Χριστοῦ = the sphere of salvation created by the gospel (i.e., the church).

While the third option may have some merit, especially seen in Paul's correlation between πίστις Χριστοῦ and ἐν Χριστῷ (Gal. 2:16–17; 3:26; cf. 3:14), a combination between the first and second options, to my mind, carries the most weight.[56]

As a preliminary point, we may note that understanding πίστις Χριστοῦ along these lines has a theological advantage over some of the difficulties of the objective genitive reading without embracing a subjective genitive reading. For instance, as I stated in the introduction, my initial difficulty with the objective genitive reading is that it makes a human act the means by which God's righteousness (his saving power) is revealed. But if ἐκ πίστεως (1:16) and διὰ πίστεως Χριστοῦ (3:22) refer to an objective event outside the anthropological sphere (i.e., the Christ-event, God's act in Christ, the gospel, etc.), then we have a reading that is, to my mind, more in tune with Paul's discourse:

> But now at the turn of the ages (νυνὶ δέ) ... the righteousness of God (δικαιοσύνη θεοῦ) has been manifested (πεφανέρωται) ... through the gospel (or "Christ-event", διὰ πίστεως Ἰησοῦ Χριστοῦ) unto all who believe in Jesus. (Rom. 3:21–22, my paraphrase)

This objective event is then depicted in more detail in the atoning sacrifice of Christ in Romans 3:24–26a. So, then, the means through which God's redeeming activity is manifested is the gospel and its content (i.e., the Christ-event). Now whether or not the "third view" can satisfy the hearts of our grammarians, or can answer more exegetical questions than it raises – or whether or not it can even come up with an adequate translation (!) – remains to be seen. But, at the very least, it does seem to resonate with Paul's theological perspective.

---

[56] With Hofius, the content of the gospel and its proclamation are not to be sharply distinguished. "Weil das gepredigte Evangelium – als Gottes eigenes Wort – »Gottes Kraft zur Rettung für jeden Glaubenden« ist, deshalb erweist sich die Predigt selbst als das ausgezeichnete Werkzeug, durch das Gott den Glaubenden die Rettung bringt" (Hofius, "Wort Gottes", 153–4); cf. Schenk, *Die Philipperbriefe*, 312.

In the remainder of this essay, I would like to: (1) look at two passages in Galatians which might support a "third view" reading (Gal. 3:2–5 and 3:22–26); and then (2) look briefly at the Greek Fathers to see how incorporating the "third view" in the discussion may help further our understanding of πίστις Χριστοῦ.

The "Third View" in Galatians

The first of the two passages we will look at in this section does not actually contain the πίστις Χριστοῦ construction, yet it has been shown to be important for the debate.[57] While πίστις Χριστοῦ is not used, πίστις is (ἀκοῆς πίστεως), and it is contrasted with "works of Law" (ἔργων νόμου) as it was in Galatians 2:16 (cf. Rom. 3:21–22; similarly Phil. 3:9).

> I only wish to learn this from you; *did you receive the Spirit by works of law or by a <u>report</u> <u>of faith</u>* (ἐξ ἔργων νόμου τὸ πνεῦμα ἐλάβετε ἢ ἐξ ἀκοῆς πίστεως)? Thus are you so foolish, having begun by the Spirit are you now being perfected by the flesh? Have you suffered such things in vain – if indeed it was in vain? Therefore, the one who supplies you with the Spirit and works miracles among you, (does he do it) *by works of law or by a <u>report</u> <u>of faith</u>* (ἐξ ἔργων νόμου ἢ ἐξ ἀκοῆς πίστεως)?

The difficulty lies in the meaning of ἀκοῆς πίστεως, which Paul contrasts on two occasions with "works of Law". Richard Hays has conveniently summarized the different interpretive options:[58] ἀκοῆς can mean: (1) act of hearing; or (2) that which is heard, a report. Πίστεως can mean: (1) act of believing; or (2) that which is believed, the gospel. These options bear four interpretive possibilities for ἀκοῆς πίστεως:

(1) "hearing with faith"
(2) "hearing the gospel".[59]

In both instances, ἀκοῆς is rendered "hearing". However, if we take ἀκοή as "message", then we can render the phrase:

---

[57] See, e.g., Debbie Hunn, "*Pistis Christou* in Galatians 2:16: Clarification from 3:1–6", *TynBul* 57 (2006): 23–33.

[58] See Hays, *The Faith of Jesus Christ*, 128.

[59] So F. Mussner renders the phrase: "aufgrund der gehorsamen Annahme der Glaubenspredigt" (*Der Galaterbrief* [HTKNT 9; Freiburg: Herder, 1974], 207 cited in Hays, *The Faith of Jesus Christ*, 127).

(3) "the message that enables, or demands, faith"
(4) "the gospel-message".

These last two options are the most probable in light of the meaning of ἀκοή, which is best rendered as "message", not "hearing". This is the dominant meaning in the LXX, and especially in prophetic literature.[60] This meaning is further supported by Paul's own use of the term. In Romans 10:16–17 ἀκοή clearly means a "message", a meaning derived from Isaiah 53:1, "Lord, who has believed our *message* (ἀκοῇ)." Paul previously used ἀκοή to refer to the gospel message in 1 Thessalonians 2:13, "Therefore we give thanks to God unceasingly, because having received the *word of God's message* (λόγον ἀκοῆς … τοῦ θεοῦ) from us, you received it not as a word of man but what is really is, the word of God which effectively works in you who believe." Moreover, in Galatians 3:1 Paul begins his argument by reminding the Galatians of the content of the gospel message; it involved a dramatic narration of the Christ-event ("… before whose eyes Jesus Christ was publicly proclaimed as crucified").[61] We are "to understand Paul here as describing his preaching to the Galatians under the figure of a public announcement or placarding of Jesus before them".[62] So ἀκοη is best rendered as "message".

But what does πίστεως refer to here? While option three is certainly possible, it is difficult to read the sense of "demands" or "enables" out of the genitival connection. The gospel of course demands faith, and it is possible that it even elicits it, but these concepts are not explicitly stated. Option four, however, has more merit since Paul has explicitly referred to the gospel message as "the faith" (the first use of πίστις in the letter) in Galatians 1:23: "only they have heard that the one who once persecuted us is now preaching *the faith* (τὴν πίστιν) which he once tried to destroy". "The faith" refers to the gospel *message*, and a few verses earlier (Gal. 1:15–16), Paul himself says that he has been commissioned

---

[60] The term occurs 50 times in the LXX and can have the meaning of "hearing" – usually translating an infinitive absolute in the Heb. ("you shall surely hear …", Exod. 15:26; 19:5; 22:22; 23:22 [2×]; Deut. 11:13, 22; 15:5; 28:1, 2; Job 37:2). It is sometimes used with "ear" to mean "hearing", "sound" (Jer. 38:18; cf. 27:43), and "ear(s)" (2 Macc. 15:39). The term also means "report" or "message", and this is the most common use in prophetic literature (Isa. 52:7; 53:1; Jer. 6:24; 10:27; 27:43; 38:18; 44:5; Ezek. 16:56; Dan. 11:44 [2×]; Hos. 7:12; Obad. 1:1; Nah. 1:12; Hab. 3:2). For non-prophetic texts, see Exod. 23:1; 1 Sam. 2:24 (2×); 2 Sam. 13:30; 1 Kgs. 2:28; 10:7 // 2 Chron. 9:6; Ps. 111:7.

[61] See Martyn, *Galatians*, 283.

[62] R. Longenecker, *Galatians*, 100–1.

to preach *Christ* (lit., him) (ἵνα εὐαγγελίζωμαι αὐτόν). Both πίστις and Christ, or "him", are used to describe the saving message about an objective event – the death and resurrection of Jesus (cf. 1:4, 11–12; cf. "the word of *faith*" (Rom. 10:8) and "the word of *Christ*" (Rom. 10:17). Πίστις does not refer to the believer's response to the gospel, but rather to the gospel itself. In short, Paul sums up what he said about the gospel in 3:1 with the phrase ἀκοῆς πίστεως, the "message of faith" (3:2, 5), a usage not far from his initial reference to πίστις in 1:23.

If ἀκοῆς πίστεως refers to the message whose content is Christ (cf. 3:1), and in light of the unambiguous designation of that message with πίστις in 1:23, then there is perhaps some credibility in re-examining Galatians 2:16 (and 2:20) with this view as a legitimate possibility. This certainly does not solve the debate, but it is at least suggestive that there is another option that has not been sufficiently considered.

The next passage in Galatians where the "third view" may gain a hearing is in Galatians 3:22–26.

> But the Scripture has shut up all things under sin, so that the promise *by Jesus Christ-faith* (ἐκ πίστεως Ἰησοῦ Χριστοῦ) might be given to those who believe.
>
> But before *this faith* came, we were kept in custody under the law, being shut up to *this faith* which was later to be apocalyptically revealed (ἀποκαλυφθῆναι). Therefore the law has become our *paidagogos* until Christ, that we may be justified *by faith*. But now that *this faith* has come, we are no longer under a *paidagogos*. For you are all sons of God in Christ Jesus, through *this faith*. (Gal. 3:22–26)

This passage is significant for the πίστις Χριστοῦ debate since the five references to πίστις in 3:23–26 are anaphoric – they all refer back to the πίστις of the πίστις Χριστοῦ construction in 3:22. The meaning that we give to the πίστις Χριστοῦ construction in 3:22, then, must be in the purview of what πίστις means in 3:23–26.

Objective genitive interpreters have a hard time reconciling the πίστις Χριστοῦ phrase in 3:22 with the following references to πίστις in 3:23–26. For instance, Dunn maintains an objective genitive of 3:22 and agrees that the references to πίστις in 3:23 and following are anaphoric, yet he argues that the latter "coming of faith" is the same "faith in Christ" of 3:22.[63] Maintaining an objective genitive

---

[63] Dunn, *Galatians*, 200.

understanding of πίστις in 3:23–26 is difficult, however, in light of the terms associated with πίστις. Not only does πίστις "come" (3:23, 25), but it is "apocalyptically revealed" (ἀποκαλυφθῆναι, 3:23b). The choice of verbs in verses 23–25 (esp. ἀποκαλύπτω) makes it difficult to understand πίστις as the religious disposition, the decision, or response of an individual believer.[64]

Ronald Fung, another objective genitive advocate, also believes that the references to πίστις in 3:23–26 refer back to the πίστις Χριστοῦ phrase. Unlike Dunn, however, Fung believes that πίστις takes on a different nuance in 3:23 and following, where it is "identical to the coming of Christ" and the "dispensation of faith" that is inaugurated with Christ.[65] But this is not very consistent. To say that πίστις refers to one's trust in Christ, or one's "subjective means of appropria[ting]" sonship with Christ,[66] is quite different from saying that it refers to the coming of Christ itself. While the objective genitive interpretation of πίστις Χριστοῦ may be a possible way to understand 3:22, it runs into difficulty in 3:23–26.

The subjective genitive view rests on firmer ground, especially in light of the parallel between 3:19 and 3:23:

> Why the law then? It was added because of transgressions, *until the seed should come* (ἄχρις οὗ ἔλθῃ τὸ σπέρμα) to whom the promise was made. (Gal. 3:19)

> *But before this faith came* (πρὸ τοῦ δὲ ἐλθεῖν), we were kept in custody under the law, being shut up to this faith which was later to be apocalyptically revealed. (Gal. 3:23)

The coming of "the seed" (*viz.* Christ) in 3:19 corresponds with the coming of "this faith" in 3:23. However, while subjective genitive advocates agree that πίστις and Christ are related to each other, they are far from uniform in their understanding of what πίστις itself refers to in 3:23–26. For instance, Sam Williams argues that πίστις Χριστοῦ refers to "Christ's own faith as prototype, Christ's faith as it now determines the

---

[64] Paul uses the verb ἀποκαλύπτω with the following objects: the righteousness of God (Rom. 1:17); the wrath of God (1:18); glory (Rom. 8:18); the wisdom of God (1 Cor. 2:10); revelation (14:30); the goal of God (Phil. 3:15); the son of God (Gal. 1:16); and only once of a human attribute (the work of the apostolic builders in 1 Cor. 3:13) (see Choi, "Πίστις in Galatians 5:5–6", 476).

[65] Fung, *Galatians*, 168.

[66] Fung, *Galatians*, 171, n.20.

personal existence of every believer".[67] Πίστις has a similar referent as in the objective genitive view, only according to Williams it applies to Christ as the exemplar of faith, and not primarily to believers. Several subjective genitive advocates understand πίστις in 3:23–26 to include both the faithfulness that Christ displayed on earth when he died on Calvary, and the faith of believers in appropriating this saving event.[68] This understanding seems closer to Paul's point than what objective genitive advocates argue.

But I think the "third view" can best account for *both* the πίστις Χριστοῦ construction in 3:22 and the following references to πίστις in 3:23–26. According to the "third view", πίστις Χριστοῦ refers not to the Son's earthly character or disposition toward the cross, nor to the believer's response of faith to the gospel; rather, πίστις Χριστοῦ refers to the *event of the gospel itself* – or, as stated earlier, to the gospel and its content. This meaning is close to the subjective genitive view in that it is centred on Christ and not on the human response to Christ. It is different, however, in that it understands πίστις Χριστοῦ (3:22) and πίστις (3:23–26) as signifying an *objective event* – God's saving act in Christ. It is not so much the Son's role or disposition within that event, but the event itself.

The "Third View" and the Fathers

The question came up a number of years ago whether the Greek Fathers had any trouble with the πίστις Χριστοῦ construction. How did they interpret it? Roy Harrisville answered this question in his 1994 study when, based on a computer search, he examined every occurrence of the πίστις Χριστοῦ construction in the Fathers.[69] Now what is clear in Harrisville's study is that he approached the question with two options in view: the objective genitive or the subjective genitive view. In the end he found no clear evidence for the subjective genitive view and thus concluded that the Greek Fathers understood the phrase as an objective genitive. The possibility of a "third view" was not presented as an option – yet it should have been. Having re-examined these passages, I

---

[67] Williams, "Again *Pistis Christou*", 444.

[68] Bruce Longenecker, *The Triumph of Abraham's God: The Transformation of Identity in Galatians* (Nashville, TN: Abingdon, 1998), 104; R. Longenecker, *Galatians*, 145; Martyn, *Galatians*, 362.

[69] Harrisville, "Witness of the Fathers".

have found a few that do not fit well into either the objective genitive or subjective genitive view. For instance, in Origen's commentary on John (*In Joannem*), he uses the πίστις Χριστοῦ construction in his comment on John 14:6:

Πάλιν ἐὰν συνῶμεν τὴν γενομένην ἐν τῷ λόγῳ ζωήν, τὸν εἰπόντα « Ἐγώ εἰμι ἡ ζωή », ἐροῦμεν μηδένα τῶν ἔξω **τῆς πίστεως Χριστοῦ** ζῆν, πάντας δὲ εἶναι νεκροὺς τοὺς μὴ ζῶντας θεῷ.

Again, if we consider the life produced in the word, which has said, "I am the life", we will say that no one who is outside **the Christ-faith** lives, but everyone who is not living to God is dead.[70]

Harrisville states that this is an objective genitive "because the context directly concerns human faith and there is an antithetical parallelism between the phrase 'faith of Christ' and 'those who do not live to God'".[71] If the subjective genitive or objective genitive were the only two options, then certainly the objective genitive view would win. But Origen's use of πίστις Χριστοῦ with the article here conveys something closer to the "third view". Those who are "outside *the* πίστις Χριστοῦ" are not simply outside "the faith in Christ" – which is awkward – but outside a certain community of believers who are living to God. Whatever exactly he means by πίστις Χριστοῦ, Origen seems to use it to refer to a *singular entity* in a way that goes beyond the objective genitive or subjective genitive views.[72] Likewise, in his commentary on the Song of Songs, Origen speaks about those who are "strangers of *the Christ-faith*" (ἀλλοτρίους τῆς πίστεως Χριστοῦ).[73] As in the previous passage, Origen uses the πίστις Χριστοῦ construction as a singular entity.[74]

---

[70] "D'autre part, si nous comprenons la vie produite dans le Verbe, (c'est-à-dire) celui qui a déclaré: «C'est moi qui suis la vie», nous dirons qu'aucun de ceux qui sont étrangers à la foi au Christ ne vit, que tous ceux qui ne vivent pas pour Dieu sont morts." *Origène: Commentaire sur Saint Jean* (SC 120; Livre I–V; Paris: Cerf, 1966), 284.

[71] Harrisville, "Witness of the Fathers", 239.

[72] Origen seems closer to the third aspect of the "third view" here, namely, that πίστις Χριστοῦ refers to the sphere of salvation created by the gospel (i.e., the church).

[73] W.A. Baehrens (ed.), *Libri X in Canticum Canticorum* (Origenes Werke, vol. 8; Die Griechischen christlichen Schriftsteller; Leipzig: Hinrich, 1925), 192–3.

[74] Harrisville himself states this in a footnote but places this passage under the heading "The Ambiguous Cases" ("Witness of the Fathers", 235, n.10).

Ignatius of Antioch, in his letter to the Philadelphians, speaks of "the faith" (ἡ πίστις) in relation to the Christ-event in a manner which seems to go beyond the objective genitive or subjective genitive views.

> But to me Jesus Christ is in the place of all that is ancient: His cross, and death, and resurrection, and *the faith which is through Him* (ἡ πίστις ἡ δι᾽ αὐτοῦ), are undefiled monuments of antiquity; by which I desire, through your prayers, to be justified. (Ign. *Phld.* 8:2)

Harrisville, again working within the objective genitive or subjective genitive options, considers this an objective genitive, or possibly a genitive of author.[75] But it seems that "the faith" here is not a person's trust in Christ, but rather an objective entity that is wrapped up, as it were, in the Christ-event.[76] Mark Elliott, in his essay in this book ("Πίστις Χριστου in the Church Fathers and Beyond"), has also noted other passages in Ignatius where "faith" is used in similar terms (see, e.g., Ign. *Trall.* 6:2; 8:1, "refresh yourselves in the faith, which is the flesh of the Lord").[77]

This brief look at the Fathers certainly does not prove that they held to a "third view" of πίστις Χριστοῦ. What it does show, however, is that there is evidence that the use of πίστις Χριστοῦ and similar constructions among some early Greek-speaking Christians cannot be clearly labeled as an objective genitive or subjective genitive. Perhaps re-examining the Fathers and other passages in Paul with the "third view" held out as a valid option may advance the debate – a debate that has been at loggerheads for quite some time.

Conclusion

By now, some may be convinced; others may wish to hear again concerning this (Acts 17:32); still others may think that only the demons can believe in a "third view" (cf. James 2 and R. Barry Matlock). In any case, I conclude with the following observations:

---

[75] Harrisville, "Witness of the Fathers", 240.

[76] I thank Mike Bird for pointing out that the same construction is actually found in Acts 3:16, "And on the basis of the faith of his name, the name of Jesus which has strengthened this man whom you see and know; and *the faith which is through him* (ἡ πίστις ἡ δι᾽ αὐτοῦ) has given him his perfect health in the presence of you all."

[77] See also Ignatius' designation of Jesus as "the perfect faith" (ἡ τελεία πίστις) in his letter to the Smyrnaeans (10:2).

(1) A steady stream of interpreters suggesting a "third view" to the πίστις Χριστοῦ debate have gone virtually unnoticed by subjective genitive and objective genitive advocates. In order for this debate to move forward – beyond its apparent stalemate position – I suggest that more interaction with this "third view" is needed, as we have seen in the case of the Greek Fathers.

(2) While the "third view" is not without its problems, it does exhibit some exegetical support. The πίστις Χριστοῦ construction in Galatians 2:16 is surrounded by two references to faith that speak of the gospel message: Galatians 1:23 – the first occurrence of πίστις in the letter – and Galatians 3:2–5, where Paul sets an anarthous genitival construction with faith as the modifier in opposition to "works of Law". We argued that the typical anthropological designation "hearing with faith" is inadequate, and that the phrase probably refers to the gospel message. As such, there is ground for suggesting that the πίστις Χριστοῦ construction in 2:16, which is also contrasted with "works of Law", is used in a similar way.

But, (3) this view does face some challenges. First, does Paul use πίστις Χριστοῦ with the kind of elasticity that the "third view" (sometimes) suggests? What exactly is πίστις Χριστοῦ? It is not uncommon for proponents of the "third view" to leave the phrase untranslated so that he[78] can fill it with whatever theological idea may fit the moment! More linguistic precision is needed. Second, it remains to be seen whether the "third view" can account for all the πίστις Χριστοῦ constructions. For instance, I find it difficult to understand Philippians 3:9 through the lens of the "third view" (I think the objective genitive view prevails here; cf. Matlock). Third, more work needs to be done on the relation between the noun, πίστις, and the verb, πιστεύειν.[79] Here, both the subjective genitive and the "third view" face a common problem: Paul argues from

---

[78] I have not found a female proponent of the "third view". Morna Hooker's view is close, but she ends up combining both objective genitive and subjective genitive views (though with a much heavier slant toward the subjective genitive).

[79] "Third view" advocates often point out that the noun is used twice as often as the verb in Paul's undisputed letters, and that the verb therefore comes from the noun. This leads Lohmeyer and others to conclude that there are two aspects of faith: (1) the objective power or metaphysical principle which Paul calls "faith" (cf. Gal. 3:23); and (2) the individual experience of that power, which Paul calls "believing" (Lohmeyer, *Grundlagen*, 117).

Abraham's *believing* experience with the ἐκ πίστεως construction (Gal.
3:6–7; cf. Rom. 4:9–16). Are we to understand that Abraham's believing
in God (Gal. 3:6) is *not* correlated with the Gentiles who are justified
by faith (Gal. 3:8)? At least here it seems that the objective genitive
interpretation wins out.

11

The Faithfulness of Jesus Christ as a Theme in Paul's Theology in Galatians

ARDEL B. CANEDAY

Introduction

Unlike earlier forays in quest of the meaning of ἐκ πίστεως Χριστοῦ, which were brief and shut down rather promptly,[1] recent monographs and essays have prompted numerous essays and monographs, inciting counter-responses, rejoinders, and counter-rejoinders.[2] This recent discussion is largely indebted to the three-decades-old perspectival shift on reading Paul's letters.[3] Some marvel that the discussion even began.

> Given such a large amount of linguistic evidence – all of which is one-sidedly in favor of the so-called objective-genitive sense – it is hardly surprising that native Greek speakers understood πίστις Ἰησοῦ Χριστοῦ to mean "faith in Jesus Christ" and *only* that. What one must find surprising is that an alternative interpretation should have been proposed in modern times and that any credence should have been given to it.[4]

PhD students, not yet chastened by the guild, are not the only ones who hold to or postulate that Paul's phrase may not be an objective genitive phrase. Scholars of renown within the guild sustain the discussion, even

---

[1] See, e.g., "Haußleiter, Der Glaube Jesu Christi", 205–30; Kittel, "πίστις Ἰησοῦ Χριστοῦ"; and Deißmann in *Paul: A Study* (1957), 161–5.

[2] See Hays, *The Faith of Jesus Christ* (1983), 158–62; idem, *The Faith of Jesus Christ*, 2nd ed., xix-lii and 249–97; idem, "What is at Stake?"; Dunn, "Once More"; Achtemeier, "Apropos the Faith"; and Tonstad, "Reading Paul in a New Paradigm".

[3] Prompted largely by E.P. Sanders, *Paul and Palestinian Judaism: A Comparison of Patterns of Religion* (Philadelphia, PA: Fortress, 1977).

[4] Silva, "Faith versus Works", 233.

dominate the debate.[5] Scholars of equal renown counter their arguments
with sustained responses.[6]

Most who translate πίστις Χριστοῦ as "the faithfulness of Christ"
are more cautious but also more numerous than earlier defenders.[7]
For example, Richard Hays and Douglas Campbell are refining
their exegetical and theological insights that began with their PhD
dissertations.[8] Ambiguity first clung to their definition of πίστις
Χριστοῦ.[9] Now, both Hays and Campbell contend that πίστις Χριστοῦ
is a *metonymy* for Christ's passion as "obedience", "blood", "death",
"cross", and "crucifixion".[10]

Few other defenders of the subjective genitive view endeavour to
show how Paul integrates the metonymical significance of the disputed
phrase throughout the given contexts or letters.[11] Often the discussion
does not advance beyond the "seven ambiguous phrases" (Gal. 2:16 [2×],
20; 3:22; Rom. 3:22, 26; Phil. 3:9).[12] This is manifest in two recent English
versions that translate πίστις Χριστοῦ as "Christ's faithfulness" (NET
and ISV).[13] Neither version extends the implications of the interpretive
decision beyond the ἐκ πίστεως Χριστοῦ phrases themselves. Thus,
for example, the NET fails to follow through on its interpretive decision
in Galatians 3:22 with the subsequent four verses, as shown in the
following translation.

---

[5] R. Barry Matlock observes, "It is remarkable in itself that seven ambiguous phrases
in Paul (Gal. 2:16 [2×], 20; 3:22; Rom. 3:22, 26; Phil. 3:9) should be expected to bear
such weight. Equally remarkable is the momentum the subjective genitive reading,
'the faithful(fulness) of Christ', has achieved. The case for the objective genitive
reading ('faith in Christ') now clearly lags behind" ("Even the Demons Believe",
300).

[6] Follow the exchange between Matlock and Hays. Matlock, "Detheologizing ΠΙΣΤΙΣ
ΧΡΙΣΤΟΥ"; Hays, *The Faith of Jesus Christ*, xliv–xlvii; Matlock, "Rhetoric".

[7] Cf. Barr, *Semantics*, 162–95.

[8] Hays, *The Faith of Jesus Christ* (1983); and Campbell, *Rhetoric of Righteousness*.

[9] E.g., see Douglas J. Moo, review of *The Faith of Jesus Christ*, by Richard B. Hays in
JETS 27 (1984): 48; and Richard Longenecker, review of *The Faith of Jesus Christ*, in
Them 10 (1984–5): 38.

[10] Hays, *The Faith of Jesus Christ*, xxx. Cf. Campbell, "The Story of Jesus in Romans",
esp. 120–3, repr. in Campbell, *Quest*, 69–94 (esp. 90–93). Achtemeier seems to miss
that Hays understands πίστις Χριστοῦ as metonymy for the whole of Christ's
passion, not just his death ("Apropos the Faith", 91).

[11] But see Choi, "Πίστις in Galatians 5:5–6".

[12] Matlock, "Even the Demons Believe", 300.

[13] Both the New English Translation and the International Standard Version translate
each of the following passages as subjective genitives – Rom. 3:22, 26; Gal. 2:16, 20;
3:22, 26; Phil. 3:9; and Eph. 3:12.

But the scripture imprisoned everything and everyone under sin so that the promise could be given – because of the faithfulness of Jesus Christ – to those who believe.

Now before *faith came* we were held in custody under the law, being kept as prisoners until *the coming faith* would be revealed. Thus the law had become our guardian until Christ, so that we could be declared righteous *by faith*. But now that *faith has come*, we are no longer under a guardian. For in Christ Jesus you are all sons of God *through faith*. (Gal. 3:22–26, emphasis mine)

If πίστις Ἰησοῦ Χριστοῦ (3:22) means "the faithfulness of Jesus Christ", why not translate each subsequent mention of the same ἡ πίστις accordingly? This is all the more true, especially since anaphora of πίστις occurs five times and the anaphoric article with πίστις occurs four times in subsequent verses, each time with evident reference to ἐκ πίστεως Ἰησοῦ Χριστοῦ (3:22).[14] To the four uses of ἡ πίστις, add Paul's formulaic expression ἐκ πίστεως δικαιθῶμεν (3:24).[15] If the NET translates ἐκ πίστεως Ἰησοῦ Χριστοῦ as the "faithfulness of Jesus Christ" (3:22), then why are the five occurrences of ἡ πίστις in 3:23–26 not translated with reference to *this faithfulness*? Yet both the NET and the ISV confuse readers with incoherency, translating subsequent mentions of ἡ πίστις with no apparent reference to *the faithfulness of Christ*.[16]

If some have made excessive exegetical claims for the subjective genitive reading, the same also flaws counter claims too frequently

---

[14] Following are the six uses of πίστις in sequence in Gal. 3:22–26 with the four phrases that employ the anaphoric article underlined:

    3:22   ἵνα ἡ ἐπαγγελία ἐκ πίστεως Ἰησοῦ Χριστοῦ δοθῇ τοῖς πιστεύουσιν
    3:23a πρὸ τοῦ ἐλθεῖν τὴν πίστιν
    3:23b εἰς τὴν μέλλουσαν πίστιν ἀποκαλυφθῆναι
    3:24   ἵνα ἐκ πίστεως δικαιωθῶμεν
    3:25   ἐλθούσης δὲ τῆς πίστεως
    3:26   διὰ τῆς πίστεως

[15] It is curious that no article occurs with the third anaphora, ἵνα ἐκ πίστεως δικαιωθῶμεν (3:24). Is the article absent because the expression is already stylized? Cf. δικαιθῶμεν ἐκ πίστεως Χριστοῦ (2:16).

[16] The ISV translates, "But the Scripture has put everything under the power of sin, so that what was promised by the faithfulness of the Messiah might be given to those who believe. Now before this faith came, we were held in custody and carefully guarded under the law in preparation for the faith that was to be revealed. And so the law was our guardian until the Messiah came, so we might be justified by faith. But now that this faith has come, we are no longer under the control of a guardian. For all of you are God's children through faith in the Messiah Jesus." Furthermore, this translation shows no awareness concerning the doubtful connections in 3:26.

marred with misunderstanding and dismissal. For example, do exegetes who take πίστις Χριστοῦ as a subjective genitive deny that Paul's gospel calls for belief in Christ Jesus to be justified?[17] Does it follow that πίστις Ἰησοῦ Χριστοῦ as "Jesus Christ's faithfulness" subverts the call for human belief in Christ for justification?[18] Does acceptance of a non-objective genitive reading entail contending that "the so-called Protestant doctrine of justification was invented by a sixteenth-century conscience-stricken monk and then imposed on the writings of Paul"?[19]

Framing the Question

Too readily scholars on both sides of the debate attempt to resolve the ambiguity of Paul's expression isolated from other complexities in his texts. For example, attempts to explain ἐκ πίστεως Χριστοῦ while assuming the meaning of Paul's juxtaposed ἐξ ἔργα νόμου in Galatians 2:16 is duly suspect.[20] Paul Achtemeier observes, concerning the SBL seminar exchange between Richard Hays and James Dunn,

---

[17] Though understandably taken as denying that Christ is the object of faith, S.K. Williams claims something different, albeit less than fully clear ("Again *Pistis Christou*", 446). Mark Reasoner, who adopts a mediating interpretation of πίστις Χριστοῦ as "including both subjective and objective senses of the genitive" in at least one passage (Rom. 3:22), raises a similar objection (*Romans*, 39). Reasoner translates Rom. 3:22 as retaining both the subjective and objective senses (31).

[18] Silva, "Faith versus Works", 227.

[19] Silva, "Faith versus Works", 227. See also *Romans*, where Reasoner asks, "Why does it matter whether we read *pistis Christou* as objective (faith in Jesus) or subjective (Jesus' faith)?" He offers four consequences to reading πίστις Χριστοῦ as a subjective genitive (39). First, those who make the case that πίστις Χριστοῦ denotes Christ's saving efficacy "will not call for a distinct, conversion-constituting act of placing one's faith in Jesus" but will instead "call people to join the church that lives out in a concentric pattern the faith that Jesus displayed" (39). Second, he observes that this interpretation will incline us "to read Paul's gospel not as primarily based around the dichotomy of works and faith, which both have a human subject, but rather as a dichotomy between law and Christ" (40). Third, he contends that the view leads to seeing justification as part of a larger theme, i.e., participation in Christ, and that "participation means that justification and sanctification refer to the same process in the life of the church" (40). Finally, Reasoner adds that this view will enlarge "the circle around those we call saved" to include individuals who do not believe in Christ Jesus. Reasoner may have over-interpreted Hooker, "Πίστις Χριστοῦ", *NTS*, 341.

[20] On this deficiency in Hays, *The Faith of Jesus Christ* (1983), see A.B. Caneday, "The Curse of the Law and the Cross: Works of the Law and Faith in Galatians 3:1–14" (PhD dissertation; Trinity Evangelical Divinity School, 1992), 47.

"What is absent in both papers ... is the contrast ... between πίστις Χριστοῦ and ἔργα νόμου."²¹ Yet, contrary to Achtemeier's complaint, a recent essay claims that "because the problem of πίστις Χριστοῦ is independent of most of the other problems in the text, including the meaning of ἔργα νόμου ('works of Law'), it is unnecessary to discuss them here".²² Exegetical focus in isolation upon πίστις Χριστοῦ renders one's argument less credible, regardless of the view one advances. Some appeal to the subjective genitive interpretation to account for Paul's antithesis between ἔργα νόμου and πίστις Χριστοῦ (Gal. 2:15–16) not as "works" versus "faith" or as "doing" versus "believing" but as "human activity" versus "Christ's faithfulness unto death". But they seem to proceed on the assumption that ἔργα νόμου depicts "human activity".²³

Contrary to this approach, helpful exegetical and theological reflections upon Paul's πίστις Χριστοῦ phrases require thoughtful examination of the phrase and its variations as entangled with other phrases such as ἐξ ἔργων νόμου, ὁ νόμος, ἐν Χριστῷ, ἐκ πίστεως, and ἡ πίστις – each of which is charged with its own significance and contributes to the fullness of Paul's themes. To isolate πίστις Χριστοῦ from these and other phrases but also to isolate it from its own prepositional phrase, with either ἐκ or διά, is to ignore crucial aspects of Paul's uses of the phrase.

Barry Matlock challenges Douglas Campbell's claim that ἐκ πίστεως in Paul's citations of Habakkuk 2:4 (Rom. 1:17; Gal. 3:12) structure the Apostle's ἐκ πίστεως Χριστοῦ formulation. Instead, Matlock proposes,

But another possibility presents itself with the observation that ἐκ enters the scene in the form of ἐξ ἔργων νόμου – a strikingly stable combination ... And rather than ask why ἐκ πίστεως only occurs in letters that cite Hab. 2:4, I would ask why the πίστις Χριστοῦ formulations only occur in contexts where "works of law" and "faith in Christ" are set in antithesis ...

---

²¹ Achtemeier, "Apropos the Faith", 87.
²² Hunn, *"Pistis Christou"*, 25. The present essay disputes both Hunn's claim and method.
²³ Hays, *The Faith of Jesus Christ* (1983), 147 and (2002), 130. Cf. idem, "Galatians", 254. It seems curious that Hays offers little exegetical discussion of ἐξ ἔργων νόμου. Instead, he seems to assume that the expression denotes "human activity". Discussion of this is missing also from his "What Is at Stake?", 35–60. Achtemeier calls attention to this lacuna ("Apropos the Faith", 87–9).

Why does πίστις Χριστοῦ belong so inseparably to that antithesis? Why, indeed, is Paul's very form of expression so bound to that contrast – as Gal. 2:16 impresses upon one?[24]

Though Matlock's question warrants consideration, his question requires adjustment to fit the evidence. Reflection shows that πίστις Χριστοῦ does not "only occur in contexts where 'works of Law' and 'faith in Christ' are set in antithesis". Πίστις Χριστοῦ occurs in three of Paul's letters; ἔργα νόμου occurs only in two (Rom. and Gal.). Thus, ἔργα νόμου does not occur everywhere πίστις Χριστοῦ does (e.g, Gal. 3:22, 26; Phil. 3:9). In the larger context of Romans 3:20–28, ἔργα νόμου occurs twice (3:20, 28), but in Romans 3:21–22, πίστις Χριστοῦ stands opposite χωρὶς νόμου, not ἐξ ἔργων νόμου. In Galatians 2:20, πίστις τῇ τοῦ υἱοῦ τοῦ θεοῦ is opposite ὁ νόμος. Only one passage juxtaposes πίστις Χριστοῦ directly with ἔργα νόμου (Gal. 2:16). Is Matlock warranted to assume that ἔργα νόμου speaks of "observing the works of the Law" so that πίστις Χριστοῦ speaks of "believing in Christ"?[25]

Given these correctives, why do we find ἡ πίστις Χριστοῦ only in contexts where Paul pairs it antithetically with variations on ἔργα νόμου and ὁ νόμος? What is the theological import of this polarity? The question is necessarily larger than this because, according to Paul, πίστις Χριστοῦ is not only juxtaposed in polarity with "works of the Law" (2:16) and "the Law" (Rom. 3:22), but also is the subject of "came" (ἐλθεῖν, ἐλθούσης, Gal. 3:23, 25); the object of "revealed" (ἀποκαλυφθῆναι, 3:23); the "origin" (ἐκ) of justification (δικαιωθῶμεν ἐκ πίστεως Χριστοῦ, Gal. 2:16; 3:24); the agency through which sonship is attained (διὰ τῆς πίστεως, Gal. 3:26); and the means by which the believer lives (ἐν πίστει ζῶ τῇ τοῦ υἱοῦ τοῦ θεοῦ, Gal. 2:20). Furthermore, πίστις Χριστοῦ is the agency through which God's righteousness is "made known" (πεφανέρωται ... διὰ πίστεως Ἰησοῦ Χριστοῦ, Rom. 3:21, 22); is the agency by which God presented Christ as the mercy-seat (ὃν προέθετο ὁ θεὸς ἱλαστήριον διὰ τῆς πίστεως, Rom. 3:25); identifies the justified person by origin (τὸν ἐκ πίστεως Ἰησοῦ, Rom. 3:26); and is the agency by which righteousness comes from God (διὰ πίστεως Χριστοῦ, Phil. 3:9). How does πίστις Χριστοῦ hold these together? Debate tends to reduce alternatives to

---

[24] Matlock, "Detheologizing ΠΙΣΤΙΣ ΧΡΙΣΤΟΥ", 21.

[25] Matlock, "Detheologizing ΠΙΣΤΙΣ ΧΡΙΣΤΟΥ", 21–2. Cf. Hunn, "*Pistis Christou*", 25; Gordon D. Fee, *Pauline Christology: An Exegetical-Theological Study* (Peabody, MA: Hendrickson, 2007), 224–6.

two – either the objective genitive ("faith in Christ") or the subjective genitive ("faith/faithfulness of Christ").[26]

Originally, this essay was to address πίστις Χριστοῦ as a theme across Paul's letters. A less ambitious approach focuses upon Paul's letter to the Galatians as indicative and suggestive concerning his theology in his letters to the Romans and the Philippians. If πίστις Χριστοῦ constitutes an integrated theme in his letter to the Galatians, what is its meaning and impact? What if Paul's phrase is best understood other than an objective genitive? What would the theme contribute to understanding Paul's gospel? Would it alter or enhance our understanding of Paul's gospel? Would the theme fit within the tradition understood by, and received from, the Reformers? Would it do injury to the place justification has in Paul's theology according to the objective genitive understanding of the phrase? Would such an understanding of Paul's phrase clarify or muddle understanding of Paul's theology?

Though this essay draws observations and conclusions concerning πίστις Χριστοῦ that distinguish it from the objective genitive reading, its principal objective is to accent Paul's phrase with greater integrated emphasis that may aid rapprochement among the various interpretations by seeing more clearly Paul's polarity between ἔργα νόμου and πίστις Χριστοῦ in terms of Torah and Christ.[27]

Πίστις Χριστοῦ as a Theme in Paul's Letter to the Galatians

Seven passages in three of Paul's letters trigger the debate concerning πίστις Χριστοῦ (Gal. 2:16 [2×], 20; 3:22; Rom. 3:22, 26; Phil. 3:9). Each passage poses distinctive exegetical decisions and theological considerations. The ensuing discussion examines the contributions of Paul's phrase to his argument in Galatians 2:15–3:29, with suggestions concerning the passages in his other letters.

Paul's terms and categories in Galatians 2:15–16 are dense, full, and redundant. Among advocates for the subjective genitive reading of

---

[26] For alternatives see Williams, "Again *Pistis Christou*", 441–7; Hultgren, "*Pistis Christou* Formulation"; Cosgrove, *The Cross*, 55–6; Seifrid, "Paul, Luther, and Justification", 218–19; idem, *Christ, Our Righteousness*, 139–46. Each argues for a kind of genitive of quality without full agreement.

[27] T. David Gordon, who adopts the objective genitive view, contends that "If we would understand the polemic of Galatians, we must describe it in terms of 'Torah or Christ' rather than in terms of 'Works or Faith'" ("The Problem at Galatia", *Int* 41 [1987]: 36–8).

πίστις Χριστοῦ, frequent appeal to tautology, to favour the subjective genitive reading, is overblown.[28] The proposal does not avoid repetition, for ἔργα νόμου occurs three times in the same passage. Yet, what if those who favour the objective genitive view conclude too easily that the verbal clause disambiguates the two noun clauses?[29] Exegetical and theological elements challenge my long inclination toward the subjective genitive but also restrain me from hasty repentance.[30]

The density, fullness, and repetition of expressions in 2:15–16 are what one reasonably expects should constitute a thesis statement that a writer intends to unpack. Undoubtedly, subsequent uses of Paul's compact expressions throughout his letter, but especially in 2:15–3:29, clarify meanings.[31] Paul's return to his πίστις Χριστοῦ formulation in 3:22 with his giving ἡ πίστις *objectivity*, even *quasi-personification*, in 3:23–26, reinforces the significance of his dense expressions in 2:15–16.

Whether ἐκ πίστεως Χριστοῦ speaks of belief in Christ is disputed, but Paul unambiguously calls for belief in Christ Jesus when he reports his rebuke of Peter – "We by nature are Jews ... even we believed in Christ Jesus in order that we might be justified" (Gal. 2:16).[32] He writes this for the Galatians' benefit because troublemakers endeavour to compel them to live as Jews, just as Peter's behavior in Antioch incited for Gentiles there (2:11–13).

The troublemakers incited questions concerning who constitutes the Israel of God (Gal. 6:16) or who are the seed of Abraham (3:1–29). Paul addresses these questions throughout 2:15–3:29 but made explicit at the apex of his reasoning (3:27–29). "For, as many as were baptized into

---

[28] The argument is that if the twice-used πίστις Χριστοῦ in Gal. 2:16 is an objective genitive, then εἰς Χριστὸν Ἰησοῦν ἐπιστεύσαμεν is tautological. Concerning Gal. 3:22, the argument is that τοῖς πιστεύουσιν is redundant if πίστις Ἰησοῦ is an objective genitive. I made this mistake in A.B. Caneday, "'Redeemed from the Curse of the Law': The Use of Deut 21:22–23 in Gal. 3:13", *TJ* 10 (1989): 189, n.19.

[29] See, e.g., Fee, *Pauline Christology*, 224. Cf. Silva, "Faith versus Works", 232–3.

[30] See Caneday, "Redeemed", 189–90, n.19; 192, n.30; also idem, "The Curse of the Law", esp. 176–201.

[31] For appeal to Paul's later uses of πίστις without the genitive qualifier to support the objective genitive interpretation, see Hunn, "*Pistis Christou*", 21–33. Hunn's thesis is that the meaning of ἐκ πίστεως Χριστοῦ (2:16) can be resolved from the difficult ἐξ ἀκοῆς πίστεως (3:5). Hunn's effort to clarify one ambiguous expression appeals to another even more ambiguous expression. On this, see Silva, "Faith versus Works", 234. See also Fee, *Pauline Christology*, 226–7.

[32] Between the two genitive constructions under question, Paul unambiguously states, ἡμεῖς εἰς Χριστὸν Ἰησοῦν ἐπιστεύσαμεν (Gal. 2:16).

Christ have put on Christ. Therefore, there is neither Jew nor Greek, nor is there slave or free, nor is there male and female, for we are all one in Christ Jesus. Now if you are of Christ, then you are of the seed of Abraham, heirs according to promise." Here, Paul's genitives (if you are *of Christ* then you are the seed *of Abraham*) depict the true lineage of Abraham. Paul's reasoning inverts the troublemakers' efforts to compel the Galatians to live as Jews that they might become Abraham's seed. The seed who trace their lineage from Abraham through the Law and circumcision hold no claim on God's promises to Abraham. Instead, theirs is the curse of Torah. Through Christ alone, the blessing of Abraham comes, namely, the Spirit and justification.[33] God's promises belong to the seed who trace their lineage through Christ Jesus to Abraham. Being baptized into Christ constitutes Jew and Greek the seed of Abraham. Because Christ is the seed of Abraham to whom the promises were spoken (3:16), all who are clothed with Christ are also the seed of Abraham (3:29).[34] Thus Paul's argument reaches its apex the way it begins in 2:15–16, by contrasting *origin from Torah* and *origin from Christ*.

With rare exception, however they read the genitive, exegetes fasten upon πίστις Χριστοῦ and gloss over two other crucial exegetical issues in Galatians 2:16. One is the force of ἐὰν μή, whether adversative (but) or exceptive (except – as it is in all of Paul's uses elsewhere). Another issue, which is bound up with the exegetical question prompted by ἐαν μή, is the ignored word order, εἰδότες ὅτι οὐ δικαιοῦται ἄνθρωπος ἐξ ἔργων νόμου. Most connect ἐξ ἔργων νόμου with the negated verb οὐ δικαιοῦται instead of with ἄνθρωπος, resulting in, "we know that a person is not justified by the works of the Law" (e.g., ESV; NRSV). This

---

[33] Cf. S.K. Williams, "Justification and the Spirit in Galatians", *JSNT* 9 (1987): 91–100.

[34] That Paul deprecates one ritual (circumcision of the flesh) while he endorses another (baptism into Christ) and that he appeals to the baptism of his readers in Galatia as virtually identifying them as belonging to Christ, and consequently as Abraham's seed, suggests that his conflict with the Judaizers is not principally over ritualism or a form of works-righteousness. Paul's concern is not principally ascribing efficaciousness to the act of circumcision to make one righteous. For, if it were, how could he escape the same charge with regard to baptism? Instead, given his argument, that he virtually merges the rite of baptism with being clothed with Christ suggests that Paul's conflict with the agitators in Galatia converges upon their failure to acknowledge that the Mosaic Law, which had a divinely-given function until Christ Jesus had come, has been displaced by Messiah to whom it pointed (Gal. 3:19–25). Now that Messiah has come, the law no longer has jurisdiction. Cf. Caneday, "The Curse of the Law", 345–8.

leads to another oversight, namely, to take ἐὰν μή not with exceptive force, as always elsewhere in Paul's letters.[35]

Mark Seifrid is an exception: "Paul argues, even the one who is 'of the works of the Law' is justified" ἐκ πίστεως Ἰησοῦ Χριστοῦ.[36] This is instructive.[37] Reading ἄνθρωπος ἐξ ἔργων νόμου as "a person from the works of the Law" takes the phrase, in context, to refer to a Jew governed by the Law. This correlates "a person from the works of the Law" with "sinners from the Gentiles" (ἐξ ἐθνῶν ἁμαρτωλοί). The flow is natural: "We by nature are Jews and *not sinners from the Gentiles*, but knowing that *a human from the deeds required by the Law* is not justified *except through* πίστεως Ἰησοῦ Χριστοῦ, even we believed in Christ Jesus in order that we might be justified from πίστεως Χριστοῦ and not from the deeds required by the Law, because no flesh shall be justified from the deeds required by the Law." A person who *originates* ἐξ ἔργων νόμου, an Israelite, is not justified before God *except through* πίστεως Ἰησοῦ Χριστοῦ. The ἐξ ἔργων νόμου and διὰ/ἐκ πίστεως Χριστοῦ antithesis concerns *spiritual origin*. Being ἐξ ἔργων νόμου does not justify anyone before God. Even an Israelite is not justified before God except διὰ/ἐκ πίστεως Χριστοῦ.

Four observations are in order. First, οἱ ἐκ περιτομῆς (Gal. 2:12), ἐξ ἐθνῶν ἁμαρτωλοί (2:15), and ἄνθρωπος ἐξ ἔργων νόμου (2:16) function idiomatically to denote origin or pedigree, not "works-righteousness".[38]

---

[35] A. Andrew Das, "Another Look at ἐὰν μή in Galatians 2:16", *JBL* (2000): 529–39. Das concludes that ἐὰν μή is "grammatically ambiguous" and opts for J.D.G. Dunn's interpretation. Richard B. Hays offers no observations concerning word order, though it would assist the case he seeks to make. See Hays, "Galatians", 236–41.

[36] Seifrid, "Paul, Luther, and Justification", 218.

[37] Matlock mentions Seifrid's solution to reading ἐαν μή as an adversative but dismisses it ("Rhetoric", 197, n.25).

[38] "A man from the works required by the law" is not pejorative but descriptive of a Jew whose whole life is circumscribed by and defined by the Law, the Old Covenant. It does not denote "works righteousness". The phrase is an idiom that denotes origin. Cf. "the ones from circumcision" (οἱ ἐκ περιτομῆς, Gal. 2:12). See also, οἱ ἐξ Ἰσραήλ (Rom. 9:6); οἱ ἐξ ἐθνῶν (Acts 15:23); οἱ ἐκ περιτομῆς (Acts 10:45; Gal. 2:12; Col. 4:12; Titus 1:10); ὁ ἐκ πίστεως Ἀβραάμ (Rom. 4:16); ὁ ἐκ πίστεως Ἰησοῦ (Rom. 3:26); and οἱ ἐκ πίστεως (Gal. 3:7, 9). Cf. Caneday, "The Curse of the Law", 220–23; Maximilian Zerwick, *Biblical Greek: Illustrated by Examples* (Rome: Scripta Pontificii Instituti Biblici, 1963), §134, 45. Zerwick observes that this Gk. idiom (ὁ ἐκ or οἱ ἐκ + the genitive) denotes a member or members of a group or sect or school of thought much as the English ending -*ist*. Zerwick's first examples are ὁ ἐκ πίστεως Ἰησοῦ (Rom. 3:26) and οἱ ἐκ πίστεως (Gal. 3:7, 9). Cf. N. Turner, *Syntax*, 260. Cf. BDAG, 3b, 296.

Later, Paul substitutes ὅσοι for ἄνθρωπος when he writes "*as many as are from the deeds required by the Law*" (ὅσοι ἐξ ἔργων νόμου, 3:10).[39] "A person from deeds required by the Law" distinguishes between Jews, as possessors of Torah, and "sinners from the Gentiles", who stand outside the Law covenant. Paul's concern with being ἐξ ἔργων νόμου is not with "works-righteousness", even when linked with δικαιόω (2:16), for Paul contends that "a person from the deeds required by the Law is not justified *except through* πίστεως Χριστοῦ". Paul contends that tracing descent from the eclipsed covenant instead of from Christ, now that Messiah has come, leaves one exposed before God. His principal distress over the subversive "gospel" in Galatia is its implicitly inherent repudiation of Christ, through whom alone the Torah's curse is removed and the blessing of Abraham comes.

Second, ἄνθρωπος ἐξ ἔργων νόμου seems purposefully juxtaposed with ἐξ ἐθνῶν ἁμαρτωλοί to counter Jewish pride in possessing Torah and circumcision. Neither Gentile ("sinners from the Gentiles") nor Jew ("a person from the deeds required by the Law") will be justified before God *except* through πίστεως Χριστοῦ, now that Messiah has come (cf. 3:22–26). Paul follows this by saying, "Now if while seeking to be justified in Christ we also were found to be sinners, then is Christ a servant of sin?" His terse argument is reminiscent of his protracted argument in Romans 2 that generates the sequence of questions in 3:1–9 where he first asks, "Then what advantage has the Jew? Or what is the value of circumcision?" (Rom. 3:1).

Third, the genitive πίστεως governed by ἐκ is integral to the sense of ἐκ/διὰ πίστεως ['Ιησου] Χριστοῦ. Given his initial use of ἐξ ἔργων νόμου in Galatians 2:16, as a reference to the Mosaic Law, to denote affiliation or origin, it is reasonable to take Paul's parallel expression, ἐκ πίστεως

---

[39] See Caneday, "The Curse of the Law", 257. James Scott, independently and later, agrees that "there is no evidence that ὅσοι means 'those who rely on works of the law'. The expression ἔργα νόμου seems to correspond to the Hebrew מעשׂי תורה (4QMMT 3.29; 4QFlor. 1.7; cf. 2 Bar. 57.2), and in Paul it refers to 'deeds of the law' in the comprehensive sense of Torah observance (cf. Rom. 3:20, 28; Gal. 2:16; 3:2, 5, 10). The expression ὅσοι denotes origin (cf. Lam. 1:7; Sir. 41:10; Acts 4:6). Hence, the phrase 'as many as are of works of the law' conveys nothing pejorative per se and should not be over interpreted" ("'For as Many as Are of Works of the Law Are under a Curse' (Galatians 3:10)", in *Paul and the Scriptures of Israel* [ed. Craig A. Evans and James A. Sanders; JSNTSup 83; Sheffield: JSOT Press, 1993], 190).

[40] For the influence of Hab. 2:4 on ἐκ πίστεως Χριστοῦ, see Campbell, "Meaning", esp. 101–3. See also Francis Watson, "By Faith (of Christ): An Exegetical Dilemma and its Scriptural Solution" in this volume.

Χριστοῦ, to denote origin or affiliation also. This is true especially since he uses the idiom οἱ ἐκ πίστεως later (3:7, 9), juxtaposed with ὅσοι ἐξ ἔργων νόμου εἰσίν (3:10) and followed by the citation of Habakkuk 2:4, ὁ δίκαιος ἐκ πίστεως (3:11).[40]

Fourth, in Galatians 2:16, ἄνθρωπος ἐξ ἔργων νόμου speaks of Peter's former affiliation with the covenant characterized by its required deeds, Torah.[41] Substitution of ὁ νόμος and Χριστός for ἐξ ἔργων νόμου and ἐκ πίστεως Χριστοῦ, respectively (2:17–21), confirms that the genitive qualifiers are the indispensable features of the two phrases. At the forefront, then, in the polarity is not "works" versus "faith" but "Torah" versus "Christ" representing two distinct covenants: (1) the one bounded by the Law, and ended by (2) the one bounded by Christ.[42] This fits the progression of Paul's argument, for at the apex (3:22–29) he contends that ἡ πίστις Χριστοῦ has ended Torah's jurisdiction. This is precisely the point he makes at the beginning of his argument by appealing to Peter's episode at Antioch.

Paul reinforces his use of ἐξ ἔργων νόμου and ἐκ πίστεως Χριστοῦ to depict contrasting affiliation with two distinct covenants when he refracts the Abraham narrative through Isaiah to contrast two covenants (Gen. 21:8–21; Isa. 54:1), which are not contemporary but sequential. Christ shares no jurisdiction with Torah. If, as the "other gospel" proclaims that the law covenant's jurisdiction is contemporaneous with Christ, in Galatians 2:15–16 Paul identifies two necessary consequences.[43] First, unless Gentiles live as Jews, the Law excludes them from the promise, as Peter's behaviour in Antioch intimated, intimidating Gentile believers who were present, such as Barnabas (Gal. 2:11–15). Second, now that Christ has come,

---

[41] On ἔργα νόμου see my "The Curse of the Law", 150–55, where I argue that Paul's expression is idiomatic for "works assigned by the law" and that because νόμος is the indispensable word in the phrase, given that it defines ἔργα, it is understandable how νόμος replaces ἔργα νόμου in Gal. 2:19, 21; 3:11, 12, and 13.

[42] Caneday, "The Curse of the Law".

[43] In Gal. 2:17–18, concerning reconstructing the Law, Paul reasons, "Now if while seeking to be justified in Christ we [Jews] ourselves are found also to be sinners, then is Christ a servant of sin? Definitely not! For if I rebuild again the things that I tore down, I establish myself as a transgressor." Using the rhetorically representative "I", Paul's reasoning seems to be that if the law no longer holds jurisdiction over himself, Peter, and fellow Christian Jews, in that Christ has now come and has torn down the law, then, for anyone who reconstructs the law, as though justification were ἐξ ἔργων νόμου, that one proves to be a transgressor against Christ. Cf. Bruce, *Galatians*, 142.

for Jew or Gentile to submit to the Law covenant's jurisdiction is to become subject to Torah's curse and to be excluded from the blessing of Abraham, for "a person from the works required by Torah is not justified except διὰ πίστεως Ἰησοῦ Χριστοῦ ... because from the works required by the Law *no flesh* will be justified" (Gal. 2:16). Thus, ἔργα νόμου and πίστις Χριστοῦ are harmonious and allied with God's purposes only in the sequential relationship of "before" and "now" (3:23, 25). Following God's promise to Abraham, the Law "was added" as a guardian and warden "until the Seed would come, to whom the promise was given" (Gal. 3:19).

In Galatians 2:17–21, where Paul begins to draw out the categories expressed in the compact phrases introduced in 2:15–16, Christ's crucifixion is central to his argument in that the demise of the Law does not nullify God's grace, "for if justification is through the Law, then Christ died gratuitously" (2:21). Yet, even in these verses, terseness marks his shortened and substituted expressions. In place of δικαιωθῶμεν ἐκ πίστεως Χριστοῦ Paul writes δικαιωθῆναι ἐν Χριστῷ. Both feature Christ rather than πίστις. Διὰ νόμου replaces ἐξ ἔργων νόμου and features Torah, not obedience to Torah. The Law lost its jurisdiction over all who believe in Christ Jesus, for Paul says, "through the Law I died to the Law, that I might live to God" (2:19). This transaction of death to the Law and new life occurs in Christ, and Paul links Christ's sacrificial death to πίστις Χριστοῦ with the cumbersome genitive construction in 2:20 (τῇ [πίστει] τοῦ υἱοῦ τοῦ θεοῦ). He says, "I was crucified with Christ. Now I live no more, but Christ lives in me. And the life I now live in the flesh I live *by faith* which is of the Son of God who loved me and gave himself on my behalf" (2:19–20). What is Paul saying in 2:20? Is the Son of God the object of faith (undisputed in 2:16)? Because we share in Christ's crucifixion we died to the Law's power to curse us. Christ died to redeem us from the Law's curse. Is πίστις to be understood as Christ's faithfulness as a metonymy for his sacrificial death and resurrection? Does "the πίστις which is of the Son of God" signify that Christ, who sacrificed himself and was raised for us is the *origin of our faith*, not only the *object of our faith*, or that πίστις is *metonymy for Christ's redeeming passion*?

Israel's incurring the curse of the Law because of unfaithfulness to the Law covenant, as narrated in Scripture, is the source of Paul's theology that provides focus upon the polarity: (1) the curse of Torah belongs to "as many as are of the works required by the Law" (ὅσοι ἐξ ἔργων νόμου εἰσίν, 3:10), and (2) the blessing of Abraham is for "those of faith/faithfulness" (οἱ ἐκ πίστεως, 3:7, 9).[44] Galatians 3:1–14 develops this dual focus upon the curse of the Law that had fallen upon Israel and the blessing of Abraham held at bay by Torah and its curse.[45] Paul's catchphrases sustain his formulaic expressions of 2:15–16. Reception of the Spirit not ἐξ ἔργων νόμου but ἐξ ἀκοῆς πίστεως proves fulfilment of "the promise of Abraham" among the Galatians (3:2–6, 14).

After introducing Abraham into his argument, Paul reasons, "We know that οἱ ἐκ πίστεως, these are the sons of Abraham. And Scripture foreseeing that ἐκ πίστεως God would justify the Gentiles, preached the gospel beforehand to Abraham, saying, 'In you shall all the nations be blessed' so that οἱ ἐκ πίστεως might be blessed with the faithful Abraham [τῷ πιστῷ Ἀβραάμ]" (3:7–9). No one disputes that following Paul's citation of Genesis 15:6 (ἐπίστευσεν τῷ θεῷ) the ἐκ πίστεως phrases imply the genitive qualifier (Χριστοῦ, 2:16). At issue is whether Paul's stylized uses of οἱ ἐκ πίστεως [Χριστοῦ] in 3:7 and 3:9 entail an idiom of origin that grounds his inferential conclusion that Christ is the exceptional one whose πίστις defines those who truly are Abraham's sons (οὗτοι υἱοί εἰσιν Ἀβραάμ, 3:7) who are blessed with faithful Abraham (εὐλογοῦνται σὺν τῷ πιστῷ Ἀβραάμ, 3:9). It seems they do and that this is crucial, given the progression of Paul's argument that if one belongs to Christ one is of Abraham's seed.

It seems reasonable to infer that Paul does not refer to the believer's πίστις but to a πίστις outside of him or herself, given his idiomatic expressions. Twice, here, Paul uses οἱ ἐκ πίστεως, earlier identified as an idiom for origin or descent, "those who are of πίστις". If he means "the one who believes", why does he not simply use the substantival participle, ὁ πιστεύων?[46] He does so later in 3:22 (τοῖς πιστεύουσιν). The

---

44 One need not embrace all that others claim concerning Paul's "narrative substructure". E.g., even Hays is "somewhat repentant about the methodological overkill of the piece [*The Faith of Jesus Christ*, 1983]". "Some of the methodological preliminaries I would now gladly consign to the flames" ("What Is at Stake?", 37, n.5). Also see Hays's qualifications of his method in *The Faith of Jesus Christ*, xxiii–xxxv. Cf. Scott, "For as Many", 221.

45 Cf. N.T. Wright, "Curse and Covenant: Galatians 3:10–14" in *The Climax of the Covenant*, 150–51.

46 Cf. discussion of οἱ ἐκ πίστεως in Gal. 3:7, 9 where Herman Ridderbos (*The Epistle of Paul to the Churches of Galatia* [trans. Henry Zylstra; Grand Rapids, MI: Eerdmans, 1953], 119), acknowledges that the expression denotes origin, but he reads the expression as "the believers". See also Bruce, *Galatians*, 155, who regards οἱ ἐκ

focus of Paul's argument seems not to be one's *act of believing* but one's *spiritual origin*, one's spiritual lineage. For Paul, these two ideas are not divorced, for those he calls οἱ ἐκ πίστεως do believe in Jesus Christ (2:16). Paul's concern here continues to be the same as in 2:16 – origin, whether one traces spiritual descent from Christ (οἱ ἐκ πίστεως [Χριστοῦ]) or from Torah (ὅσοι ἐξ ἔργων νόμου εἰσίν).[47] Does not 3:7, οὗτοι υἱοί εἰσιν Ἀβραάμ, indicate that origin or descent is Paul's principal concern as he seeks to persuade the Galatians against judaizing?[48] The question of *spiritual lineage* is the central cord that runs through Paul's entire argument (cf. 4:28–29).

The Law bears multidimensional functions. Torah, with its curse, served God's purpose (cf. 4:4) as an impediment to the fulfilment of God's sworn oath to Abraham (3:6, 8) until Messiah's coming (3:15–26).[49] As an impediment, Torah could not make good on its promise to give life (3:12) nor did it deliver justification (cf. 3:19–21) because of human sinfulness. Torah has power to energize sin (cf. 1 Cor. 15:56) and to curse (Gal. 3:10) but not to bless nor to enliven nor to justify. Torah, consisting of demands, was powerless to secure obedience but capable of imposing its curse for unfaithfulness. Torah also prophesied the coming Messiah with its multiform foreshadows and prefigurements (e.g.; cf. 3:13). Torah required satisfaction for Israel's incurrence of the curse by her lack of covenant loyalty which is typologically representative of humanity's plight under sin (3:10), recapitulating Adam's role.[50]

πίστεως (Gal. 3:7, 9) as "those who are characterized by such faith as Abraham showed when he believed God". Similarly, N. Turner, *Syntax*, 296. BDAG 3b, p. 296, translates the expression as "those who have faith". See also Rom. 3:26. Is ὁ ἐκ πίστεως Ἰησοῦ equivalent to ὁ πιστεύων, "the one who believes"? If the expression ὁ ἐκ πίστεως Ἰησοῦ in Rom. 3:26 is synonymous with ὁ πιστεύων, then why does Paul not use the substantival participle as he does in Rom. 3:22, where he uses two distinguishable expressions: (1) διὰ πίστεως Ἰησοῦ Χριστοῦ; and (2) εἰς πάντας τοὺς πιστεύοντας?

[47] Likewise, those Paul calls ὅσοι ἐξ ἔργων νόμου εἰσίν (3:10) also perform the things required by the law (5:3), though this is not the phrase's meaning.

[48] Later Paul depicts the same antithesis of origin when he says, "Just as at that time the one who is born according to the flesh persecuted the one born according to the Spirit, so also it is now" (Gal. 4:29). Paul's polarity between σάρξ and πνεῦμα in 3:3 links the two contexts.

[49] See Caneday, "The Curse of the Law", 346–7.

[50] Cf. Wright, "Curse and Covenant", 137–56; and Scott, "'For as Many", 187–221. Because completion of my dissertation preceded access to these two essays, it did not benefit from the work of Wright and Scott. It did, however, anticipate their arguments and conclusions. See Caneday, "The Curse of the Law".

As a designed impediment to the fulfilment of God's promise to Abraham, Torah also functioned typologically, pointing to its own fulfilment and termination in Messiah. Redemption stood at an impasse, for Torah could not be bypassed. Justice had to be done. Torah, which stood between promise and fulfilment, cursed its subjects but also foreshadowed redemption from its curse. It pointed forward to the one who would come to bear the curse of the violated covenant just as executed criminals of old had borne the curse in the nation's place.[51] By his curse-bearing "upon the tree", Messiah redeems from the Law's curse typologically and representatively by fulfilling the obscure and repugnant regulation of hanging a condemned and executed criminal to bear God's anger and avert his curse (Deut. 21:22–23).[52]

Christ is not opposed to the Law. Rather, Christ was born under the Law so that he might bear the Law's curse to put an end to the Law for all who believe in him (Gal. 4:4–5; 3:13; 2:16). Paul sustains his juxtaposed antithetical expressions from 2:15–16, to underscore the fact that Torah and Christ are not coexistent or coterminous allies. They are allied in God's purpose only in the sequential relationship of "before" and "now", of prefiguration and fulfilment, for Christ's bearing Torah's curse "upon the tree" is the long-awaited "Amen" to God's promise to Abraham. Now that Abraham's singular Seed has come, to whom the promises were spoken (3:16, 23), Torah, with all its covenant functions, is fulfilled and terminated. Torah's own provisions restricted the extent of its jurisdiction. By his sacrificial act "upon the tree", the True Israel (3:16), Messiah, in contrast to unfaithful Israel, supplanted Torah for all who believe in him.[53] Thus, being of Abraham is no longer a matter of affiliation with either Torah or Israel, for one who is of Christ is also of Abraham (3:29).

"Scripture incarcerated all things under sin in order that the promise ἐκ πίστεως Ἰησοῦ Χριστοῦ might be given to those who believe" (3:22).[54] What does Paul mean when he writes ἐκ πίστεως Ἰησοῦ Χριστοῦ? Contextual indicators are not lacking. The ἡ πίστις of which Paul speaks was not present until it "came" and was "revealed" (3:23), making an

---

[51] For fuller elaboration see Caneday, "Redeemed", 185–209. See also, idem, "The Curse of the Law", 302–44.

[52] See Caneday, "The Curse of the Law", 328.

[53] Cf. Wright, "Curse and Covenant", 151–2.

[54] The usual discussion deliberates whether ἐκ πίστεως κ.τ.λ. denotes "the ground on which the promise was originally made, or the grounds on which the promise is now ratified". See Hooker, "Πίστις Χριστοῦ", *NTS*, 329.

eschatological entry.[55] Πρὸ τοῦ ἐλθεῖν τὴν πίστιν (3:23) corresponds to a series of clauses, both temporal and telic, that relate the Law to the promise and to its fulfilment.[56] The Law played a temporal and purposeful role that anticipated the coming of the Seed, Messiah. The Law's own temporal and purposeful design restricted the extent of its jurisdiction, "until the Seed would come" (ἄχρις οὗ ἔλθη τὸ σπέρμα, 3:19).[57]

From the beginning, in 2:15–16, Paul's argument gives ἐκ πίστεως Χριστοῦ a certain objectivity that prepares for his arresting assertion that ἡ πίστις is *now revealed* and has *now come*. Paul's concern is to juxtapose antithetical *spiritual lineages* to argue that believers in Galatia already are Abraham's seed, for they trace their descent through Christ who is the singular Seed of Abraham to whom God spoke the promises (3:16). Crucial to Paul's argument are the words "the promises were spoken to Abraham and to his seed ... who is Christ" (3:16). Paul reasons that Messiah was present when the promises *were spoken*.[58] This is no more remarkable than his earlier claim, "And Scripture, foreseeing that God would justify the Gentiles ἐκ πίστεως, *proclaimed the gospel in advance to Abraham*: 'in you all the Gentiles will be blessed'" (3:8). Messiah is Abraham's unique Seed to whom the promises were spoken. For this

---

[55] Usually, exegetes acknowledge that the verbs ἔρχομαι and ἀποκαλύπτω give ἡ πίστις objectivity. Cf., e.g., Fung, *Galatians*, 168; and Burton, *Galatians*, 198. For various interpretations of ἡ πίστις see Betz, *Galatians*, 176, n.120. Betz is surely correct when he says that ἡ πίστις "describes the occurrence of a historical phenomenon, not the act of believing of an individual".

[56] Whether deliberate or not, πρὸ τοῦ ἐλθεῖν τὴν πίστιν echoes an aspect of Paul's address to Peter, πρὸ τοῦ ἐλθεῖν τινας ἀπὸ Ἰακώβου μετὰ ἐθνῶν συνήσθιεν (Gal. 2:12). Ponder the series of temporal and purpose clauses that relate the Law to the promise and its fulfilment.

    3:19 ὁ νόμος ... προσετέθη, ἄχρις οὗ ἔλθη τὸ σπέρμα ᾧ ἐπήγγελται
    3:22 συνέκλεισεν ἡ γραφὴ ... ἵνα ἡ ἐπαγγελία ἐκ πίστεως Ἰησοῦ Χριστοῦ δοθῇ
    3:23 ὑπὸ νόμον ἐφρουρούμεθα πρὸ τοῦ δὲ ἐλθεῖν τὴν πίστιν
    3:23 συγκλειόμενοι εἰς τὴν μέλλουσαν πίστιν ἀποκαλυφθῆναι
    3:24 ὁ νόμος παιδαγωγὸς ἡμῶν γέγονεν εἰς Χριστόν
    3:25 οὐκέτι ὑπὸ παιδαγωγόν ἐσμεν ἐλθούσης τῆς πίστεως

See Caneday, "Galatians 3:22ff.: A *Crux Interpretum*", 14–15; idem, "The Curse of the Law", 176–201. Cf. Campbell, *Quest*, 211–12.

[57] Silva observes, "The use of the verb ἐλθεῖν ... suggests strongly that Paul must be referring to Christ, an identification that is confirmed by the immediate context.... If so, we should probably understand this use of πίστις as a simple metonymy whereby the word stands for the object of faith" ("Faith versus Works", 240).

[58] Cf. the claim that Levi gave tithes to Melchizedek in Heb. 7:9.

reason Paul could write "in order that the promise ἐκ πίστεως Ἰησοῦ Χριστοῦ might be given to those who believe" (3:22). For different reasons, exegetes of opposing interpretations prefer to connect ἡ ἐπαγγελία with δοθῇ rather than with ἐκ πίστεως Ἰησοῦ Χριστοῦ.[59] Paul's word order, however, is in keeping with the idiom of origin, already used in 2:16. Torah does not originate ἐκ πίστεως [Ἰησοῦ Χριστοῦ] (3:12); the promise originates ἐκ πίστεως Ἰησοῦ Χριστοῦ (3:22). These contrasting origins correlate to God's *distance* in the giving of Torah (3:19) and his *immediacy* in speaking the promises (3:16).

Though Paul's argument does prepare for his bold assertion, he still catches readers by surprise when he says, πρὸ τοῦ δὲ ἐλθεῖν τὴν πίστιν (3:23). Given the discussion of the priority of the promise to the Law one might expect Paul to use either ὁ Χριστός or τὸ σπέρμα, but not ἡ πίστις. To emphasize his startling announcement that ἡ πίστις only now has "come", he reiterates it twice more in place of the expected ὁ Χριστός or τὸ σπέρμα (3:23b, 25). Thus, when he says "we were kept in custody under the Law εἰς τὴν μέλλουσαν πίστιν to be revealed" (3:23b), he uses ἡ πίστις to represent the eschatological revelation of the unique Seed of Abraham, Messiah. Now that ἡ πίστις "has come we are no longer under the pedagogue" (3:25). Consequently, for Paul, to speak of the revelation or entrance of ἡ πίστις into the world underscores the exceptionalism of Messiah in whom the promises have come to fulfilment.

The question is not simply whether the relationship between the nouns (πίστις Χριστοῦ) is (1) an objective genitive; (2) a genitive of quality or source; or (3) a subjective/possessive genitive. The meaning of the genitive in Paul's expression ἐκ πίστεως Χριστοῦ is not found by isolating πίστις Χριστοῦ but by tracing his whole argument through to its apex in 3:22–29. Paul gives objectivity to πίστις Χριστοῦ by writing ἡ πίστις as the object of the verbs ἔρχομαι (3:23, 25) and ἀποκαλύπτω (3:23). Paul objectifies ἡ πίστις by requiring ἡ πίστις to stand in figuratively for τὸ σπέρμα, which itself represents ὁ Χριστός. Thus, Paul wrote ἡ πίστις instead of ὁ Χριστός. Why? To answer discloses how one understands the genitive in the antecedent, πίστεως Ἰησοῦ Χριστοῦ, that gives rise to the figurative expression (3:22).[60]

---

[59] Cf. Fung, *Galatians*, 165; Hays, *The Faith of Jesus Christ* (1983), 157ff. and (2002), 143ff.; and Hooker, ibid, "Πίστις Χριστοῦ", *NTS*, 329. Contrast Matlock, "Rhetoric", 187–90.

[60] Since Paul could easily have written ὁ πιστός and not ἡ πίστις, Campbell's translation of ἡ πίστις (3:23a, 23b, 25, 26) as "the faithful one" is unlikely (*Quest*, 211).

When Paul says ἡ πίστις has been revealed, is this "a simple metonymy whereby the word stands for the object of faith", Christ?[61] Does ἡ πίστις function as a metonymy for Christ and his work as inseparable with a dual sense that "only now has Christ been given as the source and object of faith"?[62] Or, when ἡ πίστις substitutes for τὸ σπέρμα or ὁ Χριστός, is it a metonymy for Christ's faithfulness, answering Israel's unfaithfulness, in his substitutionary role of redeeming us from Torah's curse, when he put an end to Torah's impedimentary function of confining its subjects typologically representative of the whole world's imprisonment under sin (cf. Rom. 3:19–20)?[63] Theologically, all three are reasonable and not one of them, in itself, injures Paul's gospel. Exegetically speaking, attractive as the second view is, the latter seems to provide greater explanatory capability for the span of Paul's argument (2:15–3:29). Though persuadable to the contrary, I am inclined to translate ἡ πίστις as "this faithfulness", referring to πίστις Χριστοῦ as "Christ's faithfulness" (3:22).

As such, then, Christ's faithfulness is his bearing the curse of the Law as God's redemptive act in history that marks the turning point of the ages, the end of non-age under Torah's guardianship and the dawn of full sonship in Christ. Christ's faithfulness ends Torah's curse incurred by Israel's unfaithfulness and brings the blessing of Abraham – namely, life, the Spirit, and justification.

Conclusions

In Galatians, Paul's argument features Christ Jesus over against Torah, with Torah in a servant role to Christ, as preparatory for Christ who has now come. Paul's antithetical placement of ἡ πίστις Χριστοῦ with ἔργα νόμου/ὁ νόμος placards the faithfulness of Christ Jesus who accomplishes what the Law could not. Torah requires deeds; Christ's

---

[61] Silva observes, "The use of the verb ἐλθεῖν ... suggests strongly that Paul must be referring to Christ, an identification that is confirmed by the immediate context ... If so, we should probably understand this use of πίστις as a simple metonymy whereby the word stands for the object of faith" ("Faith versus Works", 240.

[62] Seifrid, "Paul, Luther, and Justification", 219.

[63] On Israel's typological representation, recapitulating Adam's representative role, see A.B. Caneday, "'They Exchanged the Glory of God for the Likeness of an Image': Idolatrous Adam and Israel as Representatives in Paul's Letter to the Romans", *SBJT* 11 (2007): 34–44.

faithfulness elicits faith in him. Life is not within Torah's power to give; life comes through death to Torah, which entails being crucified with Christ. Works required by the Law condemn; Christ's faithfulness justifies. Torah curses; Christ blesses. Torah discriminates Jews from Gentiles; Jesus Christ renders Gentiles and Jews one without distinction. Torah imprisoned unfaithful Israel under sin, representatively of the whole world; by his faithfulness, Christ gives freedom from Torah to Jew and Gentile alike. The Law exacerbates transgressions; Christ gives life and righteousness. Torah impeded fulfilment of God's promise to Abraham; Christ's faithfulness, namely his bearing the curse "upon the tree", gives the promise to those who believe in him. The Law prepared for Christ; Christ ends the Law by subjecting himself to the Law's curse on our behalf. Torah foreshadows Messiah who was to come; Christ Jesus renders Torah passé as covenant, casting the Law into the shadows, for it was appropriate only for the time before his advent but malapropos now that Abraham's Seed has come.

A few observations are in order concerning Paul's use of πίστις Χριστοῦ in Galatians with reasonable inferences that bear upon his use of the same expression in his letters to the Romans and to the Philippians. In each of Paul's three letters where we find πίστις Χριστοῦ we find a collocation of similar words and phrases: circumcision, the Law, justified, righteousness, faith, faith of Christ, and so on (Gal. 2:15–3:29; Rom. 3:21–28; Phil. 3:1–11).

When Paul mentions πίστις Χριστοῦ he does so only in polarity with the Law covenant. Though not explicitly mentioned, hints of Israel's unfaithfulness enter at the core of Paul's argument, in Galatians, with mention of the curse of the Law and redemption from that curse. Israel is more explicit in Paul's letter to the Romans, where echoes of Israel's unfaithfulness enter early, juxtaposed with echoes of Adam's disobedience.[64] Juxtaposition of Israel's unfaithfulness, untruthfulness, and unrighteousness with God's faithfulness, truthfulness, and righteousness (Rom. 3:1–8) seems to prepare for Paul's argument that "now God's righteousness, apart from the Law, has been made known … through Jesus Christ's faithfulness unto all who believe" (3:21–22). God's righteousness is revealed in Christ's faithfulness in that God displays his righteousness by presenting Christ Jesus as the atoning sacrifice on behalf of us so that God is both just and the one who justifies the one from Christ's faithfulness (3:25–26). In Romans 3, if πίστις Χριστοῦ

---

[64] See Caneday, "Idolatrous Adam and Israel".

denotes Christ's faithfulness, it is another metonymy for his redeeming work, as is "his blood" (3:25). Consideration of Paul's use of the idiom of origin in Galatians 2 prompts the question whether ὁ ἐκ πίστεως Ἰησοῦ, in Romans 3:26, substitutes for ὁ πιστεύων εἰς Ἰησοῦν Χριστόν, keeping in mind the parallel phrase ὁ ἐκ πίστεως Ἀβραάμ (Rom. 4:16).

Unlike Paul's restricted, explicit, and structured account of Adam's typological foreshadowing of Christ where he juxtaposes Adam's disobedience and Christ's obedience (Rom. 5:12–19), Israel's typological prefiguring of Christ is scattered, more subtle, and less structured – but no less present or real. Thus, we debate whether διὰ πίστεως Χριστοῦ is akin to διὰ τῆς ὑποκοῆς τοῦ ἑνὸς ἀνθρώπου (5:19). Yet, Paul draws a parallel between Adam and Israel when he connects Israel's transgression of commandments with Adam's transgression in distinction from those during the time from Adam to Moses (5:14). Furthermore, Paul seamlessly links Adam's trespass in the Garden with Israel's trespasses under the Law (5:20–21).

Also disputed is whether Philippians 2:5–11 assists in making the case that διὰ πίστεως Χριστοῦ in 3:9 speaks of Christ's faithfulness. In that passage Paul uses the adjective "obedient" (ὑπήκοος, 2:8), associated more with the Adam-Christ typology, rather than "faithful" (πιστός), which one might expect with the Israel-Christ typology. Is it plausible that Philippians melds together the Adam-Christ and Israel-Christ prefigurements with Paul's focus upon the cross?

THE WITNESS OF THE WIDER NEW TESTAMENT

12

The Faith of Jesus Christ in the Synoptic Gospels and Acts

PETER G. BOLT

Since the phrase πίστις Χριστοῦ, found (with slight variations) eight times in Paul,[1] does not occur at all in the Synoptics and Acts, what can an examination of these portions of the New Testament contribute to the Pauline debate?

Linguistically, when two nouns are brought into relationship with each other by way of a genitive, the exact relationship remains unspecified. According to Moisés Silva, greater specificity is derived from (1) the reader's lexical knowledge, especially of the first noun; and, (2) the reader's contextual or historical knowledge.[2] Given Silva's second point, the Gospels and Acts may assist the Pauline debate by providing the contextual and historical backdrop against which Paul's usage may be further understood.

This seems to be a fairly common-sense assumption. Some kind of "narrative substructure" must lie behind the epistles of Paul in general, and the various expressions within them in particular, even if its exact shape is debatable.[3] Paul self-consciously preached Jesus as the Jewish Messiah, whose life, death, and resurrection also brought eschatological blessing to the nations. Any narrative substructure would certainly have been shaped by the "narrative-shape" of these great events. Since the apostolic preaching (as recorded in Acts) and the Synoptic Gospels also share this interest – albeit providing a little more "flesh" to the "narrative shape" – it seems eminently sensible to assume some correspondence

---

[1] Rom. 3:22, 26; Gal. 2:16 (2×), 20; 3:22; Phil. 3:9; Eph. 3:12. Cf. Rom. 1:17 (with Barth) and 3:3.

[2] Silva, "Faith versus Works", 220; cf. 227.

[3] With respect to the Pauline debate about πίστις Χριστοῦ, this has been explored, of course, by Hays, *The Faith of Jesus Christ*. Note p. 274: "Paul's theology must be understood as the explication and defence of a *story*."

between the gospel proclamation of the Apostle to the Gentiles, and both the earliest apostolic preaching and the final written form of the gospel as found in the Synoptics.[4] If so, then it is sensible to ask whether there is anything in these narratives that could provide a substructure for πίστις Χριστοῦ.

There is, of course, no shortage of evidence that these portions of the New Testament not only portray faith in their various characters, but that they do so as part of their aim to promote faith in their readers. Amongst the other strategies by which this purpose is achieved, the Synoptics present Jesus as the one who chiefly urges and encourages faith (e.g., Mk. 4:40; 5:36), and Acts presents the apostles doing the same (e.g., 16:31). The portrayal of so many individuals exercising faith in Christ, in both scene and summary, makes it clear that the promotion of faith is one of the positive narrative norms. In sum, "faith in Christ" is something that is described, endorsed, and encouraged by the Synoptics and Acts. If this feeds into a narrative substructure for πίστις Χριστοῦ, it could therefore somehow endorse the opinion that the genitive is objective.

It is the contention of this essay, however, that the Synoptic Gospels and Acts also provide material that not only supports the subjective genitive, but, in fact, may make it the better option.

Rather than attempting anything comprehensive, the approach taken here is one of sampling. Three particular texts of interest to the discussion are examined, before exploring some broader christological considerations.[5]

Some Synoptic Texts of Interest

Mark 11:22

Amongst the arguments about whether the genitive in the Pauline expression is to be taken objectively or subjectively, reference is

---

[4] This trajectory was explored by C.H. Dodd, *The Apostolic Preaching and its Developments* (London: Hodder & Stoughton, 1944). See also P.G. Bolt, "The Gospel for Today's Church", in *Exploring the Missionary Church* (ed. B.G. Webb; Explorations 7; Sydney: ANZEA, 1993), 27–59.

[5] There are also theological issues underlying the debate, which I have left aside, such as the implications of the divine and human natures of Christ, esp. in relation to our salvation. See further, A. Leslie, "Christ's Faithfulness and Our Salvation", in *Donald Robinson – Selected Works – Appreciation* (ed. P.G. Bolt and M.D. Thompson; Camperdown, NSW: Australian Church Record/Moore College, 2008), 73–81.

occasionally made to the analogous expression πίστις θεοῦ in Mark 11:22. Although the only comparable expression in Romans 3:3 (τὴν πίστιν τοῦ θεοῦ) is usually regarded as a clear case of the subjective genitive (and so is translated "the faithfulness of God"),[6] the Markan instance is not usually taken this way.

The complete expression on Jesus' lips is ἔχετε πίστις θεοῦ. Unfortunately, when invoking this expression as an analogy in the wider discussion interpreters often assume that it provides a stable point of comparison, as if its meaning is absolutely clear. But this is far from true. Not only does Jesus' instruction to his disciples appear in what is probably the most difficult – and neglected[7] – paragraph in the entire gospel, it is also ambiguous in its every element.

Setting aside the textual[8] and punctuational issues, the first issue is the lexical ambiguity, an issue that similarly plagues the wider debate. πίστις could denote concepts we usually capture with the translation "faith", or those we capture with "faithfulness".[9] To give one example: although Jesus clearly encouraged "faith" (e.g., Mk. 4:40; 5:36), he also expected "faithfulness" from Israel (e.g., Matt. 23:23). This presents some difficulty to English speakers, since we operate with two separate words with different nuances, whereas πίστις does double duty. Nevertheless, good lexical practice insists that both options must be given serious consideration.

The second ambiguity is syntactical: what is the nature of the relationship between the noun in the genitive (here θεοῦ) and πίστις? Although the genitive is regularly taken as objective, the clarity of the identification of the subjective genitive in the equivalent expression in Romans 3:3 (and, indeed, in the LXX 1 Sam. 21:3) raises a fairly strong counter-argument – the inclusion of the article notwithstanding.

---

[6] S.E. Dowd, *Prayer, Power, and the Problem of Suffering: Mark 11:22–25 in the Context of Markan Theology* (SBLDS 105; Atlanta, GA: Scholars Press, 1988), 60. Its only occurrence in the LXX is as a place name, and a subjective genitive, 1 Sam 21:3: ἐν τῷ τόπῳ τῷ λεγομένῳ θεοῦ πίστις Φελλανι Αλεμωνι. This appears to be a misreading of the Heb., rather strangely followed by an alliteration of the Heb. idiom transliterated as if it is also a place name. Dowd also refers to πίστις τοῦ θεοῦ in the Western text of Acts 19:20, which she takes as objective.

[7] See Dowd, *Prayer, Power*, 2–5.

[8] A few witnesses insert εἰ before the expression, most probably due to assimilation to Lk. 17:6 or Matt. 21:21. For discussion see Lane, *Mark*, 409, n.49; Dowd, *Prayer, Power*, 59.

[9] For an early discussion of this issue, see Hebert, "Faithfulness."

The third ambiguity is grammatical – and it is rarely even noted, even though it is constantly present in the verbal form ἔχετε. For this can, of course, be either an imperative or an indicative.[10] The assumption that this is a clear imperative has sometimes provided the basis for what sounds like a "knock-down" argument, such as when Silva states that this verse does not mean "*have* the faithfulness God has", but rather "*have* faith in God".[11] However, noting that the mood is ambiguous allows that Jesus could be using an indicative to affirm a fact about God – just as Paul does in Romans 3:3. The imperative has probably been assumed because a cogent meaning for the expression in indicative mode has not been apparent. But good exegesis ought to consider all the grammatical options and failure to do so may, in fact, be why a cogent meaning has not been forthcoming.

If we decide each of these three ambiguities against the tide of usual opinion, Jesus would be reminding the disciples of a fact about God: "you have the faithfulness of God".[12] Now, although the occurrence of this phrase is unusual, its theological truth is not. By way of the expression "God is faithful" (πιστὸς [ὁ] θεός and the like), the people of both the Old (Deut. 7:9; 32:4; Isa. 49:7) and the New (1 Cor. 1:9, 18; 10:13; 2 Cor. 1:8; 1 Pet. 4:19) Covenants are encouraged to continue in their walk before him. The variation used by the writer to the Hebrews, "the one who promised is faithful" (πιστὸς ὁ ἐπαγγειλάμενος, Heb. 10:23), shows that the expression evokes the covenant promises that shaped and guided Israel's expectations for the future, and so also their present experience. Despite Dowd's contention that the context suggests that Mark 11:22 is about confidence in the power of God,[13] the context also allows for Jesus commending his disciples to the promises of God.

---

[10] Noted by Dowd, *Prayer, Power*, 60, who opts for the imperative.

[11] Silva, "Faith versus Works", 231. See also C.E.B. Cranfield's comment, *The Gospel according to St. Mark* (Cambridge: Cambridge University Press, 1959), loc. cit., that "'have the sort of faith God has' is surely a monstrosity of exegesis".

[12] So Lane, *Mark*, 409: "It is possible that it should be understood as an encouragement rather than an exhortation: 'you have the faithfulness of God' (cf. Hab. 2:4)." Although opting for "faithfulness" and a subjective genitive, D.W.B. Robinson maintains the imperative, offering the translation: "be firm as God is firm" ("The Faith of Jesus Christ", 78–9). Cf. Hooker, *Mark*, 269: "The use of the unusual expression in Mark 11:22 serves to remind us that the exhortation to have faith in God is in fact based on God's own faithfulness."

[13] Dowd, *Prayer, Power*, 60.

If these ambiguities are borne in mind, Silva's four arguments take on a different perspective.[14] Firstly, the claim that neither Mark nor the gospel tradition speaks of God believing or having faith needs to be addressed in broader perspective. Even if this objection is true *elsewhere* in the gospel tradition, this does not prove that Mark 11:22 cannot be an exception. More importantly, if we allow for God's *faithfulness*, which especially implies his *faithfulness to his promises*, then we can ask this: what portion of the gospel tradition does *not* show God's faithfulness, as it is brought to fulfilment in Christ?

Silva's second observation, that Mark and the gospel tradition speak of humans believing, is, of course, entirely correct, as is his third that ἔχω + πίστις elsewhere clearly refers to people believing (citing Matt. 17:20, 21:21; Mk. 4:40; Lk. 17:6). But it is also true that (1) a person can be reminded of the faithfulness of God by being told that it was something they "had" (to rely upon), and that (2) human faith is directed towards God's promises, and so it is in itself grounded upon God's faithfulness. When the Messiah arrives, he does so as the concrete expression of God's faithfulness to his covenant promises, and it is no surprise that he commends faith in other people. But this does not mean that he cannot also speak of God's faithfulness in the context of this commendation;[15] in fact, it makes sense that he may have done so.[16]

This leads us to Silva's final argument, that the immediate context of the expression shows Jesus teaching his disciples to believe (Mk. 11:23, using πιστεύω).[17] But, although similar expressions may well be parallel in a given context, they certainly do not have to be, and other more subtle nuances may be present instead. So, for example, rather than these being parallel statements, the recommendation for the disciples to believe

---

[14] Silva, "Faith versus Works", 231. These are similar to Dowd's objections (*Prayer, Power*, 61).

[15] The LXX version of Hab. 2:4 has God's faithfulness in view (ἐκ πίστεώς μου, "by my faith[fulness]"). The MT has the pronoun "his", which in the context may still refer to God (cf. v. 3), but the three citations of the verse in the NT (Rom. 1:17; Gal. 3:11; Heb. 10:37) appear to take it to refer to human faith (although God's faithfulness certainly seems to be in the background, esp. for Rom. 1:17). But, if we take a lead from the LXX version, it is interesting to imagine how someone might use this text to commend "the just" to live by "my (i.e., God's) faithfulness". Wouldn't this involve affirming the presence of God's faithfulness, in order to urge living by it? And wouldn't this kind of exhortation be exactly what we have here?

[16] This is the drift of Hebert's argument in "Faithfulness."

[17] This is also an important argument for Dowd, *Prayer, Power*, 61.

may well be *consequential* upon the reminder of God's faithfulness to his promises.

Resolving the ambiguities in these ways makes good sense of this difficult paragraph. In the wake of the judgment on Israel implied by the withered fig tree (v. 21), Jesus reminds his disciples that they have the faithfulness of God to his promises (v. 22). Reference to "*this mountain*" in the context of Mark 11–13 must be to the Mount of Olives, the removal of which, in turn, invokes the eschatological prophecy of Zechariah 14:4,[18] – the particular promise that Jesus has in mind. The verbs in verses 24–25 should be taken as referring to the present practice of the disciples as Jews who were expecting the coming judgment day, on the basis of this (and other) promise(s): "whatever you are asking …", "whenever you stand praying …" The new feature brought by Jesus is the age of fulfilment, making the coming kingdom imminent (Mk. 1:15), and so they are to "believe that you have received it", and "it will be yours" – as they realize who he is and what difference he has made to time. If the judgment day has drawn near, then it is important for them to forgive one another, for God's court is about to be seated.[19] This urgent forgiveness arises from a conviction that the time is short and the future judgment day is just around the corner, since the promises of God are being fulfilled by the coming of Jesus into their midst. Jesus urges this conviction upon them by reminding them of "the faithfulness of God".

Mark 9:23

A second text that is occasionally drawn into the debate is Mark 9:23. According to Mark, Jesus opened his public ministry with the announcement that "the time is fulfilled and the kingdom of God is

---

[18] See W. Manson, *Jesus the Messiah: The Synoptic Tradition of the Revelation of God in Christ: With Special Reference to Form-Criticism* (London: Hodder & Stoughton, 1943), 29–30, 39–40; R.M. Grant, *Miracle and Natural Law in Graeco-Roman and Early Christian Thought* (Amsterdam: North-Holland, 1952), 167; idem, "The Coming of the Kingdom", *JBL* 67 (1948): 297–303 (300); Lane, *Mark*, 410. Dowd, *Prayer, Power*, 72–3, discusses this interpretation – without finally agreeing.

[19] Manson, *Jesus the Messiah*, 39–40; P.G. Bolt, *The Cross from a Distance: Atonement in Mark's Gospel* (Leicester: InterVarsity Press, 2004), 88; idem, *Jesus' Defeat of Death: Persuading Mark's Early Readers* (SNTSMS 125; Cambridge: Cambridge University Press, 2003), 245–6. Note Stendahl's paraphrase, quoted by Lane, *Mark*, 411: "When you stand and pray – especially if you expect your prayer to share in the power of the messianic age – forgive if you have something against somebody."

near", with the corresponding call to "repent and believe in the gospel" (1:15). After this opening, it is no surprise that Mark's narrative shows a profound interest in people coming to faith in Jesus. Two of the most poignant stories show Jesus encouraging a parent to believe, despite overwhelming counter-evidence surrounding the circumstances of their child. Jairus' daughter had actually died, and those around him gave him the eminently sensible advice that he should refrain from bothering the teacher any further. Jesus disagreed and offered him different advice: "don't be afraid, only believe" (5:36). A few chapters later we read of a father, whose son was afflicted with a killing spirit, despairing over ever receiving any help with this life-long affliction. But Jesus' word of promise was strong: "all things are possible to the one who believes" (9:23). The man's immediate reply is redolent with honest emotion: "I believe: help me in my unbelief" (9:24).

Whereas Jesus had successfully raised the little girl from her death-bed, the disciples had been unable to help the boy and his father. Jesus, however, was able to do what had seemed impossible to everyone else on the scene. The flow of the action in this account strongly suggests that Jesus was able to do what the disciples could not do, because he is the one who epitomizes "the one who believes", and so he does the impossible.

If this logic is sound, then the lesson drawn from this unit can then be extended to the other miracles that Jesus performed in Mark. He is able to work these mighty powers because he himself is a believer. With the amount of miracle material in the Gospel of Mark, and its importance to the narrative, we would have a vast amount of material displaying Jesus exercising faith. This would then become a very strong backdrop to the gospel message which, in turn, may come to act as the "narrative substructure" for the subjective genitive in the Pauline expression πίστις Χριστοῦ.

This same logic deriving from "faith to work miracles" can also be applied to the "faith of a disciple".[20] With Christian discipleship somehow linked with following Jesus, it has long been the practice of gospel readers to view Jesus as something of a model. Ian Wallis has examined this theme at length, both in the New Testament material and in the church fathers, showing that the example of Jesus' faith played a significant role in the promotion of Christian discipleship.[21] The logic of

---

[20] See also Wallis, *Faith of Jesus Christ*, ch. 2.
[21] Wallis, *Faith of Jesus Christ*.

this *imitatio Christi* theme must also drive us to conclude that Jesus must show the kind of faith that he promotes in others. If this was a strong part of the gospel message, it could also in turn provide a "narrative substructure" for the subjective genitive in the Pauline expression.

Matthew 27:43

Amongst the additions Matthew makes to Mark's account of the passion, we find the Jewish religious leaders declaring of the crucified Jesus, πέποιθεν ἐπὶ τὸν θεόν, as the grounds for their mocking taunt: "let [God] now rescue him if he wishes, for he said 'I am the Son of God'" (Matt. 27:43).[22] Because this is clearly an ironic statement, the reader recognizes two things: first, that the chief priests *did not* believe that this statement was true and, second, that Matthew *did*. Given that this is the climax of the Gospel, these ironic words in the mouths of Jesus' opponents actually bring the reader a strong summary statement about the character of Jesus' entire life.

Much of the ironic effect of this statement comes from the fact that this mockery alludes to an important Old Testament text. Matthew's interest in scriptural fulfilment is well known, as is his tendency to draw upon a rich tapestry of scriptural material in his passion narrative. The crucifixion scene is no different, depicting "Jesus as the suffering righteous one akin to the figures in Psalm 22, Isaiah 53, and Wisdom 2", and its use of scriptural language is "perhaps its outstanding feature".[23] In particular, according to Allison and Davies, "the believing reader who knows Scripture comes away with two convictions: the death of Jesus fulfils several eschatological prophecies (Ezek. 37; Amos 8:9; Zech. 14:4–5) as well as Psalms 22 and 69 (both Davidic laments)".[24]

The main allusion of verse 43 is to Psalm 22:8 – with the perfect tense form πέποιθεν being a slightly better rendering of the Hebrew than ἤλπισεν (LXX). The English translations usually render this expression: "He trusts (or trusted) in God …", which, in English, is clearly equivalent to "he has faith in God". This meaning is borne out by its use in the Psalms, where it is used for trust in God, in the hope of not being put to

---

[22] Some MSS rescue the opponents of Jesus from making a strong assertion of fact, apparently in Jesus' favour, by adding εἰ before πέποιθεν.

[23] W.D. Davies and D.C. Allison, *Matthew* (ICC; 3 vols.; Edinburgh: T&T Clark, 1997), 3.608.

[24] Davies and Allison, *Matthew*, 3.609. There are also striking parallels with Wis. 2:10–20, which itself draws upon similar material.

shame by his enemies (Ps. 24 [ET 25]:2), or destroyed (Ps. 56:2 [ET 57:1]), as opposed to trusting in power/wealth (Ps. 48:7 [ET 49:6]), or idols (Ps. 113:16 [ET 115:8]; 134 [ET 135]:18), or mortals (Ps. 117 [ET 118]:8; 145 [ET 146]:3). Not only is it used for placing confidence in the LORD (Ps. 10 [ET 11]:1; 124 [ET 125]:1), or in the Messiah (Ps. 2:12); it is also used for the confidence of the Messiah (Ps. 22:8).

Since Matthew's Gospel has already taken great pains to demonstrate that Jesus' life and ministry fulfilled the Scriptures, this mockery at the climax of the gospel narrative is absorbed by this larger theme. In Matthew's hands, Jesus' opponents end up bearing unwitting testimony to another realm of evidence that Jesus is Messiah. When they announced that "he trusted in God", the allusion to Psalm 22:8 suggests that Jesus should be seen to be the Messiah because of his previous life of faith, and especially because of his faith as he undergoes his greatest trial.

When we realize that "he trusts in God", or "he trusted in God", is an almost exact equivalent of the expression "the faith of Jesus Christ" – with the genitive understood subjectively – and that Matthew appears to summarize the Messiah's ministry in exactly these terms, then we see that this kind of substructure could certainly be deeply embedded in the gospel message and so also underlie the Pauline expression.

The Obedient Servant

The Importance of Servant Christology

As well as noting particular passages that may be of relevance for the wider discussion, the full and rich Christology of the Synoptics and Acts should also inform any summary statements that may be made in the epistles, such as πίστις Χριστοῦ.

Even where exact correspondence of vocabulary is lacking, it is highly probable that broader christological themes inform each reference to Jesus Christ in the Epistles – at least to some degree. Since the Christology of the Synoptics and Acts shares with that of Paul the important notion that Christ was the Servant of the Lord,[25] this Christology could provide an additional "narrative substructure" for the Pauline expression "faith of Christ".

---

[25] For the importance of the Servant in the Synoptics see P.G. Bolt, "The Spirit in the Synoptic Gospels: The Equipment of the Servant", in *Spirit of the Living God* (Part 1) (ed. B.G.Webb; Explorations 5; Homebush West, NSW: Lancer, 1991), 45–75.

The "faith(fulness)" of the Servant is clearly depicted by the Servant Songs in a variety of ways (e.g., Isa. 50:4–8), even if the actual language of faithfulness is not particularly well used. The success of the Servant's mission is grounded in "the Lord, who is faithful" (49:7). Equipped with the Spirit, the servant will "in truth bring forth justice" (cf. ESV: "faithfully"; Isa. 42:3, לֶאֱמֶת; LXX: εἰς ἀλήθειαν; cf. Matt. 12:18–21, where Matthew has εἰς νῖκος). In the flow of the book, the Servant stands in contrast to the people of Israel, who have not been faithful (Isa. 59:4). The theme of his righteous suffering and the Lord's vindication also implies his faithfulness. This comes to a climax in Isaiah 53, where the Servant's faithfulness is focused upon his willingness to be sacrificed to bring about the justification of the many, and it is this willingness that is given as the reason for his ultimate vindication (Isa. 53:10–12).

The presentation of Jesus as the Servant of the Lord, long-promised by the prophet Isaiah, is a key element of the Christology of the Synoptics and Acts. The ministry of the Servant provides the form and the content for Jesus' ministry – from his baptism by John (e.g., Mk. 1:11), through his miracles and manner of ministry (e.g., Matt. 12:15–21), to his substitutionary death as the ransom for many (e.g., Mk. 10:45), and on to his resurrection from the dead (cf. Isa. 53:10–12). Jesus drew upon this Servant Christology when he reminded his disciples that the Christ had to suffer before entering his glory (Lk. 24:26). Likewise, when his apostles proclaimed the gospel in the wake of his resurrection, they named Jesus as the Servant (e.g., Acts 3:13, 26; 4:27, 30).

The Uniqueness of the Servant's Faith

The previous discussion of Jesus' faith in the context of miracle-working and discipleship also needs to be considered in the context of Christology. Jesus not only called for faith from others, but, as a – or even, *the* – faithful Israelite, it seems absolutely right to say that he also exercised this called-for faith himself. This certainly has some role in shaping and encouraging Christian discipleship, including providing some raw material for an ethic of *imitatio Christi*. But, that said, it would be a mistake to see that this is the main aim of the gospels, or that this is all that can be said about Jesus' faith.

Each person must exercise faith in the context of the unique circumstances of life given to them by God. Jesus was more than just an ordinary Israelite; he had the special vocation of the Servant of the Lord – and the Christ, the Son of Man, the Son of God. For him to exercise faith was to embark upon a mission that ended only in one place: the death of the Servant as a ransom for many. This is not a destiny that can be shared or imitated by anyone else, for his role was unique in God's purposes for redeeming a lost world.

This is also true of Jesus' miracles. Although it is almost certainly true that he performed miracles because he exercised faith in his heavenly Father, this does not mean that the power to work miracles resides in a thing called "faith". Consequently, it would be completely misguided to say that someone else who had a "faith" that approximated that of Jesus could also work similar mighty powers. His faith was exercised as the Servant of the Lord and, as such, he was the one who could perform miracles in line with the prophecies of the coming messianic age (cf. Isa. 35:5–6). The ability to perform miracles did not lie in the faith of Jesus, but in his person.

But, although it is important to clarify his faith against his unique role as messianic Servant of the Lord, this does not diminish the importance of his faith. As the Servant of the Lord, by his faith he fulfilled the will of God. And, by faithfully fulfilling the Servant's role, he brought about the salvation not only of Israel but also of the nations to the ends of the earth. This came about through his sacrificial, substitutionary death (Isa. 53) as the ransom for many (Mk. 10:45). Because he was willing to die to bring about the justification of many, God vindicated him by raising him from the dead (cf. Isa. 53:10–12).

The Servant's Faithfulness in Doing God's Will

If we take a lead from the final Servant Song, the vindication of the Servant occurs because of his willingness to die for the justification of the many. In turn, this is the means by which "the will of God shall prosper in his hand" (Isa. 53:10). It does not take much imagination to recognize the parallels between this Song and Paul's own summary statements about Christ's cross-centred work, and so to recognize this as a major passage behind his own atonement theology.

But, of course, Paul's gospel was not simply derived from his understanding of the Old Testament Scriptures. Paul's gospel was generated from his understanding of who Jesus Christ was, and what he had done – especially through being willing to be crucified on behalf of the many. Thus the intermediate step between the Servant theology of Isaiah and Paul's atonement theology was the life, death, and resurrection of the Lord Jesus Christ as the one in whom "the will of the Lord" prospered.

At this point we realize that we have stumbled across a fairly major and deep-seated theme of both the Synoptics and Acts. Here Jesus is portrayed not only as doing the will of God in some kind of ordinary way expected of any Israelite, but as bringing about *the* will of God, as promised from long ages past. This is depicted, of course, in the almost constant reference to the promises of Scripture being fulfilled in and by him, as well as by the language of divine necessity that is a feature of all the Gospels, but perhaps especially the Gospel of Luke.[26] But it is also depicted with explicit reference to Jesus fulfilling the will of God, and to the will of God being fulfilled in him.

From the moment he was baptized by John, Jesus is depicted in Mark as setting out on "the way" towards the cross in fulfilment of the Father's will. Having left Nazareth to go to his baptism (Mk. 1:9), he did not give in to his family's pressure to return (3:31–35). This would be tantamount to a denial of the direction he was thrust upon by the voice from heaven (1:11). Instead, he chose to stay amongst those who sought the will of God. In Gethsemane he faced his supreme crisis as he struggled to do the will of God on the eve of that will being done, but his intention and commitment were clear: "not what I want, but whatever you want" (14:36, οὐ τί ἐγὼ θέλω ἀλλὰ τί σύ). Since he was the Servant of God, the will of God took him to the cross so that he died as a ransom for many (10:45).

Doing the will of God is even more of a positive narrative norm for the Gospel of Matthew. Jesus not only teaches his disciples to pray that the Father's will might be done on earth (Matt. 6:10) and that no one will enter the kingdom of heaven without doing the will of God (Matt. 7:21), but the very definition of Jesus' true family is those who do the will of his Father (Matt. 12:50). In the parable of the two sons, as the application of the intra-parabolic son who does the will of his father (Matt. 21:31), Jesus taught that it was those deemed "tax-collectors and sinners" (and not the self-styled righteous) who enter the kingdom of heaven. If we chase this theme through the narrative, we see that these are the people who properly responded to John the Baptist, the forerunner, and so they also responded properly to Jesus, the Messiah (cf. 11:11–19; 17:10–13; 21:23–32). Doing the will of God involves believing in the Messiah.

But what does it involve for the Messiah himself? He stands in solidarity with those who wish to do the will of his Father (12:46–50), and he prays to his Father that it might be true in his own life that people

---

[26] See, esp., J.T. Squires, *The Plan of God in Luke–Acts* (SNTSMS 76; Cambridge: Cambridge University Press, 1993).

see the Father in the Son (11:25–30). The will of the Father is explained as being at least that none of these little ones perish (Matt. 18:14), and it is clear from Matthew's story that Jesus' Servant ministry, which took him to his death on their behalf, is the means by which they are saved from perishing. This helps us to see that the prayer that the will of God might be done on earth (Matt. 6:10) was actually fulfilled in the work of Jesus as the Servant of the Lord.

As in Mark, the classic Matthean text which confirms this must be Jesus' struggle in the garden of Gethsemane (Matt. 26:42, εἰ οὐ δύναται τοῦτο παρελθεῖν ἐὰν μὴ αὐτὸ πίω, γενηθήτω τὸ θέλημά σου). Matthew's version has the dramatic "let your will come about". Here the will of the Father is that the Son might perish as the Suffering Servant, handed over to drink the cup of wrath on behalf of the sins of the world. By the Son submitting to this "fate", we see that it is not so much the Father against the Son, but both Father and Son being perfectly tuned in to this will being done. This is God entering into his own wrath, in order that the will of God might be done willingly through the Son's actions. And those actions are both active and passive – a faith-driven determination to do the will of God, and a faithful submission to the dreadful consequences required by the will of God for the redemption of the world.

The plan of God is a central theme of Luke–Acts and, once again, it is centred around Jesus' death as the necessary prelude to the proclamation of forgiveness of sins going to the ends of the earth (cf. Lk. 24:26, 44–47). Those who resisted John resisted the plan (βουλή) of God (Lk. 7:30). It is the servant who knows his master's will (θέλημα) and who gets ready (Lk. 12:47) that he commends – and, as the gospel proceeds, it becomes clear that Israel was to get ready for the arrival of the Messiah, according to the will of God. While losing the "ransom saying" (Mk. 10:45), Luke nevertheless increases the Suffering Servant overtones behind Jesus' death by alluding to Isaiah 53:6 (Lk. 22:37–38; see also 23:35) as the passion narrative begins. After this imperative for Isaiah 53 being fulfilled, Luke immediately moves into Gethsemane (22:39–53), adds to the cosmic conflict (v. 53, "this is your hour and the power of darkness"; cf. 22:3), and shows Jesus struggling with deep emotion to embrace the path the will of God has charted for this Suffering Servant (v. 42). In fact, Luke's picture of this struggle is even more intense (with the additional strength of "testing" in vv. 40, 46; the strengthening by the angel, v. 43; the agony and tears of blood, v. 44 [if vv. 43–44 are original]).

When Luke reflects upon the crucifixion in "volume 2", he summarizes this event in terms of the Son being delivered over by "the will and foreknowledge of God" (Acts 2:23). This is also the clear understanding of the early Christians who, as they prayed for boldness, recalled that in the crucifixion the Jewish authorities and Pilate had acted "to do whatever your hand and purpose (βουλή) foreordained to occur" (4:28). Gamaliel may have questioned whether this was the will of God (5:38), but Luke's readers cannot miss the fact that the resurrection of Jesus overturned the human will for him (cf. Lk. 23:25), thus displaying that the crucifixion, far from being a mistake, was the central part of God's plans for salvation for both Jew and Gentile. Jesus had been put to death on a tree, that is, under the curse of God, but "God had raised his servant up" (Acts 3:26). Through this one, "the will of God will prosper".

The Servant Christology, prominent not only in the Synoptics and Acts but also in Paul, with its emphasis upon the Servant faithfully achieving God's will, appears to be a natural candidate for deeply informing Paul's expression "the faith of Jesus Christ", with the genitive being understood subjectively.

Conclusion

To conclude, in the context of the πίστις Χριστοῦ debate, Mark 11:22 should be treated more carefully and Mark 9:23 could be used to speak of Jesus' faith, as Matthew 27:43 in fact does. But these individual texts (and any others of relevance) need to be set within the broader context of Christology, and especially that of Jesus as the Servant of the Lord. As this occurs, the message of the Synoptics and Acts provides a serious picture of the faithfulness of Jesus Christ, and this may well provide a narrative substructure which supports, or even demands, a subjective reading of the genitive in πίστις Χριστοῦ.

13

The Obedient Son: The "Faithfulness" of Christ in the Fourth Gospel

WILLIS H. SALIER

"When he had received the drink, Jesus said, 'It is finished'." (John 19:30)

"These are written that you may believe that Jesus is the Christ, the Son of God, and that by believing you may have life in his name." (John 20:31)

The Fourth Gospel might be thought to have little to contribute to the long-running debate concerning the phrase "faith of Jesus Christ" in the Pauline writings. As is well known, the phrase itself does not occur in the Fourth Gospel, nor indeed does the noun πίστις. John will certainly refer to the importance of belief through his use of the verb and associated forms, but Jesus is almost always the object of these forms and never their subject (cf. 2:24).[1] However, one does not always need specific vocabulary to mark the presence of a concept, and it can be seen that the Fourth Gospel has a contribution with respect to the broader concepts involved in the subjective/objective genitive debate.

In terms of the objective genitive reading of the phrase πίστις Χριστοῦ there is ample evidence for this concept, believing in Christ, in the Fourth Gospel – albeit carried in the unique style of the writer with the use of the verb prominent. The purpose statement of the gospel (20:31) points us to the significance of believing in the Fourth Gospel. As to the subjective reading, the narrative of the Fourth Gospel addresses this conceptually through its presentation of the mission of the faithful Son, though it needs to be noted at the outset that "faithful" is not an adjective used of Jesus in the gospel.[2] This mission is carried out in obedience to the

---

[1] Note that all biblical references are from the Fourth Gospel unless otherwise specified.

[2] Though Jesus urges this of Thomas (20:27). The adjective is used in 1 Jn. 1:9 but the Johannine letters are not examined here and the reference is to God.

Father's will and climaxes in the declaration that "it is finished" as the Son dies on the cross. A brief exploration of both of these themes will form the bulk of the Fourth Gospel's contribution.

As the examination of these two broad areas unfolds it will be possible also to reflect on the contribution that John's presentation of Jesus makes, more generally, to issues raised by the Pauline discussion concerning the faithfulness of Christ.

The Work of the Obedient Son

In John 19:30 Jesus cries out from the cross τετέλεσται. Commentators note the triumphant note struck in the cry and how this fits in with the theme of glorification through death that John has emphasized.[3] Carson comments that the verb τελειόω denotes the carrying out of a task and, in religious contexts, the fulfilment of one's religious duties.[4] This is one of a number of statements that have resounded through the last section of the gospel indicating fulfilment and completion (13:1; 19:28). Commentators, almost universally, take this statement to refer to the completion, by the Son, of the work that the Father gave him to do (4:34; 5:36; 14:31; 17:4). This accounts, at least in part, for the note of triumph.[5] This, in turn, is the climax of the theme of the mission of Jesus that has been a prominent feature of the gospel. With respect to this theme, it is overwhelmingly the language of sonship that predominates. This usage is further marked by constant references to God as Father. It is, therefore, to the mission of the Son, who was sent by the Father to do the work of the Father, that we turn our attention initially. Of particular interest will be the conduct of that work, the context of that work, and the content of that work.

The Mission of the Son

It is Bultmann who has most emphatically drawn attention to the central place of the theme of the commissioning and sending of the Son

---

[3] Most recently C.S. Keener, *The Gospel of John: A Commentary* (2 vols.; Peabody, MA: Hendrickson, 2003), II:1147.

[4] G.R. Beasley-Murray, *John* (WBC 36; Waco, TX: Word, 1987), 621.

[5] R. Schnackenburg, *The Gospel according to John* (trans. K. Smyth; 3 vols.; Kent: Burns & Oates, 1968–82), III:284 is representative.

in the Fourth Gospel.[6] This theme is carried by several word groups, most notably the language of sending (πέμπω, ἀποστέλλω). While the theme encompasses both the Father sending the Son and the Son in turn sending the disciples, it is the group of references that refer to the former that are pertinent here (e.g., 3:16–17; 5:23, 30, 36; 10:36; 12:49; 14:24; 17:3, 18, 21, 23, 25; 20:21). Other word fields include coming (ἔρχομαι; cf. 1:9; 3:19; 8:12; 12:46; ὁ ἐρχόμενος, 6:14; 7:27, 31, 41–42; 11:27; 12:13, 15); returning (ὑπάγω, 7:33; 8:14); and the language of descending and ascending (ἀναβαίνω, καταβαίνω, 6:30–59; 3:13; 6:62; 8:28), all predicated of the Son.

Köstenberger, in his comprehensive exposition of the theme of mission in the gospel, also includes word fields concerned with the idea of calling to follow (ἀκολυθέω, 8:12; 10:4, 5; 12:26; 21:19–23); and gathering (ἄγω, 10:16; συνάγω, 11:51–52), commenting that a failure to consider all of the categories mentioned leads to an "imbalanced and incomplete" account.[7] These modes of movement are connected with a variety of purposes that are enunciated for Jesus' mission. He is sent for the purpose of salvation and judgment (3:16–17). Jesus comes into the world (and returns) in order to reveal the Father (1:14, 18); for the purpose of judgment (9:39); to both save and judge (12:47); and to bring abundant life and salvation (10:9–10). He is the coming one in fulfilment of Old Testament expectations (4:25; 6:14; 7:27, 31, 41–42; 11:27; 12, 13, 15). He has descended in order to give life (6:33, 40, 44, 47, 50–58). He calls people to believe (1:37–43; 8:12; 10:4, 5, 27; 12:26; 21:19–23); and he gathers the eschatological people of God into a unity (10:16; 11:51–52). Köstenberger notes that the language of sending correlates with the title "the Son" throughout the gospel and that the emphasis in most statements concerning sending is not so much on the purpose for being sent as it is on the mode of Jesus' behaviour in the activity of being sent. The accent falls on the Son's obedience.[8]

---

[6] So P. Borgen, "God's Agent in the Fourth Gospel", in *Religions in Antiquity: Essays in Memory of Erwin Ramsdell Goodenough* (ed. Jacob Neusner; Leiden: Brill, 1968), 137–48 (137). A concentrated exposition of the theme is found in Bultmann, *Theology*, II, 33–40.

[7] A. Köstenberger, *The Missions of Jesus and the Disciples in the Fourth Gospel: With Implications for the Fourth Gospel's Purpose and the Mission of the Contemporary Church* (Grand Rapids, MI: Eerdmans, 1998), 89.

[8] Köstenberger, *The Missions of Jesus*, 91–6.

The Obedience and Dependence of the Son

Köstenberger notes that "the sending Christology of John's Gospel appears to centre around the themes of obedience and dependence".[9] That is to say that the Son carries out his mission in obedience to, and dependence upon, the Father. This observation correlates with the more general observation that, throughout the Fourth Gospel, the Father initiates and the Son responds.

The motifs of obedience and dependence are carried by a number of different emphases. As the sent one, Jesus is to bring glory and honour to the sender (5:23; 7:18). He does the sender's will (4:34; 5:30, 38; 6:38–39). In doing this will he speaks the sender's words (3:34; 7:16; 12:49; 14:10b, 24) and does his works (5:36; 9:4). He is accountable to the sender (cf. Jn. 17, where Jesus reports back to the Father concerning the mission given him). He is to represent the sender accurately (12:44–15; 13:20; 15:18–25) and to bear witness to the sender (5:36; 7:28).

Jesus perfectly manifests all of these emphases. He claims that the sender's glory is uppermost in his mind (cf. 11:4; 12:28; 13:31; 14:13). He claims that his "food" is to do the will of the Father and accomplish his work (4:34); that he is continually about doing the work of the Father (9:4; cf. 5:17). In fact, he says he can only do what the Father has shown him and he only does this in the power of the Father (cf. 5:19–20). Jesus' words likewise emanate from the Father. His teaching is that of the Father (7:16) and he only speaks what the Father has told him to say (12:48–50; cf. 14:24). In all of these references the perfect obedience and dependence of the Son is on view. He is faithful in this task because he completes the work the Father has given him, the obedient Son.

John 5 is a key passage for this understanding. Jesus moves into a lengthy monologue in response to the charge from the Jews that he is making himself equal to God (5:18). In the dense exposition that follows, the language of Father and Son is defended and Jesus' implicit claim to equality with God is expounded. It is made clear that "Jesus is not equal with God as *another* God or as a *competing* God; the functional subordination of the Son, the utter dependence of the Son upon the Father are explicated".[10] The dependence of the Son is shown in verse 19, where Jesus says he can do nothing on his own but only what he sees the Father doing. The equality of the Son and Father is demonstrated in the way that the Son is able to do all that the Father shows him – most

---

[9] Köstenberger, *The Missions of Jesus*, 107.
[10] D.A. Carson, *The Gospel according to John* (PNTC; Leicester: InterVarsity Press, 1991), 250.

notably give life (5:21) and exercise judgment (5:22). Further, the Son is to be honoured as the Father is honoured (5:23). The basis for this is the love that the Father has for the Son (5:20). As the gospel presents it, the Son is both able and willing to do the will of the Father. He is able to do the will of the Father because he is the Son and he is willing to do the will of the Father because of the reciprocal love that exists between Father and Son.

It is often observed that behind the sending concept lies the Jewish concept of sending or agency. Borgen notes the striking similarities between halakic principles of agency and ideas in the Fourth Gospel.[11] These include the idea of the unity between agent and sender; the subordination (at the same time) of agent to sender; and the obedience of the agent to the will of the sender. A.E. Harvey makes an important contribution to this line of thinking when he emphasizes that the theme of sending in the Fourth Gospel focuses on the sending of the Son.[12] He makes the point that this thought advances and deepens the agency concept and that the sonship language points to the fact that only the son, an only son beloved by the father, could be fully trusted to promote the interests of the Father and perfectly fulfil his will. Jesus is never referred to as an agent in the Fourth Gospel and Harvey suggests that this is because calling him an agent might suggest the absence of the Father. Beasley-Murray makes a similar observation in his discussion of the mission motif when he notes that "[p]recisely because the origin of the mission of the Son is the presence of the Father, the dictum 'One sent is as he who sent him' receives an application more profound and more complete than could be so in the purely human relationship of Sender and Sent".[13]

The Context of the Work of the Son

John presents the work of the Son not only in the context of his relationship with the Father, but also in the context of the narrative of Israel and the promises of God in the Old Testament. This is suggested in John 19:28, where Jesus says "I thirst" so that (ἵνα) Scripture might

---

[11] Borgen, "God's Agent", 128–32.

[12] A.E. Harvey, "Christ as Agent", in *The Glory of Christ in the New Testament: Studies in Christology in Memory of G.B. Caird* (ed. L.D. Hurst and N.T. Wright; Oxford: Clarendon Press, 1987), 239–50.

[13] G.R. Beasley-Murray, "The Mission of the Logos-Son", in *The Four Gospels 1992: Festschrift Frans Neirynck* (ed. F. van Segbroeck, et al.; BETL; 3 vols.; Leuven: University Press, 1992), III:1865–66.

be fulfilled. The plans of God and the work of the Son occur in the context of God's dealings with his covenant people. The obedient Son is obedient in the context of a salvation-historical understanding of history. This is demonstrated by, amongst others, J. Prior, who shows how deeply embedded in the entire fabric of John's text is a salvation-historical perspective.[14] This comes through, for example, in the use of the phrase "his own" with reference to Israel in 1:11; in the allusion to God's dwelling among his Old Covenant people Israel in 1:14; in the portrayal of Jesus in Mosaic terms with the proviso that Jesus exceeds him (1:17; cf. Abraham, 8:58); in the statement in 1:51 implying that Jesus replaces Israel as the place where God's glory is revealed; in John's adaptation of covenantal terminology and patterns (e.g., to love, obey, know, and see in 14:15–24 drawing on Exodus and Deuteronomy). Tom Wright has drawn attention to John's use of the creation motif to frame his work.[15] There is also evidence of the use of broad thematic patterns as well as specific verses from the writings of Isaiah.[16]

This strand of the gospel encourages us to see that while the sending motif (and perhaps the Fourth Gospel's emphasis on revelation) might be thought to have more apocalyptic overtones, these overtones are tempered by their embedding in the more longitudinal salvation-historical understanding. The revelation of the Father by the Son and the sending of the Son by the Father are presented within a context that is always conscious of God's prior dealings with his people. The obedient Son comes and completes his work in the context of God's wider plans for his people, and indeed for the world (1:10–13; cf. 12:20–23).

The Work of the Son: What Is Finished?

"It is finished" is the cry of Jesus from the cross as he completes the work that his Father has given him to do. But what is accomplished? What is the work of the Son?

The use of the term "work" in the question gives pause to examine the use of the term ἔργον in the gospel. Twice Jesus refers to his mission in terms of the singular ἔργον (4:34; 17:4). On a number of other occasions he refers to the works (ἔργα) given him to complete (5:20, 36). The usage

---

[14] J. Prior, *John: Evangelist of the Covenant People: The Narrative and Themes of the Fourth Gospel* (London: Darton, Longman & Todd, 1992).

[15] T. Wright, *John for Everyone* (2 vols.; London: SPCK, 2002).

[16] W. Salier, *The Rhetorical Impact of the Semeia in the Gospel of John* (WUNT II: 186; Tübingen: Mohr Siebeck, 2004), 124–5.

points to Jesus' work as being conceived as a whole and also in its constituent parts. The term ἔργα is quite general. Jesus' works are the works of God (6:28; 9:3, 4; 10:37; cf. 14:10). They, therefore, testify and reveal the Father (10:25, 38) and so can be the basis of believing response (10:38; 14:11). There are many of these works (10:32). Jesus' works clearly include what the narrator and other characters in the gospel call σημεῖα. Jesus occasionally uses this term (4:48; 6:26), though not in reference to his own activity. The σημεῖα are included in the ἔργα and comprise their focal point but do not exhaust their referent.[17] At times when Jesus speaks of his works he clearly has what John will call the σημεῖα in mind (7:21; 9:3–4; 15:22–24). However, there are other more general references to Jesus' activity which could also be seen as comprising elements of his works in a broader sense. In the immediate context of 19:28, for example, his work may include the fulfilment of Scripture. In 14:2–3 Jesus says he is preparing dwelling places for the disciples, while in John 14:6 it is a way to the Father. In the context of John 5 it is giving life to the dead and executing judgment. On a wider thematic scale, the work of the Son might be said to be to represent the Father in the lawsuit against the κόσμος. We have already noted statements that the Son has been sent in order to reveal the Father (1:14, 18), to both save and judge (9:39; 12:47), and to bring abundant life and salvation (10:9–10).

The references to works, signs, and also to the words of Jesus, point to the significance of the actions of his whole life, or at least recorded ministry, as aspects of his obedience to the Father. He is obedient with respect to both what he says and what he does. He does the works the Father shows him and speaks only what the Father gives him to say. At times his obedience to the Father seems to come down to a matter of days (cf. 7:6; 11:6). However, the question remains: What is that work? What binds these many aspects together? And what do the events on the cross, which form the context for the statement "It is finished", have to contribute?

Clearly a major aspect of the work of Jesus in the Fourth Gospel is that he has come to reveal the Father.[18] It is also noted that another prominent element in the gospel is the presentation of Jesus' mission as bringing life.[19] John 17:1–5 brings these elements together as Jesus

---

[17] Salier, *Rhetorical Impact*, 81, 144–6.

[18] Most emphatically, Bultmann, *Theology*, II:49–69.

[19] See M. Labahn, *Jesus als Lebensspender: Untersuchungen zu einer Geschichte der johanneischen Tradition anhand ihrer Wundergeschichten* (BZNW 98; Berlin: Walter de Gruyter, 1999).

speaks of his work and defines life as knowing the Father. But how does he give life? And what is the connection between the death of Jesus and this life-giving purpose?

There has been a long-running discussion in Johannine scholarship as to whether the work of Jesus includes redemptive as well as revelatory aspects. It was Bultmann who famously suggested that "[t]he thought of Jesus' death as an atonement for sin has no place in John".[20] In his view, humanity exists in a plight consisting of ignorance of God and the darkness of unbelief. What is required, therefore, is revelation of the knowledge of God and light. This is Jesus' mission, which he achieves through the incarnation. The death of Jesus is the final transition to the glory that he had in his pre-existence.[21] Jesus' single work is to reveal, through word and deed, meeting the problem of ignorance. Käsemann similarly denies any redemptive aspect to Jesus' death in John, viewing it as a "mere postscript which had to be included".[22] In responding to Bultmann and Käsemann, Forestell also denies any vicarious, expiatory, or sacrificial elements to the presentation of the death of Jesus in John. However, he does understand the cross as a part of the apocalyptic disclosure of salvation that occurs in Jesus in the Fourth Gospel.[23] The cross becomes more than a mere stepping-stone to glory – rather, it is the focus of the presentation of the glory of the revelation of God's love for humankind. With variations, views that seek to downplay or reject redemptive elements of John's presentation of the death of Jesus remain a live element in Johannine studies.[24]

Responses from a variety of writers have generally pointed to a series of statements in the Fourth Gospel that give voice to a theology of atonement that moves beyond what Bultmann or Forestell have suggested. Usually this is phrased in terms of a both/and rather than an either/or approach to the question.[25] While this later approach is

---

[20] Bultmann, *Theology*, II:54.

[21] Bultmann, *Theology*, II:53.

[22] E. Käsemann, *The Testament of Jesus* (trans. G. Krodel; London: SCM Press, 1966), 7.

[23] J.T. Forestell, *The Word of the Cross: Salvation as Revelation in the Fourth Gospel* (AnBib 57; Rome: Biblical Institute Press, 1974).

[24] See the summary in J. Dennis, "Jesus' Death in John's Gospel: A Survey of Research from Bultmann to the Present with Special Reference to the Johannine Hyper-Texts", *CBR* 4 (2005–6): 331–63; 342–9.

[25] So, e.g., B. Lindars, "The Passion in the Fourth Gospel", in *Essays on John* (ed. C.M. Tuckett; Leuven: University Press, 1992), 69. M. Turner has an extended critique of Forestell in "Atonement and the Death of Jesus in John – Some Questions to Bultmann and Forestell", *EvQ* 62.2 (1990): 99–122.

no doubt correct, there still appears to be a little too much demurring at certain points as to the redemptive aspects of John's presentation. There is a series of clues in the text that prepare the reader to embrace a substitutionary understanding of the cross within the framework of vicarious sacrifice.

An initial observation is to point to how integral the death of Jesus is to the plot of the gospel. It is where the narrative leads from at least 2:21–22. The major turning point at the raising of Lazarus sets in motion the events of the death of Jesus that dominate the second "half" of the gospel. The use of the hour motif (cf. 2:4; 7:30; 8:20; 12:23, 27, 38; 13:31; 17:1) focuses attention through the gospel on the events of that hour – the death and resurrection of Jesus. Jesus refers in a variety of ways to his death and its effects, including statements concerning his lifting up (3:14–15; 8:28; 12:32–34). Death threats (5:18; 7:1, 19; 8:37, 40) and the various attempts at stoning (10:31–33; 11:8) also point to the cross.[26]

B.H. Grigsby points to three thematic elements that suggest an expiatory understanding of the cross: a paschal theme (1:29; 19:14, 29, 36); an Akedah theme (1:29; 3:16; 19:17); and a "living water" theme, whereby sin is cleansed by the outpouring of blood by the sacrificial victim or by washing with living water (4:10–15; 7:37; 13:10; 19:34).[27]

A sequence of statements and incidents prepares the reader through the gospel to understand the death of Jesus in this way. John 1:29 is a key verse in understanding John's presentation of the cross in sacrificial and atoning terms. As Turner points out, it is important due to its positioning in the gospel. It occurs in the midst of chapters 1–2, which are foundational for the rest of the gospel as Jesus is introduced. He notes that, "[f]ar from being insignificant, its position would suggest 1:29 is a doorway to the Johannine understanding of the cross".[28] Further, it is a declaration from the lips of John, who has been established in the prologue as a key witness to the light, through whose testimony all belief must come (1:7). Jesus is referred to as "the Lamb of God who takes away the sin of the world". It is, initially, an enigmatic reference.

---

[26] J. Frey, "Die '*theologia crucifixi*' des Johannesevangeliums", in *Kreuzestheologie im Neuen Testament* (ed. A. Dettwiler and J. Zumstein; WUNT I:151; Tübingen: Mohr Siebeck, 2002), 197–9. Frey suggests that Kahler's well-known statement concerning the Gospels as passion narratives with an extended introduction is even more true of John than it is of Mark (193).

[27] B.H. Grigsby, "The Cross as an Expiatory Sacrifice in the Fourth Gospel", *JSNT* 15 (1982): 51–80 (62). The Akedah references are, arguably, the most tentative and least convincing of his three broad thematic elements.

[28] Turner, "Atonement", 121–2.

What Lamb might lie in the background of this statement?[29] As the gospel progresses, it becomes clear that the primary referent of this verse is the Passover lamb. This is established by the multiple references to the Passover throughout the gospel as well as by details of the passion narrative that further hint at the role of Jesus as the Passover lamb (18:28, 39; 19:14, 29, 31–37).[30]

John 1:29 also highlights the notion of sin as the problem in the gospel. The issue of sin virtually bookends the gospel (cf. 20:23), thereby highlighting its prominence. While the concept of sin in the Fourth Gospel includes ignorance, this cannot be the restricted meaning of the concept in John. As early as the prologue we have statements of ignorance concerning the κόσμος alongside a more culpable not receiving (1:9–10). A platform is laid for an understanding of the cross in John as atoning for sin as rebellion, rejection of the Christ, rather than simply a revelation for the ignorant (cf. 8:21, 24; 20:23).[31] There is also some evidence for the atoning character of the Passover lamb in a variety of Old Testament and Jewish texts (e.g., Deut. 16; 2 Chr. 30; Philo, *Spec. Laws* 2.145; Josephus, *Ant.* 2.312).[32] The early Christian understanding is not in dispute (cf. 1 Cor. 5:7).[33]

Another clue is offered when Jesus speaks of himself as the good shepherd who lays down his life for the sheep (10:11). This action of the good shepherd is emphasized through repetition (10:15, 18). This theme is then reprised in John 18, when there is a visible re-enactment of the good shepherd motif as Jesus gives himself up to protect his sheep (18:9, 14).[34] Amongst these references are three of a number of references in the gospel where the preposition ὑπέρ is used (6:51c; 10:11, 15; 11:51–52; 15:13; 17:19; 18:14). While there is some dispute as to the extent and

---

[29] For a useful survey of the options see Carson, *John*, 148–51.

[30] Cf. G.L. Carey, "The Lamb of God and Atonement Theories", *TynBul* 32 (1981): 97–122 (102–3) and S.E. Porter, "Can Traditional Exegesis Enlighten Literary Analysis of the Fourth Gospel? An Examination of the Old Testament Fulfilment Motif and the Passover Theme", in *The Gospels and the Scriptures of Israel* (ed. C.A. Evans and W.R. Stegner; JSNTSup 104; Sheffield: Sheffield Academic Press, 1994), 396–428.

[31] See W.D. Chamberlain, "The Need of Man: The Atonement in the Fourth Gospel", *Int* 10.2 (1956): 157–66; David Adamo, "Sin in John's Gospel", *EvRTh* 13.3 (1989): 216–27; and C.K. Barrett, *The Gospel according to St. John* (2nd ed.; London: SPCK, 1978), 80–1, give some indication of the breadth of the concept.

[32] R. Metzner, *Das Verständnis der Sünde im Johannesevangelium* (WUNT 1:122; Tübingen: Mohr Siebeck, 2000), 129–30.

[33] See Schnackenberg, *John*, I.299–300. Cf. Metzner, *Sünde*, 129.

[34] See also M.G.W. Stibbe, *John as Storyteller: Narrative Criticism and the Fourth Gospel* (SNTSMS 73; Cambridge: Cambridge University Press, 1992), 102–5.

referent of the ὑπέρ passages, Frey convincingly argues that a narrative reading of these later references in the light of 1:29 will incorporates them into an overall picture of Jesus' death as vicarious and atoning.[35]

A further contribution is made in John 12:23–24, where Jesus declares that a grain of wheat must fall to the ground and die before producing much fruit. At the very least the death of Jesus is described as fruit bearing, although the application is further individuated to the believer in verse 25. Finally, in John 13:10 the death of Jesus is described as cleansing. The further insight is added in the exchange with Peter, where Jesus declares that unless he "serves" Peter by washing him Peter can have no "part" with Jesus (13:8). Herein is a further hint at the vicarious nature of Jesus' work.

All of this is ample preparation for a general substitutionary and atoning understanding of the death of Jesus. This is not to pit the importance of revelation against such an understanding. The Father who is revealed by the Son is the Father who has sent the Son to reveal and to be the Lamb of God that takes away the sin of the world.

Summary

The obedient work of Jesus is both broad and focused. It encompasses his earthly life and ministry but always with a focal point of movement towards the events of the "hour": his death and resurrection. Jesus' "faithfulness" or obedience is displayed in his life and, most especially, at the singular moment of his death and resurrection. It was for this that he came (12:27). While this correlates to what an earlier generation of theologians called the active and passive obedience of Christ, we observe that the focus on the cross via the terminology of the hour, lifting up, and glorification places the accent finally on the death and resurrection of Jesus as *the* moment of obedient action.[36]

Believing in the Fourth Gospel

How does one benefit from the work of Jesus in the Fourth Gospel? The simple answer is by believing. Belief is a major theme in the Fourth

---

[35] See Frey, "Die '*theologia crucifixi*'," 214–15, for a discussion.

[36] The movement of the various sign narratives to the cross and resurrection as the "sign of signs" is a further indication of this point. See Salier, *Rhetorical Impact*, 142–3; 148–51.

Gospel – so much so that at least one commentary is subtitled "The Gospel of Belief".[37] A number of observations can be made.

The first thing to note is that John does not use the noun πίστις at all. While this might be consistent with a preference for verbs generally, Brown echoes a general consensus when he remarks that the use of the verb marks for John a sense that faith is not an internal disposition so much as an active commitment.[38] Carter comments further that the verb and its various forms denote "an activity that constitutes and expresses an identity in an ongoing way of life … It has the sense of living faithfully and loyally, of acting with fidelity".[39] This is reflected in his suggestion that instead of "believe" the verb πιστεύω be more frequently translated "entrust" so as to communicate a dynamic sense of commitment and attachment and emphasize the activity involved.

The verb form is frequently followed by the preposition εἰς. This is a characteristic of Johannine style (36 out of the 45 NT occurrences) and appears to denote "not only recognition and acceptance of the truth but also adherence and allegiance to the Truth".[40] This is further illustrated by the occasions when the verb πιστεύω occurs in a parallel relationship to the idea of coming to (ἔρχομαι, 6:35; 7:37–8) and the observation that the clear majority of uses of the construction involving εἰς have Jesus, or the name of Jesus, governed by the preposition (35×). The verb πιστεύω is also followed by the dative, but these occurrences appear to be more general with belief in these instances directed towards the general acceptance of a message.[41] Clearly the two ideas are not unrelated in that the message is usually either spoken by Jesus or about Jesus.

Through the first section of the gospel there is a question raised as to what constitutes true belief. The answer is given in the statement in John 8:31, where the true follower is described as the one who abides in the word of Jesus. This is later fleshed out in John 15, where Jesus speaks of the character of the one who abides in him as one who both loves and obeys. The portrait of the true believer throughout the gospel is portrayed through these positive utterances and also in contrast to

---

[37] M.C. Tenney, *John: The Gospel of Belief* (Grand Rapids, MI: Eerdmans, 1948).

[38] R. Brown, *The Gospel according to John* (AB 29; 2 vols.; New York: Abingdon, 1966, 1970), I:512.

[39] W. Carter, *John: Storyteller, Interpreter, Evangelist* (Peabody, MA: Hendrickson, 2006), 94.

[40] Murray Harris, "Prepositions and Theology in the Greek New Testament", in *The New International Dictionary of New Testament Theology* (ed. C. Brown; 3 vols.; Exeter: Paternoster, 1978), III.1213. Cf. Brown, *John*, I.512–3.

[41] Brown, *John*, I.513.

paradigms of unbelief: the Jews and the world. The true believer loves and obeys, and this is shown in his or her abiding in the word (see 6:66–71 and 8:31–47 for positive and negative examples). A connection with the model of Jesus is established in John 15:10, where he presents himself as the paradigm of one who has obeyed the command of the Father and abides in his love.

The believer entrusts himself or herself to Jesus in a way that Jesus would not entrust himself to human beings (2:24). An interesting contrast is thereby set up. Jesus would not entrust himself to human beings because he knew them and what was in their hearts. By the end of the gospel, the readers of the gospel are invited to entrust themselves to Jesus because they have seen what is in the heart of Jesus; they have seen the revelation of the Father and his love and can therefore entrust themselves to both with confidence. If this insight has any truth, then the Fourth Gospel presents a classic dynamic of faith being engendered in response to the faithful work of the Son.

Concluding Observations

In writing his New Testament theology, G.B. Caird envisioned an apostolic roundtable whereby each writer in the New Testament was invited to contribute their perspective on a variety of topics.[42] What has John to contribute to the discussion concerning the debate concerning the faithfulness of Christ?

First, John's presentation of the Son emphasizes that talk of the obedience of Christ is talk about the obedience of the Son in the context of a relationship with the Father. It is obedience in the context of a relationship of dependence and love. This reinforces the observation of Richard Longenecker that all the titles and metaphors used to describe the nature and effects of Christ's work "are founded ultimately on the early Christians' conviction regarding the full obedience and entire faithfulness of Jesus of Nazareth ... with this complete filial obedience seen as having been exercised throughout his life and coming to complete expression in his death on the cross".[43]

---

[42] G.B. Caird, *New Testament Theology* (ed. L.D. Hurst; Oxford: Clarendon Press, 1994), 18–26.

[43] R. Longenecker, "Foundational Conviction", 475. Longenecker suggests that, of the evangelists, it is Matthew who has been most dominated by a consciousness of Christ's obedience (485). The above analysis suggests that more notice might be taken of the Fourth Gospel with respect to this issue.

Second, the context of Jesus' work in the Fourth Gospel is the plans of God as expressed through the Scriptures of Israel. John helps us to see afresh this aspect of Jesus' work. The "faithful" work of Christ is accomplished within a salvation-historical framework.

Third, the language of Father and Son reminds us that the Christology of the Fourth Gospel is important to consider, especially when there appears to be some nervousness in the wider Pauline debate over the christological implications of both the subjective and objective readings. On the one side some, defending an objective reading, express concern at the possible over-emphasis of the human obedience of Christ and the possibility that his obedience may become nothing more than exemplary.[44] On the other side, proponents of the subjective genitive have occasionally accused those holding to an objective reading of being docetic.[45] John gives us a model of balance in his presentation of the nature of Christ.

As M.M. Thompson points out, no passage in the Fourth Gospel "demands an interpretation which impugns the true humanity of Jesus".[46] At the same time, "the Gospel affirms Jesus' divine identity in the strongest possible terms ... (and) in confessing Jesus as 'God' the Fourth Gospel never denies Jesus' humanity".[47] John places these perspectives into a "dance" and allows them to create a reality more complete than either partner examined on its own.[48] It is not simply to a magnificent example of human obedience lived out before us that John urges allegiance. John shows us one who in true humanity obeyed and loved to the end – but always within the context of his identity as the Son who has come, been sent, into the world from above.

The Son is a model to be followed (13:14). However, the uniqueness of the person of the Son renders his obedience qualitatively different from that of any other human person and also underlines the uniqueness of his mission in the Fourth Gospel.[49] Further, John shows the centrality of the death and resurrection of Jesus and presents an understanding of that event in sacrificial and atoning terms. Both the obedient action

---

[44] Seifrid, *Christ, Our Righteousness*, 142.
[45] J.P. Pollard, "The 'Faith of Christ' in Current Discussion", *Concordia* 23 (1997): 213–28 (225).
[46] M.M. Thompson, *The Incarnate Word: Perspectives on Jesus in the Fourth Gospel* (Peabody, MA: Hendrickson, 1988), 117.
[47] Thompson, *Incarnate Word*, 127, citing Jn. 1:1 and 20:29.
[48] This metaphor was suggested in private conversation by Jennie Baddeley.
[49] Köstenberger, *The Missions of Jesus*, 46–52.

of the Son and the human response believing in the person and work of the Son find their place.

So ends this attempt at describing John's contribution to this topic. John clearly cannot adjudicate the exegetical debate in Paul, but he has interesting and important things to say on both sides of the wider issues involved. As such his voice is well worth hearing, especially as the debate in Paul continues to move beyond grammar and exegesis to consider broader implications.[50]

---

[50] Pollard, "Faith of Christ", 226–7.

14

James 2:1 in the Πίστις Χριστοῦ Debate: Irrelevant or Indispensable?

BRUCE A. LOWE

Introduction

Wesley Wachob (in his 1993 Emory dissertation) lamented that through-out the history of research James has been "maligned and neglected".[1] Such words are not true today. Since Wachob's dissertation, a wealth of new commentaries[2] and monographs (including his own),[3] has

---

[1] "'The Rich in Faith' and 'The Poor in Spirit': The Social-Rhetorical Function of a Saying of Jesus in the Epistle of James" (PhD dissertation; Emory University, 1993), 62.

[2] L.T. Johnson, *Letter of James* (AB 37A; New York: Doubleday, 1997); R.W. Wall, *Community of the Wise: The Letter of James* (Valley Forge, PA: Trinity, 1997); L.T. Johnson, *The Letter of James* (*NIB* 12; Nashville, TN: Abingdon, 1998), 177–225; G. Bray, *James, 1–2 Peter, 1–3 John, Jude* (ACCS 11; Downers Grove, IL: InterVarsity Press, 2000); C. Burchard, *Der Jakobusbrief* (HNT 15/1; Tübingen: Mohr Siebeck, 2000); D.J. Moo, *The Letter of James* (PNTC; Grand Rapids, MI: Eerdmans, 2000); W. Popkes, *Der Brief des Jakobus* (THKNT 14; Leipzig: Evangelische Verlags-Anstalt, 2001); P.J. Hartin, *James* (SP 14; Collegeville, MN: Liturgical Press, 2003); and W.F. Brosend, *James and Jude* (NCBC; Cambridge: Cambridge University Press, 2004).

[3] M. Klein, *"Ein vollkommenes Werk": Vollkommenheit, Gesetz und Gericht als theologische Themen des Jakobusbriefes* (BWANT 139; Stuttgart: W. Kohlhammer, 1995); W.R. Baker, *Personal Speech-Ethics in the Epistle of James* (WUNT 2/68; Tübingen: Mohr Siebeck, 1995); T.C. Penner, *The Epistle of James and Eschatology: Re-reading an Ancient Letter* (JSNTSup 121; Sheffield: Sheffield Academic Press, 1996); M. Tsuji, *Glaube zwischen Vollkommenheit und Verweltlichung: Eine Untersuchung zur literarischen Gestalt und zur inhaltlichen Koharenz des Jakobusbriefes* (WUNT 2/93; Tübingen: Mohr Siebeck, 1997); M. Konradt, *Christliche Existenz nach dem Jakobusbrief: Eine Studie zu seiner soteriologischen und ethischen Konzeption* (SUNT 22; Göttingen: Vandenhoeck & Ruprecht, 1998); R. Bauckham, *James: Wisdom of James, Disciple of Jesus the Sage* (New Testament Readings; London and New York: Routledge 1999); P.J. Hartin, *A Spirituality of Perfection: Faith in Action in the Letter of James* (Collegeville, MN: Liturgical Press, 1999); W.H. Wachob, *The Voice of Jesus in the Social-Rhetoric of*

appeared. And with the prospect of other important commentaries in the near future,[4] it may even be said that James is enjoying a renaissance at present which shows no sign of abruptly ending.

Such renewed interest ought to initially come as great encouragement to those hoping to use James 2:1 in the πίστις Χριστοῦ debate, Ἀδελφοί μου, μὴ ἐν προσωπολημψίαις ἔχετε τὴν πίστιν τοῦ κυρίου ἡμῶν Ἰησοῦ Χριστοῦ τῆς δόξης. ("My brethren, show no partiality as you hold *the faith of our Lord Jesus Christ*, the Lord of glory", RSV.) I use the word "encouragement" here because, while this verse has already been used in the debate,[5] such usage has been somewhat precarious. There is a well-documented point of confusion in this verse which threatens to undermine its value to either side – that is, the question of what τῆς δόξης modifies.[6] Such confusion then opens the door for a more troubling idea.[7] Some older exegetes have

---

James (SNTSMS 106; Cambridge: Cambridge University Press, 2000); A. Batten, "Unwordly Friendship: The 'Epistle of Straw' Reconsidered" (PhD dissertation; University of St. Michael's College, 2000); D.H. Edgar, *Has God Not Chosen the Poor? The Social Setting of the Epistle of James* (JSNTSup 206; Sheffield: Sheffield Academic Press, 2001); L.L. Cheung, *The Genre, Composition and Hermeneutics of the Epistle of James* (Paternoster Biblical and Theological Monographs; Carlisle: Paternoster, 2003); M.A. Jackson-McCabe, *Logos and Law in the Letter of James: The Law of Nature, the Law of Moses and the Law of Freedom* (NovTSup 100; Leiden: Brill, 2001); L.T. Johnson, *Brother of Jesus, Friend of God: Studies in the Letter of James* (Grand Rapids, MI: Eerdmans, 2004); J.P. Keenan, *The Wisdom of James: Parallels with Mahayana Buddhism* (New York: The Newman Press, 2005); and D. Lockett, *Purity and Worldview in the Epistle of James* (LNTS; London: T&T Clark, 2008). Note also: T.C. Penner, "The Epistle of James in Current Research", *CurBS* 7 (1999): 257–308. On recent discussion of authorship see esp. J. Painter, *Just James: The Brother of Jesus in History and Tradition* (Philadelphia, PA: Fortress, 1999).

[4] Besides works by Scot McKnight and Craig Blomberg, the author is aware of John Kloppenborg's forthcoming Hermeneia commentary and a new full-length commentary in the ICC series by Dale C. Allison.

[5] Along with Mk. 9:22 and Rev. 2:13 and 19:12, it has received ongoing consideration. See esp. Robinson, "The Faith of Jesus Christ", and Dunn, "Once More, ΠΙΣΤΙΣ ΧΡΙΣΤΟΥ", as well as Hays' discussion in *The Faith of Jesus Christ*, 149. It is somewhat ironic that Dunn (who favours the objective genitive in Paul) sees Jas. 2:1 as a probable example of a subjective genitive (253), while Daniel Wallace (who favours the subjective genitive in Paul), believes Jas. 2:1 is among the "two or three clear instances of πίστις + *objective personal* gen. in the NT" (*Greek Grammar*, 116).

[6] See, e.g., M. Dibelius, *James: A Commentary on the Epistle of James* (Hermeneia; Philadelphia, PA: Fortress, 1976), 127–8; R.P. Martin, *James* (WBC 48; Waco, TX: Word, 1988), 60.

[7] "Troubling" for those hoping to use this verse in the πιστίς Χριστοῦ debate, that is.

noted that if ἡμῶν Ἰησοῦ Χριστοῦ is eliminated from the text, the genitive construction then reads very neatly as "the Lord of glory", reminiscent of "king of Glory" in Psalm 24:7–8. This observation was then coupled with the fact that "Jesus" appears by name only here and in 1:1, and the resulting proposal was that ἡμῶν Ἰησοῦ Χριστοῦ is a later Christianizing of the text.[8] Such a reading never captured a majority following in its time and, it may therefore be argued, presents no argument against using James 2:1 in the present debate.[9] Nevertheless, while ever τῆς δόξης sits awkwardly some shadow remains. The current Jacobean renaissance should therefore be of initial *encouragement* to those hoping to use this verse, in that it provides hope for such a shadow to be removed.

Note, however, the words "initially" and "initial" in the paragraph above. Those hoping to employ James 2:1 in this debate should be *initially* encouraged, but only until the current literature is consulted. Having read recent articles by Allison and Kloppenborg, I anticipate that the forthcoming ICC and Hermeneia commentaries (respectively) will in fact argue for eliminating ἡμῶν Ἰησοῦ Χριστοῦ.[10] This is not to say that either Allison or Kloppenborg agree with the conclusions of the older view. But regardless of how things are nuanced, the prospect of such a textual decision being revived in two of the most prestigious English commentary series is a heavy blow indeed. Who, after all, would make this verse central in the aforementioned debate when critics may simply and easily dismiss it as textually controversial? Unless some other explanation for τῆς δόξης and its awkwardness can be found, the prospects for James 2:1 being invaluable in the πίστις Χριστοῦ debate appear poor.

---

[8] F. Spitta, "Der Brief des Jakobus", in *Zur Geschichte und Literatur des Urchristentums*, II (Göttingen: Vandenhoeck & Ruprecht, 1896), 3–8; L. Massebieau, "L'épître de Jacques: est-elle l'oeuvre d'un chrétien?" *RHR* 32 (1895): 249–50; A. Meyer, *Das Rätsel des Jacobusbriefes* (BZNW 10; Giessen: Töpelmann, 1930), 118–21.

[9] For obvious reasons, if Χριστοῦ is rubbed from this verse it is of minimal value in the πίστις Χριστοῦ debate. Note, however, that there is no serious textual evidence for such an elimination: 33 *pc* vg^ms removes τῆς δόξης altogether, and 614. 630. 2495 *al* sy sa^mss bo moves τῆς δόξης to be before τοῦ κυρίου ἡμῶν Ἰησοῦ Χριστοῦ.

[10] D.C. Allison, "The Fiction of James and its *Sitz im Leben*", *RB* 118 (2001): 529–70; J.S. Kloppenborg, "Judaeans or Judean Christians in James", in *Identity and Interaction in the Ancient Mediterranean: Jews, Christians and Others* (ed. Philip Harland and Zeba Crook; London and New York: Sheffield Phoenix, 2007); J.S. Kloppenborg, "Diaspora Discourse: The Construction of Ethos in James", *NTS* 53 (2007): 242–70.

Thus endeth this paper ... or perhaps not. Before washing our hands of this verse, we must hasten to note that among the recent spate of monographs, articles, and commentaries on James an idea has surfaced that has the potential to both explain τῆς δόξης and also provide a concrete answer for James 2:1 within the πίστις Χριστοῦ debate. Wesley Wachob's PhD dissertation (mentioned above), an independent article by Duane Watson, and Patrick Hartin's Sacra Pagina commentary all argue that James 2:1–13 is a self-contained unit.[11] But, rather than being a diatribe or sermon as Dibelius suggested,[12] Wachob, Watson, and Hartin (hereafter WWH) propose that it has the specific elements and structure of a rhetorical argument.[13] Drawing largely on *Rhetorica ad Herennium* (*Rhet. Her.*) as an ancient source, 2:1 becomes the proposition and 2:5–7 the argument which in turn draws on the Jesus tradition. This later move (by Wachob and Hartin) is crucial, because it reveals that Jesus' faith (as taught in the Jesus tradition) is the basis for why Christians should remain impartial.[14] Christians are not simply to have an empty faith without action, but rather by avoiding impartiality they should possess the faith of their glorious Lord Jesus Christ. WWH's reading, if correct, has the distinct advantage of placing ἡμῶν Ἰησοῦ Χριστοῦ (2:1) within the wider context of 2:1–13. Though not definitive, this lends some weight to these words being original. It is of further significance to the πίστις Χριστοῦ debate, however, because without even looking to speak to this issue in advance, it demands that Χριστοῦ be read as a subjective genitive.

Upon closer analysis, however, it may still appear that such a thesis misses something crucial. Like many recent works which take the text

---

[11] Wachob, *Voice of Jesus*; Duane F. Watson, "James 2 in Light of Greco-Roman Schemes of Argumentation", *NTS* 39 (1993): 94–121; and Hartin, *James*, 117–39 (note esp. 127).

[12] Dibelius, *James*, 127.

[13] Note also Duane F. Watson, "The Rhetoric of James 3:1–12 and a Classical Pattern of Argumentation", *NovT* 35 (1993): 48–64, and "An Assessment of the Rhetoric and Rhetorical Analysis of the Letter of James", in *Reading James with New Eyes: Methodological Reassessments of the Letter of James* (ed. Robert Webb and John Kloppenborg; London: T&T Clark, 2007), 99–120.

[14] D.F. Watson's excellent study complements Wachob and Hartin's work by paying even closer attention to rhetorical theory. Watson himself shows no interest in the Jesus tradition, however, and thus little interest in the issues of 2:1 (simply opting to follow the RSV [*Greco-Roman*, 102]). The choice is made to include him, however (note "WWH"), because his work in no way disagrees with that of Wachob or Hartin and provides independent affirmation (and thus credibility) on the rhetorical side of the equation.

as is, all three authors pass lightly over the issue of how τῆς δόξης should be understood. Wachob and Hartin take it as a genitive of quality modifying the entire phrase (i.e., "our glorious Lord Jesus Christ"). Yet, like others adopting this translation, Wachob sees this as merely the most expedient of an otherwise clumsy set of possibilities: "Because the last proposal seems to our modern sensibilities an easier appropriation of the established text, I shall prefer it in this enquiry."[15] But, of course, this is the entire controversy – looming as a shadow from older studies and promising to soon descend as a dark cloud. Is the established text really the original text? That is, given the admitted clumsiness of τῆς δόξης, should the words ἡμων Ἰησοῦ Χριστοῦ simply be left out?

WWH's work, however, is actually more powerful than they themselves have noted – able to explain the clumsy inclusion of τῆς δόξης in this verse in a way which is (arguably) more effective than any previous proposal. Both Wachob and Hartin note that the argument in 2:1–13 is built around *honour*, and within a first-century social context δόξα would have also been seen as an *honour*-word fitting neatly into such a context.[16] In rightly pointing out this social context, however, neither author expands on *the rhetorical context of honour*.[17] In both ancient rhetorical *theory* and rhetorical *practice*, substantial evidence exists (see below) that when an argument was constructed around *honour*, a word-clue should be given at the start of the argument to alert the audience that this is the form the argument will take.[18] Recently I have suggested that this same approach may explain the strangely abrupt introduction of "shame" in Romans 1:16, Οὐ γὰρ ἐπαισχύνομαι τὸ εὐαγγέλιον

---

[15] Wachob, *Voice of Jesus*, 68 (emphasis mine). Cf. A. Chester, "The Theology of James", in *The Theology of the Letters of James, Peter, and Jude* (ed. A. Chester and R.P. Martin; Cambridge: Cambridge University Press, 1994), 46–53 (44).

[16] Wachob, *Voice of Jesus*, 69–70 (and references), and affirmed again more recently: "The Language of 'Household' and 'Kingdom' in the Letter of James: A Socio-Rhetorical Study", in *Reading James with New Eyes*, 157. Cf. Hartin's excursus: "Honor and Shame, Patronage and Grace: Cultural Scripts behind the Letter of James", in *James*, 140–8.

[17] To be sure, Wachob does discuss "glory" in its ancient rhetorical context (*Voice of Jesus*, 69–70) – but only as part of a general discussion and not with specific application.

[18] Evidence will be presented from both rhetorical *theory* (*Rhet. Her.*) and rhetorical *practice* (near-contemporary Gk. speeches from Dionysius of Halicarnassus) – following Dean Anderson's appeal that both theory *and* practice should be used (*Ancient Rhetorical Theory and Paul* [Leuven: Peeters, rev. ed., 1999], 291). I extend my thanks to Dr Chris Forbes for directing me to the speeches of Dionysius of Halicarnassus.

("for I am *not ashamed* of the gospel").[19] In this case ἐπαισχύνομαι, an honour/shame word, is the clue that what follows will be an argument based on *honour*. Evidence can be found in Romans 1–5 that this is the case.[20] In a similar way, we will propose that in James 2:1 the otherwise clumsy inclusion of τῆς δόξης is a word-clue alerting readers that a rhetorical argument has commenced,[21] and that such an argument will be constructed around *honour*.

The distinct contribution of this current essay, therefore, is found here (see below, "Reconsidering τῆς δόξης in James 2:1"). By focusing on τῆς δόξης, an attempt is made to give James 2:1 an unwavering voice (perhaps for the first time) in the πίστις Χριστοῦ debate – since only in accounting for τῆς δόξης can ἡμων Ἰησοῦ Χριστοῦ be finally established. But what, then, does it say? WWH's failure to explain τῆς δόξης in no way diminishes their contribution. Indeed, in terms of the πίστις Χριστοῦ debate, this current essay is merely placing stones on what is otherwise WWH's construction – a rhetorical explanation in connection with the Jesus tradition, which ultimately points towards Χριστοῦ as a subjective genitive. A secondary contribution of this essay (see below, "The Meaning of Πίστις Χριστοῦ in James 2:1"), therefore, will be to further commend this reading of WWH by offering a summary of how 2:1–13 aligns with *Rhet. Her.* Thirdly, though, this essay will conclude by opening a door for further discussion. While it will be agreed that Χριστοῦ must be a subjective genitive in James 2:1, the question remains as to whether the emphasis of *Jesus' faith* is his faithful law-abiding life which Christians ought to follow (so Wachob and Hartin). The proposal will be offered instead that *Jesus' faith* in 2:1 is more a confidence in the eschatological reward of God while living in the midst of present suffering. Such a reading (it will be argued) does greater justice to how an audience would have read James synchronically, even as they read on into 2:14–26. We will then ask, in conclusion, whether such an eschatological reading may even help resolve the current deadlock over Paul's use of the same expression.

---

[19] "Romans 1:16–5:21: 'Already' Eschatology Argued Rhetorically" (paper presented at the SBL International Meeting, Edinburgh, 6 July 2006); and *A New Paradigm, Progression and Purpose for Romans: Roman Solutions to Enigmas and Building Relationships* (PhD dissertation, Macquarie University, forthcoming).

[20] See esp. H. Moxnes, "Honor and Righteousness in Romans", *JSNT* 32 (1988): 61–77; and Jewett, *Romans*, 136–9, 149–53, 165–91, 205–9, 229–37, 278–82, 290–303, 310–17, 348–57.

[21] Which for clarity's sake would seem an important clue to give, particularly in this case where a rhetorical argument commences mid-way through the letter.

Reconsidering τῆς δόξης in James 2:1

As we have said, τῆς δόξης in James 2:1 is controversial. Dale C. Allison has recently compiled nine different ways to explain what it modifies. Because his analysis is so comprehensive, we reproduce only an abridged version of his work here:[22]

(1) τῆς δόξης connects to ἐν προσωπολημψίαι to produce the translation, "partiality arising from opinion". This idea was offered by Erasmus and followed by Calvin[23] but suffers from the problems of word separation and of δόξα never meaning "opinion" elsewhere in the New Testament.

(2) τῆς δόξης connects to τὴν πίστιν to produce the translation, "faith in the glory of our Lord Jesus Christ"[24] or "Christ-given faith in the glory (we shall receive)" or "glorious faith in Christ".[25] Dibelius responds, however: "There is no intention in v. 1 to define more specifically the Christian faith – such as in the expression 'gospel of the glory of Christ' (εὐαγγέλιον τῆς δόξης τοῦ Χριστοῦ) in 2 Cor. 4:4, where this is preceded by the term 'light' (φωτισμός), but rather to stress quite simply that faith in Christ is not consistent with favoritism. Consequently, it is advisable to connect 'faith' (πίστις) directly with 'our Lord Jesus Christ' (τοῦ κυρίου ἡμων Ἰησοῦ Χριστοῦ), and this is also the most obvious way of construing the words."[26]

---

[22] "Fiction", 541–2, n.43. This article lists only eight points, but in a recent unpublished work Allison adds one further. The abridged discussion here is ultimately based on this unpublished work.

[23] See the *Collected Works of Erasmus*, vol. 44, *New Testament Scholarship* (ed. Robert Sider; Toronto/Buffalo/London: University of Toronto, 1993), 147; J. Calvin, "The Epistle of James", in *A Harmony of the Gospels Matthew, Mark and Luke, and the Epistles of James and Jude*, III (trans. A.W. Morrison; ed. D.W. Torrance and T.F. Torrance; Grand Rapids, MI: Eerdmans, 1972), 277.

[24] See T. Zahn, *Introduction to the New Testament*, I (Edinburgh: T&T Clark, 1909), 151; C. Burchard, "Zu einige christologischen Stellen des Jakobusbriefes", in *Anfänge der Christologie: Festschrift für Ferdinand Hahn zum 65. Geburtstag* (ed. C. Bretenback and H. Paulsen; Gottingen: Vandenhoeck & Ruprecht, 1991), 353–68 (357); and idem, "Gemeinde in der strohernen Epistel: Mutmaßungen über Jakobus", in *Kirche: Für Günther Bornkamm zum 75. Geburtstag* (ed. D. Lührmann and G. Strecker; Tübingen: Mohr Siebeck, 1980), 315–28 (322, n.52), where Burchard presents an alternative solution.

[25] B. Reicke, *The Epistles of James, Peter, and Jude* (AB 37; Garden City, NY: Doubleday, 1964), 26.

[26] *James*, 127.

(3) The KJV translates: "the faith of our Lord Jesus Christ, the Lord of glory". This requires that one gratuitously add τοῦ κυρίου to the final clause or assume *hyperbaton* ("the faith of Jesus Christ, our Lord of glory").[27] Alford, however, concludes this is "somewhat harsh and unusual".[28]

(4) "Glory" is in apposition to "Jesus Christ" – that is, Jesus Christ is "the Glory", the Shekinah. But, as Allison asks, "where else in Christian literature of the same period is Jesus called, without further ado, 'the Glory'?"

(5) One can insert a comma after ἡμῶν: "our Lord, Jesus Christ of glory". But this breaks up what naturally goes together – namely, "our Lord Jesus Christ".

6) The NRSV has "our glorious Lord Jesus Christ". This is the most common interpretation of today. One of its recent proponents, however, can do no more than call it "not impossible".[29] Again Allison notes: "hardly a recommendation. Where is the parallel to an attribute being added at the end of τοῦ κυρίου ἡμῶν Ἰησοῦ Χριστοῦ?"

(7) Perry rendered the words "our Lord Jesus Christ, our glory"[30] but has not been followed.

(8) Likewise, William Bowyer's "Have not the faith of our Lord Jesus Christ with regard to honourable appearances" has not been followed.[31]

(9) Adamson emends the text by moving "our" to the end of the sentence.[32]

The inability of modern exegetes to make sense of these words appears to lead Allison himself to a *tenth* possibility – that of eliminating ἡμῶν Ἰησοῦ Χριστοῦ from the text.

---

[27] William Bowyer, *Conjectures on the New Testament* (London: W. Bowyer and J. Nichols, 1772), 314.

[28] H. Alford, *The Greek Testament*, IV (Chicago, IL: Moody Press, 1958), 290. Cf. J. Brinktrine, "Zu Jak 2.1", *Bib* 35 (1954): 40–42, positing an Aramaism.

[29] Chester, "The Theology of James", 44. Cf. Wachob's similar tone, above.

[30] J. Perry, *A Discussion of the General Epistle of James* (London: C.J. Clay & Sons, 1903), 24 and 36–9.

[31] *Conjectures*, 314.

[32] J.B. Adamson, *The Epistle of James* (NICNT; Grand Rapids, MI: Eerdmans, 1976), 102–4.

But if it is assumed that 2:1–13 is a cohesive unit within James (cf. Dibelius), and if we assume with WWH that this unit is best explained using *rhetoric*, then τῆς δόξης may potentially be a *word-clue* that this will be an argument conducted according to *honour*. A theoretical basis for this last statement is found in the handbook *Rhet. Her.*[33] Here it is stated that part of the beginning of a speech "consists in *setting forth, briefly and completely,* the points we intend to discuss" (*quibus de rebus dicturi sumus exponimus breviter et absolute*).[34] Such points are later defined in terms of a hierarchy of argumentative categories which begin with Security and Honour. One step down are categories such as Right or Praiseworthy, followed by numerous different *species* of argumentation (e.g., Wisdom, Justice, Courage, and Temperance). But when the handbook finally discusses each of these categories, it again reinforces that the rhetor should reveal to the audience, right at the beginning, which categories will be used in the argument that follows:[35]

> Since in causes of this kind the end is Advantage, and Advantage is divided into the consideration of Security and the consideration of Honor, if we can prove that both ends will be served, *we shall promise to make a two-fold proof* ... if we are going to prove that one of two will be served, we shall *indicate simply the one thing we intend to affirm* ... If we say that our counsel aims at the Right, and all four categories of Right apply [i.e., Wisdom, Justice, Courage, and Temperance], we shall use them all. If these categories do not all apply, we shall in speaking *set forth as many as do.*[36]

---

[33] Discussion here is restricted to this handbook and secondarily to Cicero's *De Inventione*, mainly because the former is the source used primarily by WWH, and the latter because it is seen as reflecting the same tradition (cf. Anderson, *Ancient Rhetorical Theory*, 69–72).

[34] *Rhet. Her.* 1.10.17 (Caplan, LCL, emphasis mine). Cf. 1.4.6 and Cicero, *Inv.* 1.22.31: "Altera est in qua rerum earum de quibus erimus dicturi breviter expositio ponitur distributa" (Hubbell, LCL).

[35] *Rhet. Her.* 3.2.3. For the idea that this relates to clarity see more particularly Cicero's *Inv.* 1.22.31–23.33. Note, further, Aristotle's comment on revealing one's purpose at the beginning: "in speech and epic poems the exordia provide a sample of the subject, in order that the hearers may know beforehand what it is about, and that the mind may not be kept in suspense, for that which is undefined leads astray; so then he who puts the beginning, so to say, into the hearer's hand enables him, if he holds fast to it, to follow the story" (*Rhet.* 3.14.6).

[36] 3.4.8. For discussion on the importance of both rhetorical theory and rhetorical practice see Anderson, *Ancient Rhetorical Theory*, 291.

From such rhetorical *theory*, it can be seen that the commencement of an argument should include a *clue* for the audience of the categories to be used. For an "Advantage argument" (= a deliberative argument) this may include genera such as Security and Honour (see above). It may also include mention of subgenera such as Praiseworthy (3.4.7), or Right, but also to "set forth as many" species as will be used (e.g., Wisdom, Justice, Courage, and Temperance). This paragraph, and the fuller outline in 3.1.1–4.8, clearly reveal that in rhetorical *theory* it was appropriate to begin an argument by setting "forth, briefly and completely, the points we intend to discuss" and to do so in terms of known categories, such as those already mentioned.[37]

What is outlined in *theory*, however, is also observable in ancient rhetorical *practice* – for example, in speeches from Dionysius of Halicarnassus:

> [Valerius says] ... consider that everything the most excellent Claudius has said has been said by me also ... I for my part shall also talk to you about the motion of Claudius, showing that it is not impracticable; for that it is *disadvantageous* no one even of those who derided it has ventured to allege. And I shall show you how our territory may be made *secure*, how those who have dared to do it injury may be *punished*, how we may recover our *ancient aristocracy*, and how these things may all come about at the same time with weight concurrence of *all the citizens* and without the least opposition. All this I shall do, *not* through the display of any *wisdom* (σοφία), but by citing your own actions as precedents for you to follow; for where experience teaches what is *advantageous*, what need is there of conjectures? (*Ant. rom.* 11.19.4–20.1 [Cary, LCL])

In this near-contemporary work to James[38] it can be seen that, right at the beginning of the speech, clues are given to indicate the categories of argumentation which should follow. For example, at the beginning

---

[37] For a similar list of categories in Aristotle see *Rhet.* 1.9.1ff. and, more particularly with reference to deliberative arguments, 1.3.5. The connections with Aristotle here are important for the next part of my argument, in that Dionysius was significantly influenced by Aristotle (note Anderson, *Ancient Rhetorical Theory*, 77–83). One should not draw lines too sharply, however (as Anderson seems to do). The similarities between Aristotle and *Rhet. Her.* reflect a rhetorical tradition with much continuity between its earlier Greek forms and those of later Greek and Latin handbooks.

[38] *Roman Antiquities* is believed to have been written either late first century BCE or early first century CE.

and end of this introduction (for emphasis) it is clued that this will be an "Advantage" argument. But bracketed inside these two word-clues is also mention (by name) of the subgenus, Security, as well as the species, Wisdom. The mention of Wisdom here is of some interest in light of rhetorical theory, as it shows the importance of clarity through indicating what will *not* be used, as well as the categories that will be used.[39] Interesting also are the apparent allusions to the subgenus Praiseworthiness ("*ancient aristocracy,* and ... *all the citizens*") and to the species Justice ("those who have dared to do it injury may be *punished*") revealed not by word-clues but rather through description.[40] From this it may also be seen that great variety was allowable in the practice of how these categories were rehearsed to a hearer. The consistent picture in all of this, however, is that practice matched theory – clues (whether through specific words or descriptions) were ideally to be employed at the beginning of an argument to make the categories of argumentation abundantly clear.

In the above example, however, "Honour" is not mentioned. Is this also a category which was clued in *practice*, even as it is listed as a category in *theory*? The question is important, since it will soon be argued that τῆς δόξης is the clue in 2:1 that James 2:1–3 is an honour argument. The answer is that, in Dionysius, multiple examples exist of honour being clued near the start of a speech:[41]

> But in what manner the terms of reconciliation may prove *honourable* and *advantageous* (καλαὶ καὶ συμφέρουσαι) to both cities (for probably you have long been eager to hear this) I shall now endeavour to explain. (3.8.3)

> Tribunes and centurions, I am going to disclose to you important and unexpected things which I have hitherto been concealing; and I beg of you to keep them secret if you do not wish to ruin me, and to assist me in carrying them out if you think their realization will be *advantageous* (ἐὰν δόξῃ συνοίσειν ἐπιτελῆ γενόμενα). The present occasion does not permit of many words, as the time is short; so I shall mention only the most essential matters. I, from the time we were subordinated to the Romans up to this day,

---

[39] Again note *Inv.* 1.22.31–23.33 for discussion on the importance of such clues for clarity's sake.

[40] For descriptions of these two categories see *Rhet. Her.* 3.4.7 and 3.3.4. See below for further evidence that descriptions were permissible indicators, just like word-clues. Indeed, in an example of a speech found in *Rhet. Her.* 4.43.56–58, only descriptions are used.

[41] See also 8.48.1, 9.52.3, and 10.28.2–6.

have led a life full of *shame* and grief (αἰσχύνης μεστὸν καὶ ὀδύνης), though *honoured* by the king (τιμηθείς γε ὑπὸ τοῦ βασιλέως) with the supreme command ... [yet] we have been deprived by the Romans of our *supremacy*, I took thought how we might recover it *without experiencing any great disaster*. And although I considered many plans of every sort, the only way I could discover that promised success, and at the same time the easiest and the *least dangerous one*, was in hand a war should be started against them by the neighbouring states ... As to the next step, I assumed that it would not require much argument to convince you that it is more *glorious* (καλός) as well as more *fitting* to fight for our liberty than for the supremacy of the Romans. (3.23.6–8)

Every time these matters have been up for debate, senators, I have always been of the same opinion, never to yield to the people any one of their demands that is not *lawful* and *honourable* (ὅ τι μὴ νόμιμον μηδὲ καλόν), nor to lower *the dignity of the commonwealth*; nor do I even now change the opinion which I entertained from the beginning. (6.38.1)

But do thou, Jupiter Capitolinus, and ye guardian gods of our city, ye heroes and divinities who keep watch over the land of the Romans, grant that the return of the fugitives may be *honourable* and *advantageous* to all (καλὴ καὶ συμφέρουσα πᾶσιν), and that I may be mistaken in my forebodings regarding the future. (6.68.2)

Space does not permit a full discussion of any of the above para-graphs.[42] It may only be noted briefly that the above examples again show that "Advantage" is often flagged, or in other cases not flagged.[43] There are examples of specific word-clues being used, while in other cases the ideas are spelled out. Sometimes the clues are offered as part of a

---

[42] If space permitted, it would also be of great value to analyze the speeches of Titus Livius (BCE 59 – CE 17). In two very thorough articles, Canter has argued that Livy was also well skilled in the rhetoric of his era, as indicated from the speeches making up his volumes on Roman history. See H.V. Canter, "Rhetorical Elements in Livy's Direct Speeches: Part I", *AJP* 38 (1917): 125–51; idem, "Rhetorical Elements in Livy's Direct Speeches: Part II", *AJP* 39 (1918): 44–64. In this present essay, Dionysius was chosen over Livy because he was, like James, he wrote in Greek, making him (arguably) a better source of comparison.

[43] The way in which "advantage" and "honour" are so often juxtaposed in Dionysius evidences a formularization, or at least a favorite expression for him. This suggests he is closely following Aristotle's suggestion of indicating the nature of the argument at the beginning. In this case both Aristotle (*Rhet.* 1.3.5) and *Rhet. Her.* (3.2.3) are in agreement that "advantage" is the clue to the argument being deliberative, and "honour" the clue to the species of argumentation.

lengthy and full discussion (e.g., 3.23.6–8), but in other cases there is an economy of words and ideas (e.g., 6.38.1). All this indicates again the *flexibility* of how exactly indication might be given to an audience.[44] And such variety is important to keep in mind when considering James 2:1. What is most crucial for our present discussion, however, is that *honour* is clearly present as a *category* to be clued – again matching rhetorical theory with rhetorical practice.

But which Greek word should be used for clueing honour? Here is where the above-noted flexibility is important. The above rhetorical *practice* concurs with *theory*,[45] that καλός was the most favoured word for clueing honour. However, it is not the only word which a Greek speaker might have discerned as an appropriate clue. At the beginning of Book 1 of *Rhet. Her.* it is stated that any cause may be defined as either "honorable, discreditable, doubtful or petty" (*honestum*,[46] *turpe, dubium, humile*). This list is derived from a moral classification taken from Greek thought: ἔνδοξον, παράδοξον, ἀμφίδοξον, ἄδοξον.[47] It may readily be seen here that the -δοξ-root is used in each of these four words to express different shades of honour/dishonour. With such a list being carried over into rhetoric, a Greek speaker may then have also discerned δόξα as a word-clue for *honour*. A specific example of this, however, is also apparent in 3.23.6–8 (above). Here δόξα,[48] along with αἰσχύνη (cf. Rom. 1:16), τιμάω, and καλός, are all employed to show that the argument will be conducted according to honour.[49] Because δόξα is a synonym here, apparently also functioning as a word-clue, it should not be doubted that δόξα could be employed in James 2:1 for the same purpose.[50] In the

---

[44] On the subject of flexibility one need only consult examples within *Rhet. Her.* itself (e.g., 4.43.56–58), where ideas rather than word-clues are used from the categories previously discussed. For the early Cicero also (*Inv.* 2.51.155–169), much consideration was given to whether honour and advantage should be separate *genera* – reflected perhaps even in Dionysius' speeches and the juxtaposing of these two categories.

[45] See Caplan, *Rhet. Her.* (Loeb), 161, note "e" and references therein, but esp. Aristotle, *Rhet.* 1.3.5 and 1.9.3.

[46] Throughout *Rhet. Her.* this is the Latin word consistently used to express the idea of *honour*.

[47] See Caplan, *Rhet. Her.*, 10, note "c", and references therein.

[48] Strangely translated by Cary as "advantage" here, in a way inconsistent with the rest of Dionysius.

[49] Note again Aristotle, *Rhet.* 1.3.5.

[50] In reality James does employ καλός and then καλῶς in quick succession in 2:7–8 (note also καλῶς in 2:3 and ἀτιμάζω in 2:6) as part of the actual honour argument of this section (see further below).

final analysis, the Jewish context of the author and his audience likely meant that δόξα was the best word-clue in his specific context for clueing honour.[51]

How, then, may the clumsy τῆς δόξης be understood in James 2:1? Firstly, its clumsiness should be noted. If it was indeed in the original text, would not its clumsiness set it apart for a reader and so highlight its distinctive role as a word-clue (cf. the abruptness in Rom. 1:16)? Secondly, its placement at the end of the verse should be noted. If it was meant to be read as a word-clue rather than simply with the rest of the verse, would it not make sense to place it at the end? Thirdly, with further reference to position, it may be noted that τῆς δόξης comes after the words ἔχετε τὴν πίστιν τοῦ κυρίου ἡμῶν Ἰησοῦ Χριστοῦ, even as the words μὴ ἐν προσωπολημψίαις precede it. But what does μὴ ἐν προσωπολημψίαις do but define the *substance* of the argument, even as τῆς δόξης reveals its *nature*? The overall structure of the verse also fits with the idea that rhetoric is important. Fourthly, it may be noted that τῆς δόξης is articular. This cannot be used to prove anything decisively, but again, if τῆς δόξης is functioning to show a category of argumentation, it makes sense that it would be articular. Finally, it should be noted in reference to the above discussion from rhetorical theory and practice that if WWH are correct in seeing 2:1–13 as a rhetorical argument, then indication of such should have been given to the audience (at least for the person reading the letter publicly, if not for those hearing). How else would a reader discern that 2:1 was the beginning of such an argument, sitting as it does in the middle of the letter? A change in subject is hardly enough, given the multiple subject changes in the letter to this point, and besides this an informed reader would expect information of the kind we are suggesting to orientate expectations for what follows.[52] The very suggestion that 2:1–13 is a rhetorical argument placed in the middle of a letter implies that a word-clue, like δόξα, should be present. For all these reasons it is proposed that the presence of τῆς δόξης, and indeed even its clumsy positioning, can be accounted for when it is seen as a word-clue for an honour-argument which is to follow. But, if this is so, then there is no longer a problem with reading ἡμῶν Ἰησοῦ Χριστοῦ as original, and the way is clear to consider James 2:1 within the πίστις Χριστοῦ debate.

---

[51] See, e.g., J. Freeborn, "Lord of Glory: A Study of James 2 and 1 Corinthians 2", *ExpTim* 111 (2000): 185–9.

[52] Again see Aristotle, *Rhet.* 3.19.6, and Cicero, *Inv.* 1.22.31–23.33.

But how should 2:1 be translated? In my opinion this is an artificial question. A person outside a language is interested in *translations*, but a native speaker is not. If τῆς δόξης is a rhetorical clue then perhaps it needs to be left out of a proper translation of the verse and added as a note: *My dear brothers and sisters, here is my proposition (to be discussed according to honour): show no partiality as you possess the faith of our Lord Jesus Christ.*

The Meaning of Πίστις Χριστοῦ in James 2:1

All that is now left is to consider the meaning of πίστις Χριστοῦ within James 2:1. Throughout the history of James research, it has not been uncommon for people to conclude that the letter lacks coherent order.[53] But even people of this opinion commonly see that 2:1–13 is a coherent unit (along with 2:14–26 and 3:1–12). Such a clearly distinguishable and agreed upon unit is a perfect place to test whether rhetoric might be a factor in its structure and content. This seems to have been what drew WWH to this passage, wherein they have noted together five distinguishable parts corresponding neatly to the five parts of "the most complete and perfect argument . . . : the Proposition [=Jas. 2:1], the Reason [=Jas. 2:2–4], the Proof of Reason [=Jas. 2:5–7], the Embellishment [=Jas. 2:8–11], and the Résumé [i.e., *conplexio* =Jas. 2:12–13]".[54]

But how does such an argument express itself in detail? The argument itself is about partiality not being consistent with Christianity because it stands contrary to *honour* (δόξα, 2:1, see above). A "brief explanation subjoined [to set] forth the causal basis for the Proposition" is then given in James 2:2–4, showing that to seat a rich person in a position of *honour* (note καλῶς, v. 3) and the poor in lowly places, is an act of *unjust judgment* (note 2:4, καὶ ἐγένεσθε κριταὶ διαλογισμῶν πονηρῶν, "become *judges* with evil thoughts"). This highlighting of "justice" adds to the discussion of WWH, but only in line with *Rhet. Her.*, since Iustitia

---

[53] E.g., Luther says that James "throws things together so chaotically that it seems to me he must have been some good, pious man who took a few sayings from the disciples of the apostles and tossed them off on paper" (*Luther's Works* [ed. John Pelikan and Helmut Lehmann; 55 vols.; Philadelphia, PA: Fortress, 1955–] 35.397), quoted by D.F. Watson, "Greco-Roman", 117. See also Dibelius, *James*, 2, and, more recently, Bauckham, *James*, 61f.

[54] *Rhet. Her.* 2.18.28. References in all subsequent notes are to this section of the handbook.

is rightly a species of the larger category of honour (as we have seen above). My suggestion, then, is that the author is further refining the way the point will be argued – that is, he is using the species of "justice" as a sub-category of "honour".

James 2:5–7 should then corroborate "by means of additional arguments, the briefly presented Reason". This it does, by showing how God's judgment is that "those who are poor in the world [are] to be rich in faith and [become] heirs of the kingdom which he has promised to those who love him" (2:5). The audience, however, has not heeded such a judgment but has instead *dishonoured* (ἀτιμάξω) the poor (2:6a). Worse, they have copied the unjust behaviour of the rich, who are dragging the audience themselves into *court* (2:6b; note, again, "judicial"). By way of a third Proof of Reason, it is pointed out that such preferential treatment not only follows the injustice of the rich – it follows their example. But in so far as the rich are thereby *dishonouring* God (2:7), a sting is added for a God-fearing audience. It is (only) those who love God who will inherit the kingdom (2:5)! Here, then, is the appropriate "additional arguments" which fit perfectly with 2:5–7 being the Proof of Reason. But a perfect argument must also have "Embellishment … in order to adorn and enrich the argument, after the Proof as been established". James 2:8–11 fits with this, taking (appropriately) a slightly different (though not unrelated) approach to the issue.[55] The entire argument finishes with the Résumé (2:12–13), which rightly "draws together the parts of the argument" under the theme of *justice*. That 2:12–13 summarizes things in terms of justice only reinforces that justice has been the important species under which this "most complete and perfect [honour] argument" has been constructed.

I concur, therefore, with WWH that 2:1–13 is an extremely clear example of a known rhetoric form being used in the New Testament. The alignments (especially when "honour" and "justice" are highlighted) are quite uncanny. But this then brings us back to the matter at hand. How, if at all, does this help explain what is meant in 2:1 by "hold[ing] the faith of our Lord Jesus Christ"? Wachob and Hartin complement such rhetorical discussion by drawing attention to the Jesus tradition behind James 2:5 (cf. 1:12) and 2:8. They use the fact that both of these parts allude to Jesus' life and teaching to propose that "the faith of Jesus" in 2:1 is nothing other than "Jesus' faith" illustrated through this tradition. Such a move is clever and persuasive, given that the mention of "faith"

---

[55] Note again, however, the mention of honour, καλῶς, in v. 8!

and "Jesus" are otherwise hard to account for in 2:1. So by suggesting that these words point to the intertext behind subsequent parts of the argument, Wachob and Hartin create a neat and cohesive link which in turn explains the nature of πίστις Χριστοῦ in James 2:1 – it can only be a subjective genitive, speaking of "Jesus' faith" as illustrated by the tradition of his life and teaching.

Having affirmed this valuable work of Wachob and Hartin, however, further discussion is required to determine whether this subjective genitive ("Jesus' faith") is best taken to mean "Jesus' whole life [as] … an example of faithfulness for the believer to emulate".[56] This last turn (it will be argued) does not necessarily follow, simply because Χριστοῦ is a subjective genitive. Matthew 5:3, Luke 6:20, and *Gospel of Thomas* 54 (all of which use the same tradition as 2:5) have the common context of encouraging those who, in spite of hardship and poverty in this world, look (in faith) to the unseen realities of a better world. This is certainly true with the Gnosticism behind the *Gospel of Thomas*. But in both Matthew and Luke, too, this saying about poverty is found in the wider context of God blessing those at the eschaton who have believed in these realities, in spite of their present suffering.[57] James 2:5 is similarly consistent with such usage. In James 2:5, God will *bless* (cf. 1:12) those in the future kingdom who have faith and love towards him in spite of being *poor* in the present (cf. "trials" 1:12). The use of this tradition, therefore, is not in reference to Jesus' faithful life but rather to the faith of those who, in spite of suffering, trust in the future reward of their God. That verse 5 is the only place in the section where the word πίστις occurs (besides 2:1) adds an additional mandate that *whatever "the faith of Jesus" means in 2:5, it should also mean that in 2:1*. It cannot be maintained, therefore, that a reader would interpret the "faith of Jesus" as Jesus' faithfulness, having heard an echo of the Beatitudes but rather, like its earlier use in James 1:6–8, as *trust* in God.

Having said this, James 2:8 is also involved in bringing in a wider context to Jesus' teaching which now includes obedience. It is in this section that the Law and the need for the audience to obey the "royal commandment" are brought in. What, then, is happening here? The best explanation would seem to be that 2:8–11 is preparing the way for 2:14–26 which follows. The "faith of Jesus" in 2:1 is nothing other

---

[56] Hartin, *James*, 129; cf. Wachob, *Voice of Jesus*, 84–5.

[57] For Luke see esp. G. Strecker, "Die Makarismen der Bergpredigt", *NTS* 17 (1970–71): 255–75, and for Matthew see R.A. Guelich, "The Matthean Beatitudes: 'Entrance Requirements' or Eschatological Blessings?", *JBL* 95 (1976): 415–34.

than *trust* in God, the same definition derivable from James 1:6–8. But having made his link to the Sermon on the Mount in 2:5, the author now refers to other teachings of Jesus – which include the importance of love in action. A shift is therefore taking place wherein faith is now being qualified to *also* include deeds of love. James 2:8–11, therefore, is preparation for 2:14–26, which more fully spells out a connection between faith and deeds. In this regard it should also be noted how 2:14 picks up on the idea of someone claiming to "have" (ἔχω) faith, in parallel with having (ἔχω) the faith of our Lord Jesus Christ (2:1). Again as part of expanding the idea of faith, 2:14–26 now shows that it must be accompanied by deeds in order to be *true* faith. The problem with Wachob and Hartin's definition of "Jesus' faith" is not, therefore, that it ends in completely the wrong place. It does appear, however, to lose James' emphasis on *trust* (note again 1:6–8)[58] by glossing over the context of the Sermon on the Mount and moving too quickly to read 2:8ff. back into 2:1.[59] Instead, we should note the rhetorical flow of the argument as it has moved from faith in James 1:6–8, to faith in 2:1–5, before arriving at 2:8ff. Certainly the author of James sees the faith of Jesus as requiring more than simply trust (2:8–26), but such a qualification should not be read back and made *the substance of the definition of faith itself in 2:1*. Why, then, would James need to say "faith without deeds is dead" (2:26), if indeed faith itself has just been defined (through the Jesus tradition) as faithful behaviour?

With such qualifications noted, we nevertheless affirm that WWH have done a great service to those hoping to understand πίστις Χριστοῦ in the New Testament. By drawing upon ancient rhetoric they open the way for a neater solution to the clumsy τῆς δόξης in James 2:1, thus establishing Χριστοῦ in the text. More than this, though, such a rhetorical reading in combination with the Jesus tradition suggests convincingly that πίστις Χριστοῦ should be seen as a subjective genitive – albeit with primary reference to *trust* in God. One implication for Paul is that support can now be seen in another Christian author for taking πίστις Χριστοῦ as a subjective genitive.

In light of the discussion at the end of this essay, however, an important question emerges: Could it be that the "faith of Christ" in Paul is also a reference to the distinctly eschatological Christian faith

---

[58] For an attempt to read 1:6–8 eschatologically see Penner, *The Epistle of James and Eschatology*. Whether Penner has succeeded in his reading of the epistolary frame, however, is doubtful.

[59] In Wachob this may best be seen in his discussion, *Voice of Jesus*, 84–5.

which Paul describes as only having recently come (Gal. 3:23)? This seems a point worthy of further consideration – especially in light of Paul's overarching apocalyptic mindset.[60] But it is a point which must be left to some future discussion.[61]

---

[60] Recently and profoundly, J.C. Beker, *Paul the Apostle: The Triumph of God in Life and Thought* (Philadelphia, PA: Fortress, 1980).

[61] For at least an initial attempt to see this eschatological aspect to faith in Paul, see further my article: "Oh διά! How is Romans 4:25 to be Understood?" *JTS* 57 (2006): 149–57.

15

On the Sidelines of the Πίστις Χριστοῦ Debate: The View from Revelation

DAVID A. DESILVA

I can always count on presenting the debate surrounding the meaning of the phrase πίστις Χριστοῦ to my students in Biblical Greek without offering apologies to these ministry candidates, since I have the assurance that they will be vitally engaged in the conversation. The separate problems of the resolution of the meaning of the head noun πίστις and the relationship between this nominal and the second, Χριστοῦ, expressed by the genitive construction raise questions of profound importance for soteriology and for discipleship. Do Paul's great statements about salvation διὰ or ἐκ πίστεως Χριστοῦ speak of an attribute of Jesus as the means by which deliverance comes ("Jesus' faith" or "Jesus' faithfulness"), or do these statements speak of an attribute of the believer ("faith in Jesus" or "faithfulness toward Jesus")?[1] To be sure, other options exist as well, though these tend to be the prominent quadrants in which the camps pitch their tents.

Several scholars regard the stakes to be quite high,[2] though not all proponents of the objective genitive find this construction to be quite

---

[1] These questions have been quite adequately explicated and analyzed elsewhere. See, e.g., the reviews of research in Tonstad, "Reading Paul in a New Paradigm", esp. 37–47, and the introductory article in the present volume. See also the spirited and critical review of the basic arguments advanced in favour of the subjective genitive reading and the rejoinder in favour of the objective genitive in Matlock, "Even the Demons Believe." It is important to stress that the two questions are independent: resolving the sense of πίστις does not tilt the balance in favour of either option for the genitival relationship, as Tonstad assumes at one point (specifically, that a definition of "faithfulness" tilts the balance in favour of the subjective genitive; see "Reading Paul in a New Paradigm", 47). The texts of primary interest in the undisputed Pauline corpus are Rom. 3:22, 26; Gal. 2:16, 20; 3:22; Phil. 3:9.

[2] E.g., Richard Hays claims that reading the phrase as "faith in Christ", that is, as an objective genitive, "verges on blasphemous self-absorption in our own religious subjectivity" ("What Is at Stake?", 46), while Leander Keck understands that

so problematic.[3] Moreover, it can be shown that Paul speaks about the disciples' trust in Jesus, faithfulness toward Jesus, and Jesus' faithfulness toward both God and the disciples in many places where he does not use the particular expression πίστις Χριστοῦ, such that the overall impact of the resolution of this particular riddle one way or another may not be all that determinative for an overall theology of Paul (unless one remains fixated on these passages to the neglect of many others), with the single exception of the reading "Jesus' faith", which does give a more prominent place to Jesus' own posture of belief.

As we engage in this conversation, however, we have been quite rightly cautioned not to let our theological commitments or exuberance drive the results of our exegetical investigations, and we have been exhorted to bring all the sophistication of lexical semantics to bear on what is, quite properly, a lexical semantic question rather than, in the first instance, a theological and ethical one.[4]

What is striking about this debate from the perspective of reading Revelation is its absence, perhaps due not least to the absence of the key phrase πίστις Χριστοῦ, although one does find two equivalent occurrences: τὴν πίστιν μου in Revelation 2:13 (with Jesus portrayed as speaking) and τὴν πίστιν Ἰησοῦ in Revelation 14:12. If the Pauline corpus is the storm centre of this debate, Revelation is enjoying no more than cloudy skies. Insofar as there is any debate, it largely has to be constructed here through a comparison of the arguments set forth in the various commentaries on the relevant verses, or inferred from translations or glosses where explicit argumentation is absent.[5]

"emancipation from a subjectivist reading of justification, according to which its basis is either our 'works' or our 'believing'" is ultimately at stake ("'Jesus' in Romans", 454). Both are quoted in Matlock, "Detheologizing ΠΙΣΤΙΣ ΧΡΙΣΤΟΥ", 22.

[3] "If I say that I have faith in someone, I do not mean that I have some wonderful quality called faith, but simply that he or she is someone who can be relied upon … [T]he emphasis is still on the reliability of the object" (van Daalen, "Faith", 84). "There is no reason to suppose that a focus on 'our' faith rather than Christ's will inevitably issue in theological disaster. This is a faith that has its origin and content in God's reconciling act in the incarnate, crucified, and risen Jesus …" (Francis Watson, from the concluding paragraph of his contribution to this volume).

[4] In this regard, see Matlock's important, thorough, and convincing article: "Detheologizing ΠΙΣΤΙΣ ΧΡΙΣΤΟΥ."

[5] Ian Wallis provides one of the very few thematic treatments of one side of this investigation in his *Faith of Jesus Christ*, 161–74.

This essay seeks to establish which sense of the polysemous word πίστις is likely to be evoked within each context,[6] approaching the question first from the resolution of the use of the adjective πιστός, with its narrower range of significations, and the unqualified occurrences of the noun πίστις (2:19; 13:10). Throughout the discussion, reference will be made the specific senses of πίστις identified in the Louw-Nida lexicon:

πίστις[a], that which is completely believable, "proof" (31.43)
πίστις[b], "faith, trust" (31.85)
πίστις[c], "trustworthiness, dependability, faithfulness" (31.88)
πίστις[d], Christian believing (31.102)
πίστις[e], the body of what is believed, "the faith" (31.104)
πίστις[f], "promise, pledge to be faithful" (33.289)

A second question to be asked, then, will concern the relationship signaled by the presence of a second noun or pronoun in the genitive case within the relevant contexts. Here I find especially helpful Matlock's observation that an author can use different constructions involving cognate nouns and verbs within a single span of text, and that, in these contexts, the less ambiguous constructions will serve to clarify the more potentially ambiguous constructions.[7]

Occurrences of the πιστ-Word Group in Revelation

The noun πίστις occurs only four times in Revelation. In two instances, the word appears to connote rather directly a moral quality on the

---

[6] The question is admittedly not always so simple. Richard Hays, for example, questioned whether or not we should seek to make a distinction between πίστις *qua* "faith" and πίστις *qua* "faithfulness" – whether because the term is multivalent in Paul's usage ("What Is at Stake?", esp. 58–9) or because the "real" meaning of πίστις lies somewhere in between "faith" and "faithfulness", encompassing both (see also Robinson, "Faith of Jesus Christ", esp. 76). Nevertheless, Matlock has quite convincingly demonstrated the existence of clear and separate semantic senses utilizing the criteria developed in the field of lexical semantics (Matlock, "Detheologizing ΠΙΣΤΙΣ ΧΡΙΣΤΟΥ", 4–6; see D.A. Cruse, *Lexical Semantics* [Cambridge: Cambridge University Press, 1986], 52–61), confirming the approach also found in the Louw-Nida Lexicon (J.P. Louw and E.A. Nida [eds.], *Greek-English Lexicon of the New Testament Based on Semantic Domains* [2nd ed.; New York: United Bible Societies, 1989]), which identifies six distinct semantic senses for πίστις.
[7] See Matlock, "Even the Demons Believe", 316; idem, "Detheologizing ΠΙΣΤΙΣ ΧΡΙΣΤΟΥ", 13–16; some particularly clear examples appear on p. 15.

part of the disciples, thus either "trust" (πίστις[b]) or "faithfulness" (πίστις[c]):

> I know your works and love and faith/faithfulness and service and your endurance (τὰ ἔργα καὶ τὴν ἀγαπὴν καὶ τὴν πίστιν καὶ τὴν διακονίαν καὶ τὴν ὑπομονήν σου), and your last works are more plentiful than the first ones. (2:19)

> Here is the endurance and the faith/faithfulness (ἡ ὑπομονὴ καὶ ἡ πίστις) of the holy ones. (13:10)

The remaining two occurrences are of particular interest for the theme of this volume, since it is in these verses that the noun πίστις is brought directly into relation with Jesus through a genitive nominal:

> You held my name fast and you did not deny τὴν πίστιν μου.[8] (2:13)

> Here is the endurance of the holy ones, the ones keeping the commandments of God and τὴν πίστιν Ἰησοῦ. (14:12)

Most commentators would limit the sense of πίστις here to the same two senses given above (πίστις[b]; πίστις[c]), though a few readers attempt to make room for the sense "the body of what is to be believed" (πίστις[e]). However, in these two texts we still have to deal with the second question: namely, the significance of the genitives μου/Ἰησοῦ.

As a means of beginning to resolve the question regarding which sense of πίστις is likely to be evoked in each context, it would be fruitful to chart the remaining occurrences of words belonging to this group throughout Revelation.

The verbs πιστεύω and ἀπιστέω never appear in Revelation. This is the pair of words in the group that unambiguously communicates the sense of trusting or entrusting (or the opposite),[9] and the absence may prove significant. At the very least, it removes the possibility of the presence of statements using the verb πιστεύω parallel to statements using the noun πίστις, with the consequent influence on what sense will be evoked in the latter.[10]

The adjective πιστός, however, is the term from this word group most frequently represented in Revelation. Unlike the noun πίστις, which

---

[8] There would be little point trying to provide a translation at the outset.

[9] The entries in BDAG and L&N limit the connotations of the verb to this range.

[10] See Matlock, "Even the Demons Believe", 316; "Detheologizing ΠΙΣΤΙΣ ΧΡΙΣΤΟΥ", 13–16.

has six discrete senses, the adjective πιστός appears to be limited to two fundamental senses: "faithful, reliable, or trustworthy" (showing faithfulness *toward* another) and "trusting" (showing faith *in* another).[11] The adjective is used thrice to describe Jesus, who is "the witness, the one showing faith/faithfulness" (ὁ μάρτυς ὁ πιστός, 1:5), "the witness, the one showing faith/faithfulness and the genuine one" (ὁ μάρτυς ὁ πιστὸς καὶ ἀληθινός, 3:14), and the one who is described as "showing faith/faithfulness and genuine" (πιστὸς καὶ ἀληθινός, 19:11). It is used once to describe a particular disciple, Antipas, whom Jesus calls "my witness, my believing/faithful one" (ὁ μάρτυς μου, ὁ πιστός μου, 2:13); prescribed for a community of disciples, who are to "demonstrate trust/loyalty to the point of death" (γίνου πιστὸς ἄχρι θανάτου) so as to receive "the crown of life" (2:10); and one of the qualities ascribed to the "called and chosen and believing/faithful" host (οἱ κλητοὶ καὶ ἐκλεκτοὶ καὶ πιστοί) who appear with the Lamb to make war against the beast and his supporters (17:14). Finally, particular "words" are affirmed to be "genuine and believing/faithful": a declaration made from the throne of God, confirmed by the One sitting upon the throne as "believing/faithful and genuine" (πιστοὶ καὶ ἀληθινοί, 21:5), and a larger body of words that might include the entirety of the vision of New Jerusalem, or an even larger portion of Revelation ("these words are believing/faithful and genuine", πιστοὶ καὶ ἀληθινοί, 22:6).

The counterpart adjective describing the absence or opposite of these qualities, ἄπιστος,[12] appears only once, describing the people who are excluded from the promises of God and the community in which these promises are received and celebrated: "With regard to the cowardly and unbelieving/unfaithful (ἀπίστοις) and abominable and murderers and sexually immoral persons and sorcerers and idolaters and all liars, their portion is in the lake that continues to burn with fire and sulphur, which is the second death" (21:8).

The Semantic Evocations of πιστός in Revelation

The sense of some occurrences of the πιστ-word group can be rather readily discerned. "Words", for example, will be "reliable" or "trustworthy" (πιστός in the sense of "evocative of trust from others"),

---

[11] BDAG (820 col. 2 – 821 col. 2) and LSJ (1408 col. 2) foreground both senses.

[12] BDAG (103 col. 2 – 104 col. 1) unduly limits this to "distrustful", where LSJ (189 col. 2) properly understands this word to cover the negation of the full range of senses potentially evoked by πιστός (hence "untrustworthy/unfaithful" or "distrustful").

and so the adjective would clearly be read this way in Revelation 21:5; 22:6. The description of Jesus as "the witness, the one showing faith/faithfulness" (ὁ μάρτυς ὁ πιστός, 1:5) is not so immediately unambiguous. The proximity of the term "witness", however, suggests a process by means of which the hearer would be disposed to disambiguate the adjective πιστός. A witness bears testimony, whether by speech or by deeds. It is an essential quality for a witness to be "reliable" or "trustworthy". The second and third iterations of this description of Jesus point more decisively in this direction by means of pairing the descriptors πιστός and ἀληθινός (3:14; 19:11), thus using of Jesus the same pair of descriptors applied to the "words" of God and of the visionary communications to name them "reliable/faithful and genuine/true" (21:5; 22:6), a pair of words together communicating utter dependability evoking belief and trust in others. If, in fact, πιστός is read in 1:5 and 3:14 as an attributive adjective rather than a substantive describing Jesus as himself πιστός (rather than Jesus *qua* witness as πιστός), this is indeed the only sense that would emerge.

This discussion impinges, in turn, on the description of Antipas, a model of praiseworthy discipleship in Pergamum, as "my witness, my believing/faithful one" (ὁ μάρτυς μου, ὁ πιστός μου, 2:13), utilizing the same formula and vocabulary here as first described Jesus, the "dependable witness" or "the witness, the faithful one" (ὁ μάρτυς ὁ πιστός, 1:5). The double addition of the genitive μου here is significant, as it both introduces the question of how these roles or qualities ("witness", "trusting/trustworthy") are enacted in regard to Jesus (i.e., what the genitive signifies) and applies some pressure against resolving this phrase as an instance of attributive position. Antipas is a witness *and* a faithful/trusting person in regard to Jesus, not merely a "dependable witness". Nevertheless the clear parallel with the descriptors of Jesus, and the author's subtle commendation of the paradigm of Christ throughout the work,[13] suggest that Antipas has borne testimony to

---

[13] Compare, e.g., the paradigm of overcoming enacted by Jesus (5:1–10) and by the "brothers and sisters" (12:10–12). In regard to the presentation of Jesus *qua* faithful witness as paradigm in 1:5, Wallis (*Faith of Jesus Christ*, 165) comments: "Jesus provides a precedent for others to follow and one which entails witness to the point of death." Wallis, however, goes on to indulge a contextual fallacy in regard to the definition of "faithful": "Πιστός, therefore, does not simply mean reliable or true (cf. ἀμήν), but embraces Jesus' keeping faith in the midst of suffering and death (1:5)." While Jesus *does* remain faithful in the midst of such pressures, John tends to speak explicitly about these pressures in the context of using the language of fidelity (e.g., 2:10, 13): he does not "load" this added sense into the word πιστός.

Jesus and has shown himself dependable, reliable, and faithful in the process. In this reading, the genitive μου is essentially resolved in favour of an objective genitive: Antipas is "my witness" insofar as Antipas bore testimony about Jesus or on behalf of Jesus;[14] he is "faithful" insofar as he has demonstrated loyalty, particularly in regard to his relationship with Jesus in the midst of severe pressures that had been brought to bear on him in order to dislodge this connection.

A similar sense would be evoked in regard to the occurrence of πιστός naming the quality to be manifested by the disciples in Smyrna in the midst of their circumstances: "be πιστός to the point of death" (2:10). Those circumstances are described in terms of significant external pressure (imprisonment – brief, no doubt, because it would eventuate in execution), interpreted as a "test" of those disciples. The way to "pass" such a test, or to emerge "proven" from such a test, would be to endure in one's commitments to the end rather than allow the pressures to subvert one's commitments. In a situation in which hostile pressure from without appears to be intended to motivate the creation of distance between the Christians and Jesus – thus, disowning Jesus' name (3:8), with the result that Jesus would find it commendable for a disciple to "hold fast to my name" in the face of such pressure (2:13) – the most desirable quality for the disciples in Smyrna to demonstrate is probably "loyalty" or "faithfulness" in regard to their connection with Jesus, rather than the disposition to "trust" Jesus.[15]

The Semantic Evocations of πιστός in Revelation

Having examined the evocations of the adjectival forms of this word group (and the non-appearance of the verbal forms), we can return to the nominal forms with a better sense of the linguistic context for the uses of these forms. This is not to say that the evocations of πίστις are *limited* by the (probable) evocations of πιστός, nor to conclude that the sense of "trust" or "faith" is eliminated by the non-appearance of the

---

[14] So Colin J. Hemer, *The Letters to the Seven Churches of Asia* (Sheffield: JSOT Press, 1986), 86.

[15] If I have not, then, unduly stacked the deck in favour of hearing πιστός as "faithful, reliable", then in the context of this discourse, and particularly at its end, ἄπιστος would be heard as the negation of this quality, hence "unfaithful", and not merely "distrustful".

verbal forms.[16] However, John's uses of the adjectival forms may indicate a greater emphasis on the quality of loyalty or faithfulness in John's promotion of a particular "ethos" of discipleship than on the quality of trust or belief, and this might have some bearing on how the nominal forms are to be resolved as well.

John, as we surveyed above, uses πίστις twice without qualification (2:19; 13:10), both times in such a way as clearly connotes a moral quality exhibited by the disciples – thus either "trust" (πίστις[b]) or "faithfulness" (πίστις[c]). Telling in this regard is the fact that, in each case, πίστις is set alongside other moral qualities or manifestations of such qualities, namely "love", "service", and "endurance" in 2:19 (τὴν ἀγαπὴν καὶ τὴν πίστιν καὶ τὴν διακονίαν καὶ τὴν ὑπομονήν σου), and simply alongside "endurance" (ἡ ὑπομονὴ καὶ ἡ πίστις) in 13:10. While there is an ethical component to exhibiting "trust" in another person (πίστις[b]), since the ability to recognize virtue in others (e.g., reliability, fidelity) is related to one's own experience of virtue,[17] there is a more obvious ethical component in the exhibition of "faithfulness" (πίστις[c]).[18] The Christians in Thyatira are commended for exhibiting that same moral quality, thus, that is praised in Antipas and set before Smyrna as the ethical need of the moment. The context in which the later occurrence appears (13:10) is also telling. The beast engages in war against the holy ones, particularly

---

[16] Matlock ("Detheologizing ΠΙΣΤΙΣ ΧΡΙΣΤΟΥ", 8), who demonstrates a very high degree of acuity in regard to lexical semantics, understands all four occurrences of πίστις in Rev. to fall under Louw and Nida's πίστις[b], "faith, trust". Granted, as he himself admits, Matlock performed a quick survey of *all* occurrences of the word in the NT in order to ascertain whether or not Louw and Nida's six categories of meaning were sufficient. He did not undertake an exegetical study of each occurrence in an attempt definitively to place each occurrence under one or another of these categories. Nevertheless, his cursory categorization at least cautions me not to be too quick to dismiss the possibility that the sense of πίστις *qua* "faith, trust" will be evoked in Revelation.

[17] See, e.g., F.W. Danker's discussion of Heb. 3:12 and the "base heart of mistrust" (καρδία πονηρὰ ἀπιστίας) in his *Benefactor: Epigraphic Study of a Graeco-Roman and New Testament Semantic Field* (St. Louis, MO: Clayton Publishing House, 1982), 318; discussed further in D.A. deSilva, *Despising Shame: Honor Discourse and Community Maintenance in the Epistle to the Hebrews* (SBLDS 152; Atlanta, GA: Scholars Press, 1995), 258–59.

[18] So also Wallis (*Faith of Jesus Christ*, 167), who reads πίστις in both texts as the moral virtue of faithfulness, evoked by the context of naming other moral virtues; see David E. Aune, *Revelation 1–5* (WBC 52A; Dallas, TX: Word, 1997), 196, 202; Martin Karrer, *Die Johannesoffenbarung als Brief* (Göttingen: Vandenhoeck & Ruprecht, 1986), 204, n.283.

through the machinations of the second beast and his enforcement of imperial cult, that is, the demonstration of loyalty toward the first beast. This beast is, furthermore, in direct competition with the Lamb for the allegiance of the people comprising "every tribe and language and people and nation" (5:9; 13:7). In such a contest, endurance and loyalty (πίστις[c]) are most directly at issue.[19]

We arrive at last at Revelation 2:13 and 14:12, the two occurrences of πίστις qualified by a nominal in the genitive. Among the commentaries and other treatments of Revelation 2:13 ("You held my name fast and you did not deny τὴν πίστιν μου") surveyed, three solutions emerge as important "contenders" in the debate: Jesus commends the Pergamene churches for (1) not renouncing "trust in me" (πίστις[b]; objective genitive);[20] (2) not renouncing "loyalty toward me" (πίστις[c]; objective genitive);[21] or (3) not renouncing "the faith in its claims about me" (πίστις[c]; genitive of content).[22] Conspicuously absent are arguments promoting a subjective reading of the genitive μου, i.e., "you have not renounced my trust" (πίστις[b]; subjective genitive) or "you have not renounced my faithfulness" (πίστις[c]; subjective genitive).

Towards which of these readings would the context dispose the hearers? Following Matlock's lead in regard to contextual selection of senses, we should pay particular attention to the parallel comment

---

[19] This, in turn, confirms our suggestion concerning the sense of ἄπιστοι in 21:8: if "patient endurance" (a facet of the virtue of courage) and "loyalty" characterize the holy ones in their contest with the beast (13:10), resulting in that victory that leads to the enjoyment of God's promises, then "the cowardly and disloyal" are most at risk of falling short of those promises.

[20] G.K. Beale, *The Book of Revelation* (NIGTC; Grand Rapids, MI: Eerdmans, 1999), 246; Ian Boxall, *The Revelation of Saint John* (BNTC; Peabody, MA: Hendrickson, 2006), 59; Grant Osborne, *Revelation* (BECNT; Grand Rapids, MI: Baker Academic, 2002), 142; Ben Witherington, III, *Revelation* (NCBC; Cambridge: Cambridge University Press, 2003), 88; Robert H. Mounce, *Revelation* (NICNT; Grand Rapids, MI: Eerdmans, 1998), 80.

[21] Wilhelm Bousset, *Die Offenbarung Johannis* (6th ed.; Kritisch-exegetischer Kommentar über das Neue Testament; 1906; repr. Göttingen: Vandenhoeck & Ruprecht, 1966), 212; R.H. Charles, *A Critical and Exegetical Commentary on the Revelation of St. John* (ICC; Edinburgh: T&T Clark, 1920), 1:61; Donald S. Deer, "Whose Faith/Loyalty in Revelation 2:13 and 14:12?", *BT* 38 (1987): 328–30; Aune, *Revelation 1–5*, 177; Craig Keener, *Revelation* (NIVAC; Grand Rapids, MI: Zondervan, 2000), 123; G.B. Caird, *Revelation* (BNTC; Peabody, MA: Hendrickson, 1966), 38; Stephen S. Smalley, *The Revelation of John* (Downers Grove, IL: InterVarsity Press, 2005), 69.

[22] Jürgen Roloff, *The Revelation of John* (Continental Commentaries; Philadelphia, PA: Fortress, 1993), 50–51; both Beale (*Revelation*, 766) and Smalley (*Revelation*, 69) also make room for this interpretation.

about Antipas as "my witness, my faithful one" (ὁ πιστός μου, 2:13) in the attempt to resolve the meaning of not denying τὴν πίστιν μου. The importance of this parallel is not lost on proponents of a variety of solutions.

As part of his argument in favour of reading μου as an objective genitive in the phrase in question, Beale draws attention to the close proximity of the genitive pronouns in "my witness, my faithful one" (ὁ μάρτυς μου, ὁ πιστός μου, 2:13), since these also are applied to a substantive adjective related to the head noun πίστις.[23] Reading the genitive in ὁ πιστός μου as objective ("the one who was faithful toward me"), he suggests that this would clarify the significance of the genitive in τὴν πίστιν μου. This makes good sense, but Beale only applies this contextual information to the second question (what is the sense of the genitive?), and not to the first (in what sense would πίστις be heard?).

Osborne also looks to the larger context of usage in Revelation to decide between the two possibilities he lists for τὴν πίστιν μου: "the Christian faith" or "faith in me".[24] He claims that "in the context of the book, where πίστις always refers to an active and persevering trust in Christ (cf. 2:19; 13:10; 14:12) and is equivalent to πιστός (*pistos*, faithful)", readers would favour the objective genitive, "faith in me". Again, sensitivity to contextual factors in regard to the meaning of τὴν πίστιν μου yields helpful results in regard to the sense of the genitive. Striking, however, is Osborne's willingness only to consider definitions of πίστις as "faith" (specifically as the disposition of trust; πίστις[b]) rather than as "faithfulness", particularly in light of his correct translation of πιστός and his correct instinct to look to such parallel expressions in close context (2:10, 13, 19) as formative for the reader's understanding of the genitive in τὴν πίστιν μου (again, especially ὁ πιστός μου in 2:13). A gloss on Antipas's faithfulness as "a persevering *trust* in Christ in the midst of persecution and martyrdom" effectively replaces πίστις[c] with πίστις[b].[25]

The contextual observations made by both Beale and Osborne ought to raise questions about "faith in me" as a better rendering of τὴν πίστιν μου than "faithfulness toward me". As we have already attempted to show, the occurrences of the adjective πιστός in 2:10 and 2:13 speak of the display of loyalty toward Jesus as that which is praiseworthy

---

[23] Beale, *Revelation*, 246.

[24] Osborne, *Revelation*, 142.

[25] Osborne, *Revelation*, 142.

(2:13) or that which is the desideratum of the moment (2:10). The pressures brought to bear on Antipas, the Christians in Pergamum, and the Christians in Smyrna were instrumental in motivating dissociation from Jesus; the larger contest between the beast and the Lamb for the allegiance of humanity, dividing the tribes, language groups, peoples, and nations among them, provides the backdrop for these local "tests" of the disciples' loyalty.[26] In such a context, the verb ἀρνέομαι (2:13; 3:8) is likely to signify "deny[ing] any relationship of association with someone" (L&N 34.48), such that the Philadelphians are to be commended for not denying Christ's name (3:8) – that is, for not hiding or denying their association with him. The corollary of this is the positive testimony – the confession – that Jesus will make on behalf of the loyal disciple: "I will confess his or her name before my father and before his angels" (3:5).

John envisions not that the disciples' inner disposition of "trust" will be threatened in these circumstances, but rather their ongoing manifestation of association with this Jesus ("my name"). At stake is their display of loyalty. Displays of loyalty can, of course, be fueled by the inner disposition of trusting Jesus, but, again, it is the former that is most directly under attack, and that John most desires to reinforce. Those scholars who promote the translation "you have not renounced your loyalty toward me" (or the like) are reading τὴν πίστιν μου most fully in line with the context not only of the parallel uses of words from the πιστ-group (and their accompanying genitives, notably ὁ πιστός μου, 2:13),[27] but also in the context of parallel uses of the verb ἀρνέομαι, the larger context of the visionary part of the book, and of the socio-historical pressures with which the Christian communities are wrestling.[28]

---

[26] As Caird (*Revelation*, 38) observes, "Peter denied his Master without being charged in a lawcourt, and there must have been many occasions in the public life of Pergamum when it was safer not to be openly recognized as a Christian."

[27] "The one showing faith toward me" is one of those "who have not renounced faithfulness toward me" (2:13): in effect, ὁ πιστός μου describes the person who does not deny τὴν πίστιν μου.

[28] Reading πίστις here in the sense of "the body of doctrine" (πίστις^e) seems furthest removed from the contextual indicators in its emphasis on "confession" as the profession of specific beliefs about Jesus. Smalley's suggestion (*Revelation*, 69) that the Pergamene Christians "have not denied my (the Christian) faith", specifically "a balanced faith in his person as both human and divine", is an outgrowth of Smalley's reading of Revelation fully in the orbit of 1 John and the Fourth Gospel, and an obvious import of this sense of "faith" from John and 1 John. Revelation lacks the explicit discussion of such christological statements such as could possibly trump the other contextual indicators for hearing πίστις in a relational rather than a doctrinal sense.

Scholars have suggested a greater variety of solutions to the joint problem of the sense of πίστις and the nature of the relationship intimated by the genitive case in Revelation 14:12. While some commentators do not address this question explicitly,[29] those who do attempt to explicate the matter propose one (or more) of five possibilities: the holy ones are defined as (1) those who keep the trust shown by Jesus (πίστις[b]; subjective genitive);[30] (2) those who keep the faithfulness shown by Jesus (πίστις[c]; subjective genitive);[31] (3) those who keep faith in Jesus (πίστις[b]; objective genitive);[32] (4) those who keep faith with Jesus (πίστις[c]; objective genitive);[33] and (5) those who keep "the faith" as communicated by Jesus (πίστις[e]; genitive of source).[34]

---

[29] J.M. Ford (*Revelation* [AB; New York: Doubleday, 1975], 231), e.g., translates the phrase in question as "who keep the commandments of God and the faith of Jesus", providing no further comment *ad locum* (1975: 249). Similarly, Witherington (*Revelation*, 188) translates "those who keep the commandments of God and hold fast to the faith of Jesus" (14:12), but does not follow this with comment, in part no doubt because discussion of every interesting point of grammar would be to some extent impossible within the scope envisioned for that mid-range commentary series. See also Edmondo Lupieri, *A Commentary on the Apocalypse of John* (Grand Rapids, MI: Eerdmans, 2006), 51, 75, 120, 227. The translations offered both reflect the RSV ("keep ... the faith of Jesus"), which replicates the formal ambiguity, although in English one is less likely to construe "of x" as a kind of object, and thus this may prejudice readers toward a subjective genitive.

[30] Wallis, *Faith of Jesus Christ*, 168–9.

[31] Tonstad, "Reading Paul in a New Paradigm", 58; Boxall, *Revelation*, 210. Tonstad posits that the context of the cosmic struggle militates against readings that have concern with individual salvation, and he prefers to read this as a subjective genitive with the force of commending Jesus' faithfulness as a model for imitation: "hold firm to the way of God as it was revealed by the faithfulness of Jesus". In this paraphrase, the second element of the sentence (the faithfulness of Jesus) becomes a modal qualifier of the first (the commandments of God): the second shows *how* to fulfil the first.

[32] Caird, *Revelation*, 188. Substantial argumentation in favour of this reading is not presented.

[33] David E. Aune, *Revelation 6–16* (WBC 52B; Dallas, TX: Word, 1998), 783, 837–8; Smalley, *Revelation*, 368–9; Roloff, *Revelation*, 173; Osborne, *Revelation*, 543–4; Mounce, *Revelation* (rev. ed.; NICNT; Grand Rapids, MI: Eerdmans, 1998), 275. This interpretation is also reflected in the NIV ("remain faithful to Jesus") and GNB ("are faithful to Jesus").

[34] Beale, *Revelation*, 766. Beale goes on to talk about possible intentional ambiguity on John's part, making room for both a genitive of source and objective genitive, eventually with a little subjective genitive mixed in ("Jesus' faith", specifically as something to be imitated; *Revelation*, 767–8). Making room for three simultaneous senses for this genitive – the genitive of source, objective genitive, and subjective

Attention to contextual indicators is not wanting in the arguments of proponents of several different possibilities. Wallis, for example, observes the importance of the phrase τὴν μαρτυρίαν Ἰησοῦ ("the testimony of / witness to Jesus") throughout Revelation (1:2, 9; 6:9; 19:10; 20:4), and particularly in 12:17, a verse that closely parallels 14:12. He reads τὴν μαρτυρίαν Ἰησοῦ as a subjective genitive, in parallel with "the word of God" *qua* "God's word", "the word God uttered",[35] which, in turn, informs the sense of τὴν πίστιν Ἰησου: "Jesus' life of faith, lived in response to God's word and in the midst of persecution",[36] a life to be imitated by the Christians in the midst of their pressures.[37]

However, it is David Aune who provides the strongest linguistic evidence satisfying Matlock's argument that particular contexts will evoke particular senses, especially with regard to the immediate context of the expression:[38]

> The phrase πίστιν τηρεῖν occurs a few times in Josephus with the meaning "to keep a pledge" (*Ant.* 13.207; *J.W.* 6.345) ... The phrase πίστιν τηρεῖν, "to keep faith, to remain loyal", was a common Greek expression (Polybius 6.56.13; 10.37.9; Jos. *J.W.* 2.121; 6.345; *Ant.* 13.207, 415 [*var. lect.*]; BMI 3:587b, lines 5ff.) ... Since πίστιν τηρεῖν was a widespread idiom with this recognized meaning, it is likely that in Revelation 14:12 it means "to remain loyal, to be faithful".[39]

---

genitive – certainly opens up creative homiletical possibilities, but it hardly helps resolve the exegetical issues here. It seems rather to come dangerously close to the fallacy that reads all senses of a word or a syntactical relationship as being evoked simultaneously in a particular context. (On the matter of multiple senses of a given word, see, e.g., Silva, *Biblical Words*, 149–56.)

[35] *Faith of Jesus Christ*, 169.

[36] *Faith of Jesus Christ*, 172.

[37] Smalley uses the same parallel expression in 12:17 as a basis for his discussion of 14:12 (*Revelation*, 368), however he concludes that "the genitive [in 12:17] ... is most probably objective, meaning the testimony which needs to be given by believers *to* Jesus", and so supports rendering 14:12 as "keeping God's commandments and remaining faithful to Jesus".

[38] See Matlock, "Detheologizing ΠΙΣΤΙΣ ΧΡΙΣΤΟΥ", 5, n.15.

[39] Aune, *Revelation 6–16*, 838. Osborne (*Revelation*, 544) includes discussion of "faithful" as a semantic option for πίστις here, aligning closely with Aune's position: "the saints remain firmly 'faithful to Jesus'". Aune (*Revelation 6–16*, 837) argues that τὴν πίστιν Ἰησοῦ, "and faithfulness to Jesus", is "a gloss added during the revisions made for the second edition since πίστις is used in Revelation only in 2:13, 19, in the two ὧδε sayings (which are probably glosses) in 13:10, and here in 14:12. It also appears to be somewhat awkward in this context for the noun τὴν

As an object of the verb τηρεῖν, then, πίστιν will likely be heard in the sense of "faithfulness" or "loyalty" (πίστις^c), which is also entirely in keeping with the other uses of the πιστ-group throughout Revelation, with the necessary corollary that the genitive Ἰησοῦ denotes the object toward which such loyalty is directed. Once again, the narrative context of the contest between beast and Lamb over the inhabitants of the earth, who are being drawn into two camps, as it were, also favours this sense of πίστις, since staying true to the Lamb in the midst of the pressures orchestrated by the beast and his accomplice is the primary challenge identified in that narrative.

Although reading τὴν πίστιν μου in Revelation 2:13 as "faith in me" in his commentary ad loc.,[40] Beale changes his mind about 2:13 by the time he comments on 14:12:

> Ἰησοῦ is a genitive of source, so that τὴν πίστιν Ἰησοῦ is best rendered "faith from Jesus" (though objective genitive, "faith in Jesus", is possible and is preferred by most commentators). This refers specifically to the objective gospel traditions having their origin in Jesus, since it is parallel with the preceding "commandments of God" … That πίστις refers to the doctrinal content of the Christian faith (cf. Jude 3) is further evident from 2:13, where the word occurs with the same meaning. In fact, "keeping the faith of Jesus" … is synonymous with "not denying my faith" in 2:13.[41]

I would question this argument, beginning with the explicated rationale for reading "the faith of Jesus" in 14:12 as a reference to the gospel traditions, "since it is parallel with the preceding 'commandments of God'".[42] The logic seems to be that, because the first member of this descriptive pair ("those who keep the commandments of God and the faith of Jesus") concerns written/fixed traditions, so must also the second,

---

πίστιν, "faithfulness", to be used as the object of the verb τηρεῖν, "keep", since τηρεῖν must then be understood to have two simultaneous meanings, "obey" with τὰς ἐντολάς, "the commandments", and "remain with τὴν πίστιν". I do not find the second sentence to present a true obstacle to reading "faithfulness" as an original component of this saying. We can say quite easily in English, and without confusion, "who keep the commandments of God and faith with Jesus", understanding the first "keeping" to involve walking in line with rules and the second to involve preserving a relationship. The Gk. sentence demands no more flexibility of τηρεῖν than that.

[40] Beale, *Revelation*, 246.
[41] Beale, *Revelation*, 766.
[42] Beale, *Revelation*, 766.

despite the immediate availability of clearer ways of communicating this (e.g., "the sayings of Jesus", "the traditions of Jesus", "the words of Jesus"). "Faith" refers to a *depositum credendi* a very precious few times in the New Testament; in the less disputed instances (e.g., Gal. 1:23; Jude 3), it appears as such without a qualifying genitive. In light of Aune's linguistic evidence favouring the sense of "faithfulness" coupled with an objective genitive (a virtue demonstrated toward Jesus), Beale's promotion of hearing πίστις as "belief" (a trust placed in Jesus, let alone beliefs about Jesus) is difficult to maintain.

In regard to Beale's insight that the two members ought to have sufficient commonality to be held in parallel with one another, "keeping the commandments of God" and "keeping faith with Jesus" both define a way of living, a set of responses in real-life situations constrained by certain guidelines. A body of regulations ("the commandments of God") and the ethical conduct consonant with safeguarding a particular relationship ("keeping faith with Jesus") are sufficiently parallel conceptual entities. In other words, the latter does not need to be understood as a body of fixed traditions in order to be an intelligible parallel to "the commandments of God", and other factors would strongly favour taking πίστις in a different sense than "that which is to be believed".

Conclusion

Revelation never uses the language of πίστις or πιστεύω to speak about believing in Jesus or even trusting in Jesus.[43] That the sense of "faith" is not evoked in regard to the former and that the latter verb never appears in the book may be more than a coincidence, for it is the prevalence of the verb in Pauline texts that has tended to be an important contextual factor in the evocation of the sense "faith" for the noun.[44] To be sure, the author presumes a shared commitment to some

---

[43] Hebrews similarly never uses the language of πίστις or πιστεύω to speak about believing in Jesus or trusting in Jesus; all occurrences of the latter are squarely theocentric (see, e.g., Heb. 6:1; 11:6 and compare also affirmations of God's trustworthiness, esp. Sarah's example of "considering reliable the one who promised" [= trusting] in Heb. 10:23; 11:11). This is not to say that the concept of trusting Jesus (particularly as "mediator" or "broker") is not present or assumed at several points throughout the sermon, only that the nominal and verbal forms of this word group are not used to evoke the concept.

[44] On this, see further Matlock, "Detheologizing ΠΙΣΤΙΣ ΧΡΙΣΤΟΥ", 13–16.

basic convictions about the significance of Jesus' life, death, resurrection, ascension, and coming again in judgment (see, e.g., 1:5–7, 17b–18; 5:9–10; 12:5; 14:14–20; 19:11–16; 22:7, 12, 20) but does not explicitly talk about such shared conviction using this terminology. Presenting Jesus as a reliable witness (1:5; 3:14) is surely evocative of trust in Jesus' words (both those available through the Jesus tradition and those presented as uttered by Jesus in the context of Revelation), as is the presentation of other words as πιστός (21:5; 22:6), but John again does not use πιστ-terminology to talk explicitly about this inner disposition of trust in regard to the trustworthy. Disciples are commended for imitating the pattern of Jesus, particularly in regard to Jesus' own faithfulness (in what direction, whether toward God or the disciples, is never specified, and such attempts to limit or qualify faithfulness might indeed be out of place), but this is not directly fostered by the two references to "the faith(fulness) of Christ" (2:13; 14:12), and only indirectly through the repetitive patterns involving the adjective πιστός.[45]

Rather, this word group is used primarily to express the value of loyalty, dependability, trustworthiness. John portrays a world at war in a contest for allegiance and for the tokens of allegiance (e.g., worship). The broader canvas displays two powers dividing humanity between them. Who will stand alongside the Lamb? Who will gather under the aegis of the beast, paying homage before his image? John invites the hearers to see the pressures within their local situations against this larger backdrop, and so the question he puts continually before them is this: Will they exhibit faithfulness toward Jesus in the face of whatever pressures they face, or will they hide or deny their allegiance to him in order to escape those pressures? The two occurrences of the relevant phrase, ἡ πίστις Ἰησοῦ or ἡ πίστις μου, employ an objective genitive, with the noun evoking the meaning "faithfulness" shown toward Jesus, as part of John's larger agenda to foster this core value of Christian discipleship, and to preserve the witness that the Christian community has to bear to the One God in imitation of its Lord.

---

[45] These mimetic patterns emerge as, e.g., John describes Jesus as πιστός, then commends those who have been themselves πιστοί in ways recalling Jesus' demonstration of faithfulness (as in the case of Antipas, 2:13) or prescribes the stance of remaining πιστός as the advantageous and honorable course for disciples (as in the charge given to the Christians in Smyrna, 2:10), rather than in the phrase τὴν πίστιν Ἰησοῦ as the paradigm of Jesus' faith or faithfulness to be imitated (hence, "kept") by the disciples, as argued by Wallis (*Faith of Jesus Christ*, 168–9) or Tonstad ("Reading Paul in a New Paradigm", 58).

HISTORICAL AND
THEOLOGICAL REFLECTIONS

16

Πίστις Χριστοῦ in the Church Fathers
and Beyond

MARK W. ELLIOTT

In this essay I shall make use of two previous useful attempts to marshal the evidence from early Christian writers up to Augustine in order to arrive at contrasting and even conflicting opinions. I shall review this evidence, add to it a sketch of the medieval view of the question and finish by looking at more recent "dogmatic" writers whose work might be helpfully considered in the attempt of exegetes to "sift" the evidence.

The Patristic Period

In the dispute over how to understand *pistis Christou*, two writers have investigated how this idea has fared in the history of interpretation in the early church of the first four centuries or so. Ian Wallis has a chapter in his monograph which argued for "the faith *of* Jesus Christ". Roy Harrisville's essay appeared at about the same time.[1]

We begin with Harrisville, whose approach is more cautious and whose method is more of an evidentiary nature. He lists three classes of the early Christian writers' use of this phrase as thrown up by the *TLG*. The third class of cases are the clear objective genitive ones which include an example from the Acts of Peter, and Origen on Psalm 17 (MT 18) verse 24: "It says the righteousness of faith of Jesus Christ

---

[1] Wallis, *Faith of Jesus Christ*; Harrisville, "Witness of the Fathers". Harrisville's 2006 essay ("Before ΠΙΣΤΙΣ ΧΡΙΣΤΟΥ"), in which he traces the preponderance of the objective genitive in the classical Gk. sources, ends by making the theological point that Jesus is not to be missed in our faith: faith is directed towards him and God, not away from him towards God as Hays and others say. On this, see Wallis, *Faith of Jesus Christ*, 129, as approved by Foster, "First Contribution", 93.

(πίστις Ἰησοῦ Χριστοῦ) which has appeared to all who believe. For those who rightly believe faith is reckoned as righteousness".[2] Having just translated the Greek words as "the faith of Jesus Christ" Harrisville then comments: "Origen thus understands the πίστις Ἰησοῦ Χριστοῦ as objective. Otherwise, how could he state in the next sentence that the faith of 'those [plural] who rightly believe' is reckoned as righteousness? If he understood it as Jesus' faith, he would have used the singular."[3] Indeed, when one looks at the text one finds that Origen is discussing how the righteousness of God exceeds the law of nature's capacity, though Christ does not have a righteousness which is "without" the Law of Moses and the prophets; faith and the Law go together. It seems pretty clear that Origen means the objective genitive; "faith in his blood" is in parallel. The examples from Chrysostom seem clearly "objective" and Augustine is quite explicit that "there is not meant the faith with which Christ Himself believes" (*De spiritu et littera* ch. 9; CSEL 60, 167).

In the second category of cases the meaning is clearly about human faith (Abraham's faith, not faith in him). It is therefore only Harrisville's first class of cases which is interesting.

For a start there is Clement Paedagogos I, 8 (73),[4] which seems a possible witness for the subjective genitive case in its use of Romans 3:21f. (διὰ πίστεως Ἰησοῦ Χριστοῦ), since Clement uses this phrase in the wider christological context of a passage where he is focusing on the virtue and goodness of the son who prays to the Father ("if the Lord is the Son of the Creator, then the Lord is the son of the Righteous"). It is not certain, however, because Clement just juxtaposes two quotations (Rom. 3:21f. and 3:26) and says very little about them. Again, it might or might not be a problem that his variant of Romans 3:26 reads ἐκ πίστεως Ἰησοῦν, that is, Jesus in the accusative, although this might only reflect a textual variant and not reflect any intention or even understanding by Clement that it is an objective genitive. As Harrisville says, it is ambiguous.

Yet Origen is much more transparent. Where the fragment on the Song of Songs contains a line saying that the spiritual sense of Song of Songs 2:5 is either the faithful who respect the church or those who are "strangers to the faith of Christ" (ἀλλοτρίους τῆς πίστεως Χριστοῦ), this can hardly be anything other than an objective

---

[2] PG 12, 1233.
[3] Harrisville, "Witness of the Fathers", 238.
[4] SC 70, 240.

genitive. Direct references to Romans 3:22 and 26 are not found outside Origen's Romans commentary, which is a sign that these verses were not of great importance to him. Nor does his Romans commentary on these verses contain any real discussion of the phrase. Origen's chief interest is simply in explaining what a "righteousness apart from the Law" might mean. Lastly, at PG 12, 1412 on Psalm 39 (40):10, he writes of the great church "in whom/which he proclaimed righteousness through faith in Jesus" (ἐν ἧ εὐηγγελίζετο δικαιοσύνην τὴν διὰ πίστεως Ἰησοῦ).

As for the third author listed by Harrisville as providing "ambiguous cases", Basil – the quickest of looks at his *De Baptismo*'s use of Philippians 3:8–10 (and that of the *Moralia*, Rule 43) reveals that he simply quotes that passage on three occasions and says nothing about what it means.[5] Although I trust the results of Harrisville's *TLG* search, just to make sure that perhaps even where the exact phrase did not appear there was not some echo of "the faith of Jesus Christ" in the commentary on the key verses, I checked Biblia Patristica. I was interested to note that Romans 3:22, 26 and Galatians 2:16 are hardly mentioned: not at all in the volume *Troisième Siècle (Origène excepté)*;[6] and in the volume on the fourth century nothing was said about the faith of Jesus on the three occasions (in Epiphanius) where these verses were mentioned. My sense is that both ante- and post-Nicene fathers, from Origen to Chrysostom, were united in the view that this is an objective genitive; Augustine is even clearer about it. In other words, Harrisville's conclusions could be made stronger.

However, before we jump to premature conclusions, let us consider the other side of the argument over how the early Christian writers line up on the question. Wallis's two significant ante-Nicene figures (apart from Ignatius, to whom we shall return) are Clement and Tertullian. As we have seen in reviewing Harrisville's article, Clement does not think in terms of Jesus' own faith as being significant, and Tertullian's *De carne Christi*, which Wallis adduces as one of his chief witnesses, is far off what he claims for it. The phrase "therefore return to Christ his faith" (*redde igitur Christo fidem suam ...*) is followed by: "that he willed to walk the earth as a man". This means precisely that we are to give to Christ the belief due him. It is not that, as Wallis concludes: "It appears that Tertullian considered faith to be a key characteristic of

---

[5] PG 31, 764 (for *Moralia*) and SC 357, 164, 142, 260 (for *De Baptismo*).
[6] Paris: CNRS, 1977.

human being and, in consequence, one which Christ needed to exercise if he was to secure salvation for all people through his incarnation and resurrection."[7]

In any case, Wallis argues that the idea "the faith of Jesus Christ" was alive and well in the early church and got lost only with Athanasius, who referred *pistos* in Hebrews 3:2 to the unchangeability of the Eternal Son, so that *pistos* could not be applied to Jesus the man's faith. In fact, "Athanasius declined a golden opportunity to underline the completeness of the incarnation"[8] when he described Christ as "faithful, not as sharing faith with us, nor as having faith in anyone as we have, but as deserving to receive faith in all He says and does, and as offering a faithful sacrifice" (*Contra Arianos* II.9; *NPNF*[2] 4.353).[9] This was an overreaction to Arianism, Wallis thinks. It is, he muses, "interesting" that Hilary in *De Trinitate* III, 26 spoke of Christ "as simultaneously the author and witness of true faith in God".[10] But no! This is clearly about God, not Jesus, as the words show: ***cum hoc solum de Deo bene credi intellegeamus ad quod*** *de se credendum ipse sibi nobiscum et testis et auctor existat.*[11] Perhaps the more convincing one in Hilary for Wallis's case is in the context of how Jesus' body was able to transcend his suffering owing to the action of "his soul, warned [*sic.*] by the happy glow of its own heavenly faith and hope" *(quae ubi coelestis spei ac fidei suae beato calore) –* in *De Trinitate* X.44. Whatever Hilary meant by that, there is little sense of a Jesus Christ exercising faith as believers would, but rather of one who prayed for others from a position of strength.[12]

Wallis's lament is that the Cappadocian fathers and then Augustine allowed that faith was a gift from Jesus, but not something he had while on earth. "Augustine ... could still interpret Hebrews 12:2 in

---

[7] Wallis, *Faith of Jesus Christ*, 193.

[8] Wallis, *Faith of Jesus Christ*, 206.

[9] Quoted by Wallis, *Faith of Jesus Christ*, 205.

[10] Wallis, *Faith of Jesus Christ*, 209.

[11] "Since we should understand that this only is to be believed of God, for which he is both witness and author to himself with us of that which is to be believed." See SC 443 (Hilaire de Poitiers, *La Trinité, Livres I–III*), 386.

[12] The full citation (SC 462, 242) reads: *quae ubi coelestis spei ac fidei suae beato calore terrenae in corpore suo originis despexit exordium, sui quoque sensus ac spiritus corpus efficitur in dolorem ut pati se desinat sentire quod patitur.* This follows a few lines after this startlingly "Apollinarian" sounding sentence: *Et extra terreni est corporis mala non terrenis inchoatum corpus elementis, etsi originem filii hominis sanctus Spiritus per sacramentum conceptionis invexit.* Cf. L.F. Ladaria, *Cristologiá de Hilario de Poitiers* (Roma: Pontificia Università Gregoriana, 1989), 66.

terms of Christ as the source and goal of faith but not its exemplar."[13] Wallis claims, however, that there is a glimmer of the other view in Augustine's *De praedestinatione sanctorum* 31's *"ille facit in hominibus principium fidei et perfectionem in Jesum, qui fecit hominem principem fidei et perfectorem Jesum"*. (PG 44, 983: "He who made Jesus to be the prince of faith and perfector, makes the principle of faith and perfection in Jesus.") Perhaps – or perhaps it simply means that the man Jesus was a prince of faith in the sense of leading faith (and then perfecting it). Augustine usually opted for the objective genitive. Both Wallis and Harrisville were agreed on that. Wallis laments: "it seems, therefore, that the paradigmatic significance of Jesus' faith – of the way in which his life and passion inform the practice of faith – was a casualty of the movement towards establishing Christ's divinity ... [with] implications for the church's understanding of the relationship between *fides quae* and *fides qua creditor"*.[14]

It seems that Wallis thinks that only as exemplar can Jesus be the author of faith. The only footnote in his "Concluding Remarks" is to recent works of modern theology by the strange bedfellows of the Torrances, John Macquarrie, and James Mackey as pointing in a new direction that will take the faith of Christ seriously.[15] The thesis of the book as a whole is that the pre-Easter Jesus should not be submerged by the post-Easter one.

To arrive at a more reliable interpretation, a community that the New Testament writers would have approved of, we could do worse, as Markus Bockmuehl has recently suggested, than to look to those who carried the living memory of the apostles which extended into the second century.[16] This allows a tradition of interpretation as a *viva vox* for interpretation (up to about the time of Irenaeus) for those who stuck to the persons and the texts stemming from the apostles and Jesus among them. Significantly for our purposes we have no less a personage than Ignatius of Antioch using the phrase πίστις Χριστοῦ.

For Ignatius, even if it is primarily the faith of believers which concerns him, nevertheless that faith somehow comes to them through him (Ignatius, *Philadelphians* 8: ἡ πίστις ἡ δι' αὐτοῦ). This is clearly faith which is through him and nothing more (or less). The letter to the *Trallians* 8, 1 has: "renew yourself in the faith which is the flesh of the

---

13 Wallis, *Faith of Jesus Christ*, 212.
14 Wallis, *Faith of Jesus Christ*, 212.
15 Wallis, *Faith of Jesus Christ*, 220.
16 Markus Bockmuehl, *Seeing the Word* (Grand Rapids, MI: Baker, 2006), 169.

Lord and in love which is the blood of Jesus Christ" – but again this is not suggestive of Jesus Christ having a faith.

In the letter to the *Ephesians* Ignatius speaks of those "destroyers through bad teaching of the faith for which Christ was crucified" (16:1–2), although that is more about the *fides quae* ("the content of the faith") which Christ taught and stood for than asserting that Christ had faith as *fides qua*. Perhaps the strongest case is that provided by *Ephesians* 20, 1: "in his faith and in his love, in his suffering and resurrection" (ἐν τῇ αὐτοῦ πίστει καὶ ἐν τῇ αὐτοῦ ἀγάπῃ, ἐν πάθει αὐτοῦ καὶ ἀναστάσει).[17] Yet U. Körtner translates: "*im Glauben an ihn und in der Liebe an seinem Leiden und Auferstehung*" ("in faith in him and in the love in his suffering and resurrection").[18] The point is that the full sentence is a promise to describe in a second book the plan of salvation which the following sentence describes in terms of Christians living their faith in unity. So what we do have is Jesus as the author of faith, and faithful as God is faithful, but not as one who himself had faith. "Faith which is through him", as we find it in Ignatius, is perhaps a good compromise.

Medieval Developments

It might at first glance appear interesting that it took a millennium for translations of the Bible to catch up and translate the key passages clearly with "faith in Jesus Christ".[19] "Although it would have to be proven by an exhaustive study of all NT versions, it appears that Luther was the first in the history of NT translators to render *pistis Christou* as an objective genitive. He consistently (except for Galatians 2:20) translated the Greek *Glauben an Christum*."[20] Yet it is not the case that a pre-Luther any more than post-Luther interpretation from Lyra to Joseph Hall took this to be a subjective genitive. Indeed, after looking at the Syriac and the Latin Vulgate and Sahidic, one could safely claim that although translators throughout the Middle Ages up to the KJV used "the faith of Christ" (*fides Iesu Christi* – at Rom. 3:2 and Gal. 3), that was nothing more significant than just translators' literalism and a reluctance to

---

[17] Cf. F. Bergamelli, "'Fede di Gesù Cristo' nelle letter di Ignazio di Antiochia", *Salesianum* 66 (2004): 649–64.

[18] U. Körtner, *Die Apostolische Väter* (Darmstadt: Wissenschaftliche Buchgesellschaft, 1981), 159.

[19] Howard, "Faith of Christ", 759.

[20] Howard, "Faith of Christ", 759.

make changes to that which Jerome (or Rabbula, for that matter) had established.

Now the medieval consensus was that to speak of Jesus Christ as having faith was to speak unworthily of him. For Bonaventure, Christ's human knowledge was not comprehensive of his divine knowledge and was not created able to know the infinite, but was given ecstatic experiential grace that drew it towards the latter (*Disputed Questions VI & VII*). The grace of union placed his soul in an infinite hypostasis and allowed him comprehensive knowledge of the finite. During this discussion the way of faith is seen as something far beneath that of Christ; it is not even up for discussion.[21] A century previously Hugh of St. Victor had insisted, against those who stressed too much an *"assumptus homo"* Christology, that the soul of Christ was "graced" by the divine Word so that it possessed the latter's omniscience.[22]

Yet for the later Franciscan Matthew of Aquasparta, God is infinite even to saints in heaven – so faith will endure. Did Christ, already possessing what the blessed will have, need faith then – even if it included vision? For obscurity of faith means there is more of a free moral choice, which was all-important for the Franciscan theological tradition. Yet even the Dominican Thomas had to admit from Scripture that Christ was freely obedient. Karl Rahner concludes that, for the tradition flowing from Thomas, Jesus' obedience seems to have come not so much out of his faith as out of his knowledge.[23]

In his commentary on Hebrews, Thomas writes on Hebrews 12:2 ("the author and perfecter of our faith"):[24]

> He is the author of our faith in two ways. First, by teaching faith in words. Above 1:2 *Hath spoken to us by his Son.* Jn 1:18: *The only begotten Son is in the bosom of the Father, He hath declared Him.* Second, by impressing faith in our hearts. Phil. 1:29: *For unto you it is given for Christ, not only to believe in Him* ... Likewise he is the consummation of faith in two ways. In one way

---

[21] See *Works of Saint Bonaventure: Disputed Questions on the Knowledge of Christ* (intro. and trans. Zachary Hayes; New York: Franciscan Institute, 1992), 161–97.

[22] See H. Santiago-Otero, "La Sabiduría del Alma de Cristo", *RTAM* 34 (1967): 131–58.

[23] "Die ewige Bedeutung der Menschheit Jesu für unser Gottesverhältnis", in K. Rahner, *Schriften zur Theologie* III (Zürich: Benzinger, 1961), 47–61.

[24] Thomas Aquinas, *Commentary on Hebrews* (South Bend, IN: St. Augustine's Press, 2006), 270, sec. 664.

by confirming it with miracles. Jn 10:38. In the other way by rewarding faith. For since faith is imperfect knowledge, its reward consists in the perfection of that knowledge: Jn 14:21 *I will love him, and will manifest myself to him.* This was signified in Zach 4:9, where it is said, *the hands of Zorobabel have laid the foundations of this house,* namely the church, whose foundation is faith, *and his hands shall finish it.* For the hands of Christ, Who descended from the line of Zorobabel, founded the Church in faith and consummates that faith with glory. (1 Cor. 13:12) ... Augustine says in *On the Trinity* (I,10) "Contemplation is the reward of faith, for which reward hearts are cleansed by faith, as it is written, *Cleansing their hearts by faith."*

Christ is the author of our faith "only" in the sense of teaching it, and rewarding it. John's Gospel offers us something of the *contemplative* life of Jesus, according to Aquinas.[25]

Christ had unlimited knowledge (despite Mk. 5:30; 13:32). For Thomas, Jesus could have this beatific vision while also having imperfect prophetic vision as *viator* (*Summa Theologiae* IIIa, q7, a8 and q11, a1). Prophetic light elevated his capacities for abstracting from sensible images the reality which he must transmit (with an amalgam of Aristotle and Augustine here) so that humanity can thus know to whom he belongs. In this highest prophetic knowledge there is a "christic" event. Moreover, Jesus' knowledge is not just occasional but permanent, constant (*STh* IIIa, q11, a5) and thus God the Word can love God humanly through such a humanity.

Thomas is quite clear about this. Since the incarnation is for salvation, the fountain must be full of water. When John 8:55 is used in *Summa Theologiae* (III, q9 a2), "For I know him and keep his word ...", the point is that the cause has to be more powerful than the effect (Christian faith), as outlined in Hebrews 2:10, according to which through suffering Christ was made "pioneer of our salvation". If Christ's baptism is the ground "form and content" of ours, he is as man the exemplary cause (*causa exemplaris*) of our salvation (except for faith: well, Jesus has to be different and not only in his being without sin).[26] In q7 Thomas had already ruled that Jesus had hope and love but not the faith; for faith implies a deficiency. Christ did not need, by being

---

[25] B. Ashley, "The Extent of Jesus' Human Knowledge according to the Fourth Gospel", in *Reading John with St. Thomas Aquinas* (ed. M. Levering-Dauphinais; Washington, DC: CUA Press, 2005), 241–53.

[26] G. Lohaus, *Die Geheimnisse des Lebens Jesu* (Freiburg: Herder, 1985).

faithful, to merit the glory he would receive but received the grace of faith for others. For himself he had knowledge. B. Ashley interprets Thomas to mean that Jesus' possession of full vision, just as in the case of the blessed in heaven, did not make him any less human. In Jesus' case this knowledge was a background, horizon awareness, although contra Rahner this was not an *a priori* knowledge independent of the senses. He did learn things as a human, but he taught a lot more.[27] At III, q10 a1 on John 8:55 ("I know him") the *perfect* comprehension of the Father is achieved by the Word, not the human soul, and so Thomas agrees with Bonaventura. He was a perfect revealer of the Father; he did not have merely faith.[28]

When Thomas comes (in late career) to Romans 1:17 (*iustitia dei in eo revelatur ex fidem in fidem*), he emphasizes that this is the righteousness by which God is righteous and the righteousness by which God justifies, and that this is quite different to the self-justifying righteousness of human beings. As for "from faith to faith",[29] Thomas's interest is in the faith of those before Christ and those after towards Christ – it is *not* in Christ's own faith as part of that transmission. There is continuity because as both Old and New Testament believers look to Christ, they meet in him. (This is a very different view from some more modern Catholic theologians who deem that the faith of Israel was ruined ["*gescheitert*"] and therefore also that the revelation had to start anew.[30]) Faith was something prepared as a condition for revelation, and the Old Testament as a school of faith. Jesus therefore seems to have expected faith from Jewish Nazareth (Mk. 6:5).[31] Likewise the commentary on Hebrews 12 (considered above) is more about looking back to Jewish forms of faith so that Thomas can make the case that Christian faith is just like the Old Testament faith, only more urgent. The faith of Jesus Christ is not the issue.

---

[27] *In Ioann* 6, lect. 2, n.868.

[28] J.-P. Torrell, "Saint Thomas d'Aquin et la science du Christ", in idem, *Recherches Thomasiennes* (Paris: Librairie Philosophique J. Vrin, 2000), 198–213.

[29] *Comm in Romanos, 1, 17*: "Ex fide in fidem; id est, ex fide veteris testamenti procedendo in fidem novi testamenti: quia ab utroque homines justificantur, et salvantur per fidem Christi: quia eadem fide crediderunt venturum qua nos venisse credimus: et ideo dicitur II Corinth. IV, 13: *Habentes eamdem speciem fidei ... credimus propter quod loquimur.*"

[30] H. Urs Von Balthasar, *Herrlichkeit* III/2: Neues Bund (Einsiedeln: Johannes, 1969), "Einleitung."

[31] R. Schnackenburg, "Glaubensgewißheit", in *Die Freude an Gott-unsere Kraft: Festschrift B. Knoch* (Stuttgart: Katholisches Bibelwerk, 1991), 252–62.

Modern Theology

Should we then shrug our shoulders and say "so much the worse for tradition"? Is this a case where divine providence has used the instrument of modern professional exegesis so that more light has shone forth from his word, ever since the "discovery" of J. Hausleiter and the Barthian appropriation thereof [32] through to more recent exponents?

For Protestant theologians there is no doubt about the strength of the theme of *God's* faithfulness in Paul. Gerhard Ebeling argued that Jesus Christ is not simply one *credendum* among others. In other words, Christ is not (just) the object but the source and ground of faith.[33] A broadly similar position is arrived at by E. Jüngel, for whom the key idea seems to be Jesus as *Gewährsmann* (vouchsafer) of (the) faith.[34] Although in his 1969 article Markus Barth tried to suggest otherwise, for Karl Barth in his *Römerbrief*[35] Paul is speaking of *God's* faithfulness, not that of Jesus. Albert Vanhoye has shown that M. Barth and T.F. Torrance went a step further than A. Hebert's view that it meant the faithfulness of the incarnate God in Jesus Christ – they said it meant the faith of Jesus.[36]

More of the subjective genitive interpretation can be seen in Catholic circles. Romano Guardini had insisted that Jesus himself was so preoccupied with love for God there was no room for "faith".[37] But how, asked Balthasar, could Jesus enable our faith except by having faith himself so as to stamp belief in us? Jesus prays, so he must have faith. Furthermore, Balthasar in *Sponsa Verbi* maintained that it was not enough for Christ to be the object or ground of "our prayer", but he

---

[32] Torrance, "One Aspect"; Barth "Faith of the Messiah."

[33] G. Ebeling, "Jesus und Glaube", in *Wort und Glaube* III (Beiträge zur Fundamentaltheologie, Soteriologie und Ekklesiologie; Tübingen: Mohr Siebeck, 1975), 64–110.

[34] E. Jüngel, *Paulus und Jesus* (Tübingen: Mohr Siebeck, 1962), 277: "*Von einem Glauben an Jesus kann dabei vorerst keine* Rede *sein. Wohl aber von einem Glauben, der sich Jesus verdankt. Der als Teilgabe am Sein Gottes verstandene Glaube ist die Gabe des historischen Jesus, dessen Worte zwar keinen Glauben fordern, dessen Verhalten aber Glauben gewährte.*" And then at 282: "*Dieses Ereignis der Identität von Geschichte und Eschaton macht Jesus als den Christus zum Grund des Glaubens. Der durch Jesus gewährte Glaube wird zum Glauben an Jesus, weil dieses Identitäts-Ereignis des den Glauben gewährenden Jesus fortan als die Tat Gottes für uns zu Worte kommen läßt.*"

[35] 5. Aufl. (München: Kaiser, 1928), 70. *Gerechtigkeit offenbart sich "durch seine Treue in Jesus Christus"*. Then on p. 79 he translates Rom. 3:26 "*der in der Treue, die in Jesus sich bewährt, begründet ist*".

[36] Vanhoye, "Fede in Cristo."

[37] *Der Herr* (Würzburg: Werkbund, 1951), 16f.

must also be the subject in which we participate.[38] Thus Balthasar spoke in favour of a subjective genitive interpretation of *fides Christi*. Christ does what Abraham did, but he does much more. With A. Deißmann he sees this as a *"mystische Genitiv"* – not in the Schweitzerian sense of something mystical in which we "make ourselves participate", but rather something given (as E. Lohmeyer suggested). Faith is a *forma substantialis* that shapes believers.[39] *Christus-Glaube* is the metaphysical principle of that faith. Balthasar comes close to saying that it is not just the faith Christ has but the faith that he is that does the shaping. Yet when we inspect this language it concerns the risen Christ and the paradigm is the ascended High Priest. This "playing both parts" is necessary (as it was for T.F. Torrance) in a way that it was not for Rahner, though both Rahner and Balthasar share the view of revelation and faith as two sides of an encounter rather than a giving and taking of information.[40] In some ways, for Balthasar all is revelation, if it can only be seen, whereas for Rahner human nature is able to work some of the way towards meeting God so that special experience joins with experience (cf. the first two ways of the Ignatian *Exercises*), and a believer's faith has to be authentically his or her own.

Matthew 27:43 is the only place where it says that Jesus believed or trusted in God. But this comes from the mouths of the priests and scribes and elders. Yet for catholic *Neutestamentler* Jesus does seem to be less the object than the cause or catalyst of faith, perhaps that which draws faith out. In Hebrews 12:2, ἀρχηγός means not just the causal *"Urheber"* but *"Anführer"* (leader) as *"der, der anfängt"* – "he who begins". Thus, as Thüsing has it, that is not merely as exemplary but as originary, although again it does seem that Hebrews is the place to go to find a clear teaching that Christ was faith's pioneer.[41] It was part of his project that mountains would be moved

---

38 *"Der Äon des Glaubens hat Jesus nicht nur vorbildlich sondern urbildlich vorgekämpft und damit nicht nur den neutestamentlichen, sondern ebenso allen Glauben des Alten Bundes ermöglicht, grundgelegt und vollendet"* (Guardini, *Der Herr*, 57).

39 Guardini, *Der Herr*, 58.

40 See Werner Schreer, *Der Begriff des Glaubens: Das Verständnis des Glaubenartikels in den Dokumenten des Vatikanum II und in den theologischen Entwürfen Karl Rahners und Hans Urs von Balthasars* (Frankfurt: Peter Lang, 1992), 641.

41 William Thüsing in *Christologie-Systematisch und Exegetisch*, QD55 (Freiburg: Herder, 1974), 212: *"Das ist jedoch nicht bloß exemplarisch zu verstehen, sondern urbild und ursprungshaft: Als der, der diesen 'Glauben' in singulären Weise gelebt hat und dessen Glaube jetzt in die 'Bleibendheit' gelangt ist, gibt er den Seinen die Kraft zu diesem Glauben."*

"eschatologically" through his faith/obedience.[42] Vanhoye thinks that "faithfulness" as "trustworthiness" (*affidabilità*) of the incarnate faithful One is possible for the sense of πίστος in Hebrews (but not in Galatians where the genitive is objective!), since it makes Jesus "a steady, trustworthy support" for believers' faith.[43]

Something of the preservation of the traditional position on the question concerning the contribution of Christ's humanity was reflected in the Galtier-Parente debate on the broader subject of Christology.[44] The former claimed that, in Jesus, while there were two "I's", the human "I" was merely an expression of the divine Person and he (the human "I") knew this through the beatific vision. Parente responded that no, there is only one, *divine*, "I" and it is the human mind which knows this, the human soul having beatific *union* and not vision as an intellect would. Admittedly Galtier managed to hold to only one subsistence so that ontologically, although not "merely psychologically" (*saltem psychologice*), Christ's "I" was ultimately one, and Galtier stayed just on the right side of the final version of *Sempiternus Rex* (1951). Jean Galot preferred to nuance this by arguing that there was only one "I" – a divine one – known by Christ's human mind not through any hypostatic union or beatific vision but through a mystical experience. Since then, however, there have been challenges to this traditional "metaphysical" way of doing Christology with a more "bottom-up" approach used to vindicate a high Christology in the work of Gerald O'Collins, perhaps most controversially in an article co-authored with Daniel Kendall in 1992, which was encouraged by the International Theological Commission's remaining silent on whether Jesus had beatific vision in its treatment of Jesus' human knowledge of his divine identity.[45] To conclude (implicitly!) that Jesus' *fides quae* was a bit less than that of the early church (since much of the content of the second and third articles of the Creed was yet to be revealed) would necessitate a more

---

[42] William Thüsing, *Die neutestamentliche Theologien und Jesus Christus: Grundlegung einer Theologie des Neuten Testaments: I Kriterien aufgrund der Rückfrage nach Jesus und des Glaubens an seine Auferweckung* (Münster: Aschendorff, 1996); *II Programm einer Theologie des Neuen Testaments mit Perspektiven für eine Biblische Theologie* (Münster: Aschendorff, 1998), 91.

[43] Vanhoye, "Fede in Cristo", esp. 16–21.

[44] P. Parente, *L'Io di Cristo* (Brescia, 1951), P. Galtier, "La conscience humaine du Christ", *Greg* 35 (1954): 225–46; P. Inchaurraga, "La unidad psicologica de Cristo en la controversia Galtier-Parentein", *Lum* 3 (1954): 215–39.

[45] G. O'Collins, SJ and Daniel Kendall, SJ, "The Faith of Jesus", *TS* 53 (1992): 403–23 (410).

active, forward-looking *fides qua* on his part.[46] This is a bold move, but its consequences are that, with Hebrews, Jesus is the exemplar of faith – *not,* as the Protestant equivalents (above) have argued, that, with Paul, "we" are justified by his faith(fulness).

Conclusion

The faith *of* Jesus Christ movement was originally an attempt to reintroduce the earthly humanity of Jesus of Nazareth as a factor in salvation. This emphasis revealed a predilection for a "Jesus" as one who had to struggle not to doubt and whose contribution one could identify not so much at the level of his meritorious human action or redemptive suffering, but in the very psychology of the one whose human deliberations as a means to passive obedience to the divine will are glimpsed in the gospels, particularly the Synoptics. In that sense we can speak of a desire to have Christology listen to exegesis and for a canonical approach to biblical theology which takes the synoptic Christology seriously. The more recent form of the movement, represented by a number of eminent New Testament scholars, prefers to view it as Jesus' *faithfulness* which he shares with God the Father, as part of a biblical theology of divine reliability. Yet as with the older form, it amounts to the divine agent playing a part in the economy of salvation traditionally reserved for the believer, or rather for the *ecclesia* of believers, guided by the Holy Spirit. In any case, any "reintroduction" of "the faith of Jesus Christ" will occur, it seems, *despite* the evidence of the witness of the tradition of Christian theology.

---

[46] O'Collins and Kendall, "Faith", 419ff.

17

From Faithfulness to Faith in the Theology of Karl Barth[1]

BENJAMIN MYTERS

In one of his remarkable essays on Galatians, J. Louis Martyn relates an anecdote about Karl Barth: "Oral tradition ... tells of a priest who made an appointment with K. Barth on a personal matter. Coming after a while to the point, he said, 'The problem, Dr Barth, is that I have lost my faith.' The response: 'But what on earth gave you the impression that it was yours to lose?'"[2] This anecdote neatly encapsulates Barth's whole understanding of πίστις: faith arises from the faithfulness of God in Jesus Christ.

While Barry Matlock has called for a "de-theologizing" of the πίστις Χριστοῦ debate,[3] my own aim in this essay is to "re-theologize" the debate – not because it has ever ceased to be theological, but simply because my purpose is to bring theology to the foreground quite explicitly. There is, I believe, a good deal of truth in Richard Hays' observation that the πίστις Χριστοῦ debate involves a conflict over the fundamental shape of Paul's theology. Our concern is not only with words, but with what Karl Barth might have called the *Sache*; at bottom, it is not merely a question of grammar, but of Jesus Christ himself. And, as I hope to demonstrate, Barth's theology can offer a unique contribution to this particular exegetical debate.[4]

In the introduction to the second edition of his dissertation, Richard Hays provides some advice about how to interpret his book. His first and

---

[1] I am indebted to Douglas Campbell, Douglas Harink, Michael Lattke, and Adam Neder for reading a draft of this paper and providing valuable comments and suggestions.
[2] Martyn, "Apocalyptic Gospel", 250, n.10.
[3] Matlock, "Detheologizing ΠΙΣΤΙΣ ΧΡΙΣΤΟΥ".
[4] To date, the fullest analysis of Barth's relation to the debate is Harink, *Paul among the Postliberals*, 25–65. I am deeply indebted to Harink's study, even if my own reading of Barth and Paul places much greater emphasis on the category of the *subject*.

most fundamental point is that *The Faith of Jesus Christ* is a book about narrative theology – it is an argument for "the story-shaped character of Paul's theology". He explains that his interest in a narrative approach was shaped by his deeply Barthian studies at Yale in the 1970s, where he came into contact with David Kelsey's narrative interpretation of Barth, together with Hans Frei's Barthian project of retrieving the category of realistic narrative. On top of all this, Hays tells us that he himself was "appreciatively read[ing] great chunks of Karl Barth" at the time.[5] In short, Barth's theology was already lurking in the background when Hays was writing his great dissertation on the faith of Jesus Christ.

In any event, I am not concerned here with the question of Barth's historical influence on the πίστις Χριστοῦ debate. Instead, I want to focus on Barth's own interpretation of Paul – first in his famous commentary on Romans,[6] and then in the final volume of the *Church Dogmatics*.[7] In the discussion that follows, I will trace a movement in Barth's thought from πίστις (understood as "faithfulness"), to participation in Christ, and finally to the creation of a new subject. In the nexus of these three concepts – faithfulness, participation, subject – we can begin to grasp the distinctive character of Barth's interpretation of Paul, and the distinctive Paulinism of his mature dogmatic thought.

ΠΙΣΤΙΣ in the Commentary on Romans

Throughout the second edition of his commentary on Romans, Barth's preferred translation of πίστις is not *Glaube* but *Treue Gottes*, so that the accent falls not on a human act of faith, but on God's own act of faithfulness towards humanity. In Barth's translation of Romans 1:17, the gospel reveals "the righteousness of God from faithfulness to faith [*aus Treue dem Glauben*]".[8] He translates the genitive in Romans 3:22 as "the righteousness of God through his faithfulness in Jesus Christ [*die Gerechtigkeit Gottes durch seine Treue in Jesus Christus*] unto all who believe";[9] and the genitive in 3:26 is rendered as "the faithfulness which

---

[5] Hays, *The Faith of Jesus Christ*, xxiii–xxiv.

[6] Karl Barth, *Der Römerbrief 1922* (Zurich: EVZ, 1940); ET *Romans*.

[7] Karl Barth, *Die kirchliche Dogmatik* (Zurich: EVZ, 1932–70), hereafter cited as *KD*; ET *Church Dogmatics* (ed. G.W. Bromiley and T.F. Torrance; Edinburgh: T&T Clark, 1956–75).

[8] Barth, *Der Römerbrief 1922*, 10; ET 35.

[9] Barth, *Der Römerbrief 1922*, 66; ET 91.

abides in Jesus".[10] Again, Barth's rendering of Romans 3:28 foregrounds faithfulness rather than faith: "For we reckon that a person is justified by the faithfulness of God [*Treue Gottes*] apart from the works of the Law."[11] Similarly, his translation of Romans 10:6 speaks of "the righteousness which comes by the faithfulness of God [*die Gerechtigkeit, die aus der Treue Gottes kommt*]";[12] and he translates 10:8 as "the word of the faithfulness of God, which we preach".[13] This recurring translation of πίστις as *Treue Gottes* had been even more pervasive in the first edition of Barth's commentary, but in the second edition he significantly reduced the frequency of this rendering, in response to criticisms by professional exegetes.[14]

Although in some cases (such as Romans 1:17)[15] Barth's translation has been endorsed by recent scholarship, it is not my intention to defend or critique these specific translations of πίστις. At this point, I only want to note that, for Barth, it is (divine) faithfulness rather than (human) faith which lies at the heart of Paul's theology.[16] In Barth's reading, the epistle to the Romans is concerned not with any particular human action which conditions or appropriates salvation from our side, but rather with God's own faithful action which invades the cosmos and sets things right. In Barth's words (and this could serve as a summary of the entire commentary): "Above the rise and fall of the waves of history, in spite of human unfaithfulness – yes, *in* this unfaithfulness itself – there remains the faithfulness of God."[17]

The rendering of πίστις as *Treue Gottes* is thus more than mere semantics for Barth. The theme of God's faithfulness runs like a red thread through the whole commentary – indeed, it is scarcely an exaggeration to say that the *Römerbrief* is nothing other than a vigorous apocalyptic announcement of God's triumphant faithfulness. I use the

---

[10] Barth, *Der Römerbrief 1922*, 79; ET 104.

[11] Barth, *Der Römerbrief 1922*, 82; ET 107.

[12] Barth, *Der Römerbrief 1922*, 361; ET 377.

[13] Barth, *Der Römerbrief 1922*, 361; ET 377.

[14] See Barth's account in the preface to the 2nd ed., *Der Römerbrief 1922*, 17; ET 13–14; and cf. Reasoner, *Romans*, 5–7.

[15] See, e.g., Dunn, *Romans 1–8*, 43–4.

[16] In later works, Barth explicitly defended the subjective genitive reading of other disputed πίστις Χριστοῦ texts as well: e.g., in *The Epistle to the Philippians* (trans. James W. Leitch; Louisville, KY: Westminster John Knox, 2002), 99–103, he offers a detailed argument for the subjective genitive reading of Phil. 3:9; and in *KD* II/2, 620–21 (ET 559), he defends the subjective genitive reading of Gal. 2:20.

[17] Barth, *Der Römerbrief 1922*, 55; ET 81.

term "apocalyptic" here in J. Louis Martyn's sense: Barth is concerned not with *spiritual salvation*, but with *cosmic invasion*; his theme is "the death of one world, and the advent of another",[18] and thus with "God's invasive movement ... *from* the new creation *into* the present evil age".[19] Barth's announcement of the dissolution of all the finest achievements of European cultural religion is precisely an announcement of the faithfulness of God; the shattering apocalyptic "No" is the form of God's invincible "Yes".

What, then, is God's faithfulness? Barth's answer is simple but revolutionary: the divine act of faithfulness is identified with the human act of Jesus' own faithfulness. In total obedience, Jesus descends into the "deepest darkness of human ambiguity". This obedient act is "*the* faithfulness", the perfect human correspondence to "the will of the faithful God".[20] Jesus' movement of self-emptying obedience culminates in his death on the cross. Here, Jesus' entire existence is pared down to a single point. At this point, the whole human race is dissolved in order to be recreated; human history is shattered and "done away with".[21] Here, at the end of history, the faithfulness of God shines from the abyss. "The Messiah", Barth writes, "is the end of humanity, and here also God is found faithful." As Jesus dies condemned and abandoned, "we see the faithfulness of God in the depths of hell".[22]

Barth thus takes the death of Jesus as the sole event by which πίστις is defined. He rejects the notion that there is a general psychological or religious attitude of "faith" which also happens to be instantiated in the history of Jesus. There is no such generic faith, no "psychological condition" of faith.[23] On the contrary, in Barth's view faith must be understood *sui generis*. Strictly speaking, it is something which takes place only in one event, in the obedient death of Jesus. The faith of Jesus is the unique locus of human faithfulness; our own faith in God becomes

---

[18] J. Louis Martyn, "Apocalyptic Antinomies", in *Theological Issues in the Letters of Paul* (Edinburgh: T&T Clark, 1997), 117.

[19] Martyn, *Galatians*, 100. J. Christiaan Beker is, I believe, mistaken to charge Barth with reducing God's apocalypse to a "noetic-hermeneutical tool" rather than an "ontic event"; Barth's early eschatological thought aims at a reconfiguration of all history around the κρίσις of the Christ-event, rather than a reconfiguration of the event itself as a mere signifier of existential or spiritual transcendence within the present. See Beker, *Paul the Apostle*, 139–43.

[20] Barth, *Der Römerbrief 1922*, 71–2; ET 97.

[21] Barth, *Der Römerbrief 1922*, 51; ET 77.

[22] Barth, *Der Römerbrief 1922*, 72; ET 97.

[23] Barth, *Der Römerbrief 1922*, 72; ET 98.

possible only in so far as we participate in this event – and that means participating in Jesus' *death*.

Protestant theologians before Barth often spoke of the "empty hands" of faith. Traditionally, this metaphor of "emptiness" accentuated the Lutheran antithesis between the passivity of faith and the activity of works. But when Barth speaks of faith's emptiness, he radicalizes the metaphor. For Barth, this is not a distinction merely between two different psychological conditions (active striving and passive reception). Nor would he agree with James Dunn's claim that Paul articulates a "fundamental distinction between (human) faith and (human) works".[24] Instead, Barth sees a much more radical antithesis at work in Paul's thought: *human religion* versus *divine action*. This antithesis – which corresponds precisely to Martyn's reading of an "antinomy between apocalypse and religion"[25] – is central to Barth's interpretation of Romans, and it is fundamental to his understanding of πίστις. Like Luther, Barth can remark that faith takes place only when the human being stands "naked" and "impoverished" before God. But, for Barth, this naked poverty is not a psychological condition: it is Jesus' own nakedness, his own obedient abasement before God. Thus faith takes place not where one passively receives God's gift, but only where one's entire self is dissolved and done away with in the event of Jesus' death.[26]

Faith is not the opposite of works, therefore; it is the opposite of *religion*. So Barth contrasts faith with "devout contemplation" and "experience" and whatever can be "handed down by tradition" – in a word, he opposes faith to "every positive religious achievement".[27] Indeed, he insists that there is no "way of salvation" (*Heilsweg*) at all[28] – there is only the darkness and scandal of Jesus' death. And by the faithful action of God, we are made to participate in this death. Our existence is seized and displaced, and we are situated within Jesus' own history. In short: "Grace ... means neither that human beings can or should do something, nor that they can or should do nothing. Grace means that *God* does something."[29] Thus the real contrast, for Barth, is

---

[24] J.D.G. Dunn, "The Theology of Galatians: The Issue of Covenantal Nomism", in *Pauline Theology I: Thessalonians, Philippians, Galatians, Philemon* (ed. Jouette M. Bassler; Minneapolis, MN: Fortress, 1991), 125–46 (141, n.54).

[25] Martyn, *Galatians*, 39.

[26] Barth, *Der Römerbrief 1922*, 72; ET 98.

[27] Barth, *Der Römerbrief 1922*, 72–3; ET 98.

[28] Barth, *Der Römerbrief 1922*, 74; ET 99.

[29] Barth, *Der Römerbrief 1922*, 196; ET 215.

not between faith and works but between the faithful "action of God" on the one hand and "all human doing or not-doing" on the other.[30]

With its sharp concentration on the death of Jesus, Barth's reading of Paul clearly takes the side of contemporary scholars who interpret the obedient faithfulness of Jesus – his faithfulness unto death – as the fundamental "act of πίστις".[31] And in the *Römerbrief*, Barth's concentration on the death of Jesus is radically singular, apocalyptic, non-historical. In contrast to all covenantal or *heilsgeschichtlich* interpretations of Paul, Barth insists that God has intervened in an *event* which intersects history. The event touches history only "as a tangent touches a circle";[32] or, in Martyn's terminology, it is "punctiliar" rather than "linear".[33] Jesus' enactment of πίστις is compressed into the single point of death by crucifixion.[34] So, too, Barth argues that God's vindication of Jesus in the resurrection "is not an event in history elongated so as to remain an event in the midst of other events"; rather, the resurrection is a strictly "non-historical" (*unhistorische*) event, even though its function is to "relate ... the whole historical life of Jesus to its origin in God".[35]

History is thus restructured and reconstituted by the retroactive power of this event; but the act of God does not belong to history as such, nor does it emerge from any larger process of salvation-history. Barth's interpretation of Paul thus stands in stark contrast to N.T. Wright's characterization of Christ as "the climax, the denouement, of a story ... which had been steadily unfolding" throughout history.[36] In Barth's view, the faithfulness of God does not unfold in history as covenant or *Heilsgeschichte*, but it *interrupts* and *intersects* history apocalyptically. The result, then, is not merely the removal of certain boundary markers or the redefinition of how one "gets in" to the covenant community; rather,

---

[30] Barth, *Der Römerbrief 1922*, 417; ET 432.

[31] Hays, *The Faith of Jesus Christ*, 282.

[32] Barth, *Der Römerbrief 1922*, 6; ET 30.

[33] J. Louis Martyn, "Events in Galatia: Modified Covenantal Nomism versus God's Invasion of the Cosmos in the Singular Gospel: A Response to J.D.G. Dunn and B.R. Gaventa", in *Pauline Theology I: Thessalonians, Philippians, Galatians, Philemon* (ed. Jouette M. Bassler; Minneapolis, MN: Fortress, 1991), 173.

[34] Cf. Hays' important observation: "for Paul, πίστις Χριστοῦ refers to Jesus' obedience to death on the cross: in other words, the meaning of the phrase is focused on the kerygma's narration of his self-giving death, not on the whole ministry of Jesus of Nazareth. This narrow punctiliar sense – focused on the cross – is the only meaning supported by Paul's usage" (Hays, *The Faith of Jesus Christ*, 297, n.58).

[35] Barth, *Der Römerbrief 1922*, 175; ET 195.

[36] Wright, *Paul*, 134.

the result is "new creation" (Gal. 6:15). For Barth, the death of Jesus is the dissolution of the cosmos, and the resurrection is sheer *creatio ex nihilo* – an event of *creatio* which now reorganizes history around itself, so that the continuities between Israel and Christ on the one hand, and nature and grace on the other, are established by the event itself. In short, Barth finds in Paul a framework which is close to Douglas Campbell's "retrospective account of salvation"[37] – although one might rather describe this as a *retroactive* account of salvation, since, for Barth, history itself "works backwards" as it is reconfigured by the resurrection, so that all continuities with history and creation are established only in the radical contingence and singularity of this event.

Further, the new creation is in Barth's view not some separate entity which Christ produces as an external effect of his action. On the contrary, the new creation takes place as an event *within* the space of Christ's own faithful action. Thus, in his exegesis of Romans 5, Barth can speak of Christ as "the new subject, the 'I' of the coming world". This new "I" is the justified subject, the one who "receives and bears and reveals the divine justification and election". The new human subject is "directly created" by the justifying action of God; this, for Barth, is what it means to be "in Christ".[38] And so we have arrived at the decisive formulation: salvation as *participation*. Barth's whole understanding of the relation between faithfulness and faith hinges on this point – on the real participation of human existence in Christ.

But what can it mean to say that we participate in Christ? Here in the *Römerbrief* Barth has not yet attempted to answer this question systematically. At this point, he is content simply to affirm that Jesus' history has a unique place and function vis-à-vis all other history. It is uniquely "pregnant" with significance; precisely in its irreducible particularity, it is also universal, so that all times are included within its own temporality. The time of Jesus is time fitted for eternity; the existence of Jesus is "humanity filled with God's speech".[39] These are, to be sure, only rudimentary hints of what it might mean for humanity to participate in the faithful action of Jesus. But we can already glimpse here some of the fundamental decisions that will be worked out in Barth's mature theology.

Readers moving from the *Römerbrief* to the *Church Dogmatics* are usually struck by the rhetorical and theological differences between

---

37 Campbell, *Quest*, 142.
38 Barth, *Der Römerbrief 1922*, 160; ET 181–2.
39 Barth, *Der Römerbrief 1922*, 78–9; ET 103–5.

the two works. I do not want to suggest that these discontinuities are unimportant; but my argument is that there is a profound undercurrent of Paulinism which continues to shape Barth's mature dogmatic thought. Indeed, I believe this Paulinism finds its fullest expression not in Barth's explicitly exegetical work, but in the dogmatics itself, and above all in the great final volume on the doctrine of reconciliation. So I will now highlight this continuity by examining the way in which Barth's early exegetical themes of "the faithfulness of Christ" and "participation in Christ" come to function as part of the fundamental architecture of his late dogmatic thought.

Participation in Christ in the *Church Dogmatics*

A Pauline Ontology

In 1977, E.P. Sanders pointed out that the interpretation of Paul's theology seems to demand a participatory vision of reality:

> It seems to me best to understand Paul as saying what he meant and meaning what he said: Christians really are one body and Spirit with Christ ... But what does this mean? How are we to understand it? We seem to lack [the necessary] category of "reality" – real participation in Christ, real possession of the Spirit ... I must confess that I do not have a new category of perception to propose here. This does not mean, however, that Paul did not have one.[40]

In this remarkable passage, Sanders raises the question whether there might be some ontological framework, some "category of reality", which makes it possible to grasp the sheer realism with which Paul speaks of participation. Even if Barth's theology is not the only way of imagining Paul's realism, I think Barth remains a valuable resource for Pauline interpretation at this point, since his dogmatics represents a sustained attempt to work out exactly the kind of "category of reality" that Sanders calls for.

The *Church Dogmatics* could be read as an increasingly concentrated and expansive reflection on the eventfulness of Jesus' history. David Ford has described Barth's dogmatics as a "monism of the Gospel story"[41] –

---

[40] Sanders, *Paul and Palestinian Judaism*, 522–3.
[41] David F. Ford, *Barth and God's Story: Biblical Narrative and the Theological Method of Karl Barth in the Church Dogmatics* (Frankfurt am Main: Peter Lang, 1985), 13.

an exaggeration, no doubt, but one which vividly captures the essential dynamic of Barth's thought. Barth wants to show that the history of Jesus is the site in which all other histories take place. As Robert W. Jenson puts it, Barth's vision is of a temporal reality "bracketed not by Timelessness but by one of the temporal entities it contains".[42] By a divine act of "transtemporalization",[43] the temporal existence of Jesus becomes the time of all times, the history which enfolds all other histories within itself.[44] In short, Barth's dogmatic thought includes the development of a thoroughgoing participatory ontology: all human beings are said to participate in the history of Jesus; "we ourselves *are* what we are in *him*".[45]

The emphasis here is perhaps not as uncompromisingly "punctiliar" as the anti-historical formulations of the *Römerbrief*. Instead of concentrating solely on death-and-resurrection, Barth now envisions the whole historical existence of Jesus as God's decisive apocalyptic act. Nevertheless, this vision of the history of Jesus hinges entirely on the single moment of *resurrection*. It is in this event that God universalizes the history of Jesus, so that all humanity is enfolded ἐν Χριστῷ. The resurrection of Jesus from the dead does not merely belong to the past, therefore, but it "fills and determines the whole present".[46] It is "our own true history", our "true and actual today", and it is "incomparably more direct and intimate than anything we think we know as our history".[47] To speak of Jesus is thus to make "an ontological declaration about all other human beings"[48] – indeed, it is to make an ontological statement about the entire cosmos which has been dissolved and recreated in the resurrection-event. Here, the fundamental theme of Barth's commentary on Romans – resurrection as God's world-altering, apocalyptic invasion – has been expanded into a vast ontological vision of the significance of the resurrection. Because Jesus has been raised from the dead, all

---

[42] Robert W. Jenson, "Karl Barth", in *The Modern Theologians: An Introduction to Christian Theology in the Twentieth Century*, I (ed. David F. Ford; Oxford: Blackwell, 1989), 41.

[43] Ford, *Barth and God's Story*, 166.

[44] For a brilliant analysis of Barth's theology of time in connection with Giorgio Agamben's "messianic time", see Douglas Harink, "The Time of the Gospel and the History of the World" (paper presented at the SBL Annual Meeting, November 2007).

[45] *KD* IV/2, 299; ET 270.

[46] *KD* IV/1, 345; ET 313.

[47] *KD* IV/1, 611–12; ET 548.

[48] *KD* IV/2, 305; ET 275.

humanity now participates in him. If we were to invoke the terminology of classical metaphysics, we could say that, for Barth, the resurrection functions as the "ground of being".[49]

My argument is that this is a profoundly *Pauline* ontology – or, to put it another way, I think the radical apocalyptic Paulinism of the *Römerbrief* has now been translated into the form of dogmatic theological ontology. To demonstrate this claim, I want to offer a fairly close reading of the fragment on baptism (*KD* IV/4) with which Barth's doctrine of reconciliation ends.

Our own Heilsgeschichte

In his doctrine of baptism, Barth articulates his understanding of participation in Christ by coordinating the work of the Spirit with the history of Jesus. "In the work of the Holy Spirit, the history manifested to all people in the resurrection of Jesus Christ is manifest and present to a specific person as his or her own *Heilsgeschichte*."[50] This terminology of *Heilsgeschichte* (and, elsewhere, of "covenant") should not lead us to imagine that Barth has mitigated the apocalyptic radicalism of the commentary on Romans. While scholars like Wright and Dunn speak of "salvation history" and "covenant" as an already-existing relation between God and Israel into which Jesus' history is subsequently inserted, Barth understands *Heilsgeschichte* strictly as that which takes place in Jesus himself – Jesus *is* the covenant, he *is* the history of salvation. Here in the *Church Dogmatics*, then, Barth's conception of *Heilsgeschichte* is still much closer to Martyn's concept of "apocalypse" than it is to the covenantal interpretations of Wright or Dunn. More importantly, Barth's crucial emphasis here is on our participation within the *heilsgeschichtlich* occurrence of Jesus' death and resurrection. Through the Spirit we are inserted into Jesus' history, so that the history of Jesus becomes our "own *Heilsgeschichte*". This is how Barth understands baptism with the Spirit: we are plunged into the history of Jesus, incorporated in his death and resurrection. Through the Spirit, we participate in Jesus' own faithfulness to God, with the result that we also "turn to faithfulness in God".[51]

Barth thus insists that participation in Christ is not merely the production of new "religious and moral impulses", nor an infusion

---

[49] Cf. Jenson, "Karl Barth", 41.

[50] *KD* IV/4, 30; ET 27.

[51] *KD* IV/4, 1; ET, 2.

of supernatural capacities, nor again a mere forensic declaration that leaves us essentially unaltered. Such conceptions, Barth observes, all share one thing in common: they fail to explain "how the Christian comes into existence, the person who responds to God's faithfulness with faithfulness".[52] In contrast, the reality of Christian existence is to be explained by the *Spirit* as the power of participation. Through the Spirit, the Christian is caught up in the history of Jesus; she participates in Jesus' own faithful obedience, and the event of this participation launches her into a new freedom, the freedom "to be faithful to God as God is faithful to her".[53] The history of Jesus is the space (or better, the *time*) in which a faithful response to God is enacted; here, "the turning of all from unfaithfulness to faithfulness took place".[54] Jesus stepped into the space of our own ἀπιστία, and in that space he enacted authentic πίστις on our behalf: he was "faithful to God in our place, in the place of those who previously were unfaithful to God".[55] And this enactment of πίστις has a transformative effect. Though we are still marked by our own unfaithfulness, Jesus "creates in the history of each person the beginning of a new history, the history of a person who has become faithful to God".[56] This is our own *Heilsgeschichte*: the repetition in our own lives of the faithfulness of Christ.

Drawing on Paul's language in Galatians 2 ("crucified with Christ"), Romans 6 ("in the likeness of his death") and 2 Corinthians 5 ("one died for all – then all are dead"), Barth thus argues that our salvation took place in the death of Christ itself, and not in some subsequent appropriation of this death. The crucified Christ "appropriated [us] and took [us] up into his death", in an event of "supreme actuality" (*in höchster Realität*).[57] It is not a matter of our reception of Christ, therefore, but of Christ's appropriation of us: he grasps us and enfolds us within his own history, putting us to death so that we may be raised to life. Nevertheless, the history of Jesus does not negate or displace our own personal histories; our histories are *created* by their participation in Christ. We are set free for a faithful response to God's faithfulness – and this is indeed our own proper faithfulness, our own decision and act.[58]

---

[52] *KD* IV/4, 4–5; ET 4–5.
[53] *KD* IV/4, 14; ET 13.
[54] *KD* IV/4, 15; ET 13.
[55] *KD* IV/4, 23; ET 21.
[56] *KD* IV/4, 23; ET 21.
[57] *KD* IV/4, 18; ET 17.
[58] *KD* IV/4, 25; ET 23.

Barth also returns here to Romans 1:17 – a key text in his early exegesis of Paul – and his reading of this verse remains exactly the same as in the *Römerbrief*. Within the death and resurrection of Jesus, "there is movement ἐκ πίστεως, from the depth and power of the faithfulness of God, εἰς πίστιν, to the corresponding faithfulness of human beings". And this movement is not merely *possible*, but it really *takes place* in Jesus.[59]

In all this, we are far removed from S.K. Williams' proposal – based on the subjective genitive reading of πίστις Χριστοῦ – that Christ is merely the "supreme exemplar" of faith;[60] and we are equally far from what Douglas Campbell calls "Arminian" readings of Paul, in which the human agent is merely given the formal possibility of faithful action.[61] Instead, Barth's position is much closer to Alain Badiou's brilliant philosophical reading of Paul, in which the event of resurrection creates (or "subjectivates") new subjects who are *constituted* by their radical fidelity to the event, so that it is impossible even to distinguish between the subject and the subject's fidelity.[62] For Badiou, faithfulness *is* subjectivity. Or as Barth puts it, the essence of faith is *obedience* – faith is our participation in Jesus' own "enslavement" to the will of God, and this enslavement is precisely our subjectivation as free agents.[63]

Evental Participation: Barth and Torrance

Further, Barth lays great emphasis on the fact that participation in Christ is always an *event*. It is a "concrete and dynamic" occurrence, not "a timeless or supratemporal relation".[64] We can perhaps best grasp the shape of Barth's thought here if we juxtapose it with the work of his great Scottish pupil, T.F. Torrance. Under the influence of Barth's theology, Torrance has developed a full-blown doctrine of the vicarious

---

[59] *KD* IV/4, 18; ET 17.

[60] Williams, "Again *Pistis Christou*", 446.

[61] Campbell, *Quest*, 100.

[62] Alain Badiou, *Saint Paul: The Foundation of Universalism* (trans. Ray Brassier; Stanford, CA: Stanford University Press, 2003). See also idem, *Ethics: An Essay on the Understanding of Evil* (trans. Peter Hallward; London: Verso, 2001), 43: "I call 'subject' the bearer [*le support*] of a fidelity, the one who bears a truth process. The subject, therefore, in no way pre-exists the process. He is absolutely nonexistent in the situation 'before' the event. We might say that the process of truth *induces* a subject."

[63] *KD* III/3, 279–86; ET 247–52.

[64] *KD* IV/4, 25; ET 23.

humanity of Jesus. He speaks of Jesus as "our human response to God",[65] and as the embodied "polarity between the faithfulness of God and the answering faithfulness of man".[66] He argues that Jesus is both "the incarnation of the divine *pistis*" and "the embodiment of man's *pistis* in covenant with God",[67] and he stresses that Jesus believes "on our behalf and in our place".[68] On the surface, this appears to be a very Barthian construal of πίστις – indeed, Hays himself has spoken approvingly of Torrance's "unmistakably Barthian" approach.[69] However, the most distinctive feature of Barth's understanding of πίστις is completely effaced in Torrance's account. Where Barth's thought is structured by actualistic categories, Torrance's interpretation of faithfulness rests on a substantialist conception of atonement. For Torrance, God's faithfulness has become embedded in "the incarnate medium" of Jesus' human flesh as such;[70] our human essence has been "interpenetrate[d]" and thus sanctified.[71] Torrance's whole vision of atonement is shaped by this conception of a generic human substance which is healed and restored through its incarnational union with the Son of God. One might describe this as a kind of anthropological transubstantiation: Christ assumes and penetrates the substance of our humanity in order to redeem it and elevate it to a new status.

Against the backdrop of Torrance's substantialist ontology, Barth's radical Paulinism is thrown into sharp relief. It is axiomatic for Barth that our humanness is not "a substance with certain qualities or functions";[72] it is rather an *event* in which our faithful action corresponds to God's faithfulness. Human beings do not "have a kind of nature in which they are then addressed by God". They do not have "something different and earlier and more intrinsic, a deeper stratum or more original substance of being".[73] Indeed, in Barth's view there is no human essence at all – or rather, essence is *history*; it is a trajectory of action set in motion by the prevenient action of Jesus Christ. As Adam Neder demonstrates in his important study, Barth does not envisage any

---

[65] T.F. Torrance, *The Mediation of Christ* (2nd ed.; Edinburgh: T&T Clark, 1992), 80.
[66] Torrance, *The Mediation of Christ*, 82.
[67] Torrance, "One Aspect", 113.
[68] Torrance, *The Mediation of Christ*, 82–3.
[69] Hays, *The Faith of Jesus Christ*, 146.
[70] Torrance, *The Mediation of Christ*, 82.
[71] Torrance, *The Mediation of Christ*, 88.
[72] *KD* III/2, 233; ET 196.
[73] *KD* III/2, 179; ET 150.

"healing of human 'nature', conceived as a substance which underlies human actions"; instead, human action itself is made to participate in Christ. Jesus *does* our humanness; he *enacts* it and so brings it into being. We become human by participating in his acts of faithful obedience. In Neder's words, "human nature is as Jesus Christ does it, not as he does something to 'it'".[74] So if Torrance regards the faithfulness of God as an object which is inscribed in Jesus' incarnate flesh, Barth sees πίστις as an event which takes place apocalyptically in Jesus' death and resurrection. Within the framework of Barth's ontology, participation in Christ can only be an *eventual* participation in the faithful action of Jesus. There is no human "essence" or "nature" which could participate in the divine being, but only "a common history" which takes place between God and humanity in the action of one agent, Jesus Christ.[75]

A Universal Event

At the heart of Barth's theological ontology, therefore, is an event: a singular occurrence which becomes universal. I am reminded here of Badiou's conception of a "universal singularity",[76] a contingent event which is so utterly singular that it imprints itself on infinity. As for Badiou, so too for Barth: the particularity of the event is not effaced by its universal trajectory, since the event becomes universal precisely *in* the full realization of its particularity; the singular is pregnant with the universal. Barth thus speaks of a trajectory from the particular to the universal; the "particular history" (*partikulare Geschichte*) of Jesus' death and resurrection has "a universal goal and direction" (*universaler Absicht und Tendenz*). "In its very limitation, [Jesus' history] reaches beyond itself. It comprehends the world."[77]

This "reaching beyond itself" is a crucial structuring principle of Barth's participatory ontology. The pure event of Jesus' history is so

---

[74] Adam Neder, *Participation in Christ in Karl Barth's Church Dogmatics* (Louisville, KY: Westminster John Knox, forthcoming), ch. 2.

[75] Bruce L. McCormack, "Participation in God, Yes, Deification, No: Two Modern Protestant Responses to an Ancient Question", in *Denkwürdiges Geheimnis: Beiträge zur Gotteslehre: Festschrift für Eberhard Jüngel zum 70. Geburtstag* (ed. I.U. Dalferth, J. Fischer, and H.-P. Großhans; Tübingen: Mohr Siebeck, 2004), 359. On the actualistic structure of Barth's theological anthropology, see also Paul T. Nimmo, *Being in Action: The Theological Shape of Barth's Ethical Vision* (London: T&T Clark, 2007).

[76] Badiou, *Saint Paul*, 13.

[77] *KD* IV/4, 23; ET 21.

singular and so "eventful" that it imprints itself, so to speak, on eternity. Without effacing its own historical particularity, it "reaches beyond itself" (*über sich selbst hinausgreift*), folding out into history and then folding all other human histories back into itself. In this movement beyond itself, it never leaves its own temporal boundaries – it remains precisely the same particular event – but it now includes all other histories within itself. Such is the infinite eventfulness of this finite history.

If Badiou's theory of universality helps to shed light on Barth's ontology, we must immediately add that Barth's focus is sharper and more radical than Badiou's. While Badiou interprets the resurrection merely as an exemplary instance of a more general class of "events", Barth understands Jesus' resurrection as *the* event. Indeed, Barth has no interest in developing an ontology for its own sake; the one thing that concerns him is the profoundly Pauline thought that God has raised Jesus from the dead, and that all reality now stands under the light of that event. Through the resurrection, God has universalized the singularity of Jesus' existence.[78] For Barth, the resurrection dissolves the "transience" of Jesus' history, "its imprisonment in its temporal, spatial and personal singularity".[79] This event does not introduce any new, subsequent phase of Jesus' history, nor does it elevate Jesus' existence to some "higher, otherworldly plane".[80] Instead, the resurrection is nothing other than the manifestation of the sheer *once-for-all-ness* of Jesus' particularity (*Einmaligkeit*). The history of Jesus remains localized in its own particular time and space, but "what took place on the third day after [Jesus'] death lifted up the whole of what took place before in all its *particularity* (not in spite of but because of its particularity!) into something that took place once and *for all*".[81] There is thus no longer any historical distance, no ugly ditch, between Jesus' history and our own; through the resurrection, his history has drawn near to us all – "too near", as Barth says rather uncannily.[82] In the resurrection, the singularity of Jesus' history has integrated all other histories within itself. Thus Barth can even say that "to be human" means "to be a participant in the history of Jesus Christ which took place once, then and there".[83]

---

[78] For a detailed study of this important theme, see R. Dale Dawson, *The Resurrection in Karl Barth* (Aldershot: Ashgate, 2007).

[79] *KD* IV/4, 27; ET 24.

[80] *KD* IV/4, 27; ET 24.

[81] *KD* IV/1, 345; ET 313.

[82] *KD* IV/4, 28; ET 26.

[83] *KD* IV/4, 28–9; ET 26.

The New Subject

In as much as Jesus' history now incorporates all other histories within its own space and time, it also acts on these histories – or rather, these histories *become* histories only as this event acts on them. Thus the justifying action of God not only takes place *extra nos*, but also *in nobis*, forming us from within as new subjects.[84] And so, in Barth's thought, the trajectory from "the faithfulness of Christ" to "participation in Christ" finally leads here: to the creation of the subject. The subjectivity of Jesus is the event within which new subjects are generated. This is Barth's dogmatic exposition of the Pauline theme of "new creation".

As I have already noted, Barth understands the creation of subjects as the work of the *Spirit*. If the resurrection is the universalization of Jesus' particular history, then the work of the Spirit is the making-present of this history to specific human persons. It is the Spirit's work to manifest the history of Jesus to each specific person, and to open each person to the reality of Jesus' history "as his or her own *Heilsgeschichte*".[85] The history of Jesus thus becomes "internal" to the new subject[86] – and in this event of internalization, a dramatic alteration takes place in which "a person, in virtue of God's faithfulness, becomes faithful to God in return".[87] Here, there is a real subjective response to God's faithfulness; and, at the same time, this response is structured by the form of Jesus' own history as it has been imprinted on the subject. Barth thus insists that the new creation involves no mechanical causation, no mere setting of the cogs in motion; there is no *causal* relation between divine action and human response.[88] Instead, there is a *creative* relation: God forms a new subject from within, and this act of formation is a liberation of the subject to say "Yes" to God in faithfulness.

We have seen, then, that the trajectory of Barth's Paulinism runs from *faithfulness* to *participation* and finally to the *subject*. Through participation in the faithfulness of Christ, we become new subjects, set free to correspond to God with our own faithful action. There is – as Barth had already emphasized in the *Römerbrief* – a new subject who now acts within the "space" of Jesus' own history.

---

[84] *KD* IV/4, 23; ET 21.
[85] *KD* IV/4, 31; ET 28.
[86] *KD* IV/4, 32; ET 29.
[87] *KD* IV/4, 36–7; ET 33.
[88] *KD* IV/4, 39; ET 35–6.

Conclusion: "I, yet not I"

The πίστις Χριστοῦ debate has often been construed as a contest between "anthropological" and "christological" readings of Paul:[89] but I think this is a mistake. There need be no conflict between the anthropological and the christological; the human subject need not be erased in order to make room for divine action. On the contrary, the lesson of Barth's theology is that there is no competition between the divine and the human. While various traditional accounts of divine and human action have run aground on the assumption that God and humans are like separate substances which can never co-exist in the same space, Barth dissolves this competitive model, and in its place he develops a radically actualistic ontology. God simply *is* an event of action; and the human subject *is* the history which this action generates. As Francis Watson has perceptively remarked, the human response of faith therefore "falls within the scope of the ongoing divine action";[90] there is no division of labour between divine faithfulness and human faith, since the latter is included within the scope of the former.

There is, in short, a real "I" who believes – yet at the same time, it is "not I, but Christ" (Gal. 2:20). Barth's whole doctrine of reconciliation could be read as one massive theological exposition of this Pauline dictum. I participate in the history of Jesus; I am activated by the event of his faithful existence. Within his history, I become a new creature, a new subject liberated for faithful response to God. Within his death and resurrection, I live – yet not I, but Christ, since *his* faithfulness to God is the internal determining principle of my own subjectivity. My history is imprinted with Christ's, so that even the *imitatio Christi* is not my own work, but his – and in just that way, it is truly *my* work.

"I live – yet not I, but Christ." In Barth's hands, this paradox becomes a christological rendering of the nature of subjectivity itself. All Christian existence is *imitatio Christi*, since the Spirit has fashioned us from the mould of Jesus' faithful existence. Through the power of the Spirit, the history of Jesus generates its own corresponding *imitatio* – and it is true *imitatio* just because it is real *participatio*. The Christian is a real "I" who responds faithfully to God, but this "I" is always already formed by Jesus' own history of πίστις before God.

---

[89] E.g., Hays, *The Faith of Jesus Christ*, 277.

[90] Francis Watson, "The Triune Divine Identity: Reflections on Pauline God-Language, in Disagreement with J.D.G. Dunn", *JSNT* 80 (2000): 110.

Indeed, Barth envisages the creation of new subjects whose very existence is nothing other than an enactment of the faithfulness of Christ through a participation in the history of his agency. Christ is here no mere exemplar. He is the event which determines a trajectory of faithful action; he is the subjectivation of faithfulness to God in our own histories. He is – to return to Paul's language – the powerful movement ἐκ πίστεως εἰς πίστιν, from God's faithfulness to our faith (Rom. 1:17). And, for Barth, *ontological participation* is the means by which this movement is carried out.

The final section of the *Church Dogmatics* thus brings us back to the central theme of the *Römerbrief*. Here, the great movement of Barth's thought ends where it began: in a passionate and uncompromising attempt to hear Paul, and to follow Paul – "even to the very last word".[91]

---

[91] Barth, *Der Römerbrief 1922*, 20; ET 17.

Bibliography

Achtemeier, Paul J. "Apropos the Faith of/in Christ: A Response to Hays and Dunn", in *Pauline Theology*. IV. *Looking Back, Pressing On* (ed. David M. Hay and E. Elizabeth Johnson; Atlanta, GA: Scholars Press, 1997), 82–92.

Adamo, David. "Sin in John's Gospel", *EvRTh* 13.3 (1989): 216–27.

Adamson, J.B. *The Epistle of James* (NICNT; Grand Rapids, MI: Eerdmans, 1976).

Alford, H. *The Greek Testament*, IV (Chicago, IL: Moody Press, 1958).

Allison, D.C. "The Fiction of James and its *Sitz im Leben*", *RB* 118 (2001): 529–70.

Anderson, Dean. *Ancient Rhetorical Theory and Paul* (Leuven: Peeters, rev. ed., 1999).

Aquinas, Thomas. *Commentary on Hebrews* (South Bend, IN: St. Augustine's Press, 2006).

Ashley, B. "The Extent of Jesus' Human Knowledge according to the Fourth Gospel", in *Reading John with St. Thomas Aquinas* (ed. M. Levering-Dauphinais; Washington, DC: CUA Press, 2005), 241–53.

Aune, David E. *Revelation 1–5* (WBC 52A; Dallas, TX: Word, 1997).

——. *Revelation 6–16* (WBC 52B; Dallas, TX: Word, 1998).

Badiou, Alain. *Saint Paul: The Foundation of Universalism* (trans. Ray Brassier; Stanford, CA: Stanford University Press, 2003).

——. *Ethics: An Essay on the Understanding of Evil* (trans. Peter Hallward; London: Verso, 2001).

Baehrens, W.A., ed. *Libri X in Canticum Canticorum* (Origenes Werke, vol. 8; Die Griechischen christlichen Schriftsteller; Leipzig: Hinrich, 1925).

Baker, W.R. *Personal Speech-Ethics in the Epistle of James* (WUNT 2/68; Tübingen: Mohr Siebeck, 1995).

Barr, James. "Faith and Truth: An Examination of Some Linguistic Arguments", in *Semantics of Biblical Language* (London: Oxford University Press, 1961), 161–205.

——. *Semantics of Biblical Language* (London: Oxford University Press, 1961).

Barrett, C.K. *The Acts of the Apostles* (ICC; Edinburgh: T&T Clark, 1994).

——. *The Gospel according to St. John* (2nd ed.; London: SPCK, 1978).

Barth, K. *Church Dogmatics* (ed. G.W. Bromiley and T.F. Torrance; Edinburgh: T&T Clark, 1956–75).

——. *The Epistle to the Philippians* (trans. James W. Leitch; Louisville, KY: Westminster John Knox, 2002).

——. *The Epistle to the Romans* (trans. E.C. Hoskyns; Oxford: Oxford University Press, 1933).

——. *Die kirchliche Dogmatik* (Zurich: EVZ, 1932–70).

——. *Der Römerbrief* (München: Kaiser, 1928).

——. *Der Römerbrief 1922* (Zurich: EVZ, 1940).

Barth, Markus. *Ephesians: Introduction, Translation, and Commentary on Chapters 1–3* (AB 34; Garden City, NY: Doubleday, 1974).

——. "The Faith of the Messiah", *HeyJ* 10 (1969): 363–70.

——. "Jews and Gentiles: The Social Character of Justification in Paul", *JES* 5 (1968): 241–67.

——. "The Kerygma of Galatians", *Int* 21 (1967): 131–46.

Batten, A. "Unwordly Friendship: The 'Epistle of Straw' Reconsidered" (PhD dissertation; University of St. Michael's College, 2000).

Bauckham, Richard. *God Crucified: Monotheism and Christology in the New Testament* (Carlisle: Paternoster, 1998).

——. *James: Wisdom of James, Disciple of Jesus the Sage* (New Testament Readings; London and New York: Routledge 1999).

Bayer, O. *Schöpfung als Anrede: Zu einer Hermeneutik der Schöpfung* (Tübingen: Mohr Siebeck, 1990).

Beale, G.K. *The Book of Revelation* (NIGTC; Grand Rapids, MI: Eerdmans, 1999).

Beare, F.W. *A Commentary on the Epistle to the Philippians* (BNTC; London: A&C Black, 1959).

Beasley-Murray, G.R. *John* (WBC 36; Waco, TX: Word, 1987).

——. "The Mission of the Logos-Son", in *The Four Gospels 1992: Festschrift Frans Neirynck*, III (ed. F. van Segbroeck, et al.; BETL; 3 vols.; Leuven: University Press, 1992), 1865–6.

Beker, J.C. *Paul the Apostle: The Triumph of God in Life and Thought* (Philadelphia, PA: Fortress, 1980).

Bell, Richard H. *Deliver Us from Evil: Interpreting the Redemption from the Power of Satan in New Testament Theology* (WUNT 216; Tübingen: Mohr Siebeck, 2007).

——. *The Irrevocable Call of God: An Inquiry into Paul's Theology of Israel* (WUNT 184; Tübingen: Mohr Siebeck, 2005).

——. *Provoked to Jealousy: The Origin and Purpose of the Jealousy Motif in Romans 9–11* (WUNT 2.63; Tübingen: Mohr Siebeck, 1994).

——. "Sacrifice and Christology in Paul", *JTS* 53 (2002): 1–27.

Bergamelli, F. "'Fede di Gesù Cristo' nelle letter di Ignazio di Antiochia", *Salesianum* 66 (2004): 649–64.

Best, Ernest. *A Critical and Exegetical Commentary on Ephesians* (ICC; Edinburgh: T&T Clark, 1998).

Betz, H.D. *Galatians* (Hermeneia; Philadelphia, PA: Fortress, 1979).

Binder, Hermann. *Der Glaube bei Paulus (Berlin: Evangelische Verlagsanstalt, 1968).*

Bird, Michael F. *The Saving Righteousness of God: Studies on Paul, Justification, and the New Perspective* (Carlisle: Paternoster: 2007).

Blake, B.J. *Case* (Cambridge: Cambridge University Press, 1994).

Bligh, J. "Did Jesus Live by Faith?" *HeyJ* 9 (1968): 414–19.

Bockmuehl, Markus. *The Epistle to the Philippians* (BNTC; Peabody, MA: Hendrickson, 1998).

——. *Seeing the Word* (Grand Rapids, MI: Baker, 2006).

Bolt, P.G. *The Cross from a Distance: Atonement in Mark's Gospel* (Leicester: InterVarsity Press, 2004).

——. "The Gospel for Today's Church", in *Exploring the Missionary Church* (ed. B.G. Webb; Explorations 7; Sydney: ANZEA, 1993), 27–59.

——. *Jesus' Defeat of Death: Persuading Mark's Early Readers* (SNTSMS 125; Cambridge: Cambridge University Press, 2003).

——. "The Spirit in the Synoptic Gospels: The Equipment of the Servant", in *Spirit of the Living God* (Part 1) (ed. B.G. Webb; Explorations 5; Homebush West, NSW: Lancer, 1991), 45–75.

Bonaventure, *Works of Saint Bonaventure: Disputed Questions on the Knowledge of Christ* (intro. and trans. Zachary Hayes; New York: Franciscan Institute, 1992).

Borgen, P. "God's Agent in the Fourth Gospel", in *Religions in Antiquity: Essays in Memory of Erwin Ramsdell Goodenough* (ed. Jacob Neusner; Leiden: Brill, 1968), 137–48.

Bousset, Wilhelm. *Die Offenbarung Johannis* (6th ed.; Kritisch-exegetischer Kommentar über das Neue Testament; 1906; repr. Göttingen: Vandenhoeck & Ruprecht, 1966).

Bowyer, William. *Conjectures on the New Testament* (London: W. Bowyer and J. Nichols, 1772).

Boxall, Ian. *The Revelation of Saint John* (BNTC; Peabody, MA: Hendrickson, 2006).

Bray, G. *James, 1–2 Peter, 1–3 John, Jude* (ACCS 11; Downers Grove, IL: InterVarsity Press, 2000).

Brinktrine, J. "Zu Jak 2.1", *Bib* 35 (1954): 40–42.

Brosend, W.F. *James and Jude* (NCBC; Cambridge: Cambridge University Press, 2004).

Brown, Raymond. *The Gospel according to John* (AB 29; 2 vols.; New York: Abingdon, 1966, 1970).

Brown, Raymond. *Introduction to the New Testament* (ABRL; New York: Doubleday, 1997).

Bruce, F.F. *The Epistle to the Galatians* (NIGTC; Grand Rapids, MI: Eerdmans, 1982).

Bultmann, Rudolf. *Theology of the New Testament* (trans. K. Grobel; 2 vols.; London: SCM Press, 1955).

Burchard, C. *Der Jakobusbrief* (HNT 15/1; Tübingen: Mohr Siebeck, 2000).

———."Gemeinde in der strohernen Epistel: Mutmaßungen über Jakobus", in *Kirche: Für Günther Bornkamm zum 75. Geburtstag* (ed. D. Lührmann and G. Strecker; Tübingen: Mohr Siebeck, 1980), 315–28.

———."Zu einige christologischen Stellen des Jakobusbriefes", in *Anfänge der Christologie: Festschrift für Ferdinand Hahn zum 65. Geburtstag* (ed. C. Bretenback and H. Paulsen; Gottingen: Vandenhoeck & Ruprecht, 1991), 353–68.

Burton, E.D. *A Critical and Exegetical Commentary on the Epistle to the Galatians* (ICC; New York: Scribner's Sons, 1920; Edinburgh: T&T Clark, 1921).

Butt, M. *Theories of Case* (Cambridge: Cambridge University Press, 2006).

Caird, G.B. *New Testament Theology* (ed. L.D. Hurst; Oxford: Clarendon Press, 1994).

———. *Revelation* (BNTC; Peabody, MA: Hendrickson, 1966).

Calvin, J. "The Epistle of James", in *A Harmony of the Gospels Matthew, Mark and Luke, and the Epistles of James and Jude*, III (trans. A.W. Morrison; ed. D.W. Torrance and T.F. Torrance; Grand Rapids, MI: Eerdmans, 1972).

Campbell, Douglas A. *The Deliverance of God: An Apocalyptic Rereading of Justification in Paul* (Grand Rapids, MI: Eerdmans, 2009).

———. "False Presuppositions in the ΠΙΣΤΙΣ ΧΡΙΣΤΟΥ Debate: A Response to Brian Dodd", *JBL* 116 (1997): 713–19.

———. "The Meaning of πίστις and νόμος in Paul: A Linguistic and Structural Investigation", *JBL* 111 (1992): 85–103.

———. *The Quest for Paul's Gospel: A Suggested Strategy* (JSNTSup 274; London: T&T Clark, 2005).

———. *The Rhetoric of Righteousness in Romans 3:21–26* (JSNTSup 65; Sheffield: JSOT Press, 1992).

———. "Romans 1:17 – A *Crux Interpretum* for the ΠΙΣΤΙΣ ΧΡΙΣΤΟΥ Dispute", *JBL* 113 (1994): 265–85.

———. "The Story of Jesus in Romans and Galatians", in *Narrative Dynamics in Paul: A Critical Assessment* (ed. B.W. Longenecker; Louisville, KY: Westminster John Knox, 2002), 97–124.

Caneday, Ardel B. "The Curse of the Law and the Cross: Works of the Law and Faith in Galatians 3:1–14" (PhD dissertation; Trinity Evangelical Divinity School, 1992).

Caneday, Ardel B. "Galatians 3:22ff.: A *Crux Interpretum* for ΠΙΣΤΙΣ ΧΡΙΣΤΟΥ in Paul's Thought" (conference paper, Evangelical Theological Society, Philadelphia, 16–18 November 1995; available from Theological Research Exchange Network [http://tren.com]).

——. "'Redeemed from the Curse of the Law': The Use of Deut. 21:22–23 in Gal. 3:13", *TJ* 10 (1989): 189–209.

——. "'They Exchanged the Glory of God for the Likeness of an Image': Idolatrous Adam and Israel as Representatives in Paul's Letter to the Romans", *SBJT* 11 (2007): 34–44.

Canter, H.V. "Rhetorical Elements in Livy's Direct Speeches: Part I", *AJP* 38 (1917): 125–51.

——. "Rhetorical Elements in Livy's Direct Speeches: Part II", *AJP* 39 (1918): 44–64.

Carey, G.L. "The Lamb of God and Atonement Theories", *TynBul* 32 (1981): 97–122.

Carson, D.A. *The Gospel according to John* (PNTC; Leicester: InterVarsity Press, 1991).

Carter, W. *John: Storyteller, Interpreter, Evangelist* (Peabody, MA: Hendrickson, 2006).

Chamberlain, W.D. "The Need of Man: The Atonement in the Fourth Gospel", *Int* 10.2 (1956): 157–66.

Charles, R.H. *A Critical and Exegetical Commentary on the Revelation of St. John* (ICC; Edinburgh: T&T Clark, 1920).

Charlesworth, J.H., ed. *Old Testament Pseudepigrapha* (London: Darton, Longman & Todd, 1985).

Chester, A. "The Theology of James", in *The Theology of the Letters of James, Peter, and Jude* (ed. A. Chester and R.P. Martin; Cambridge: Cambridge University Press, 1994), 46–53.

Cheung, L.L. *The Genre, Composition and Hermeneutics of the Epistle of James* (Paternoster Biblical and Theological Monographs; Carlisle: Paternoster, 2003).

Choi, Hung-Sik. "Πίστις in Galatians 5:5–6: Neglected Evidence for the Faithfulness of Christ", *JBL* 124 (2005): 467–90.

Corsani, Bruno. "Ἐκ πίστεως in the Letters of Paul", in *The New Testament Age: Essays in Honor of Bo Reicke* (ed. W.C. Weinrich; Macon, GA: Mercer University Press, 1984), 87–93.

Cosgrove, Charles H. *The Cross and the Spirit: A Study in the Argument and Theology of Galatians* (Macon, GA: Mercer University Press, 1988).

Cranfield, C.E.B. *A Critical and Exegetical Commentary on the Epistle to the Romans*, I–II (ICC; Edinburgh: T&T Clark, 2004 [1975]).

——. *The Gospel according to St. Mark* (Cambridge: Cambridge University Press, 1959).

Cranfield, C.E.B. "On the Πίστις Χριστοῦ Question", in *On Romans and Other New Testament Essays* (Edinburgh: T&T Clark, 1998), 81–97.

Croft, W., and D.A. Cruse. *Cognitive Linguistics* (Cambridge: Cambridge University Press, 2004).

Cruse, D.A. *Lexical Semantics* (Cambridge: Cambridge University Press, 1986).

Daalen, D.H. van. "'Faith' according to Paul", *ExpTim* 87 (1975): 83–5.

Danker, F.W. *Benefactor: Epigraphic Study of a Graeco-Roman and New Testament Semantic Field* (St. Louis, MO: Clayton Publishing House, 1982).

Das, A. Andrew. "Another Look at ἐὰν μή in Galatians 2:16", *JBL* (2000): 529–39.

Davies, W.D., and D.C. Allison. *Matthew* (ICC; 3 vols.; Edinburgh: T&T Clark, 1997).

Dawson, R. Dale. *The Resurrection in Karl Barth* (Aldershot: Ashgate, 2007).

Deer, Donald S. "Whose Faith/Loyalty in Revelation 2:13 and 14:12?", *BT* 38 (1987): 328–30.

Deißmann, A. *Paulus: Eine Kultur- und Religionsgeschichtliche Skizze* (2nd ed.; Tübingen: Mohr Siebeck, 1925).

——. *St. Paul: A Study in Social and Religious History* (trans. L.R.M. Strachan; London: Hodder & Stoughton, 1912; 2nd ed. trans. W.E. Wilson; New York: Harper & Row, 1957).

Dennis, J. "Jesus' Death in John's Gospel: A Survey of Research from Bultmann to the Present with Special Reference to the Johannine Hyper-Texts", *CBR* 4 (2005–6): 331–63; 342–9.

deSilva, D.A. *Despising Shame: Honor Discourse and Community Maintenance in the Epistle to the Hebrews* (SBLDS 152; Atlanta, GA: Scholars Press, 1995).

Dibelius, M. *James: A Commentary on the Epistle of James* (Hermeneia; Philadelphia, PA: Fortress, 1976).

Dodd, Brian J. "Romans 1:17: A *Crux Interpretum* for the πίστις Χριστοῦ Debate?" *JBL* 114 (1995): 470–3.

——. "The Story of Christ and the Imitation of Paul in Philippians 2–3", in *Where Christology Began: Essays on Philippians 2* (ed. Ralph P. Martin and Brian J. Dodd; Louisville, KY: Westminster John Knox, 1998), 154–61.

Dodd, C.H. *The Apostolic Preaching and its Developments* (London: Hodder & Stoughton, 1944).

Dowd, S.E. *Prayer, Power, and the Problem of Suffering: Mark 11:22–25 in the Context of Markan Theology* (SBLDS 105; Atlanta, GA: Scholars Press, 1988).

Dunn, James D.G. *The Epistle to the Galatians* (BNTC; Peabody, MA: Hendrickson, 1993): 351–66.

——. "*EK PISTEŌS*: A Key to the Meaning of *PISTIS CHRISTOU*", in *The Word Leaps the Gap: Essays on Scripture and Theology in Honor of Richard B. Hays* (ed. J.R. Wagner, et al.; Grand Rapids, MI: Eerdmans, 2008), 351–66.

Dunn, James D.G. *Jesus, Paul and the Law* (London: SPCK/Louisville, KY: Westminster John Knox, 1990).

———. *Jesus Remembered* (Grand Rapids, MI: Eerdmans, 2003).

———. "The New Perspective on Paul", *BJRL* 65 (1983): 95–122.

———. *The New Perspective on Paul* (WUNT 185; Tübingen: Mohr Siebeck, 2005/ Grand Rapids, MI: Eerdmans, 2008).

———. "Once More, ΠΙΣΤΙΣ ΧΡΙΣΤΟΥ", in *Pauline Theology. IV. Looking Back, Pressing On* (ed. David M. Hay and E. Elizabeth Johnson; SBL Symposium Series; Atlanta, GA: Scholars Press, 1997; first published in *SBLSP* 30 [1991]: 730–44), 61–81. (Also Appendix 1 in D. Hays, *The Faith of Jesus Christ* [2002], 249–71.)

———. "Paul's Letter to Rome: Reason and Rationale", in *Logos – Logik – Lyrik: Engagierte exegetische Studien zum biblischen Reden Gottes* (ed. V.A. Lehnert and U. Rüsen-Weinhold; Leipzig: Evangelische Verlagsanstalt, 2007), 185–200.

———. *Romans 1–8* (WBC 38A; Waco, TX: Word, 1988).

———. *Romans 9–16* (WBC 38B; Waco, TX: Word, 1988).

———. "The Theology of Galatians: The Issue of Covenantal Nomism", in *Pauline Theology I: Thessalonians, Philippians, Galatians, Philemon* (ed. Jouette M. Bassler; Minneapolis, MN: Fortress, 1991), 125–46.

Ebeling, G. "Jesus und Glaube", in *Wort und Glaube* III (Beiträge zur Fundamentaltheologie, Soteriologie und Ekklesiologie; Tübingen: Mohr Siebeck, 1975).

Edgar, D.H. *Has God Not Chosen the Poor? The Social Setting of the Epistle of James* (JSNTSup 206; Sheffield: Sheffield Academic Press, 2001).

Eichholz, Georg. *Die Theologie des Paulus im Umriß* (Neukirchen-Vluyn: Neukirchener, 1985 [1972]).

Evans, C.A. *Mark 8:27–16:20* (WBC 34B; Nashville, TN: Thomas Nelson, 2001).

Fee, Gordon D. *Pauline Christology: An Exegetical-Theological Study* (Peabody, MA: Hendrickson, 2007).

Fitzmyer, J.A. *According to Paul: Studies in the Theology of the Apostle* (New York: Paulist Press, 1993).

———. "Paul's Jewish Background and the Deeds of the Law", in idem, *According to Paul*, 19–35.

———. *Romans* (AB 33; New York: Doubleday, 1993).

Ford, David F. *Barth and God's Story: Biblical Narrative and the Theological Method of Karl Barth in the Church Dogmatics* (Frankfurt am Main: Peter Lang, 1985).

Ford, J.M. *Revelation* (AB; New York: Doubleday, 1975).

Forestell, J.T. *The Word of the Cross: Salvation as Revelation in the Fourth Gospel* (AnBib 57; Rome: Biblical Institute Press, 1974).

Foster, P. "The First Contribution to the πίστις Χριστοῦ Debate: A Study of Ephesians 3:12", *JSNT* 85 (2002): 75–96.

Freeborn, J. "Lord of Glory: A Study of James 2 and 1 Corinthians 2", *ExpTim* 111 (2000): 185–9.

Frey, J. "Die '*theologia crucifixi*' des Johannesevangeliums", in *Kreuzestheologie im Neuen Testament* (ed. A. Dettwiler and J. Zumstein; WUNT I:151; Tübingen: Mohr Siebeck, 2002), 197–9.

Fuchs, E. "Jesu und der Glaube", *ZTK* 55 (1958): 170–85.

Fung, Ronald Y.K. *The Epistle to the Galatians* (NICNT; Grand Rapids, MI: Eerdmans, 1988).

Galtier, P. "La conscience humaine du Christ", *Greg* 35 (1954): 225–46.

Garlington, Don. *Faith, Obedience, and Perseverance: Aspects of Paul's Letter to the Romans* (WUNT II.79; Tübingen: Mohr Siebeck, 1994).

——. *"The Obedience of Faith:" A Pauline Phrase in Historical Context* (WUNT II.38; Tübingen: Mohr Siebeck, 1991).

——. "Role Reversal and Paul's Use of Scripture in Galatians 3:10–13", *JSNT* (1997): 85–121.

Gaston, L. *Paul and the Torah* (Vancouver: University of British Columbia Press, 1987).

Gathercole, Simon. *Where Is Boasting? Early Jewish Soteriology and Paul's Response in Romans 1–5* (Grand Rapids, MI: Eerdmans, 2002).

Goodenough, Erwin R., and A.T. Kraabel. "Paul and the Hellenization of Christianity", in *Religions in Antiquity: Essays in Memory of Erwin Ramsdell Goodenough* (ed. Jacob Neusner; Leiden: Brill, 1968; repr. 1970), 35–80.

Gordon, T. David. "The Problem at Galatia", *Int* 41 (1987): 36–8.

Gnilka, Joachim. *Der Philipperbrief* (HTKNT 10.3; Freiburg/Basel/Wien: Herder, 1987 [1968]).

Goppelt, Leonhard. *A Commentary on I Peter* (ET; Grand Rapids, MI: Eerdmans, 1993).

Gotteri, N.J.C. "A Note on Bulgarian Verb Systems", *JMALS* ns 8 (1983): 49–60.

Grant, R.M. *Miracle and Natural Law in Graeco-Roman and Early Christian Thought* (Amsterdam: North-Holland, 1952).

——. "The Coming of the Kingdom", *JBL* 67 (1948): 297–303.

Green, S.G. *Handbook to the Grammar of the Greek Testament* (London: Religious Tract Society, n.d.).

Grigsby, B.H. "The Cross as an Expiatory Sacrifice in the Fourth Gospel", *JSNT* 15 (1982): 51–80.

Guardini, Romano. *Der Herr* (Würzburg: Werkbund, 1951).

Guelich, R.A. "The Matthean Beatitudes: 'Entrance Requirements' or Eschatological Blessings?" *JBL* 95 (1976): 415–34.

Haacker, Klaus. *Der Brief des Paulus an die Römer* (THKNT; 3rd ed.; Leipzig: Evangelische Verlagsanstalt, 2006).

———. "Glaube II: Altes und Neues Testament", in *Theologische Realenzyklopädie*, XIII (ed. G. Krause and G. Müller; Berlin: Walter de Gruyter, 1997–).

Halliday, M.A.K. "On the Ineffability of Grammatical Categories", in *Linguistics in Systemic Perspective* (ed. J.D. Benson, M.J. Cummings, and W.S. Greaves; Amsterdam: Benjamins, 1988), 27–51.

———. "The Form of a Functional Grammar", in *Halliday: System and Function in Language* (ed. G. Kress; Oxford: Oxford University Press, 1976), 7–25.

Hanson, A.T. *Studies in Paul's Technique and Theology* (Grand Rapids, MI: Eerdmans, 1974).

Harink, Douglas. *Paul among the Postliberals: Pauline Theology beyond Christendom and Modernity* (Grand Rapids, MI: Brazos, 2003).

———. "The Time of the Gospel and the History of the World" (paper presented at the SBL Annual Meeting, November 2007).

Harkins, Paul W., ed. *St. John Chrysostom: On the Incomprehensible Nature of God* (FC 72; Washington, DC: Catholic University of America, 1982).

Harris, Murray. "Prepositions and Theology in the Greek New Testament", in *The New International Dictionary of New Testament Theology* (ed. C. Brown; 3 vols.; Exeter: Paternoster, 1978).

Harrisville, Roy A., III. "Before ΠΙΣΤΙΣ ΧΡΙΣΤΟΥ: The Objective Genitive as Good Greek", *NovT* 48 (2006): 353–8.

———. "ΠΙΣΤΙΣ ΧΡΙΣΤΟΥ: Witness of the Fathers", *NovT* 36 (1994): 233–41.

Hartin, P.J. *James* (SP 14; Collegeville, MN: Liturgical Press, 2003).

———. *A Spirituality of Perfection: Faith in Action in the Letter of James* (Collegeville, MN: Liturgical Press, 1999).

Harvey, A.E. "Christ as Agent", in *The Glory of Christ in the New Testament: Studies in Christology in Memory of G.B. Caird* (ed. L.D. Hurst and N.T. Wright; Oxford: Clarendon Press, 1987), 239–50.

Haußleiter, Johannes. "Der Glaube Jesu Christi und der christliche Glaube: Ein Beitrag zur Erklärung des Römerbriefes", *NKZ* 2 (1891).

———. *Der Glaube Jesu Christi und der christliche Glaube: Ein Beitrag zur Erklärung des Römerbriefes* (Erlangen: Deichert, 1891).

———. "Was versteht Paulus unter christlichen Glauben?", in *Theologische Abhandlungen* (Festschrift H. Cremer; Gütersloh: Bertelsmann, 1895), 159–81.

Hawthorne, Gerald F. *Philippians* (WBC 43; Waco, TX: 1983).

Hay, David M. "*Pistis* as 'Ground for Faith' in Hellenized Judaism and Paul", *JBL* 108 (1989): 461–76.

———, and E. Elizabeth Johnson, eds. *Pauline Theology IV. Looking Back, Pressing On* (Atlanta, GA: Scholars Press, 1997).

Hays, Richard B. "Apocalyptic Hermeneutics: Habakkuk Proclaims 'the Righteous One'," in idem, *The Conversion of the Imagination*, 119–42.

——. "*EK PISTEŌS*: A Key to the Meaning of *PISTIS CHRISTOU*", in *The Word Leaps the Gap: Essays on Scripture and Theology in Honor of Richard B. Hays* (ed. J.R. Wagner, et al.; Grand Rapids, MI: Eerdmans, 2008.

——. *The Conversion of the Imagination: Paul as Interpreter of Israel's Scriptures* (Grand Rapids, MI: Eerdmans, 2005).

——. *The Faith of Jesus Christ: The Narrative Substructure of Galatians 3:1–4:11* (SBLDS 56; 2nd ed.; Chico, CA: Scholars Press, 1983; Grand Rapids, MI: Eerdmans, 2002).

——. "Justification", in *ABD* (New York: Doubleday, 1992), 3:1131.

——. "The Letter to the Galatians: Introduction, Commentary, and Reflections" (*NIB* 11; Nashville, TN: Abingdon, 2000), 181–348.

——. "ΠΙΣΤΙΣ and Pauline Christology: What Is at Stake?", in Hay and Johnson, eds., *Pauline Theology IV. Looking Back, Pressing On* (first published in *SBLSP* 30 [1991]: 714–29), 35–60. (Also Appendix 2 in D. Hays, *The Faith of Jesus Christ* [2002], 272–98.)

——. "Psalm 143 and the Logic of Romans 3", *JBL* 99 (1980): 107–15.

——. "'The Righteous One' as Eschatological Deliverer: A Case Study in Paul's Apocalyptic Hermeneutics", in *Apocalyptic and the New Testament: Essays in Honour of J. Louis Martyn* (ed. J. Marcus and M. Soards; Sheffield: JSOT, 1988), 191–215.

Hebert, Gabriel. "'Faithfulness' and 'Faith'", *RTR* 14 (1955): 33–40; also in *Theol* 58 (1955): 373–9.

Heliso, Desta. *Pistis and the Righteous One: A Study of Romans 1:17 against the Background of Scripture and Second Temple Jewish Literature* (WUNT 2.235; Tübingen: Mohr Siebeck, 2007).

Hemer, Colin J. *The Letters to the Seven Churches of Asia* (Sheffield: JSOT Press, 1986).

Hilgard, A., ed. *Grammatici Graeci* (Leipzig: Teubner, 1889–94; repr. Hildesheim: Olms, 1965).

Hoehner, Harold W. *Ephesians: An Exegetical Commentary* (Grand Rapids, MI: Baker, 2002).

Hoffmann, E.G., and H. v. Siebenthal. *Griechische Grammatik zum Neuen Testament* (Riehen, Schweiz: Immanuel-Verlag, 1990).

Hofius, Otfried. *Der Christushymnus Philipper 2,6–11: Untersuchungen zu Gestalt und Aussage eines urchristlichen Psalms* (WUNT 17; Tübingen: Mohr Siebeck, 1991 [1976]).

——. "'Die Wahrheit des Evangeliums'", in *Paulusstudien II* (Tübingen: Mohr Siebeck, 2002), 17–37.

——. "Wort Gottes und Glaube bei Paulus", in *Paulusstudien* (WUNT 51; Tübingen: Mohr Siebeck, 1989), 150–60.

Hooker, Morna D. "Glaube. III. Neues Testament", in *Religion in Geschichte und Gegenwart* (ed. Hans D. Betz, et al.; 4th ed.; 8 vols.; Tübingen: Mohr Siebeck, 1998–2007).

Hooker, Morna D. "Πίστις Χριστοῦ", in *From Adam to Christ: Essays on Paul* (Cambridge: Cambridge University Press, 1990; first published in *NTS* 35 [1989]: 321–42), 165–84.

——. *The Gospel according to Saint Mark* (London: A&C Black, 1991).

Howard, George E. "Faith of Christ", in *ABD* 2 (New York: Doubleday, 1992), 758–60.

——. "The 'Faith of Christ'," *ExpTim* 85 (1973–74): 212–15.

——. "Notes and Observations on the 'Faith of Christ'," *HTR* 60 (1967): 459–65.

——. *Paul: Crisis in Galatia* (SNTSMS 35; Cambridge: Cambridge University Press, 1979).

——. "Romans 3:21–31 and the Inclusion of the Gentiles", *HTR* 63 (1970): 228–31.

Hultgren, Arland J. "The *Pistis Christou* Formulation in Paul", *NovT* 22 (1980): 248–63.

Hunn, Debbie. "*Pistis Christou* in Galatians 2:16: Clarification from 3:1–6", *TynBul* 57 (2006): 23–33.

Hurtado, Larry W. *Lord Jesus Christ: Devotion to Jesus in Earliest Christianity* (Grand Rapids, MI: Eerdmans, 2003).

Inchaurraga, P. "La unidad psicologica de Cristo en la controversia Galtier-Parentein", *Lum* 3 (1954): 215–39.

Jackson-McCabe, M.A. *Logos and Law in the Letter of James: The Law of Nature, the Law of Moses and the Law of Freedom* (NovTSup 100; Leiden: Brill, 2001).

Jenson, Robert W. "Karl Barth", in *The Modern Theologians: An Introduction to Christian Theology in the Twentieth Century*, I (ed. David F. Ford; Oxford: Blackwell, 1989), 41.

Jewett, R. *Romans* (Hermeneia; Minneapolis, MN: Fortress, 2007).

Johnson, Luke Timothy. *Brother of Jesus, Friend of God: Studies in the Letter of James* (Grand Rapids, MI: Eerdmans, 2004).

——. *Letter of James* (AB 37A; New York: Doubleday, 1997).

——. *The Letter of James* (*NIB* 12; Nashville, TN: Abingdon, 1998).

——. *Reading Romans: A Literary and Theological Commentary* (New York: Crossroad, 1997).

——. "Romans 3:21–26 and the Faith of Jesus", *CBQ* 44 (1982): 77–90.

Juel, Donald H. *Messianic Exegesis: Christological Interpretation in the Old Testament and Early Christianity* (2nd ed.; Minneapolis, MN: Augsburg Fortress, 1998 [1988]).

Jüngel, Eberhard. *Das Evangelium von der Rechtfertigung des Gottlosen als Zentrum des christlichen Glaubens. Eine theologische Studie in ökumenischer Absicht* (Tübingen: Mohr Siebeck, 1999 [1998]).

———. *Paulus und Jesus* (Tübingen: Mohr Siebeck, 1962).

Karrer, Martin. *Die Johannesoffenbarung als Brief* (Göttingen: Vandenhoeck & Ruprecht, 1986).

Käsemann, Ernst. "The Righteousness of God in Paul", in *New Testament Questions of Today* (London: SCM Press, 1969 [1965]), 168–93.

———. *The Testament of Jesus* (trans. G. Krodel; London: SCM Press, 1966).

Keck, L.E. "'Jesus' in Romans", *JBL* 108 (1989): 443–60.

Keenan, J.P. *The Wisdom of James: Parallels with Mahayana Buddhism* (New York: The Newman Press, 2005).

Keener, Craig S. *The Gospel of John: A Commentary* (2 vols.; Peabody, MA: Hendrickson, 2003).

———. *Revelation* (NIVAC; Grand Rapids, MI: Zondervan, 2000).

Kertelge, K. *Rechtfertigung bei Paulus* (Münster: Aschendorff, 1967).

Kinneavy, James L. *The Greek Rhetorical Origins of Christian Faith* (Oxford: Oxford University Press, 1987).

Kittel, Gerhard. "Πίστις Ἰησοῦ Χριστοῦ bei Paulus", *TSK* 79 (1906): 419–36.

Klein, M. *"Ein vollkommenes Werk:" Vollkommenheit, Gesetz und Gericht als theologische Themen des Jakobusbriefes* (BWANT 139; Stuttgart: W. Kohlhammer, 1995).

Kloppenborg, J.S. "Diaspora Discourse: The Construction of Ethos in James", *NTS* 53 (2007): 242–70.

———. "Judaeans or Judean Christians in James", in *Identity and Interaction in the Ancient Mediterranean: Jews, Christians and Others* (ed. Philip Harland and Zeba Crook; London and New York: Sheffield Phoenix, 2007).

Konradt, M. *Christliche Existenz nach dem Jakobusbrief: Eine Studie zu seiner soteriloogischen und ethischen Konzeption* (SUNT 22; Göttingen: Vandenhoeck & Ruprecht, 1998).

Koperski, Veronica. "The Meaning of *Pistis Christou* in Philippians 3:9", *LS* 18 (1993): 202–14.

Körtner, U. *Die Apostolische Väter* (Darmstadt: Wissenschaftliche Buchgesellschaft, 1981).

Köstenberger, A. *The Missions of Jesus and the Disciples in the Fourth Gospel: With Implications for the Fourth Gospel's Purpose and the Mission of the Contemporary Church* (Grand Rapids, MI: Eerdmans, 1998).

Kühner, R., and B. Gerth. *Ausführliche Grammatik der griechischen Sprache* (Hannover/Leipzig: Hahn, 1898; Darmstadt, 1966).

Labahn, M. *Jesus als Lebensspender: Untersuchungen zu einer Geschichte der johanneischen Tradition anhand ihrer Wundergeschichten* (BZNW 98; Berlin: Walter de Gruyter, 1999).

Ladaria, L.F. *Cristologiá de Hilario de Poitiers* (Roma: Pontificia Università Gregoriana, 1989).

Lane, W.L. *The Gospel of Mark* (Grand Rapids, MI: Eerdmans, 1974).

Lange, Johann P. *Romans* (trans. Philip Schaff; n.p., 1865; repr. Grand Rapids, MI: Zondervan, ca. 1950).

Leslie, A. "Christ's Faithfulness and Our Salvation", in *Donald Robinson – Selected Works – Appreciation* (ed. P.G. Bolt and M.D. Thompson; Camperdown, NSW: Australian Church Record / Moore College, 2008), 73–81.

Lietzmann, Hans. *An die Römer* (HNT; Tübingen: Mohr Siebeck, 1933).

Lightfoot, Joseph B. *St. Paul's Epistle to the Philippians* (Peabody, MA: Hendrickson, 1993 [1868]).

Lincoln, A.T. *Ephesians* (WBC 42; Dallas, TX: Word, 1990).

Lindemann, A., and H. Paulsen, eds. and trans. *Die Apostolischen Väter griechisch-deutsche Parallelausgabe auf der Grundlage der Ausgaben von Franz Xaver Funk/Karl Bihlmeyer und Molly Whittaker* (Tübingen: Mohr Siebeck, 1992).

Lindars, B. "The Passion in the Fourth Gospel", in *Essays on John* (ed. C.M. Tuckett; Leuven: University Press, 1992).

Lindsay, Dennis R. "Works of Law, Hearing of Faith and Πίστις Χριστοῦ in Galatians 2:16–3:5", *SCJ* 3 (2000): 87.

Lipsius, R.A. "Die Briefe an die Galater, Römer, Philipper", in *Hand-Commentar zum Neuen Testament, Band 2.2* (ed. H.J. Holtzmann, et al.; Freiburg: Mohr Siebeck, 1891).

Ljungman, H.J. *Pistis: A Study of its Presuppositions and its Meaning in Pauline Use* (Lund: Gleerup, 1964).

Lockett, D. *Purity and Worldview in the Epistle of James* (LNTS; London: T&T Clark, 2008).

Lohaus, G. *Die Geheimnisse des Lebens Jesu* (Freiburg: Herder, 1985).

Lohmeyer, Ernst. *Grundlagen paulinischer Theologie* (BHT 1; Tübingen: Mohr Siebeck, 1929).

Longenecker, Bruce W. "Defining the Faithful Character of the Covenant Community: Galatians 2.15–21 and Beyond", in *Paul and the Mosaic Law* (ed. J.D.G. Dunn; Tübingen: Mohr Siebeck, 1996), 75–97.

——. "Πίστις in Romans 3:25: Neglected Evidence for the 'Faithfulness of Christ'?" *NTS* 39 (1993): 478–80.

——., ed. *Narrative Dynamics in Paul: A Critical Assessment* (Louisville, KY: Westminster John Knox, 2002).

——. *The Triumph of Abraham's God: The Transformation of Identity in Galatians* (Nashville, TN: Abingdon, 1998).

Longenecker, Richard. *The Christology of Early Jewish Christianity* (London: SCM Press, 1970).

Longenecker, Richard. "The Foundational Conviction of New Testament Christology: The Obedience/Faithfulness/Sonship of Christ", in *Jesus of Nazareth Lord and Christ: Essays on the Historical Jesus and New Testament Christology* (ed. Joel B. Green and Max Turner; Grand Rapids, MI: Eerdmans, 1994), 473–88.

Longenecker, Richard. *Galatians* (WBC 41; Dallas, TX: Word, 1990).

——. "The Obedience of Christ in the Theology of the Early Church", in *Reconciliation and Hope: New Testament Essays on Atonement and Eschatology Presented to L.L. Morris on his 60th Birthday* (ed. R. Banks; Exeter: Paternoster/ Grand Rapids, MI: Eerdmans, 1974), 142–52.

——. *Paul, Apostle of Liberty* (New York: Harper & Row, 1964).

——. Review of *The Faith of Jesus Christ*, in *Them* 10 (1984–5): 38.

Louw, J.P. "Linguistic Theory and the Greek Case System", *Acta Classica* 9 (1966): 73–88.

——. and E.A. Nida, eds. *Greek-English Lexicon of the New Testament Based on Semantic Domains* (2nd ed.; New York: United Bible Societies, 1989).

Lowe, Bruce A. "Oh διά! How is Romans 4:25 to be Understood?" *JTS* 57 (2006): 149–57.

——. *A New Paradigm, Progression and Purpose for Romans: Roman Solutions to Enigmas and Building Relationships* (PhD dissertation, Macquarie University, forthcoming).

——. "Romans 1:16–5:21: 'Already' Eschatology Argued Rhetorically" (paper presented at the SBL International Meeting, Edinburgh, 6 July 2006).

Lupieri, Edmondo. *A Commentary on the Apocalypse of John* (Grand Rapids, MI: Eerdmans, 2006).

Luther, Martin. *Luther's Works* (ed. John Pelikan and Helmut Lehmann; 55 vols.; Philadelphia, PA: Fortress, 1955–).

Lyons, J. *Introduction to Theoretical Linguistics* (Cambridge: Cambridge University Press, 1968).

Manson, W. *Jesus the Messiah: The Synoptic Tradition of the Revelation of God in Christ: With Special Reference to Form-Criticism* (London: Hodder & Stoughton, 1943).

Marcus, Joel. *The Way of the Lord: Christological Exegesis of the Old Testament in the Gospel of Mark* (Louisville, KY: Westminster John Knox, 1992).

Martin, R.P. *James* (WBC 48; Waco, TX: Word, 1988).

Martyn, J. Louis. "Apocalyptic Antinomies", in *Theological Issues in the Letters of Paul* (Edinburgh: T&T Clark, 1997).

——. "The Apocalyptic Gospel in Galatians", *Int* 54 (2000): 250.

——. "Events in Galatia: Modified Covenantal Nomism versus God's Invasion of the Cosmos in the Singular Gospel: A Response to J.D.G. Dunn and B.R. Gaventa", in *Pauline Theology I: Thessalonians, Philippians, Galatians, Philemon* (ed. Jouette M. Bassler; Minneapolis, MN: Fortress, 1991).

Martyn, J. Louis. *Galatians: A New Translation with Introduction and Commentary* (AB 33A; New York: Doubleday, 1997).

Massebieau, L. "L'épître de Jacques: est-elle l'oeuvre d'un chrétien?" *RHR* 32 (1895): 249–50.

Matera, F.J. *Galatians* (SP 9; Collegeville, MN: Liturgical Press, 1983).

Matlock, R. Barry. "Afterword" to "The Arrow and the Web: Critical Reflections on a Narrative Approach to Paul", in *Narrative Dynamics in Paul: A Critical Assessment* (ed. Bruce W. Longenecker; Louisville, KY: Westminster John Knox, 2002), 54–7.

——. "Beyond the Great Divide? History, Theology, and the Secular Academy", in *Moving Beyond New Testament Theology? Essays in Conversation with Heikki Räisänen* (ed. Todd Penner and Caroline Vander Stichele; Publications of the Finnish Exegetical Society 88; Göttingen: Vandenhoeck & Ruprecht, 2005), 369–99.

——. "Detheologizing the ΠΙΣΤΙΣ ΧΡΙΣΤΟΥ Debate: Cautionary Remarks from a Lexical Semantic Perspective", *NovT* 42 (2000): 1–23.

——. "'Even the Demons Believe': Paul and πίστις Χριστοῦ", *CBQ* 64 (2002): 300–18.

——. "Πίστις in Galatians 3:26: Neglected Evidence for 'Faith in Christ'?", *NTS* 49 (2003): 433–9.

——. "The Rhetoric of πίστις in Paul: Galatians 2:16, 3:22, Romans 3:22, and Philippians 3:9", *JSNT* 30.2 (2007): 173–203.

McCormack, Bruce L. "Participation in God, Yes, Deification, No: Two Modern Protestant Responses to an Ancient Question", in *Denkwürdiges Geheimnis: Beiträge zur Gotteslehre: Festschrift für Eberhard Jüngel zum 70. Geburtstag* (ed. I.U. Dalferth, J. Fischer, and H.-P. Großhans; Tübingen: Mohr Siebeck, 2004).

Menge, Hermann. *Die Heilige Schrift des Alten und Neuen Testaments* (11th ed.; Stuttgart: Württembergische Bibelanstalt, 1949).

Metzner, R. *Das Verständnis der Sünde im Johannesevangelium* (WUNT 1:122; Tübingen: Mohr Siebeck, 2000), 129–30.

Meyer, A. *Das Rätsel des Jacobusbriefes* (BZNW 10; Giessen: Töpelmann, 1930), 118–21.

Mitton, C. Leslie. *The Epistle to the Ephesians: Its Authorship, Origin and Purpose* (Oxford: Clarendon, 1951).

Moo, Douglas J. *The Epistle to the Romans* (NICNT; Grand Rapids, MI: Eerdmans, 1996).

——. *The Letter of James* (PNTC; Grand Rapids, MI: Eerdmans, 2000).

——. Review of *The Faith of Jesus Christ* by Richard B. Hays in *JETS* 27 (1984): 48.

Moorhouse, A.C. "The Role of the Accusative Case", in *In the Footsteps of Raphael Kühner* (ed. A. Rijksbaron, H.A. Mulder, and G.C. Wakker; Amsterdam: Gieben, 1988), 209–18.

Mounce, Robert H. *Revelation* (NICNT; Grand Rapids, MI: Eerdmans, rev. ed., 1998).

Moule, C.F.D. "The Biblical Conception of 'Faith'," *ExpTim* 68 (1957): 222.

Moule, C.F.D. "Further Reflections on Philippians 2:5–11", in *Apostolic History and the Gospel* (ed. W. Ward Gasque and Ralph P. Martin; Exeter: Paternoster, 1970), 274–5.

Moulton, J.H. *Prolegomena*, vol. 1 of *A Grammar of New Testament Greek* (3rd ed.; Edinburgh: T&T Clark, 1908).

Moxnes, H. "Honor and Righteousness in Romans", *JSNT* 32 (1988): 61–77.

Mussner, F. *Der Galaterbrief* (HTKNT 9; Freiburg: Herder, 1974).

Musurillo, H.A., ed., *The Acts of the Pagan Martyrs* (Oxford: Acta Alexandrinorum, 1954).

———. *The Acts of the Christian Martyrs* (Oxford: Acta Alexandrinorum, 1972).

Neder, Adam. *Participation in Christ in Karl Barth's Church Dogmatics* (Louisville, KY: Westminster John Knox, forthcoming).

Neugebauer, Fritz. *In Christus = En Christoi: Eine Untersuchung zum paulinischen Glaubenverständnis* (Göttingen: Vandenhoeck & Ruprecht, 1961).

Nimmo, Paul T. *Being in Action: The Theological Shape of Barth's Ethical Vision* (London: T&T Clark, 2007).

O'Brien, Peter T. *The Epistle to the Philippians: A Commentary on the Greek Text* (NIGTC; Grand Rapids, MI: Eerdmans, 1991).

———. *The Letter to the Ephesians* (PNTC; Grand Rapids, MI: Eerdmans, 1999).

O'Collins, G., SJ, and Daniel Kendall, SJ. "The Faith of Jesus", *TS* 53 (1992): 403–23.

O'Donnell, M.B. *Corpus Linguistics and the Greek of the New Testament* (Sheffield: Sheffield Phoenix Press, 2005).

Origène: Commentaire sur Saint Jean (SC 120; Livre I–V; Paris: Cerf, 1966).

O'Rourke, J.J. "πίστις", *CBQ* 36 (1973): 188–94.

Osborne, Grant. *Revelation* (BECNT; Grand Rapids, MI: Baker Academic, 2002).

Ota, Shuji. "Absolute Use of PISTIS and PISTIS XRISTOU in Paul", *AJBI* 23 (1997): 64–82.

———. "πίστις Ἰησοῦ Χριστοῦ – Consideration Based on Survey of Uses of πίστις and πιστεύειν in LXX, OT Pseudepigrapha, and Philo", *Seishogakuu Ronshu* 26 (1993): 132–63.

———. "*Pistis* of Jesus Christ in Galatians", *Nihon-no-Sishogaku* 1 (1995): 123–46.

———. "Structure of Pauline *Pistis*", *Shinyakagaku Kenkyu* 24 (1996): 1–12.

Painter, J. *Just James: The Brother of Jesus in History and Tradition* (Philadelphia, PA: Fortress, 1999).

Parente, P. *L'Io di Cristo* (Brescia, 1951).

Partington, A. *Patterns and Meanings: Using Corpora for English Language Research and Teaching* (Amsterdam: Benjamins, 1998).

Penner, T.C. *The Epistle of James and Eschatology: Re-reading an Ancient Letter* (JSNTSup 121; Sheffield: Sheffield Academic Press, 1996).

Penner, T.C. "The Epistle of James in Current Research", *CurBS* 7 (1999): 257–308.

Perry, J. *A Discussion of the General Epistle of James* (London: C.J. Clay and Sons, 1903).

Plevnik, Joseph. "The Understanding of God at the Basis of Pauline Theology", *CBQ* 65 (2003): 567.

Pollard, Jesse Paul. "The Problem of the Faith of Christ" (PhD dissertation, Baylor University, 1982).

——. "The 'Faith of Christ' in Current Discussion", *Concordia* 23 (1997): 213–28.

Popkes, W. *Der Brief des Jakobus* (THKNT 14; Leipzig: Evangelische Verlags-Anstalt, 2001).

Porter, S.E. "Can Traditional Exegesis Enlighten Literary Analysis of the Fourth Gospel? An Examination of the Old Testament Fulfilment Motif and the Passover Theme", in *The Gospels and the Scriptures of Israel* (ed. C.A. Evans and W.R. Stegner; JSNTSup 104; Sheffield: Sheffield Academic Press, 1994), 396–428.

——. *Idioms of the Greek New Testament* (Biblical Language: Greek 2; 2nd ed.; Sheffield: Sheffield Academic Press, 1994).

——. "The Rhetorical Scribe: Textual Variants in Romans and their Possible Rhetorical Purpose", in *Rhetorical Criticism and the Bible* (ed. S.E. Porter and D.L. Stamps; JSNTSup 195; London: Sheffield Academic Press, 2002), 403–19.

——. *Verbal Aspect in the Greek of the New Testament, with Reference to Tense and Mood* (New York: Lang, 1989).

——., and M.B. O'Donnell. "'On the Shoulders of Giants' – The Expansion and Application of the Louw-Nida Lexicon" (paper presented at the SBL 2005 Annual Meeting, Biblical Greek Language and Linguistics/Lexicography Sections Joint Session, Philadelphia, 19–22 November 2005).

Prior, J. *John: Evangelist of the Covenant People: The Narrative and Themes of the Fourth Gospel* (London: Darton, Longman & Todd, 1992).

Quarles, Charles. "From Faith to Faith: A Fresh Examination of the Prepositional Series in Romans 1:17", *NovT* 45 (2003): 1–21.

Rahner, K. *Schriften zur Theologie* III (Zürich: Benzinger, 1961).

Reasoner, Mark. *Romans in Full Circle: A History of Interpretation* (Louisville, KY: Westminster John Knox, 2005).

Reicke, B. *The Epistles of James, Peter, and Jude* (AB 37; Garden City, NY: Doubleday, 1964).

Ridderbos, Herman. *The Epistle of Paul to the Churches of Galatia* (trans. Henry Zylstra; Grand Rapids, MI: Eerdmans, 1953).

Robertson, A.T. *A Grammar of the Greek New Testament in the Light of Historical Research* (4th ed.; Nashville, TN: Broadman, 1934).

Robinson, Donald W.B. "'The Faith of Jesus Christ': A New Testament Debate", *RTR* 29 (1970): 71–81.

Roloff, Jürgen. *The Revelation of John* (Continental Commentaries; Philadelphia, PA: Fortress, 1993).

Roo, Jacqueline de. *Works of Law at Qumran and in Paul* (Sheffield: Sheffield Phoenix, 2007).

Salier, W. *The Rhetorical Impact of the Semeia in the Gospel of John* (WUNT II: 186; Tübingen: Mohr Siebeck, 2004).

Sanders, E.P. *Paul and Palestinian Judaism: A Comparison of Patterns of Religion* (Philadelphia, PA: Fortress, 1977).

Santiago-Otero, H. "La Sabiduría del Alma de Cristo", *RTAM* 34 (1967): 131–58.

Schenk, Wolfgang. "Die Gerechtigkeit Gottes und der Glaube Christi" *TLZ* 97 (1972): 161–74.

———. *Die Philipperbriefe des Paulus* (Stuttgart: Kohlhammer, 1984).

Schlatter, A. *Der Glaube im Neuen Testament* (3rd ed.; Calv/Stuttgart: Vereinsbuchhandlung, 1905 [1885]).

———. *Romans: The Righteousness of God* (trans. S. Schatzmann; Peabody, MA: Hendrickson, 1995 [1935]).

Schließer, Benjamin. *Abraham's Faith in Romans 4: Paul's Concept of Faith in Light of the History of Reception of Genesis 15:6* (WUNT 2.224; Tübingen: Mohr Siebeck, 2007).

Schlier, Heinrich. *Der Römerbrief* (HTKNT 6; Freiburg/Basel/Wien: Herder, 1987 [1977]).

Schmitz, Otto. *Die Christus-Gemeinschaft des Paulus im Lichte seines Genetivgebrauchs* (NTF 1. Reihe. Paulusstudien 2; Gütersloh: C. Bertelsmann, 1924).

Schnackenburg, R. *The Epistle to the Ephesians: A Commentary* (Edinburgh: T&T Clark, 1991).

———. "Glaubensgewißheit", in *Die Freude an Gott-unsere Kraft: Festschrift B. Knoch* (Stuttgart: Katholisches Bibelwerk, 1991).

———. *The Gospel according to John* (trans. K. Smyth; 3 vols.; Kent: Burns & Oates, 1968–82).

Schreer, Werner. *Der Begriff des Glaubens: Das Verständnis des Glaubenartikels in den Dokumenten des Vatikanum II und in den theologischen Entwürfen Karl Rahners und Hans Urs von Balthasars* (Frankfurt: Peter Lang, 1992).

Schreiner, Thomas R. *Paul, Apostle of God's Glory in Christ: A Pauline Theology* (Downers Grove, IL: InterVarsity Press, 2001).

Schreiner, Thomas R.. *Romans* (BECNT; Grand Rapids, MI: Baker, 1998).

Scott, James. "'For as Many as Are of Works of the Law Are under a Curse' (Galatians 3:10)", in *Paul and the Scriptures of Israel* (ed. Craig A. Evans and James A. Sanders; JSNTSup 83; Sheffield: JSOT Press, 1993), 187–221.

Scroggs, R. "Rom. 6.7 ὁ γὰρ ἀποθανὼν δεδικαίωται ἀπὸ τῆς ἁμαρτίας", *NTS* 10 (1963): 104–8.

Seifrid, Mark A. *Christ, Our Righteousness: Paul's Theology of Justification* (NSBT 9; Leicester: Apollos/Downers Grove, IL: InterVarsity Press, 2000).

——. "Paul, Luther, and Justification in Galatians 2:15–21", *WTJ* 65 (2003): 215–30.

Sider, Robert, ed. *Collected Works of Erasmus*, vol. 44. *New Testament Scholarship* (Toronto/Buffalo/London: University of Toronto, 1993).

Silva, Moisés. *Biblical Words and their Meaning: An Introduction to Lexical Semantics* (Grand Rapids, MI: Zondervan, 1983).

——. "Faith versus Works of Law in Galatians", in *Justification and Variegated Nomism, II, The Paradoxes of Paul* (ed. D.A. Carson, P.T. O'Brien, and M.A. Seifred; WUNT 2.181; Tübingen: Mohr Siebeck, 2004), 230–47.

——. *God, Language and Scripture: Reading the Bible in the Light of General Linguistics* (FCI 4; Leicester: Apollos, 1990).

——. *Philippians* (BECNT; 2nd ed.; Grand Rapids, MI: Baker, 2005 [WEC, 1988]).

Smalley, Stephen S. *The Revelation of John* (Downers Grove, IL: InterVarsity Press, 2005).

Smith, D. Moody. "Ο ΔΕ ΔΙΚΑΙΟΣ ΕΚ ΠΙΣΤΕΩΣ ΖΗΣΕΤΑΙ", in *Studies in the History and Text of the New Testament in Honor of Kenneth Willis Clark* (ed. Boyd L. Daniels and M. Jack Suggs; Salt Lake City, UT: University of Utah, 1967), 13–25.

Spitta, F. "Der Brief des Jakobus", in *Zur Geschichte und Literatur des Urchristentums*, II (Göttingen: Vandenhoeck & Ruprecht, 1896), 3–8.

Sprinkle, Preston. "'Two's Company, Three's a Crowd?': Another Option for the '*PISTIS CHRISTOU*' Debate" (conference paper, Far West Region of the Evangelical Theological Society, Sun Valley, CA; 2 May 2003).

Squires, J.T. *The Plan of God in Luke–Acts* (SNTSMS 76; Cambridge: Cambridge University Press, 1993).

Stegman, Thomas. "Ἐπίστευσα διὸ ἐλάλησα (2 Corinthians 4:13): Paul's Christological Reading of Psalm 115:1a Lxx", *CBQ* 69 (2007): 725–45.

Stibbe, M.G.W. *John as Storyteller: Narrative Criticism and the Fourth Gospel* (SNTSMS 73; Cambridge: Cambridge University Press, 1992).

Still, Todd D. "*Christos* as *Pistos*: The Faith(fulness) of Jesus in the Epistle to the Hebrews", *CBQ* 69 (2007): 746–55.

Stowers, S.K. "ἐκ πίστεως and διὰ τῆς πίστεως in Romans 3:30", *JBL* 108 (1989): 665–74.

Stowers, S.K. *A Rereading of Romans: Justice, Jews, and Gentiles* (New Haven, CT: Yale University Press, 1994).

Strecker, G. "Die Makarismen der Bergpredigt", *NTS* 17 (1970–71): 255–75.

Suggs, M.J. "Wisdom 2:10–5: A Homily Based on the Fourth Servant Song", *JBL* 76 (1957): 26–53.

Taylor, Greer M. "The Function of πίστις Χριστοῦ in Galatians", *JBL* 85 (1966): 58–76.

Taylor, John W. "From Faith to Faith: Romans 1:17 in the Light of Greek Idiom", *NTS* 50 (2004): 337–48.

Taylor, V. *The Gospel according to St. Mark* (2nd ed.; London: Macmillan, 1966).

Tenney, M.C. *John: The Gospel of Belief* (Grand Rapids, MI: Eerdmans, 1948).

Thompson, M.M. *The Incarnate Word: Perspectives on Jesus in the Fourth Gospel* (Peabody, MA: Hendrickson, 1988).

Thurston, B.B., and J.M. Ryan, *Philippians and Philemon* (SP 10; Collegeville, MN: Liturgical Press, 2005).

Thüsing, William. *Christologie-Systematisch und Exegetisch*, *QD*55 (Freiburg: Herder, 1974).

——. *Die neutestamentliche Theologien und Jesus Christus: Grundlegung einer Theologie des Neuten Testaments: I Kriterien aufgrund der Rückfrage nach Jesus und des Glaubens an seine Auferweckung* (Münster: Aschendorff, 1996).

——. *Die neutestamentliche Theologien und Jesus Christus: Grundlegung einer Theologie des Neuten Testaments: II Programm einer Theologie des Neuen Testaments mit Perspektiven für eine Biblische Theologie* (Münster: Aschendorff, 1998).

Tonstad, Sigve. "πιστις χριστου: Reading Paul in a New Paradigm", *AUSS* 40 (2002): 37–59.

Torrance, T.F. "The Biblical Conception of 'Faith'," *ExpTim* 68 (1957): 221–2.

——. *The Mediation of Christ* (2nd ed.; Edinburgh: T&T Clark, 1992).

——. "One Aspect of the Biblical Conception of Faith", *ExpTim* 68 (1957): 111–14.

Torrell, J.-P. "Saint Thomas d'Aquin et la science du Christ", in idem, *Recherches Thomasiennes* (Paris: Librairie Philosophique J. Vrin, 2000), 198–213.

Tsuji, M. *Glaube zwischen Vollkommenheit und Verweltlichung: Eine Untersuchung zur literarischen Gestalt und zur inhaltlichen Koharenz des Jakobusbriefes* (WUNT 2/93; Tübingen: Mohr Siebeck, 1997).

Turner, M. "Atonement and the Death of Jesus in John – Some Questions to Bultmann and Forestell", *EvQ* 62.2 (1990): 99–122.

Turner, Nigel. *Syntax*, III, *A Grammar of New Testament Greek* (ed. J.H. Moulton; Edinburgh: T&T Clark, 1963).

Ulrichs, Karl Friedrich. *Christusglaube: Studien zum Syntagma pistis Christou und zum paulinischen Verständnis von Glaube und Rechtfertigung* (WUNT 2.227; Tübingen: Mohr Siebeck, 2007).

Valloton, P. *Le Christ et la foi: Etude de théologie biblique* (Geneva: Labor & Fides, 1960).

Vanderkam, James C. "Righteous One, Messiah, Chosen One, and Son of Man in 1 Enoch 37–71", in *The Messiah: Developments in Earliest Judaism and Christianity* (ed. James H. Charlesworth; Minneapolis, MN: Fortress, 1992), 169–91.

Vanhoye, Albert. "Πίστις Χριστοῦ: Fede in Christo o affidabilità di Cristo", *Bib* 80 (1999): 1–21.

Von Balthasar, H. Urs. *Herrlichkeit* III/2: Neues Bund (Einsiedeln: Johannes, 1969).

Wachob, Wesley. "The Language of 'Household' and 'Kingdom' in the Letter of James: A Socio-Rhetorical Study", in Webb and Kloppenborg, eds., *Reading James with New Eyes*.

——. "'The Rich in Faith' and 'The Poor in Spirit': The Social-Rhetorical Function of a Saying of Jesus in the Epistle of James" (PhD dissertation; Emory University, 1993).

——. *The Voice of Jesus in the Social-Rhetoric of James* (SNTSMS 106; Cambridge: Cambridge University Press, 2000).

Wagner, J.R., et al., eds., *The Word Leaps the Gap: Essays on Scripture and Theology in Honor of Richard B. Hays* (Grand Rapids, MI: Eerdmans, 2008).

Wall, R.W. *Community of the Wise: The Letter of James* (Valley Forge, PA: Trinity, 1997).

Wallace, Daniel B. *Greek Grammar beyond the Basics: An Exegetical Syntax of the New Testament* (Grand Rapids, MI: Zondervan, 1996).

Wallace, S. "Figure and Ground: The Interrelationships of Linguistic Categories", in *Tense-Aspect: Between Semantics and Pragmatics* (ed. P.J. Hopper; Amsterdam: Benjamins, 1982), 201–23.

Wallis, Ian G. *The Faith of Jesus Christ in Early Christian Traditions* (SNTSMS 84; Cambridge and New York: Cambridge University Press, 1995).

Watson, Duane F. "An Assessment of the Rhetoric and Rhetorical Analysis of the Letter of James", in Webb and Kloppenborg, eds., *Reading James with New Eyes*, 99–120.

——. "James 2 in Light of Greco-Roman Schemes of Argumentation", *NTS* 39 (1993): 94–121.

——. "The Rhetoric of James 3:1–12 and a Classical Pattern of Argumentation", *NovT* 35 (1993): 48–64.

Watson, Francis. *Paul and the Hermeneutics of Faith* (London & New York: T&T Clark, 2004).

——. *Paul, Judaism, and the Gentiles: Beyond the New Perspective* (2nd ed.; Grand Rapids, MI: Eerdmans, 2007).

Watson, Francis. "The Triune Divine Identity: Reflections on Pauline God-Language, in Disagreement with J.D.G. Dunn", *JSNT* 80 (2000): 110.

Webb, Robert, and John Kloppenborg, eds. *Reading James with New Eyes: Methodological Reassessments of the Letter of James* (London: T&T Clark, 2007).

Wilckens, U. *Der Brief an die Römer* (EKKNT VI/1; Zurich/Neukirchen-Vluyn: Benziger Verlag/Neukirchener Verlag, 1978).

Williams, Sam K. "Again *Pistis Christou*", *CBQ* 49 (1987): 431–47.

———. *Galatians* (ANTC; Nashville, TN: Abingdon, 1997).

———. *Jesus' Death as Saving Event: The Background and Origin of a Concept* (HDR 2; Missoula, MT: Scholars Press, 1975).

———. "Justification and the Spirit in Galatians", *JSNT* 9 (1987): 91–100.

———. "The 'Righteousness of God' in Romans", *JBL* 99 (1980): 241–90.

Winer, G.B. *A Treatise on the Grammar of New Testament Greek* (trans. W.F. Moulton; Edinburgh: T&T Clark, 1882).

Witherington, Ben, III. *Revelation* (NCBC; Cambridge: Cambridge University Press, 2003).

Wright, N.T. *The Climax of the Covenant: Christ and the Law in Pauline Theology* (London: T&T Clark, 1991; Minneapolis, MN: Fortress, 1994).

———. "Curse and Covenant: Galatians 3:10–14", in idem, *The Climax of the Covenant*, 137–56.

———. "Jesus Christ is Lord: Philippians 2:5–11", in idem, *The Climax of the Covenant*.

———. *John for Everyone* (2 vols.; London: SPCK, 2002).

———. *Paul: In Fresh Perspective* (Minneapolis, MN: Fortress, 2005).

———. "Romans and the Theology of Paul", in *Pauline Theology*. III. *Romans* (ed. D.M. Hay and E.E. Johnson; Minneapolis, MN: Fortress, 1995), 30–67.

Zahn, T. *Introduction to the New Testament*, I (Edinburgh: T&T Clark, 1909).

Zerwick, Maximilian. *Biblical Greek: Illustrated by Examples* (Rome: Scripta Pontificii Instituti Biblici, 1963).

Index of References to the Bible or Related Ancient Writings

OT APOCRYPHA and PSEUDEPIGRAPHA

NT APOCRYPHA

DEAD SEA SCROLLS

Index of Modern Authors
(since 1500)